Personal Conflict Management

Theory and Practice

Suzanne McCorkle

Boise State University

Melanie J. Reese

Boise State University

Allyn & Bacon

Boston • New York • San Francisco

Mexico City • Montreal • Toronto • London • Madrid • Munich • Paris

Hong Kong • Singapore • Tokyo • Cape Town • Sydney

Acquisitions Editor: Jeanne Zalesky
Assistant Editor: Megan Lentz
Marketing Manager: Blair Tuckman
Production Supervisor: Beth Houston
Editorial Production Service: Integra
Manufacturing Buyer: JoAnne Sweeney
Electronic Composition: Integra
Cover Administrator: Joel Gendron
Cover Photograph: Boise State University Photographic Services

Library of Congress Cataloging-in-Publication Data

McCorkle, Suzanne.
  Personal conflict management/Suzanne McCorkle, Melanie J. Reese.—1st ed.
    p. cm.
  ISBN-13: 978-0-205-49988-5 (alk. paper)
  ISBN-10:   0-205-49988-0 (alk. paper)
  1. Conflict management. 2. Problem solving. 3. Interpersonal relations.
I. Reese, Melanie. II. Title.
HM1126.M396 2009
303.6'9—dc22

                                 2009002667

10 9 8 7 6 5 4 3 2 1   13 12 11 10 09

Allyn & Bacon
is an imprint of

www.pearsonhighered.com

ISBN-10:   0-205-49988-0
ISBN-13: 978-0-205-49988-5

Contents

12 *Managing the Aftermath: Anger, Apology, Forgiveness, and Reconciliation* 213

SECTION IV • *Conflict in Context* 233

13 *Family Communication and Conflict* 234

14 *Conflict at the Workplace* 258

Toolbox Resources

List of Cases

Mastery Cases

Preface

In our combined fifty-plus years of teaching conflict management, mediation, and related coursework, we have used many resources. We found that over the years our conceptualization of the course differed from what was available in existing textbooks.

Specifically, we were interested in demonstrating the value of collaborative models for resolving conflict and the necessity and benefits in understanding competitive approaches. Our experience as mediators and organizational facilitators also influenced much of our curriculum and expanded our conceptualization of conflict management.

Finally, having taught a course in conflict management at three different universities, we discovered the value of differing approaches to the course: those that focus entirely on interpersonal conflict theory, those that combine theory and application, and those that span from interpersonal conflict to other settings. Our aim was to create a text that represented innovations in curriculum and cutting-edge concepts arising from research.

We believe that a text should be accessible and inviting to the students. Toward that end we have included many examples, case studies, and application exercises. At the beginning of each chapter, vocabulary terms and chapter objectives identify key concepts for students to master. As we field-tested the book, we found the discussion questions within the chapters helpful guides for classroom interaction. They also enhance students' ability to integrate the concepts with their lives. Our goal is to support an interactive environment that optimizes opportunities for learning.

Exercises, case analyses, and project/essay suggestions at the end of each chapter provide a focus for class or group discussion, as well as potential topics for student assignments. For writing intensive courses, we include a mastery case at the end of most chapters that can be used as the subject of analytical writing assignments.

We believe conflict management is one of the most critical topics a student can study. We want to make this course enjoyable and thought-provoking for students and instructors. We would love to hear back from you about ways to improve the course or suggestions for making this material more meaningful to your students.

Suzanne McCorkle and Melanie Reese

Acknowledgments

We would like to thank all those who assisted in the creation of this book. In particular, we thank the students in Communication 390, whose comments inspired many of the cases and who helped field-test the chapters. We also thank graduate students Christine Lukas and Catherine Nailon, who assisted with the research on the text.

We thank our copyeditor, Anne Lesser, and those who reviewed the text–Amy Bippus, California State University-Long Beach; Wendy Bjorklund, St. Cloud State University; Chris R. Logan, Southern Methodist University; Richard K. Olsen, Jr., University of North Carolina, Wilmington, and Heidi Reeder, Boise State University. Their comments led to innumerable improvements as the project unfolded.

Interpersonal Conflict Causes and Patterns

Even though we cannot change others, we are not powerless in the face of conflict. *Managing Personal Conflict* explores the dynamic world of interpersonal conflict management. We believe that competent conflict managers can better reach career goals and have more successful relationships than those who do not cope well with conflict.

Successful conflict management stands on a three-part foundation built with knowledge, attitudes, and skills. First, the competent conflict manager must have knowledge about conflict theory, causes, patterns, and tactics. Second, the best conflict managers embrace the productive and creative energy of conflict. Finally, flexible conflict managers develop a toolbox of skills to engage in competitive conflict (when one must) and cooperative conflict (when one can). Although it may take two to tango, it only takes one person to create the opportunity to change a conflict pattern. One person, with knowledge, skill, and the right attitude, can enhance the probability of transforming an unproductive conflict into an opportunity for everyone. No set of skills can promise to resolve every conflict, but we can guarantee one trend: Many conflicts will not get better on their own.

Section I first begins with an examination of the nature of interpersonal conflict and how it differs from other communication contexts. The section continues with a discussion of the dominant theories that guide the study of interpersonal conflict, the contrast between competitive and cooperative approaches to interpersonal conflict, an elaboration of conflict causes, and research on common conflict variables.

1

Conflict in Everyday Life

Vocabulary

Argument
Barnlund's six views
Connotative meaning
Denotative meaning
Face goals

Interdependence
Interpersonal conflict
Intrapersonal conflict
Latent conflict
Process goals

Pseudo-conflict
Relationship goal
Substantive goals

Objectives

After reading the chapter, you should be able to:

1. Explain why conflict is an inherent and crucial part of the human condition

2. Identify the components in the definition of interpersonal conflict

3. Explore the role of perception in communication and conflict

Why Study Conflict?

How people react to conflict makes all the difference. In Case 1.1, Beth may be clueless that a problem even exists. Rachel avoids talking with Beth about job expectations, but she becomes angry when her expectations aren't met. Avoidance, overreaction, and lashing out can turn a minor disagreement into a full-blown conflict.

The range of skills, attitudes, and assumptions that individuals bring to everyday problems underscores the fact that people do not have one uniform experience of conflict. Some individuals fear conflict; others seem to thrive on it. Yet research indicates that when asked to recall past conflicts, respondents almost uniformly talk about events that were negative and painful (McCorkle & Mills, 1992; Zweibel, Goldstein, Manwaring, & Marks, 2008). Even though personal experiences of conflict differ and people tend to view conflict as negative, several facts summarized in Table 1.1 make the study of conflict important.

CASE 1.1 • *Let's Switch Jobs*

Rachel and Beth are coworkers. Beth has been working for the company for over three years. Rachel was hired as part-time help about a year ago. Both work at the front desk as receptionists. Every morning when Rachel arrives there is a pile of customer service requests, files to be processed, and appointments that need to be scheduled. When Beth comes in, she goes to the back room to help other coworkers with general filing.

It is June 29, and the end of the month is the busiest time in the company. Rachel is stressing that she won't get through all the customer requests by the end of the day, which could really be bad for some of the customers. Rachel enters the back office to ask Beth if she will help at the front desk. As Rachel entered the back room, she sees Beth shopping on the Internet for new flip-flops.

Rachel: "Beth, could you help me up front? I don't think I'm going to get through all the paperwork by the end of the day."

Beth: "I can't right now. I'm waiting for Brent to get off the phone to help me lift boxes in the filing room."

Disgusted, Rachel walks to the front desk where she continues to slog through the customer service requests. After a while, the FedEx man arrives to drop off a pile of mail and boxes. One of the packages is addressed to Beth from Eddie Bauer. Rachel gets up and goes to the back room to hand out what FedEx has delivered. She saves Beth's delivery for last.

Rachel: "Beth, you have a delivery."

Beth: "Really, who from?"

Rachel: "Eddie Bauer."

Beth: "Oh awesome! I ordered my husband a nice lunch box to take to work."

Rachel: "It must be nice to have the time to shop while you're at work. Is that all you ever do back here?"

Beth: "I only shop when I have some downtime."

Rachel: "Well, you want to switch places for a while? I'd love to be paid to shop on the Internet!"

Rachel drops the package onto the floor and stomps back to the front desk. Beth glares at her as she walks away.

General Assumptions About Interpersonal Conflict

First, *conflict is an inevitable and integral part of life.* As the author of *The Coward's Guide to Conflict* remarks, conflict is inescapable: "we can run, but we cannot hide! We can sprint, jog, scream, deny, avoid, and make any other desperate attempt to get away from conflict, but we cannot make conflict disappear from our lives. Conflict is a part of life. And, like it or not, you will have to deal with it in some way" (Ursiny, 2003, p. xvii). Knowing that conflict is an integral part of the human experience, we examine the attitudes, knowledge, analytical abilities, and skills that differentiate productive from destructive conflict experiences. Studying conflict is crucial because it is a part of everyday life. When prepared to engage conflict productively, you may discover choices that previously were hidden.

Second, *conflict can be invigorating.* Some people find it so exciting that they constantly stir things up to create conflict. Conflict can be invigorating in both good and hurtful ways. Protracted negative conflict literally can make a person ill (Blase & Blase, 2003; Glendinning,

TABLE 1.1   *Why Study Conflict?*

Conflict is an inevitable part of life.
Conflict can be invigorating.
Overusing any one strategy is a weakness.
We need to be ready to compete and to cooperate.
The cost to relationships of poorly managed conflict is high.
Lack of conflict management skills is related to abuse.
The cost of poorly managed conflicts at work is severe.

2001; Workplace Bullying and Trauma Institute, 2003). Conversely, safely managed conflict can stimulate creativity or renew an at-risk relationship. Conflict can lead to personal and societal change.

Third, *overuse of any one strategy is a weakness.* People who only know one response to a conflict situation continue to reuse the same strategies and tactics—even when those behaviors do not have desirable outcomes. Studying interpersonal conflict helps us gain the capacity to analyze the nature of conflict, build an understanding of one's choices, and develop a repertoire of skills suitable to many different conflict situations.

Fourth, Americans live in a culture in which *cooperative and competitive conflict management systems exist side by side.* Persons aware of only one conflict perspective—cooperative or competitive—lack the knowledge and skills to be effective when conflict arises with a person operating in the opposite system. We examine how these two systems differ. We provide strategies to approach conflict productively when competition is necessary and techniques to collaborate when cooperation is desirable. Knowledge of both cooperative and competitive approaches will help you navigate through confusing conflict situations with skill and confidence.

Fifth, *the cost of poorly managed conflict in relationships is high.* "By 2 years of age, children are highly familiar with conflict interchanges, and by the age of 4, they are veteran observers of, and participants in, family conflicts" (Stein & Albro, 2001, p. 115). Children learn about conflict management from many sources, including parental modeling. For intimate partners, the quality and type of communication during conflict is related to relationship satisfaction and long-term commitment (Cramer, 2002; Gottman & Silver, 1999; Stanley, Markman, & Whitton, 2002). Other effects of unregulated conflict in relationships include loss of friendship or intimacy, avoidance, stress, illness, decreased self-confidence, relationship breakup/divorce, and sometimes violence. The ability to maintain important relationships is improved through the study of interpersonal conflict.

Sixth, *the cost of poorly managed conflict to employers and employees is severe.* The Dana Measure of Financial Cost of Conflict itemizes the hidden costs of workplace conflict, including the monetary value of wasted time, lost opportunity, lower motivation, decreased productivity, absenteeism, conflict-incited theft, and illness. Dana (2003) concluded that even a relatively simple conflict among employees that consumes two hours per week of a manager's time can have direct costs of $30,000 to a business. Some estimate that managers spend as much as 20 percent of their total time dealing with conflict (Marin, Sherblom, & Shipps, 1994).

INSERT 1.1

Is My Conflict Normal?

"I seem to experience conflict frequently with my friends and spouse; is there something wrong with me?"

"I just ignore conflicts whenever they come up; is that a good strategy?"

"Why do I always feel like I'm the one who lost, even when I get my way?"

"I like to keep things stirred up because it helps me feel alive; is that wrong?"

"I don't like conflict, so I let the other person have his or her way; is there a problem with that?"

Bullying (discussed in Chapter 10) probably is the most underrecognized kind of workplace conflict and stress (Boucaut, 2003). One sixth of all U.S. workers experience bullying (Coloroso, 2003; *Today Show,* 2004). An increasingly diverse workplace exposes employees, sometimes for the first time, to other social, racial, ethnic, or religious groups—enhancing opportunities for misunderstandings that may grow into conflicts. Effects of conflict or bullying in organizations may include lack of productivity, stress, absenteeism, health issues, decreased self-confidence, poor work relationships, customer service erosion, increased turnover, a tarnished company reputation, legal actions, and sometimes violence. Studying interpersonal conflict is important to maintain a productive workplace.

Lastly, *a lack of conflict management skills is related to verbal and physical aggression* (Olson, 2002). Although aggression and violence are complex phenomenon, acquiring conflict management skills creates the potential for less aggression when difficulties arise. Many people act aggressively because they feel they have no other options to get their needs met. Acquiring skills in conflict management broadens choices and is instrumental in reducing violence and aggression.

Discussion Question 1.1

Which of the seven reasons to study conflict is most important to you personally at this stage of your life? Which of the four benefits do you most wish to have?

A strong understanding of conflict is critical because the financial and personal costs are too high if we do not. Unmanaged and unproductive conflict affects our families, our friendships, and our work. Equipped with the right attitude, knowledge, and skills, interpersonal conflicts can be approached with less fear, more confidence, and better outcomes.

Beneficial Aspects of Interpersonal Conflict

There are also numerous advantages to the better management of interpersonal conflict that merit attention (summarized in Table 1.2). First, *knowledge of how to manage conflict and the ability to solve problems is a source of power.* Organizations place value on people who

TABLE 1.2 *Beneficial Aspects of Conflict*

Managing conflicts productively is a source of personal power.
Managing conflicts saves money.
Managing conflicts builds confidence.
Managing conflicts creates opportunity.

can solve problems (Plowman, 1998). Employers would rather hire someone who knows how to manage conflict and solve problems than someone adept at creating conflict or pretending that conflicts don't exist. Supervisors who manage conflict successfully avoid the inefficiencies of unproductive conflict.

Second, *conflict management saves money.* Great Britain claims to have saved over 6 million pounds (about $12 million) by initiating conflict management and alternative dispute resolution processes in government agencies (Millar, 2003). U.S. companies that use internal dispute resolution systems or professional conflict managers, called ombudsmen, claim up to 90 percent of employee disputes are settled quickly—reducing long appeals, wrongful termination lawsuits, and other productivity losses (Saleh, 2003; Wexler & Zimmerman, 2000).

> ### *Discussion Question 1.2*
> Deutsch's crude law of social relationships suggests that your behaviors will lead others to behave in similar ways. That is, what goes around comes around. Have you experienced situations in which negative attitudes bred more negative attitudes or productive and positive behaviors led others to be more productive and positive?

Third, *conflict management can build personal confidence and competence.* In the personal realm, the successful management of conflict offers similar advantages as those in the world of work. Ursiny (2003) asserts that dealing with conflict productively may lead to better relationships, increased confidence, less anger, less depression, greater respect for others, increased intimacy, career enhancements, less fear, and a greater sense of personal strength. Skilled conflict managers develop a greater sense of confidence when conflict arises and know that they have choices in how to respond, which is an improvement over the helpless, trapped, or out-of-control feelings that some experience during conflict.

Finally, *conflict management creates opportunity.* The issues raised during conflict present individuals with choices—not only in how to communicate and what tactics will be chosen, but also in what the future will become. We can assess if goals should be changed or determine what a relationship should be like in the future. These and other important choices arise in conflict and create forks in the road of a relationship. Our actions create our future. Clearly, conflict management is an integral skill for making people's lives better. In the next section, we explore the term *interpersonal conflict.*

Defining Interpersonal Conflict

In this text, **interpersonal conflict** is defined as a struggle among a small number of interdependent people (usually two) arising from perceived interference with goal achievement. Interpersonal conflict occurs when one person perceives interference from another. Interference is seen as a threat to goal achievement. The drive for goal achievement creates a feeling of disequilibrium that then affects behavior toward the other person.

The definition of interpersonal conflict recognizes that conflict is both internal and external. Internally, when an individual *feels* a struggle between personal goals and someone else's actions, conflict is germinated. The external dimension of interpersonal conflict inextricably is tied with the internal. The internal feeling of struggle affects how one *behaves* externally. Even though the conflict may not be an obvious topic of conversation, communication is different than before the conflict germinated because of the feeling of disequilibrium. Most individuals have experienced the feeling that something is wrong when talking with a friend or acquaintance. Even though no discussions have occurred about the topic of concern and no obvious conflict strategies have been applied, a conflict is being expressed through the nuances of nonverbal communication. The internal disequilibrium is leaking through to external behavior.

At other times, there is no doubt that a conflict exists. Direct expression of conflict can take many forms—some productive and some less so. A discussion of each part of the definition of interpersonal conflict will highlight these means of conflict expression.

Interpersonal Conflicts Are a Struggle

The term *struggle,* popularized by Keltner (1987) as it relates to interpersonal conflict, is an apt description of how conflict differs from casual disagreements, mild differences, or intellectual argument. Not all differences among persons rise to the level of interpersonal conflict. An interpersonal conflict is hallmarked by a feeling of struggle, meaning participants in an interpersonal conflict care about the outcome. In casual disagreements, mild differences, or intellectual arguments, the participants have little emotional or relational investment in the outcome or may argue as a type of entertainment. Two friends may call each other "pig," "stupid," "brat," or even profane names in a ritual of good-natured banter. What might be fighting words in another context is a type of bonding for these friends. Sports fans may argue passionately about which quarterback is the all-time best as a type of entertainment and a way to practice their command of statistics, facts, and sports trivia. The conversation, unless it takes a negative turn and becomes personal, is not an interpersonal conflict. For instance,

---

INSERT 1.2

Interpersonal Conflict

Interpersonal conflict is defined as a struggle among a small number of interdependent people (usually two) arising from perceived interference with goal achievement.

banter can turn into interpersonal conflict when one fan is invested deeply in his perception of himself as a sports expert and has an emotional connection to the Denver Broncos. When his sports expertise is questioned, even playfully, he may see the challenger as interfering with his role as a defender of quarterback John Elway's record. To be an interpersonal conflict, the participants must feel invested in the outcome—emotionally and/or relationally.

Discussion Question 1.3

How is conflict expressed by Rachel in Case 1.1? How does Jerod in Case 1.2 express conflict? Is Rachel or Jerod emotionally invested in the outcome of their conflict?

Interpersonal Conflict Occurs Among a Small Number of People

The minimum number is two. The maximum number is open but limited to a number less than when group dynamics begin to alter communicative processes or when the individuals do not have enough awareness of each other to exert mutual influence. Group communication contains many of the characteristics of interpersonal processes, but it also includes unique dynamics such as group leadership, specialized role development, or coalition formation (see Chapter 14). Although this book examines interpersonal conflict in a variety of settings (friendship, family, and work), the primary focus is the dynamic interplay of two individuals.

Even though **intrapersonal conflicts**—purely internal musings about what one wants—do occur, they are not the primary interest of this book. Psychologists are interested in internal states and may focus on conflict completely within the self. The feeling that two of one's cherished goals are in conflict is not unusual. A person may believe that exercise is important to long-term health and have a goal of staying fit yet spend free time watching television. Internal conversations, called *intrapersonal communication,* may occur where the "internal athlete" chews out the "couch potato" in a tussle among competing goals.

Interpersonal Conflict Requires at Least a Minimal Amount of Interdependence

Interdependence can be understood as the level to which people need each other to attain their goals. Few goals can be achieved totally alone. Students cannot get A's in a class without someone to evaluate their work; teachers and students are interdependent. Bosses need employees to complete tasks, and employees need bosses to write paychecks: They are interdependent.

Discussion Question 1.4

Are strangers waiting for a bus interdependent? If so, how? If not, what would have to change for them to become interdependent in a significant way?

Interdependence is tied inextricably to perceptions of goal interference. If one person doesn't need another to reach a goal, there is no interdependence and no reason to care. Without some perceived interdependence, there is no reason to engage in conflict.

Some authors claim that interdependence must be significant and urgent for interpersonal conflict to exist. Lulofs and Cahn (2000) distinguish between conflict, disagreements, bickering, and aggression on the basis of interdependence. They assert that in conflict: (1) People perceive they have different means or seek different outcomes, (2) they realize the conflict could negatively impact the relationship if not addressed, and (3) there is a sense of urgency. Although urgency affects intensity, within the definition in this book, the parties to a conflict must have mutual dependency only to the extent that one party thinks the other is interfering with goal achievement. What moves conflict to be fully expressed or not is the individuals' weighing of the importance of their relationship to the importance of the goal interference.

Interdependence exists in Case 1.2, "The Deli Dill." Emma is the owner of the deli, and Jerod loves the deli's food. Jerod wants to go there frequently for lunch. He depends on the deli to meet his needs for a particular type and quality of food. Emma depends on Jerod as a customer. Jerod and Emma are interdependent: They need each other to obtain their goals.

If the case of the Deli Dill occurred in a distant town that Jerod would never visit again, the exchange might not seem to be an interpersonal conflict. The parties would

CASE 1.2 • *The Deli Dill*

Jerod examined the deli menu carefully and selected one of his favorite lunches—a Reuben sandwich with turkey instead of corned beef. It included a dill pickle slice and chips for $6.50. Jerod asked for a Reuben made with turkey instead of corned beef and a whole pickle instead of chips.

Emma was busy taking orders, making sandwiches, and delivering them to tables. She delivered his order, with chips and a slice of pickle.

Jerod: "This isn't my order."

Emma: "Rueben with turkey, that's you."

Jerod: "I wanted a whole pickle."

Emma: "That's a dollar extra."

Jerod: "I don't want these chips."

Emma: "Do you want me to take them off?"

Jerod: "I don't want them."

Emma shrugged and took the plate behind the counter, where she dumped the chips into the trash. She carried the rest of the plate back to Jerod.

Emma: "Happy now, sport?"

Jerod: "Where's my pickle?"

Emma: "On your plate."

Jerod: "I wanted a whole pickle."

Emma picked up the plate again and went behind the counter, commenting to everyone else in line as she passed by about how "special" some people thought they were. She put a whole pickle on the plate with the now cold sandwich and returned to slam it on Jerod's table.

Emma: "Here you go, sport. That will be one dollar."

Jerod: "I can't believe this. Here's your stupid dollar."

Jerod threw a pocketful of change on the table and stomped out, taking his cold sandwich and whole pickle.

never see each other again and might judge the interference as "not worth the effort"—in which case the conflict would seem to end when Jerod left the premises and their momentary interdependence dissipated. Does this mean that strangers cannot have an interpersonal conflict? No. Even if Jerod and Emma have no long-term relationship, either party may be offended enough at the other's behavior to create a perception of interference with self-image goals. A perception of important goal interference might lead either party to escalate the situation—elevating it to the level of a fully expressed interpersonal conflict. Long-term relationships are not a requirement for interpersonal conflict to occur. Conflicts require a minimal amount of interdependence—just enough to allow a perception of interference with goals.

Conflicts Include Interference with Goal Achievement

Every individual has goals. These goals may be profound or simple. Goals relate to tangible resources (**substantive goals**), how things should be done (**process goals**), who the parties are to each other (**relationship goals**), or one's sense of self-worth, pride, self-respect, or power (**face goals**). For example, in the Deli Dill case, Jerod's substantive goal is to have lunch, but the spectators watching the confrontation with Emma may threaten his sense of self by causing him embarrassment, evoking face goals. If Jerod and Emma begin a discussion of how to resolve their differences, process goals may be involved. If the two are friends and Jerod perceives that friends don't charge an extra dollar for a pickle, the nature of the relationship may become an issue. Goals, a key construct in understanding the nature of conflict, are discussed in depth in Chapter 3.

> **Discussion Question 1.5**
>
> Which of the four goal types is most evident in Case 1.3, "Daryl's Time-Bound Friendship"?

CASE 1.3 • *Daryl's Time-Bound Friendship*

Back in high school, Mark was a good friend. But like a lot of relationships, I suppose, we grew apart and went our own ways. Years later we still see each other sometimes and go to a football game or do something together, but we don't hang out every day.

This is the way I see it. I wanted to change myself when I went away—to grow, to learn new things about life. Mark didn't. It's almost like Mark is still doing the same things and thinking the same ways, like he's locked in a time warp or something. He still looks at me and sees me as I was years ago. His opinions haven't changed much. Anytime I mention something I learned at college, he calls me a "know-it-all college boy" and tells me to live in the real world. He acts like we are still buddies in school who don't have any other responsibilities. When I say I have to study or go to my part-time job, Mark tells me to blow it off and calls me a punk if I won't. I think that if I hadn't known Mark all these years, I'd never choose him as a friend now.

Conflict Is Perceived

The word *perceived* is critical to our understanding of interpersonal conflict. The act of communication is not an exact transference of meaning from one person to another. To the contrary, the meaning of any message or act is interpreted by the receiver of the message. Words carry different meanings for different individuals. The **denotative meaning** (dictionary definition) of a word is different from the **connotative meaning** (personal association). For a teenager, the words *MP3 player* may be associated with the freedom to listen to music and be a part of a music culture group. For a parent, the words *MP3 player* may be associated with a time-wasting, conversation-killing device. In addition, messages are perceived differently than intended more often than we think. Inconsequential acts can be perceived as intentional slights. With all the many ways messages can go astray, it is amazing that more conflicts do not erupt.

> ### Discussion Question 1.6
> Discuss the six views possible in Case 1.2, "The Deli Dill."

Barnlund (1970), in his classic analysis of interpersonal communication, proposed that every conversation between two people really involves six views:

1. How you view yourself
2. How you view the other person
3. How you believe the other person views you
4. How the other person views himself or herself
5. How the other person views you
6. How the other person believes you view her or him

The interplay among **Barnlund's six views** provides fertile ground for interpersonal conflict. Mack may see himself as the workplace clown who makes everyone happy by telling jokes. He may believe that others see him as a good person who is well intentioned with his jokes. Mack thinks Maria is too serious and needs to loosen up a little and not work so hard, so he drops by her area every day to bring a little cheer into her life. Maria actually may view Mack as an insensitive sexist because he wastes work time telling off-color jokes. She sees herself as a professional who has a sense of humor but not for jokes that put down people, particularly women. Maria thinks Mack views her as inferior or a sex object because of the jokes he tells about women. The interplay among the six views in a simple communicative encounter highlights two aspects of communication: How one is perceived can vary; communication is not always received the way it was intended.

> ### Discussion Question 1.7
> Describe a recent interpersonal conflict. Then, diagram the six views that two individuals may hold about that conflict and each other.

For purposes of the definition of interpersonal conflict, you must understand that conflict occurs when one party *perceives* that the other party is standing between him or her

TABLE 1.3 *Perception in Conflict Definitions*

Cahn and Abigail (2007): Interpersonal conflict is "a *problematic situation* with the following four unique characteristics:
1. the conflicting parties are interdependent,
2. they have the perception that they seek incompatible goals or outcomes or they favor incompatible means to the same ends,
3. the perceived incompatibility has the potential to adversely affect the relationship if not addressed, and
4. there is a sense of urgency about the need to resolve the difference" (p. 3).

Folger, Poole, and Stutman (2005): "Conflict is the interaction of interdependent people who perceive incompatibility and the possibility of interference from others as a result of this incompatibility" (p. 4).

Wilmot and Hocker (2007): Interpersonal conflict is "an expressed struggle between at least two interdependent parties who perceive incompatible goals, scarce resources, and interference from others in achieving their goals" (p. 9).

and the attainment of an important goal. When the perception of goal interference is not activated, the conversation may be bantering or mild disagreement without rising to the level where interpersonal conflict manifests.

Perception is tricky business and, unless telepathy is achieved, requires skillful vigilance during conflict. That is why most modern definitions of conflict, as illustrated in Table 1.3, have adopted perception as a key element.

What each individual perceives is her or his reality. An objective observer may study individuals and conclude that two people have different goals and are, in fact, interfering with each other's goal achievement—but the participants don't yet perceive it. So interpersonal conflict does not yet exist; it is **latent conflict.** Conversely, two individuals may be embroiled in conflict when no goal interference objectively exists or is intended. The goal interference is based on miscommunication or inaccurate perceptions of another person's intentions. Some scholars label these events **pseudo-conflicts** (Beebe & Masterson, 2006), yet the struggles that ensue are not less hurtful or time consuming than objectively "real" differences. When perceived goal interference occurs, the conflict occurs. As Folger, Poole, and Stutman (2005) comment, "Regardless of whether incompatibility actually exists, if the parties believe incompatibility exists, then conditions are ripe for conflict" (p. 5).

> ### Discussion Question 1.8
> Compare the definition of conflict in this text to other definitions of conflict. How are the definitions different? What common threads run through all of the definitions?

Interpersonal Conflict Is Different from Argument

You may be surprised to learn that skillful arguing does not equate to skillful conflict management (Stein & Albro, 2001). To the contrary, stern dedication to logic may contribute to the creation of considerable interpersonal conflict. Someone who tells an angry coworker not "to be so emotional" is valuing rationality over feelings. **Argument** is a rational weighing of facts and evidence using the rules of logic. Simply put, *to argue is to provide reasoned support leading to a conclusion* (Herrick, 2009). Thus argumentation is like a game played by a set of formal rules, much like chess. Arguments need not be emotional or even about topics that the debaters particularly care about. Some people just like to argue. Members of a college debate team research and argue both sides of an issue with equal vigor. Those who love argument find something to disagree about no matter the topic. They enjoy the tussle of logic. Using agreed-upon rules, the debaters can be judged on which side presented the best argument, whether or not the debaters believe their own facts and claims. The antiseptic purity of logic may work well when both parties value it equally, but it won't work with those who lead with their heart rather than their head. For more emotional individuals, rational responses deny the legitimacy of feelings and may make the conflict worse.

Summary

Although each person may experience interpersonal conflict differently, seven general assumptions of conflict apply to everyone: (1) Conflict is inevitable, (2) conflict can be invigorating, (3) overuse of any one conflict strategy is a weakness, (4) cooperative and competitive conflict perspectives exist in modern life, (5) the cost of poorly managed conflict on relationships is high, (6) lack of conflict management skill is related to verbal and physical aggression, and (7) the cost of poorly managed conflict at work also is substantial. Unmanaged conflict can affect virtually all aspects of life in a negative way.

Interpersonal conflict is defined as a struggle among a small number of interdependent people stemming from perceived goal interference. Argument and mild disagreement do not fit the definition. Goals can be substantive, relationship, face, or process focused. The definition of interpersonal conflict is based in the individual who perceives goal interference and, subsequently, alters his or her behavior.

Chapter Resources _____

Exercises

1. In groups, select two people willing to talk about their first impressions of each other. As they discuss their first impressions, diagram their personal interpretations of Barnlund's six views.

2. As a group, discuss instances during past encounters where misperception or lack of communication played a role in the conflict.

Journal/Essay Topics

1. What disagreement from your past had the greatest impression on you? Describe the conflict and then compare what occurred to the definition of interpersonal conflict. According to the definition of conflict in the text, is your example an interpersonal conflict?

2. What internal and external factors contribute to the six views that Barnlund describes? How are the personalities and values of each of the six views constructed? Can the six views be altered? If so, how?

Research Topic

Consult textbooks or journal articles to learn more about group or organizational conflict. Write a paper that describes how group or organizational conflict differs from interpersonal conflict.

Mastery Case

Examine the Mastery Mini-Cases. Mark each item as C, N, or M: **Clearly** a conflict using the definition of interpersonal conflict, **Not** a conflict using the definition, or **Maybe** a conflict. State the reasoning behind your classification of each case.

1. A driver in the car behind you moves into the right lane, speeds up, and passes you—cutting you off where the two lanes come together and forcing you to brake sharply. You are very annoyed.

2. You have been planning for months to go home with your roommate over the holiday break and visit his family. One day, your roommate says you should "Find something else to do over break because I'm going skiing with some friends." You can't believe he said this and hotly reply, "Hey, we've been planning our trip for months. If you switch out now because you got a better deal, you are a scumbag."

3. You are house training your puppy. He is far enough along to know what you want him to do, but he gets mad when you are gone all day and urinates on the kitchen floor.

4. A newly married couple differs on what to do with their money. He wants to save and invest to build wealth and buy items only when enough cash is saved to make the purchase. She wants to borrow money and get a new plasma television right now. They have the same conversation several nights in a row, and they each wind up saying the other doesn't care. After the last episode, he slept on the couch.

5. Two members of the debate team argue for and against changing Social Security to private accounts at a debate tournament.

6. You trip over an uneven sidewalk in front of the county courthouse and break your ankle. You are trying to decide whether to sue the city for damages.

7. Upon hanging up the phone with your sister, you realize that the reason she told you about her car problems was because she wanted to borrow your car again. You don't want to lend it to her, so you actively avoid answering her calls or going places she might be for the next week.

8. Your professor makes a comment that people of "your generation," as a whole, are less patriotic than her generation. You are offended and tell your friend about it.

2

Major Approaches to Conflict Management

Vocabulary

Approach-approach conflict
Approach-avoid conflict
Attribution error
Attribution theory
Avoid-avoid conflict
Boundary management theory/
    Communication privacy
    management theory
Constructive conflict
Constructivism

Destructive conflict
Dialectical tensions theory
Emotional intelligence
Field theory
Game theory
Interaction theory
Interdependence
Mechanical process
Mixed-motive situation
Nature theory

Negative interdependence
Nurture theory
Positive interdependence
Psychodynamic theory
Self-serving bias
Social exchange theory
Systems theory
Transactional process

Objectives

After reading the chapter, you should be able to:

1. Understand the historical background of conflict theories
2. Differentiate between nature and nurture theories
3. Differentiate between constructive and destructive conflict
4. Explain attribution theory as it applies to conflict management

The Purpose of Theory

In the middle of a conflict, have you ever wondered, "Am I the only person this happens to? What is going on here? Why are we at odds?" Be assured: Conflict definitely happens to everyone! Friends who discuss conflicts find they have similar experiences. When patterns emerge, people wonder why. Speculation about why things occur is a theory-creating activity.

CASE 2.1 • *Lamont and Latisha's Happy Holiday*

When Lamont and I were married, we moved away from home to go to college. After two years, we were able to get enough money to go home for Christmas for a week. On Christmas Eve, we were at my in-laws. My sister-in-law wanted me to look at some pictures of her niece. I was so tired; I said I would look at them tomorrow. She threw the pictures across the room and said, "Lamont, I need to talk to you now!" I knew this could not be good. An hour later, Lamont came back upstairs and we left.

In the car, I asked what the scene was all about. He said that his mother and sister wanted him to divorce me. I was shocked and couldn't understand why they didn't like me. Lamont said he didn't want a divorce, but I needed to be more involved with his family. I told him his family should be more considerate of my needs. As we drove to my sister's house, we both got angrier and started to pick at each other's faults. By the time we reached my sister's house, we were both fuming in silence. This incident started an argument that went on for two years every time we visited his family. Finally, we stopped going home to visit.

Generally speaking, *theories* are not facts but rather tentative explanations for observed behaviors. They provide rich tools for analyzing conflict. Conflict managers use theory to provide insight into the root causes of conflict, identify patterns in interactions, and provide hints for how best to proceed toward a positive outcome.

Most theories applied to interpersonal conflict management originally were developed in some other context and have since been adapted to interpersonal conflict. The scientific study of interpersonal conflict management is relatively new—beginning after World War II—and the first interpersonal conflict textbooks emerged in the 1970s. Table 2.1 summarizes the types of questions that conflict theorists and researchers commonly address.

TABLE 2.1 *Questions for Conflict Theorists and Researchers*

1. What determines if a conflict becomes destructive or constructive?
2. What are the sources of possible injustice in questions of fairness?
3. What causes the continuation of conflict?
4. What processes lead to trust or lack of trust?
5. What is the difference between effective communication and communication that leads to misunderstandings?
6. How do attribution errors contribute to conflict?
7. How do attempts to persuade each other affect the conflict process?
8. What helps individuals keep focused on their goals rather than being distracted by unexpected emotions (rage, anxiety, or wounded pride)?
9. How do the parties in a conflict use power to influence each other?
10. What contributes to violent behavior, and how can violence be reduced?
11. What gives rise to judgmental biases and the misunderstandings that result?
12. What role does personality play in conflict?
13. At what age do children develop specific types of conflict management strategies?
14. How do intergroup processes differ from interpersonal conflict?
15. How does culture, age, sex, or status affect negotiation and conflict management?
16. What methods can be applied to long-term intractable conflict?
17. What tactics work better than others during interpersonal conflict?

Source: Adapted from Deutsch (2000a).

Nature versus Nurture

Since humans began to ask "why?" a debate has ensued about whether behavior is learned (**nurture**) or determined by biology (**nature**). Geneticists, biologists, psychologists, and social scientists, among many others, support one side or the other of the nature versus nurture debate. Do genetics, chemical balances, hormones, brain functioning, and other innate factors cause us to behave in certain ways (nature), or are we born into this world as a blank slate to be written on by our environment (nurture)? If the consensus among scholars were that people behaved in conflicts entirely based on their genetic predisposition or entirely based on chemical and/or hormonal influences, there would be little need for classes in conflict management. The means to influence conflict behavior would be gene therapy, drugs, or hormone suppression/injection. If genes, drugs, or hormones determined conflict behaviors, communication training would be useless. Why learn new communication skills if behavior is predetermined?

Those in the nurture camp believe that most behavior comes from interaction with the environment. People learn conflict behaviors from parents, peers, mass media, and culture. Regardless of sex, genetic code, hormones, or body chemistry, individuals would act the same way in a conflict situation if all had the same environmental influences. Theorists from the nurture viewpoint consider humans to be a blank slate at birth (or earlier) written on by their surroundings.

> ### *Discussion Question 2.1*
> What personal experiences or observations lead you to believe that behaviors are caused by nature or nurture? Do you believe any conflict management behaviors could be caused by biological or genetic influences?

Some scholars argue for a combined approach—a bit of biology blended with some learning and environmental influences. For example, researchers determined that in *some* situations, genetics, chemical balances, or hormones may prompt *some* tendencies toward aggressive behavior, but the influence is not strong enough to explain why some people are much more aggressive than others.

In Case 2.1, a couple discovers that Latisha is not fitting into Lamont's family. A "nature" explanation might argue that part of the problem is that men and women are genetically or biologically programmed to behave differently. However, to attribute all explanations to biology would be to ignore social relationships and culture. Conversely, social scientists have developed theories that might explain this conflict by saying Latisha grew up in a family that had different rules than Lamont's family—and those differences are causing the conflict.

Most researchers recognize that neither side of the nature/nurture debate can explain all behavior. Subsequently, multiple theories abound to explain different facets of conflict.

Communication Theory

Before we focus specifically on conflict management theories, we will examine the nature of communication. Early theorists, such as Shannon and Weaver (1949), represented communication as a **mechanical process**—as if communication were like a machine with discrete parts that functioned in preset sequences. Implicit in a mechanical model is the idea that communication occurs in a series of one-way messages. Person A talks and is the message sender to Person B. In turn, Person B talks and becomes the sender, making Person A the new receiver. In a mechanical model of communication, meaning resides in the message. Communication is like an intercom system—you can talk or you can listen, but you can't do both at the same time. In the 1960s, theorists such as Watzlawick, Beavin, and Jackson (1967) rejected the mechanical approach and proposed that communication is a complex **transactional process** that occurs continuously and simultaneously. While Person A talks, Person B is listening and reacting nonverbally. Both parties are communicating simultaneously because each is giving feedback to the other. When Lamont's sister threw the pictures across the room, everyone's reactions were instantly obvious. Additionally, the transactional view posits that communication is ongoing, meaning that one "cannot *not* communicate." Even refusing to participate in a discussion is an act of communication. When Lamont and Latisha stopped talking to each other, their silence still was communicating volumes of hurt, anger, and frustration.

"Meanings are in people" is another truism for modern communication scholars. Words and gestures have no inherent meanings. Meanings must be interpreted by those who perceive them. There is no connection between most words and their meanings. The words *cell phone* refer to a portable communication device. Because humans invent words, the cell phone could just as well have been labeled a telephone without a cord (TWC) or a clooh—a sound that has no assigned meaning. Words are symbols to which humans attach meaning.

To make matters more complex, words have denotative and connotative meanings (as discussed in Chapter 1). For Lamont's sisters, in Case 2.1, being more involved meant (connotatively) looking at pictures of babies, helping with cooking, and creating a sisterly friendship. For Latisha, being involved meant showing up during holidays.

> ### Discussion Question 2.2
> Describe a conversation where people were using the same words but attaching different connotative meanings.

Theories Influencing Conflict Management Studies

Early Ideas About Conflict

The earliest theories of conflict management focused on the most visible and dramatic aspects of conflict. They shared a common view of life as a struggle that often led to aggression and violence. Darwin theorized that life is built on competition among species, implying that aggressive competition is an inherent part of survival. Marx's social theory saw inevitable struggles for resources between classes that would simmer and then erupt in violent revolution against the rich. Freud's **psychodynamic theory** conceived an internal struggle between the id and the superego (see Deutsch, 2000a; Lulofs & Cahn, 2000). Early theorists suggested that psychologically, socially, or genetically, people were driven by aggression. Later theorists such as Lewin began to divert from this assumption.

Field theory was proposed by Lewin and others in the pre–World War II era of 1920 to 1940. Lewin suggested that within any system there are forces that drive conflicts and forces that restrain conflicts. Deutsch (2000a) explained that these forces create tensions leading to three basic types of conflict. When there are two choices of equal positive value, an **approach-approach conflict** exists. For example, in a company downsizing employees, one individual might be given the choice of taking a promotion at the same location (which is seen as desirable) or moving to another state (where the individual has close relatives and friends). When there are two choices of equal negative value, an **avoid-avoid conflict** emerges. In this situation, an employee would be forced to choose between being downsized or a demotion to a job he or she considers less valuable. When there are opposing negative and positive values, an **approach-avoid conflict** is created. An employee might be given a promotion, but only if he or she moves to a detested location. A field theorist would look at Lamont and Latisha in Case 2.1 and speculate that Latisha's holidays were an avoid-avoid conflict: She could offend Lamont's family by not going to holiday dinners or she could offend them by not acting "the right way" when she did attend.

> ### Discussion Question 2.3
> Describe a time when you felt torn by an approach-avoid or an avoid-avoid conflict.

Post–World War II Influences on Theory

Game theory evolved in the 1940s as a mathematical way to calculate projected gains and losses while playing games to simulate human choice making. Social scientists adapted game theory to the idea that people in a conflict are interdependent and exhibit a mix of cooperative and competitive impulses. Schelling created the term **mixed-motive situation** to refer to the competitive and cooperative nature of conflict. Game theory works well in areas where resources and choices are limited (Deutsch, 2000a; Schelling, 1960). It can involve sophisticated mathematical analysis and is useful to detect the structure and rules for behaviors that operate in existing relationships and organizations (Jost & Weitzel, 2007). Its limitation is the assumption that people in conflicts always act rationally and predictably.

The prisoner's dilemma illustrates a classic situation used by game theorists. Two people are caught outside a convenience store after it is robbed. The police try to get a confession. The suspects are separated, and each is told the same thing. If one confesses and implicates her partner, she would get a lighter sentence and perhaps be set free. Table 2.2 details their choices and possible outcomes. If each stays mute, both may be set free. If one implicates the other, the confessor will be released and the other will be prosecuted. If both rat on the other, the police will prosecute both and they probably will be convicted. In a totally rational world, both should stay silent.

TABLE 2.2   *The Prisoner's Dilemma*

		Ralph the Robber	
		Stay Silent	*Confess*
Bertha the Burglar	*Stay Silent*	Both go free	Ralph goes to jail
	Confess	Bertha goes to jail	Both go to jail

The gambling game of Texas Hold' Em illustrates the limits of game theory. Like many card games, each individual is competing to see who wins based on the relative rank order of the hands. In a purely rational world, each player would assess the statistical probability of the cards being the winning combination and would bet accordingly. If that were all that occurred, poker would be predictable—and boring. What makes poker exciting is the unknown. In Texas Hold 'Em, people bluff. Even though a player knows his or her cards probably are not the best at the gaming table, a gambler may pretend to be strong and win by getting others to throw away their "winning" hands. Because people don't always play by the rational rules, predicting their behavior is challenging.

Constructive and Destructive Conflict

The concept of **constructive versus destructive conflict** was developed from field theory in the 1940s and still is used today. Deutsch's theory of constructive and destructive conflict identified two core concepts in scholarly thinking about conflict management. First, people's goals are **interdependent**—meaning the probability of one's goal attainment is linked to the probability of the other's goal attainment. If the connection is positive, each person's goals are moving in the same direction; if one attains his or her goals, so will the other person (**positive interdependence**). Goals can be positively linked for many reasons, such as liking the other person, sharing resources, common group membership, common values, culture, common enemies, or division of labor. If the connection is negative, attainment of one person's goals means that the other will not attain his or her goals. **Negative interdependence** of goals can result from factors such as disliking the other person or a competitive reward structure. As Deutsch (2000b) notes, "if you're positively linked with another, then you sink or swim together; with negative linkage, if the other sinks, you swim, and if the other swims, you sink" (p. 22).

> ***Discussion Question 2.4***
>
> In Case 2.1, "Lamont and Latisha's Happy Holiday," what factors made this conflict destructive?

The second dimension is that actions to achieve goals are either effective or bungling (Deutsch, 2000b). The actions that people take to reach their goals can be well chosen and effective or ill advised and ineffective. Had Case 2.1 participants attempted to discuss how

Latisha could become a member of the extended family, constructive conflict might have been possible. By demanding that Lamont divorce his wife, a negative competitive situation was created. Lamont ultimately had to choose between his wife and his family.

Situations often are *mixed motive:* The goals are more or less positive or more or less negatively related and the actions are more or less effective. For example, a salesperson may work in a company that gives cash awards to the employee who sells the most during a month. The situation seems purely competitive. In reality, if the sales staff like each other, motives are mixed—each wants to win the bonus but not to offend coworkers who also are friends.

Deutsch's theory may seem to suggest that only cooperative conflicts can be productive. To the contrary, Deutsch, and other modern theorists, believe that competition also can be productive. He states,

> I do not mean to suggest that competition produces no benefits. Competition is part of everyday life. Acquiring the skills necessary to compete effectively can be of considerable value. Moreover, competition in a cooperative, playful context can be fun. It enables one to enact and experience, in a non-serious setting, symbolic emotional dramas relating to victory and defeat, life and death, power and helplessness, dominance and submission; these dramas have deep personal and cultural roots. (Deutsch, 2000b, p. 28)

Chapter 3 delves into cooperative and competitive conflict in more detail.

Attribution Theory

Attribution theory advances the concept that people consistently attempt to make sense of the world around them (Manusov & Spitzberg, 2008). As individuals observe the world, they are attributing meaning. Danny sees two of his friends, Sally and Sam, walking side by side down the street. They are very close together, and Sam is holding Sally's arm. Both are in committed relationships with other people. Attribution theory suggests that Danny will make sense of his observation by attributing meaning to the situation. It is as if the mind asks, "What does this piece of information mean?" The answer is then treated as if it were truth. Danny will infer a meaning to what he saw. He might infer that Sally and Sam are having an affair. In reality, Sally might be unwell and Sam is helping her back to her car. If Danny talks to Sally or Sam, using a suspicious tone of voice, he acts on his attribution rather than seeking information to determine the real truth.

Discussion Question 2.5

What attributions have you made recently about people you have met? How do attributions contribute to conflict?

Attribution theory was adapted to interpersonal conflict and how individuals look at the other person as the source of conflict (Sillars, 1980). From an interpersonal conflict viewpoint, attributions about the other person—and the subsequent interpretation of those attributions—drive a conflict. Two types of attributions can be made about behavior: Internal or external. *Internal* attributions label behavior as arising from the other person's personality, values, or characteristics. For example, Lamont's sister took Latisha's statement that she wanted to look at the pictures later as meaning Latisha was stuck-up, unfriendly, and uncaring (internal to her personality). However, when Latisha didn't look at the pictures, the sister could have interpreted her choice as a result of being tired after a long drive (external or outside of her personality). *Externalizations* assume that the behavior is caused by some situation outside the individual's control. After a hurricane and breakdown of civil order in New Orleans in 2005, some people attributed the subsequent looting to a criminal predisposition and the low moral character of New Orleans residents (internal). Others attributed the events as caused by the deprivation of the situation or by historic patterns of poverty (external).

Attribution theory helps explain a behavioral pattern of assigning personality flaws to others' failings while assigning external reasons to one's own faults. Assigning internal or external causation without a factual base is called an **attribution error.** A **self-serving bias** occurs when we assign internal attributions to our successes ("I studied hard and that's why I got an A.") and external factors to our shortcomings ("The teacher doesn't like me, that's why I only got a C–.") In general, we are much more complimentary of our own behaviors than we are of others, according to attribution theorists.

In conflict, how one attributes motive to the other person makes a difference in how one behaves. If a group sees another group as not trustworthy (an internal attribution), they act toward that group with suspicion. Not being trusted may lead to resentment and misjudgments, which creates more defensiveness. Defensiveness is seen as a personality flaw in others (internal attribution).

Attribution theory is useful because it raises awareness about how people make sense of others' behaviors. People who are optimists may attribute good in people; pessimists may see the bad. Both might be wrong.

Exchange Theories

Exchange theories posit that individuals make relationship choices on a cost-benefit tally system. Exchange theory is built on the metaphor of an economic marketplace and assumes that people will make choices that are the most beneficial to them.

Social exchange theory proposes that people evaluate the costs and rewards of a relationship by the amount of effort required to attain rewards and avoid costs (see West & Turner, 2000). Social exchange theory explains the occasional feeling that another person is too calculating—assessing what he or she can get out of it before investing anything in the relationship. When rewards are perceived as too low and the other party is viewed as interfering with reward attainment, conflict is likely. One spouse may see constant bickering and high tension as too much of a cost (to personal happiness) and decide to get a divorce. In Case 2.1, if Lamont uses exchange theory to judge his relationship, he may break up with Latisha if he feels he is sacrificing more than the overall relationship brings back to him in rewards.

> ### Discussion Question 2.6
> Consider the "economic" language used to describe relationships. "You owe me one." "This isn't worth the hassle." "What's the payoff?" Do you think most relationships really use a social exchange theory model?

All relationships take time, which is an investment cost within exchange theory. Relationships also provide a variety of rewards—esteem, security, resource access, and so forth. In a committed relationship where both are going to college, time can be a rare commodity. Time for romance may conflict with time to study. Socializing with a partner's friends may interfere with time to go to the library. Going to a movie may be at the cost of lost sleep or a poorly written assignment. Within social exchange theory, each individual calculates the costs and benefits to the relationship and to career ambitions before making choices.

Interaction Theories

Interaction theories focus attention on the communication and interactions among people rather than on the individual. To interaction theorists, conflict management must involve the perspectives of all parties to the conflict, not just one side (Olson & Braithwaite, 2004). **Constructivism,** one type of interaction theory advanced by Delia, states that people create meaning through a series of personal constructs (or schemas) (Delia & Crockett, 1973). Each person's construct of what it means to be friends, patriotic, or a good worker may be significantly different. How, then, can people manage to communicate at all?

According to constructivists, an agreed-upon social construction is created through human interaction. By talking about our views and ideals, a common interpretation can emerge. Students' constructs of a "good teacher" vary considerably. One student may construct the concept of a good teacher versus a bad teacher based on workload:

Good Teacher	*Bad Teacher*
Understands I have a life	Thinks only his or her class is important
Gives little homework	Gives too much homework
Gives high grades	Grades too hard

A second student may construct the concept of a good teacher versus a bad teacher quite differently, based on outcome:

Good Teacher	*Bad Teacher*
Motivates me to learn	Doesn't care about my learning
Gives meaningful assignments	Gives busywork assignments
Makes me think	Is too easy

As we learn and gain experience, constructs change. Only through interaction can individuals work to create a shared meaning, or construct, about important issues. For conflict managers, constructivist theories suggest that the right way to manage conflict is a socially created concept. To succeed, those in conflict need to create a shared construction of meaning, not only about the issues being negotiated but also about how to behave during conflict. Each individual has a personal construction of what it means to be a good parent, boss, or romantic partner. If personal constructions are not shared with others, conflict occurs because each individual is pushing toward a different ideal.

> ### Discussion Question 2.7
> What is your construct of a good teacher or a good friend? What is your construct of a good conflict manager?

Systems Theory

In contrast to theories that focus on processes within the individual, **systems theory** includes all of our relationships and interactions. The most fundamental idea in systems theory is that one cannot understand the whole system just by looking at its composite parts (von Bertalanffly, 1968). In other words, the system is more than the sum of its parts. Applied to conflict, systems theory suggests looking at the interaction between the parties over time and in context rather than focusing on just one side or at just one moment in time. For example, a systems theorist would need to know more about Lamont and Latisha in Case 2.1 before analyzing their situation: What has occurred in the past during holidays? What are the norms for Lamont's family during holidays? What are the norms for Latisha's family of origin during holidays? What type of relationship do Lamont and Latisha have? What has the relationship been between Lamont and his sisters and between Latisha and the sisters-in-law before this event? Are any cultural influences at play in the system? Only by looking at the entire system could the meaning in a single episode be made clear.

Systems have identities that go beyond their individual parts. Lamont's sisters and parents have an identity as a family system. A newcomer, such as Latisha, not only unknowingly may break the customs in her partner's family, but she can also be seen as a threat to that family. When threatened, a system moves to enforce its rules or protect its identity—in Lamont's case, by asking him to divorce his wife.

Emerging Theories

Each year, new theories emerge that help us understand aspects of conflict. We have selected several that represent a range of perspectives.

Communication Privacy Management

How privacy is established and regulated is the topic of Petronio's **communication privacy management theory.** Petronio (2000, 2002) posits that individuals manage the disclosure of private information by creating boundaries of what they will tell and what they will withhold. In one application, communication privacy management theory was used to explain children's distancing from parents as the child tries to establish independence. Researchers tested how adolescents use "fortification" of their rooms to create privacy or adopt evasive tactics to keep parents from discovering what they do. Children also set boundaries through topic avoidance and deception as responses to parental questions (Mazur & Hubbard, 2004). A parent asks her high school sophomore daughter how school was today, to which the daughter responds with, "Fine." Mom knows the girl was called into the principal's office for skipping class, but she is hoping the daughter will self-disclose the specifics. The daughter is attempting to maintain a boundary between her school life and her home life. She is unlikely to volunteer information that bridges those two worlds, unless pressed.

Discussion Question 2.8

What boundary management techniques did you attempt as a teenager? How did those strategies prevent or cause conflict?

Boundary management goes beyond teenage angst and has broad implications for conflict management. Determining what individuals perceive to be invasions of privacy and how they respond to perceived privacy violations is helpful to prevent and to manage conflict in many contexts, including the workplace and virtually any type of new relationship. For example, Jana worked in a physician's office with several other women. The staff shared information with each other about families, boyfriends, husbands, and children. Jana didn't engage in these conversations because she wanted to keep her personal life private. At her first performance evaluation, she was marked down for not being a "team player" and was told that the other employees thought she was standoffish. Jana's boundary management strategy created a conflict in the office.

Surveillance in the workplace is an emerging practice in which employees and employers may differ over who controls information boundaries. What employees think is private communication via e-mail or phone may be overtly or covertly recorded, studied, and appear in reports given to management. Allen, Coopman, Hart, and Walker (2007) explore how employees perceive boundary management at work and the effort made to avoid inadvertent disclosure of so-called private information.

The context of premarriage/commitment counseling can address the issue of how much privacy each partner should expect after moving in together. Many new relationships start without negotiating boundaries and later trip over boundary issues. Healthy discussions to negotiate boundaries would help many new couples and all new college roommates. For example, couples might wish to discuss these questions: How does each party view assets—private or mutually owned? How will the other partner be included in purchases—as a co-decider, or do individuals make major purchases without consultation? Will the individuals spend time alone with former friends, or will the couple do everything together? Can partners keep secrets from each other? Roommates might discuss issues such as: Can roommates borrow clothes from each other without explicit permission? Is food put in the refrigerator available to everyone? Is any space in the apartment/dormitory room private, or does everyone have access everywhere? What level of cleanliness is appropriate?

Emotional Intelligence

The realization that intellectual intelligence (often expressed as IQ) had little to do with interpersonal competence led to a search for a companion concept to fill in the rest of the picture. **Emotional intelligence (EQ)** encompasses self-awareness, managing emotions, self-motivation, recognizing emotions in others, and handling relationships (Cherniss & Adler, 2000).

TOOLBOX 2.1

Negotiating Roommate Boundaries

When roommates live in close contact over time, they usually discover that each person has different ideas in some important areas. Rooming together involves mutually negotiating behaviors and being able to bring difficulties to your roommate's attention in a constructive way. Privately answer these questions where roommates have encountered difficulty in the past. Then initiate a discussion with your roommate to negotiate boundaries that will work for both of you.

1. How do you feel about your private possessions—clothes, books, CDs, shoes, toiletries, snacks? How would you feel if your roommate "borrowed" any of your personal items?
   - If it is OK with you to borrow specific things, how should the borrowing take place? Do you need to know each time in advance? Can your roommate borrow the item without asking in advance? Would a note be enough?
   - Are there conditions on borrowing things? If clothes are borrowed, do they need to be washed/dry cleaned before being returned? What if the item is damaged while it is borrowed?
2. What are your expectations on spending time socializing together? What does it mean to be roommates?

3. What are your expectations on how your common space will be used?
   - How often should one person's friends be over to visit in the room/common area? Can they stay over?
   - Is it reasonable to ask your roommate to be gone from the room/home for a while, all evening, or even all night?
   - Are there times when it is OK/not OK to play electronic equipment without headphones?
   - Are there specific times set aside for studying?
4. Will you keep the area clean?
   - Describe your view of what "clean" or "dirty" means.
   - How often does the area need to be cleaned?
   - Who will clean what and how often?
5. How do you want to bring up topics that the two of you need to discuss? *It is better to discuss things directly with your roommate than to tell all of your other friends.*
   - How can you raise the issue if your roommate isn't doing what you thought was the agreement on keeping the room clean, borrowing things, having visitors over, or honoring study time?

Behind EQ theory is the notion that emotions create energy. Positive energy comes with positive emotions; negative energy comes with negative emotions. Those who test low in EQ have little self-awareness and ability to manage their emotions, are not self-motivating, cannot recognize emotions in others, and don't handle relationships well. People with the opposite characteristics test higher in EQ (Bagshaw, 2000).

In recent years, training programs have emerged to help the low emotionally intelligent individual understand and work with highly emotional intelligent friends and colleagues. Bagshaw's (2000) training program focuses on five elements called CARES (see Table 2.3).

EQ is an interesting concept for conflict managers, because low EQ may explain the insensitive patterns of interaction that precipitate some conflicts. It also helps explain why

TABLE 2.3 *Dimensions of Emotional Intelligence Training*

Creative Tension means managing the present and creating the future. One focuses on both the immediate goal and the future relationship.

Active Choice involves living with the choices one has made, being proactive, and not being anxious about personal risks.

Resilience Under Pressure is stress management to deal with feelings.

Empathic Relationship involves understanding the other person before expecting them to understand you, developing relationships, and trust.

Self-Awareness and **Self-Control** mean being honest with oneself.

---

some individuals could, with good intentions, believe that everything would work out if the other person would just not be so emotional.

Culture Theories

Some theorists observe that culture influences how people think and what they expect. Much of this theorizing and research revolves around the concept of collectivist versus individualistic cultures (see Cai & Fink, 2002). Simplistically put, *collectivist cultures* value the group over the individual. *Individualistic cultures* value the individual over the group. China, Taiwan, and Japan typically are viewed as collectivist cultures, and most European and North American countries are seen as primarily individualistic. The collectivist/individualistic theories have been criticized as being too general and not analyzing the influential subcultures at play in each country. However, examining the influences of culture may provide conflict managers valuable insight as they seek understanding in

---

TOOLBOX 2.2

What's Your Emotional Intelligence?

Reflect back on past interactions with a specific individual. Then answer each of the following while thinking about that relationship. The more "Yes" answers you give, the higher your emotional intelligence.

1. Are you aware of your own feelings?
2. Do you usually sense what others are feeling, even when they don't verbalize them?
3. Does an awareness of how others feel lead you to have compassion or empathy for them?
4. Can you get the things done that you want when you experience stress, or do your feelings keep you from moving forward?
5. When you are angry, can you still interact with civility and not make the situation worse?
6. Can you focus on the long-term goal without getting distracted or sidetracked?
7. Do you keep trying to reach your goals, even if it is tempting to give up?
8. Can you use your feelings to help make decisions?

Source: Excerpted from Bagshaw (2000), pp. 61–62.

conflict situations. Chapter 4 examines how this and other cultural perspectives are used to illuminate differences or similarities in conflict styles, strategies, and tactics.

> **Discussion Question 2.9**
>
> Which theory of interpersonal conflict makes the most sense to you? Which theory appeals to you the least?

Dialectical Tensions Theory

As we navigate relationships at work or in personal life, we often experience pulls in opposite directions, examined in **dialectical tensions theory.** These dialectical tensions lay the groundwork for conflict. Researchers (Baxter, 1988; Pawlowski, 1998) studied the dominant tensions that relational partners experience as they navigate their lives together. Baxter and Mongomery (1996) identified three dialectical tensions that couples experience within their relationship and three that they feel with their community.

First, *connectedness versus separateness* is the tension between presenting a united front as a couple versus maintaining individuality and separate identities. For Lamont and Latisha, she may struggle with wanting to appear to her in-laws as happily married and part of a couple versus wanting to have space, apart from Lamont, where she can be alone.

Second, the desire to predict what one's partner will do versus the desire to live spontaneously is summed up in the dialectical tension of *certainty versus uncertainty.* We want the security of familiarity and dependability, but at the same time we don't want so much predictability that the relationship becomes boring. Finally, the dialectical tension of *openness versus closedness* encompasses how much information we let the other know. Although we may want our partners to know us intimately, we still may hold on to private thoughts and not share everything. Some partners expect full disclosure; others may believe the past is past and need not be shared. The goal in relationships is to find the equilibrium or balance point within these tensions. The challenge is heightened by the fact that as relationships grow and change, so do their balance points. Relationships can be in continual flux searching for the right balance; without care, flux can create conflict.

A couple may experience dialectical tension with their community as they form a combined identity. These dialectical tensions are inclusion versus seclusion in relationships, conventionality versus uniqueness in traditions, and revealed versus concealed information (see Table 2.4).

The first community tension, *inclusion versus seclusion*, attempts to balance the desire of the couple to join with others (such as Lamont's family) yet maintain their own autonomy. Lamont and Latisha opted for seclusion instead of the continued strife precipitated by Lamont's family gatherings.

As couples break away from their families of origin, they may strive to develop new traditions. The second external dialectic is the *conventionality versus uniqueness* tension. Will a couple follow the conventional family traditions or will they develop new ways of celebrating holidays? Third, couples may struggle with how much information to share with others about their relationship—is information *revealed or*

TABLE 2.4 *Dialectical Tensions*

Relationship Dialectics	Community Dialectics
Connectedness vs. separateness	Inclusion vs. seclusion
Certainty vs. uncertainty	Conventionality vs. uniqueness
Openness vs. closedness	Revealed vs. concealed

concealed? One couple allows the husband's mother, who is an accountant, to prepare their annual tax returns. Before this arrangement, the couple set out a rule with Mom that she wasn't to give advice on financial decisions unless asked. This rule has helped maintain a balance between the dialectical tensions of revelation versus concealment of personal matters.

Conflict is a common outcome in situations where dialectical tensions are at odds. Dialectical tensions have been studied in contexts other than romantic partnerships. Determining the appropriate balance is relevant at the workplace, with friends, as well as with families.

Summary

A theory is a tentative explanation for behavior. Modern communication theories represent the communication process as more transactional than mechanical. Theories of human behavior tend to represent one of two basic positions: Behaviors result from inherent or biological causes (nature) or behaviors result from culture and context (nurture).

The first conflict management theories, such as psychodynamic and field theory, focused on human aggression and internal psychological states. Later theories, such as game theory, developed an interest in conflict strategies and tactics or, in the case of Deutsch, the components of destructive and constructive outcomes and the nature of interdependence.

Attribution theory explains how individuals perceive others' motives and behaviors. Exchange theory posits that individuals make decisions based on a cost and reward evaluation. Interaction theories focus on the conflict pair rather than the individual. Constructivists examine the mental structures that individuals use to judge behaviors. Systems theory expands awareness to the macro level by looking at the entire context in which conflict is embedded.

Several emerging theories are gaining interest among conflict scholars. Boundary management theory proposes that individuals enact specific strategies to gain independence. Emotional intelligence theory attempts to explain differences in social sensitivity. Cultural theories describe the differences among geographic or otherwise established groups with common identities. Finally, dialectical tensions theory aims to understand the contrasting tensions that individuals may have with others and that couples may have with their community.

Chapter Resources _____

Exercises

1. Assess a current relationship using exchange theory. What are the benefits of the relationship? What are the costs?

2. Develop a "rule" about how conflict should be managed between teachers and students. Is the rule you create similar to or different from what has occurred in the past when students and teachers disagree?

3. Analyze the film *The Family Stone*. Which theory best explains the conflict between the uptight girlfriend Meredith (played by Sarah Jessica Parker) and the Stone family members?

4. Explore the dialectical tensions in one of your significant relationships.

Journal/Essay Topics

1. Identify a pattern of behavior you are curious about. Which theory in the chapter helps explain what you have observed?

2. How might your emotional intelligence affect your conflict management abilities?

Research Topics

1. Select two theories from the chapter. Review published research to understand more about the two theories. Write a paper that compares the theories' assumptions and the type of research questions that arise from each perspective.

2. Select an emerging theory other than the ones mentioned in this chapter, such as standpoint theory, the coordinated management of meaning theory, or narrative theory. What insights about conflict can be gained from the theory you selected?

Mastery Case

Examine Mastery Case 2, "Holly the Hun," using one of the theories in this chapter. Explain how the theory sheds light on this case.

Holly the Hun

Holly worked on the assembly line at the packing plant for five years before she became a manager. The line typically had ten workers, some men and some women. When she first got the promotion, most people were happy for her—except Walter, who thought he had worked for the company longer and deserved the promotion. Time has passed, and now all of the line employees hate her. She used to be friendly with her staff, but now she avoids them. Holly rarely leaves her cubicle near the plant manager's office and frequently is seen having lunch with him. Holly sends e-mail messages instructing the assembly-line workers to follow new procedures. When she does talk to people, she tells people what to do and doesn't seem to listen when anyone else has an idea. She carefully plots interactions with the line workers to maintain control of every minute, so nobody else has a chance to speak much. In discussions among themselves, the line workers say that Holly has a bizarre idea of what supervisors should do and that she thinks she is superior to them now.

3

Competitive and Cooperative Conflict Approaches

Vocabulary

Accommodation
Argumentativeness
Avoidance
Communication climate
Competitive conflict
Cooperative conflict
Creating value

Defensive climates
"I" statements
Interest-based conflict
Interests
Mixed-motive situation
Mutual gains
Neutrality

Passive aggression
Positions
Supportive climate
Taking value
Verbal aggression

Objectives

After reading the chapter, you should be able to:

1. Explain the assumptions of competitive and cooperative approaches
2. Discriminate between situations that require competition and those where cooperation might result in better outcomes
3. Explain the four myths of competition
4. Explain the difference between supportive and defensive climates

There are two approaches to conflict: competition and cooperation. This chapter explores how the assumptions of these two views affect the strategies, tactics, and probable outcomes of interpersonal conflict; discusses what happens when the counterparts in a conflict are firmly fixed in opposite views; and illustrates how most conflicts involve both competitive and cooperative aspects.

CASE 3.1 • *Sibling Rivalry*

Sergio and Antoine are brothers. Their folks provided the teens with a car to use, leaving the scheduling up to the two of them to figure out. Sergio, the oldest, drives them both to school and has claimed first dibs on the car during weekends. Antoine has tried to talk to Sergio about sharing the car more equitably. Sergio says it was his car first and his brother needs to live with it until he moves out next year. Antoine tried again, this time with a schedule in hand that had each of them sharing the driving during the week (even giving Sergio an extra day) and alternating Friday and Saturday nights each weekend. Sergio responded by laughing at Antoine and told him, "Get over it already."

Antoine came up with a new plan of attack. He drew up a list of all of the items that belonged to him that Sergio regularly borrows. The list included clothes, sporting equipment, video games, and his MP3 player (after Sergio accidentally laundered his own). Antoine also listed ways that he had helped Sergio in the past with chores, homework, and occasionally lending him money. He also wrote down the few times that he had covered for Sergio when he's come in after curfew. When he finished his lists, he approached Sergio again.

Antoine presented Sergio with the lists he'd created and said, "Look, bro, if you want to be completely independent from each other, that certainly would have some benefits for me. But I'd rather continue to help each other out and share stuff. So, now about that car schedule . . ."

The Competitive World

Individuals steeped in the competitive paradigm believe there are only three choices in conflict: win, lose, or draw. Table 3.1 presents some of the assumptions brought to conflict by those with a competitive versus a cooperative approach. For diehard competitors, winning is tied inextricably to face—the *best* player wins. In a competitive view, goal attainment is mutually exclusive. If you win; I lose. If the "opponent" in conflict is equally powerful and skilled, compromise to achieve a tie is an acceptable outcome. Going for a draw makes the situation even: The compromise splits the difference so both win (or lose) equally (Withers, 2002). At its extreme, the competitive view is driven by fear of loss in a world dominated by limitation.

TABLE 3.1   *Assumptions about Conflict*

Competitive Worldview	*Cooperative Worldview*
• Winning is the goal	• Meeting needs of all parties while maintaining a relationship is the goal
• Zero-sum resources	• Expandable resources
• View *other* as the opponent	• View the *issue* as the opponent
• Strategic in moving toward one's desired solution	• Open to creative problem solving
• Position focused	• Interest focused

Competitive conflict sometimes is initiated by a perception that one party has a right to seek compliance from another person—based on perceived authority, status, or prejudice. Hullett and Tamborini (2001) explain, "The perception of high rights involves the perception that the actor is justified in seeking compliance. . . . Of course, having the right to seek compliance does not necessarily mean that the target will see the situation in the same way and thus not resist the attempt" (p. 4). McLaughlin posits four types of resistance strategies by those who see a compliance demand as unjust: stating one will not comply, managing self-identity by attacking the other's authority, presenting reasons for noncompliance, and entering into bargaining about the request (Hullett & Tamborini, 2001). For example, at bedtime a child may assert, "I will not go to bed" (non-negotiation). The rebellious child may bluster to a babysitter, "You are not the boss of me" (attack the other's authority). If the father is putting a child to bed, the boy may say, "Mom lets me stay up later on weekends" (justification for noncompliance). After not succeeding at other strategies, a child may switch to the last strategy and say, "I'll be good if you let me stay up" (negotiation).

> "If it doesn't matter who wins or loses, then why do they keep score?"
>
> —Football coach, Vincent Lombardi

Inherent at the extreme range of the competitive view is the role of loser, as defined by either or both parties. Losers may receive fewer resources, be left with less power, be one down in the relationship, or suffer loss of face. When complying, they may choose strategies of **avoidance** (removing oneself from the controversy), **passive aggression** (begrudging compliance, perhaps with a plan to get even), or **accommodation** (submission). Losers may develop so-called amnesia and forget to take actions that benefit the winner or comply with surly indifference. Those who are about to lose a conflict that deeply threatens a cherished goal may apply extreme strategies, such as severing the relationship or violence. Those in stable relationships who lose small conflicts may retaliate in other ways. Cedric and Jasmine may differ over a simple issue like what movie to see on Friday night. Cedric may prevail, saying, "Since I am paying for the tickets, I get to decide." The situation is a classic win/lose scenario. If Jasmine decides she doesn't like being the loser, she may take actions to ensure Cedric doesn't have a good time at "his" movie. She might stall so they miss the beginning of the film and get bad seats, talk during exciting car chases, or insist they leave early. Because she doesn't like the role of loser, Jasmine turns the win/lose outcome into a lose/lose situation.

> ### Discussion Question 3.1
>
> What lessons about competition did you learn as a child (such as "losing builds character" or "It doesn't matter if you win or lose, it's how you play the game.")? What did these lessons teach you about winning and losing, cooperating and competing?

At its extreme, classic tactics of competition include verbal aggressiveness and argumentativeness. **Argumentativeness** is defending one's positions and attacking the other party's positions. Stein and Albro (2001) note that although winning for one's side is the general goal of argument, some arguments are to determine who is the dominant individual in the situation, group, or relationship. **Verbal aggression** attacks others and their positions

(Rogan & La France, 2003). Name-calling, sneering tones, and demeaning evaluative statements are verbally aggressive tactics. These tactics subvert the esteem of the other person and create a face conflict. Even if the initial conflict was about process or scarce resource issues, it now is about pride or self-image. (You can read more about face conflict in Chapter 4.)

The competitive approach sees power as a zero-sum resource—believing that there is a finite amount power to go around. Bacharach and Lawler (1986) analyzed the fallacies in that perspective. First, it is a fallacy that power only can be developed by withholding resources to make the other person dependent. Power is based on a connection with the other party where one person has something that the other desires. From a profoundly competitive drive, power is gained by making someone more dependent or blocking his or her ability to acquire a desired goal. Although people can go to extremes, as in spousal abuse where money and contact with other people are withheld to create absolute dependence, the effort to sustain negative dependence typically is not proportionate to the payoff. A secretary who unnecessarily is miserly with office supplies tries to get power by creating scarcity. The ill will created through this strategy probably outweighs the benefits.

Second, it is a fallacy to view coercion as a rightful entitlement of the powerful. Firstborns may give orders to their younger siblings because they believe an older child automatically has authority, as in Case 3.1, "Sibling Rivalry." One spouse may coerce a desired behavior in a partner by withdrawing intimacy. Instead of complying, the partner may also pull away in an attempt to balance power. In a spiral of negative action and reaction, the couple grows further apart. Reducing intimacy also reduces the interdependence of the couple, and a spurned partner may look elsewhere for intimacy. An interesting aside is the paradox of coercive power: Overusing coercive power often leads to losing that source of power. A teen who constantly has his allowance taken as a punishment for breaking house rules may decide he can make money elsewhere and deny his parents that source of power.

> ### Discussion Question 3.2
>
> How might a reliance on coercion by a boss or a parent actually reduce the boss/parent's power in the future?

Kohn (1986), a critic of the competitive influence, claims North Americans are socialized to believe in the universal virtues of competition based on four assumptions that actually are myths. Myth 1 states *competition is an unavoidable part of human nature.* The

CASE 3.2 • *Your Call*

On a foggy night, a navy ship suddenly sees a blip appear on its radar screen. A story is told that the following conversation occurred (Seymour, 1997):

Navy Ship: "Unknown radar contact. Alter your course 10 degrees."

Reply: "Alter your course 10 degrees south."

Navy Ship: "Alter your course 10 degrees north. This is the captain in command."

Reply: "Alter your course 10 degrees south. I am a seaman second class."

Navy Ship: "I order you to change course immediately. We are a battleship."

Reply: "We are a lighthouse. Your call."

success of cooperative and mutual gains systems seems to belie that assumption, as do anthropological studies of collaborative cultures such as the Zuni Indians.

Myth 2 claims that *competition encourages people to do their best, and without competition, mediocrity would rule.* Kohn believes that energy, creativity, and wealth are wasted through unnecessary competition. Modern management theories that encourage cooperation are transforming the workplace. In education, competitive grading systems assume that if only two students can receive an "A" in a class of thirty, the best students will rise to the top of the academic heap. Competitive grading systems deter collaboration, study groups, or other ventures that might help all students learn the course concepts more effectively.

Myth 3 asserts that *competitive games are the best way to have a good time.* This probably is true for the few individuals who excel and win. In contrast, those who cannot win at games typically drop out. Mandy loves the game Trivial Pursuit and almost always wins. She really enjoys the game; her friends who always lose do not enjoy it. They now refuse to play with her. Similarly, individuals who know they cannot win a bonus in a competitive salary schedule may slack off because they know the reward is unattainable.

Myth 4 proposes that *competition builds character.* Although competition may help build positive self-esteem in some individuals, the opposite effect probably occurs for those who are habitual losers. Critics argue that cooperation provides more room for success and is a better promoter of healthy self-esteem.

> ### Discussion Question 3.3
> Do Kohn's four myths match up with your life experiences? Provide examples from school, work, family, and/or personal relationships that show these myths in action.

Competition exists along a continuum, however. Most people influenced by North American or European-based cultures were socialized to compete to one extent or another. Although loving competition too much may not be good, knowledge of competitive systems and how to bargain competitively is a necessary life skill. Benefits to competition include positive stimulation for those who prefer the style, ensuring a share of available resources when resources are scarce, and motivating high performance. Chapter 8 presents productive strategies for competitive bargaining.

At its best, competition is an appropriate response to genuine scarce resources and is manifested through strategies that do not rely on verbal aggression and personal attacks. For those higher on the competitiveness scale, it may be an exciting pastime. If conflict is a dance, the competitive dance "is usually not the waltz but the aggressive and spicy tango" (Cohen, 2003, p. 435). At its worst, however, competitors can adopt a win-at-all-costs view or believe the ultimate goal is to prevent the other from winning.

The Cooperative Approach

The cooperative approach, sometimes called a mutual gains perspective or interest-based bargaining, seeks creative and innovative solutions that maximally meet the needs of all parties. **Mutual gains** encompass the concept that the goals of all parties in a conflict

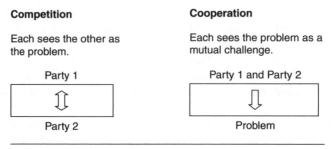

FIGURE 3.1 *Competitive and Cooperative Approaches*

might be met if creative strategies are applied to the problem. The term **interest-based conflict** arises from a focus on the underlying needs (interests) of each of the parties rather than on their surface demands. At the extreme, those holding a mutual gains view believe all conflicts can be settled in ways that maximize each person's needs and that many conflicts are about resources that are not genuinely scarce.

> ### Discussion Question 3.4
> What conflict situations are appropriate or inappropriate for competitive strategies? What conflict situations are appropriate or inappropriate for cooperative strategies?

A business theorist early in the twentieth century, Mary Parker Follett, popularized looking beyond the obvious in conflict. She tells a story of two sisters squabbling over one orange. The mother suggested they split the orange and each take half—a traditional compromise solution. "They both refused this compromise, so the mother asked them what they needed the orange for. One sister needed the orange to make juice, and half an orange was hardly enough. The other needed the orange for a cake she was baking and needed the entire peel. Of course, the clever mother helped the two daughters see that they could both be satisfied. One got the peel, the other got the fruit" (Withers, 2002). Mutual gains bargainers live in a world of abundance dominated by potential. Contrary to the competitive assumption that the other is the opponent who struggles to advance his or her solution in an either/or contest, those who take an interest-based approach shift the focus to the problem as the mutual opponent.

Interests versus Positions

Positions are demands, proposed solutions, or other fixed outcome statements. Taking a position is like standing on top of the hill and daring others to force you to come down. Once an eighteen-year-old student takes the position that she will live away from home while going to college and demands financial support from her parents, it is challenging to find a solution that all parties will find acceptable. Those who start negotiation with an unyielding position find it difficult to compromise or think creatively. Changing one's mind is perceived as backing down, creating a loss of face.

Interests are needs. Each position has underlying interests that may be obscured or unexpressed. Beneath the demand to live off campus may be an array of unexpressed interests: a desire for independence, a need for a quiet space to study, a fear of being socially isolated from college life, or a distaste for daily commuting. Likewise, the parents who say "No" and make a counterpositional demand that the daughter remain in the home during all of her college years have unexpressed interests: fear for their child's safety, lack of money, or sadness that children eventually will make their own way in the world. As long as positions are competitively exchanged, the outcome probably will be influenced more by power than by a genuine seeking of a solution that will maximize the needs of all parties. In contrast, those with an interest-based perspective turn the competitive world on its head and begin with a discussion of needs. With less ego and face involved in defending positions and more information about each party's goals, a mutually acceptable solution becomes possible.

The key difference between competitive and cooperative approaches is how conflict is framed. Competitors focus on self-centered outcomes. Cooperators focus on the processes that can lead to positive outcomes for both. Katz and Block (2000) believe people with outcome goals are focused on their positions—the outcome they want. People focused on process goals are interested in a strategy leading to a successful conflict resolution. Research shows people with process goals are more invested in the interaction and more likely to take risks. They are less anxious and are more rewarded by a variety of solutions. In contrast, outcome-focused individuals are more personally invested in one particular outcome, may not use good problem-solving skills, are rigid in their thinking, and see the inability to achieve desired positions as a lack of personal ability. Because achieving all of one's goals in every conflict is unlikely, outcome oriented goals lead to less satisfaction with conflict.

> ### Discussion Question 3.5
> What are the positions of the parties in Case 3.1? What interests might underlie each of the positions you identified?

When Worlds Collide

A weakness of the interest-based view can be the naive belief that a creative outcome always is possible. Although individuals in conflict do have more choices than may seem apparent at first glance, not all situations respond to creative problem solving. If after numerous attempts, the other person simply will not engage in **cooperative conflict** management, competition may be required. In some cases, the other party in the conflict takes an extremely competitive position and refuses to respond to cooperative overtures. Perhaps the resources in the situation genuinely are scarce and worth competing for—one promotion or one bonus. In these cases, having cooperative tunnel vision is just as limiting as overzealous competitiveness. In Case 3.1, Antoine would continue to hit a wall in trying to engage in collaboration with his brother. However, by adopting a competitive stance, and showing he's willing to play "hardball," he may be able to move Sergio into interest-based negotiations after all.

> ### *Discussion Question 3.6*
>
> How do you react to comments that are phrased with the word *You* as opposed to comments that avoid the word? For example, which phrasing would you react better to? "When you play your music so loud, I can't get my work done" or "When the music is so loud, I can't get my work done."

Extreme competitors may manipulate individuals who put all of their faith in cooperative conflict management. Some pop culture books suggest all conflict can be managed if the individuals simply follow preset steps. Generally speaking, formulaic steps are less effective if the other person doesn't follow the same rule book. As discussed in Chapter 8, the two processes in bargaining are creating value and taking value. Interest-based conflict managers are adept at **creating value.** They are creative, innovative, and capable of making numerous suggestions for solving a problem. Competitors are masters at **taking value.** Lax and Sebenius (1986) comment, "Value creators see the essence of negotiating as expanding the pie, as pursuing joint gains. This is aided by openness, clear communication, sharing information, creativity, an attitude of joint problem solving, and cultivating common interests. . . . Value claimers, on the other hand, tend to see this drive for joint gain as naive and weak-minded" (p. 32). Competitors may play along while the other is disclosing and creating value. Then they use the information to their own advantage and leave the table with the lion's share of resources. Table 3.2 summarizes the characteristics of competitive and cooperative conflict approaches.

TABLE 3.2   *Characteristics of Competitive and Cooperative Conflict*

Competition at Its Worst	*Cooperative Conflict at Its Best*
• Dominating	• Trusting
• Manipulative	• Realistic
• Aggressive	• Self-controlled
• Argumentative	• Open to suggestions
• Hostile	• Cooperative
• Ego centered	• Look for interests of both parties
• Rigid	• Flexible
• Passive-aggressive	• Direct
• Conceals interests	• Reveals interests
• Use threats, bluffs, lies	• Asks questions
• Focuses on personal outcome	• Uses criteria of fairness

Competitive at Its Best	*Cooperative Conflict at Its Worst*
• Efficient	• Time consuming
• Motivating	• Laborious
• Decisive	• Overly idealistic
• Fun	• Process rather than outcome focused
• Energizing	• Puts relationships before substance
	• May make one party too vulnerable

Case 3.1 illustrates one scenario where extreme competition and extreme cooperation meet. Sergio, the competitor, used aggressiveness and persistence in an attempt to wear down cooperative Antoine, whom he viewed as weak. Antoine was frustrated by his lack of success using interest-based tactics. Antoine could have given up and acquiesced to Sergio's demands. Instead, he recognized the clash between the competitive and cooperative approaches and changed to a competitive strategy. After proving that he "understood the game" and was able to compete, Sergio was motivated to change his strategy and engage in problem solving.

Whereas individuals may prefer either competitive or cooperative approaches to conflict, successful conflict managers are skilled at both. As stated in Chapter 2, conflict can be a **mixed-motive situation**—open to interest-based creativity but containing some goals that genuinely are in opposition. Employees may sit down together to work out the vacation schedule and have success in bringing creative problem solving to 95 percent of the calendar. The last 5 percent, however, contains sticky issues where several employees want exactly the same days off. The employees need productive skills to uphold their goals for the part of the issue that is competitive because resources are scarce and goals are in conflict.

Supportive and Defensive Climates

Communication climates are associated with cooperative and competitive tactics. Like meteorological climates, communicative climates can be hot and stormy, cold and chilling, or warm and temperate. Gibb (1961) introduced the concept of supportive and defensive climates. In defensive climates, individuals feel threatened and react to others negatively. In supportive climates, individuals feel safer, believe they are valued, and are more likely to engage in productive problem solving and conflict management. Gibb identified dichotomous clusters of behaviors that are likely to produce **defensive climates** or **supportive climates** (Table 3.3).

Descriptive language is less likely to cause defensiveness than evaluative language. Many statements beginning with "You are . . ." become negative evaluations about the other person: "You are a jerk"; "You are not listening"; "You are inconsiderate." Descriptive statements make observations about behaviors. "When the music is so loud, I find it difficult to get

TABLE 3.3 *Supportive and Defensive Climates*

Supportive Behaviors	Defense-Provoking Behaviors
Description	Evaluation
Problem solving	Control
Spontaneity	Strategy
Empathy	Neutrality
Equality	Superiority
Provisionalism	Certainty

TOOLBOX 3.1

Transforming Defensiveness

For each example, label the type of defensive statement (evaluation, certainty, superiority, neutral, strategy, or control). Rewrite the statement using the opposing supportive strategy (description, provisionalism, equality, empathy, spontaneity, or equality). The first one is done for you.

Defensive Provoking	*More Supportive*
Example:	
1. "You are a hypocrite." (EVALUATION)	"I'm bothered when you tell me that I should eat more healthily and you're eating junk food for breakfast." (DESCRIPTION)
2. (In response to the question: "Do you want to go see a movie?") "I don't care." *neutrality*	_____ _____
3. "We've tried something like that before. It didn't work then, and it won't work now." *evaluation*	_____ _____
4. "I'm the oldest so I'm driving." *superiority*	_____
5. "You tell me your offer first and I'll see if I'm still interested. *strategy*	_____ _____
6. "You just think everyone should do your work." *certainty*	_____ _____
7. "I can't believe you would consider voting for someone like *him* for president!" *control*	_____ _____

---

my work done." "When I hear derogatory comments about women, I feel uncomfortable." One way to describe rather than evaluate is to use **"I" statements,** which present the description from the perspective of the speaker. "I felt . . ." "I thought . . ." "I observed . . ." *Evaluative* statements judge and can incite the other to become defensive and to engage in competition; descriptive statements invite cooperation. A good test that a descriptive statement has not become evaluative is if the other would be unable to argue with it. For example, Randy said to Sara, "You gave me a dirty look, then stomped off and slammed the door." Sara could argue in response it wasn't a "dirty look," that she doesn't "stomp," and the wind caught the door; she didn't "slam" anything. Randy could instead remove the evaluative terms and describe what he observed and felt: "When I asked if you were going out with your friends, you looked at me but didn't answer. I felt in trouble for asking. Then you went to your room, closed the door, and haven't talked to me all evening." Description invites discussion; evaluation invites defensiveness.

> ### Discussion Question 3.7
>
> Have you been employed in a workplace that had a particularly defensive or supportive climate? In Gibb's terms, what kinds of communication characterized the workplace? Did the climate in the workplace affect how conflict occurred?

Statements that try to *control* someone's behavior prompt more defensiveness than those engaging the other in *problem solving*. A supervisor may notice two employees who are not getting along and order them to "Quit bickering and get back to work." An order is less likely to result in the desired behavior than saying, "I've noticed you two are having some challenges working together" (a *descriptive statement*). "What do the two of you think can be done about that in a way that is good for both of you and the unit as a whole?" (a *problem-solving statement*). Attempting to control another person elicits competitiveness and resistance; mutual problem solving solicits cooperation.

Car salespeople may say nice things about you, but these comments typically are perceived as a *strategy*—a manipulative tactic to gain an advantage. Any tactics that seem based on a preplanned campaign may garner a defensive reaction. *Spontaneity* means responding to the moment. Asking questions in a genuine attempt to find out how goals are in conflict or inviting the other person to engage in mutual and spontaneous problem solving will build a warmer climate.

In the way Gibb uses the term, neutrality carries with it a lack of caring or interest in the other person. George Bernard Shaw commented, "Indifference is the essence of inhumanity." Jodi asks Harrison if he wants to do something special for their anniversary. His response is an indifferent, "Whatever." Jodi is left feeling hurt and devalued by Harrison. In contrast, *empathy* shows interest in the other person's needs, goals, or values. Harrison, who is a quick learner, shows Jodi he values her by acknowledging her message: "I can't believe it's been five years already." Recognizing that Harrison cares, Jodi presses on with, "I'm thinking that we could take a cruise." Empathetic Harrison does not want to spend money on a cruise, but fortunately for him empathy does not mean the same thing as agreement. He is able to tell Jodi that he is worried about the cost of a cruise, but he agrees they should figure out a way to celebrate.

> "The opposite of love is not hate, it's indifference. The opposite of art is not ugliness, it's indifference. The opposite of faith is not heresy, it's indifference. And the opposite of life is not death, it's indifference."
>
> —Nobel Prize for Peace Winner, Elie Wiesel

A tone of voice that conveys "I am better than you" or "I know more than you" carries an implied superior-to-inferior relationship. *Superiority* triggers defensiveness. Morrell and Fauntelle are a couple nearing retirement. Morrell always handles the finances and investments for the couple, and Fauntelle knows little about the state of their retirement nest egg. Over dinner she broaches the topic with her husband. He gives her a patronizing air and says, "Don't worry your pretty little head about it, dear. I have it under control." Exhibiting superiority can be a competitive tactic to gain advantage; valuing the other regardless of status is more associated with cooperative conflict management. A tone and approach that demonstrates *equality*—or at least less superiority— opens the door to more congenial and less competitive behaviors. Morrell could have said, "It's actually quite complicated. I have investments in multiple places that will supplement our Social Security. How much do you want to know?" Sharing information with another is one way of creating more equality in a relationship. Susan is a manager who lets her employees know that she's heard some policy changes are coming down the pike from corporate, although she's not sure what they'll be yet. This disclosure serves to develop trust with her employees. Giving others access to information or a voice does not translate into a direct loss of power. In fact, in Susan's case, she gains power in the improved relationship with her staff.

Gibb's term *certainty* describes those who approach a conversation as if they know all the answers, are dogmatic about their rightness, and downgrade ideas that are contrary to their own. Conversely, exhibiting *provisionalism* is being open to change and considering opposing views. This does not mean that one can't have an opinion, a strong belief, or a favorite solution. Provisionalism is about being willing to consider the veracity of another perspective. Instead of saying, "That idea won't work," a provisional reply might be, "Explain to me how that idea would work. I don't understand." Several years ago, a university held a community improvement conference for religious leaders in the state. Spiritual leaders from a wide range of faith traditions attended, and much of the conference required considerable group work and discussion. Several of the religious leaders came from faith traditions that held their church's beliefs were "the truth," and that others who didn't ascribe to the same traditions, history, or core beliefs were missing the whole picture or were wrong—subsequently leading their members astray. Although each of the attendees was strong in his or her beliefs, perhaps certain in the correctness of their spiritual truths, they did not display certainty in their conversations. Discussions were marked by provisional statements like this: "In our church, we believe _____; how does your religion think about _____?" Participant reviews of the conference were consistent in their praise for the welcoming atmosphere and how much they learned—mostly from the other participants. Provisional dialogue is about being willing to hear and explore differing ideas, yet it does not require people to abandon their own.

Just as conflicts can be more or less competitive or cooperative (mixed motive), climates typically are not purely defensive or supportive. Nor are defensiveness and competition uniquely bound together. "Friendly" competition can occur in supportive climates. For example, a friendship group may gather to play small-stakes poker. At the end of evening, one player may walk away with the majority of the money (a scarce resource). The situation is competitive but friendly and supportive. Likewise, employers may use competitive rewards to motivate employee performance. In a supportive climate, coworkers can compete without rancor. It is not as likely, however, that cooperative conflict management will prosper in a defensive climate where trust is lacking.

Summary

Competition and cooperation are dichotomous approaches that affect attitudes and behaviors during interpersonal conflict. Competitive and cooperative conflict management approaches have advantages and disadvantages. The competent conflict manager develops skills for all contingencies and situations.

Competitors envision three possible outcomes: win, lose, or draw. Those who lose in competition may evoke a fourth option: Both parties lose. Competition may entail argumentativeness and aggressiveness. Resources in the competitive view are perceived as zero sum. There are two fallacies of the competitive approach: (1) Power can only be developed by withholding resources to create dependence, and (2) coercion is a rightful entitlement of the powerful. Kohn proposed four myths that lead to the acceptance of competition: Competition is a part of human nature, competition is required to do our best, competitive games are the best way to have a good time, and competition builds character.

The cooperative view holds that mutual gains are the most productive outcomes and the needs of all parties in most conflicts can be met with a little creativity. Instead of focusing on positional demands, cooperative conflict managers seek underlying needs or interests. A weakness of cooperative conflict management is moving beyond creating value to taking value. Many conflict situations contain motivations for competition and for cooperation: They are mixed-motive situations.

Interpersonal conflicts also occur in climates that are more or less supportive or defensive. Evaluation, control, strategy, neutrality, superiority, and certainty sustain defensive climates. Supportive climates are created through empathy, problem solving, spontaneity, empathy, equality, and provisionalism.

Chapter Resources

Exercises

1. Some board games can be converted to a noncompetitive mode by using a *universal team approach*. In games like Trivial Pursuit, no matter how many individuals are playing, select two tokens and put them on the game board. When it is the first token's turn, all four individuals work together to answer the question. The first token advances or loses its turn depending on whether the team can deduce the answer. When it is the second token's turn, the entire team again answers the question. The game is to race the tokens around the board. The tokens can be tied to some other outcome, such as "If the blue peg wins we'll have chicken for dinner; if red wins, we'll make spaghetti." In your groups, identify a favorite game. How can the game be converted from a competitive model to a group-based or cooperative model? What would be gained or lost if the game were played noncompetitively?

2. "It's a dog eat dog world." Is this cliché competitive or cooperative? Create a list of competitive and cooperative conflict sayings.

3. Analyze Case 3.2., "Your Call." Which approach to conflict is each party embracing? How do you know?

4. Change the following "You" statements into "I" statements.
   A. "You are so inconsiderate. You never think about my feelings."
   B. "You need to finish one thing before you start another."
   C. "What you need is a good attitude adjustment. You are so negative."
   D. "We wouldn't be having this argument if you would just do what you say you were going to do."

Journal/Essay Topics

1. Write an essay about the approach to conflict you learned as a child. Were you taught to use more competition or cooperation? Give specific examples of how you were taught those lessons.

2. Analyze your reactions to defense-provoking behaviors. Are there specific aspects of Gibb's defensive communication climates that seem to elicit a negative reaction from you?

Research Topic

1. Investigate the writing of Mary Parker Follett, reprinted at her foundation's website, http://www.follettfoundation.org. Summarize and evaluate her perspective on conflict.

Mastery Case

Analyze Mastery Case 3, "It's a Jungle Out There." Which concepts from this chapter best explain what is occurring in the case?

It's a Jungle Out There

Dale knows it's a dog-eat-dog world. His father taught him as a small child to be tough and always in control. When the stakes are high, anything goes. In the words of the famous coach Vince Lombardi, "Winning isn't everything; it's the only thing." Dale shouts during meetings because he knows his colleagues will back down when things get a little rough. Dale is very loyal to his employer, however, and knows that he must follow the lead of his boss.

At home Dale uses the same verbal tactics to run his family, whom he loves dearly. His wife, Adele, and kids avoid any confrontations with him. They all withhold information that might set Dale off. Adele uses the silent treatment when she wants something from Dale, like money for the kids to go to summer camp. If Adele is really mad at Dale, she'll cook food she knows he doesn't like for a week or pretend to be sick to avoid intimacy.

4

Causes of Conflict

Vocabulary

Expectancy violation theory
Face
Flash point
Future focus
Goal
Metacommunication

Process goals
Relationship goals
Retrospective goals
Scarce resources
Self-concept
Self-identity

Self-serving bias
Sense-making
Social learning theory
Substantive goals
Values
Zero-sum resource

Objectives

After reading the chapter, you should be able to:

1. Differentiate among conflict causes and topics
2. Relate the process of sense-making to conflict flash points
3. Understand common causes of conflict
4. Differentiate among types of goals
5. Explain the dynamic nature of goals

In Case 4.1, Aidan and Abigail seem to have the same long-range goal: saving for retirement. Their conversation about retirement planning, however, is less than harmonious. They may not even understand how their conversation turned into conflict. Many times a conflict emerges about one issue. Through the ensuing interaction, goals change, new goals emerge, and the nature of the conflict seems to shift.

This chapter explores the causes of conflict. Our discussion is guided by several assumptions: (1) Topics of conflict are not the same as causes of conflict, (2) people's behaviors in conflict are motivated by reasons that make sense to them, (3) conflict behaviors are more learned than biological, (4) conflict causes arise from goal interference, (5) goals are dynamic, and (6) effective conflict managers focus on the future more than on

CASE 4.1 • *It's My Money*

Aidan and Abigail have been married since starting college and are beginning their first professional jobs. Abigail is a book-keeper and pays all the family bills. Aidan's new job has a 401(k) plan, and they have been trying to find time to look over his investment choices. Tonight, they are watching television.

Abigail: "This might be a good time to look at the retirement paperwork and get that done."

Aidan: "I took care of it."

Abigail: "What do you mean, you took care of it?"

Aidan: "I turned it in."

Abigail: "But we were going to go over it together and talk about it."

Aidan: "Talk, talk, talk. I took care of it so we don't need to 'talk' about it."

Abigail: "You always tell me you don't know anything about finance and you just turned in your retirement paperwork? I'm the one who knows about our family budget and finance. What did you set up?"

Aidan: "I took care of it. I don't have time to talk about this stuff."

Abigail: "You don't have time. What about having time to pay the rent and buy groceries? What's going to happen if we don't have enough money?"

Aidan: "You're so dramatic! Don't worry about it. It's my money; I'll do what I want with it."

Abigail: "It's your money! I can't believe you said that. Maybe we should get separate checkbooks and split all our expenses if that is 'your' retirement?"

Aidan: "You always have to overreact." He turns up the volume on the television.

past causes. After explaining the assumptions that guide the search for conflict causes and examining the nature of goals in conflict, we conclude with some preliminary skills for goal analysis.

Conflict Topics Are Not Necessarily Conflict Causes

If asked "What caused a conflict?" people respond with topics like money, parenting styles, cleaning the house, or not returning a phone call. At first glance, Abigail and Aidan's conflict in Case 4.1 seems to be about money, but in reality the conflict is about something else.

Typically, *topics* are what the conflict was *about* rather than an identification of what gave rise to the conflict—its cause. Confusing a conflict topic with its underlying cause is easy. A **flash point** is the event that precipitates a conflict. For example, when Simone sees that her roommate Dom has left his stinky pizza boxes all over the living room, she may chastise him verbally the next time they meet. The pizza boxes are not the cause of the conflict. They merely are the stimulus that precipitates a struggle over some other issue—perhaps standards of cleanliness for their house, who cleans the house, or when the house is cleaned. The same conflict could be about pizza boxes, shirts left on a chair, or dishes in the sink.

Table 4.1 presents common conflict topics. Married/committed couples' conflict topics center around money and children (Cupach & Canary, 1977; Stanley et al., 2002).

TABLE 4.1 *What Conflicts Are About*

Relationship Type	Conflict Topics
Married couples	➢ Money ➢ Children ➢ In-laws ➢ Social issues ➢ Values ➢ Politics ➢ Personality flaws ➢ How to spend time ➢ Intimacy/sex ➢ Independence
Nonmarried couples	➢ Relationship commitment ➢ Love/emotional involvement ➢ Jealousy ➢ Friends ➢ Relatives ➢ Trust ➢ Possibility of separation ➢ Compatibility ➢ Frequency/satisfaction with sex ➢ Balance of power ➢ Self-esteem ➢ Male's manhood/female's womanhood ➢ Egocentrism ➢ Control ➢ Perception of self ➢ Sex roles
Children	➢ Rules ➢ What allowed to do ➢ What to wear ➢ Hair/grooming ➢ Sleep ➢ Dating ➢ Autonomy
Friends	➢ Friendship violations ➢ Sharing activities ➢ Sharing space/possessions ➢ Rival relationships ➢ Specific topic disagreements ➢ Annoying behaviors
College students	➢ Relationships ➢ Education/grades ➢ Group projects ➢ Work ➢ Money ➢ Time ➢ Parenting ➢ Sex ➢ Religion ➢ Drug/alcohol use

Ex-spouses predominantly clash over child custody, visitation rights, rules, child support, resentments, and interference (Cupach & Canary, 1977). Dating couples most often experience conflict over commitment to the relationship, love, and jealousy (Gottman, 1999; Lulofs & Cahn, 2000). Children's conflict topics revolve around behaviors and rules (Cupach & Canary, 1977). A teenager may have seven conflicts a day about issues such as control of resources, wanting more attention, trust violations, and exclusion from social groups (Scott, 2008). College students' conflicts tend to emerge around relationships, education, grades, and group projects (McCorkle & Mills, 1992; Salgado, 2005).

> ### Discussion Question 4.1
> What flash points precipitate your conflicts? Do you react to flash points or look to discover the real cause hidden behind the flashpoint?

Sometimes one conflict is played out through several topics. Two employees may clash one day about proper procedure, the next day about whose job it was to deliver a product, and a third day about who should take a weekend shift. All of these topics may be manifestations of the same underlying conflict cause—perhaps hurt feelings or a power struggle. A supervisor who takes conflict topics one at a time may miss the underlying cause—the real issue. The conflict will continue to pop up over and over again in different disguises. Dealing with the topic of the moment does not necessarily address the underlying issue in a conflict.

Conflict Behaviors Are Motivated by Reasons That Make Sense

The behaviors of people during conflict may seem odd and irrational. Regardless of how it may seem, those who engage in conflict do so for reasons that make good sense—to them. **Sense-making** is how we weave together knowledge, feelings, intuitions, and background to make sense of the world. Through sense-making, humans leap from perception, to interpretation, to action.

In Case 4.2, Juan combines his past experiences, biases, and knowledge of his neighbors to make sense of what happened. To Juan, the note was intended to deface his car because of the type of adhesive that was used. Juan *assumes* that Pete left the note. Juan makes an internal attribution about Pete: He is dangerous and surly. Pete's actions are judged as intentional—to show Juan that he can't be bullied and to cause Juan embarrassment because all the other neighbors saw the note as they walked down the sidewalk.

Assuming there is no rational justification for the other person's behavior is common in conflict situations. What does the situation seem like, however, from Tony's viewpoint, the actual writer of the note? Based on his assumption that he has a right to park on the street, each of Tony's actions make sense—to him.

An objective observer may point to the false assumptions made by Juan and Tony. Both men are acting on incomplete or bad information and are making judgments

CASE 4.2 • *Neighborhood Attribution Errors: Part I*

Juan is proud that he bikes and gets exercise while saving the environment from the carbon dioxide exhaust if he drove the five miles to work every day. Juan lives in an older part of town where the garage to his house has been converted to an apartment, which Juan rents to a college student. When Juan arrives home, he notices a very large message on his car, which is parked on the street. The note is so large, he—and all of this neighbors!—can read it from the sidewalk. The note says: "To the jerk who owns this heap of rust. You've left this eyesore in front of my house for a week. Move it or lose it! This is your last warning." The note is fastened on the car with duct tape that discolors the paint when Juan removes it. Juan doesn't know his neighbors well. He does know that Pete and Maria live in one of the houses near where the car is parked. Pete has been glaring at Juan whenever Pete walks his dog. Pete lets his dog poop in his neighbor's yards and never cleans up afterward. Juan calls the police and blames Pete for the damage to his car.

based on personal views of right and wrong. Like most people caught in the vortex of conflict, Juan and Tony do not take the time to sit back and analyze the situation. They are applying an *internal rationalizing process.* Conflicts arise, in part, because individuals do not have the same criteria or standards for what makes sense. Factors that influence sense-making include sense of self, attitudes, beliefs, biases, morals, values, philosophies, past experiences, physiological states, gender, age, education, culture, religion/spirituality, prior relationships, knowledge of the subject matter, family upbringing, conflict style, competitiveness versus cooperativeness, and the list could go on.

CASE 4.2 • *Neighborhood Attribution Errors: Part II*

Pete is a little nearsighted, which causes him to squint. Although his daily walks with his dog are famous for leaving dog poop in his wake, Pete is a pretty good neighbor. Or he was until the police visited and interviewed him about Juan's car.

Tony actually wrote the note. Tony has two cars. His frail 85-year-old mother visits every Sunday for dinner. The last two times she visited, he had to park his car a block away, and his mother had to walk in the snow all the way to his house. Everyone seems to park in front of Tony's house. Most of the neighbor's have garages, so Tony doesn't understand why they don't park in their garages, especially if they aren't going to use their car very often. Every time his mother visited this winter, the same car was parked by his house, and Tony blames the owner for his mother's discomfort. This is the third note that Tony has left. He did find one of them in the gutter and doesn't know if the rude car owner threw it there or it blew away, so this time he wrote the note large enough to see and taped it so it wouldn't blow off. Tony is really mad and may try to push the car into the street if it is there the next time his mother visits.

> ### Discussion Question 4.2
>
> Identify a conflict you've observed or been a participant in. Choose a behavior during that conflict that to an outsider would seem irrational. Discuss the internal rationalizing process that may have supported the behavior.

Competent conflict managers attempt to view others as acting from reasons that make sense to them, rather than acting in arbitrary ways from mean-spirited motives. By asking questions, conflict managers try to discover the needs and rationale that others bring to a situation.

Before leaving the discussion of how individuals make sense of their behaviors, it is necessary to distinguish between creating a rationale for a behavior and behaviors that are illegal, unethical, or unwise. During the writing of this book, someone has been poisoning dogs in our community. Poisoned meat is left for a dog in the middle of the night. The poisoner probably has some reason that makes sense to him or her for these illegal and cruel slayings. Perhaps the person can't sleep at night when dogs bark, was bitten by a dog as a child, thinks dogs are dangerous, or wants attention. Standards of a civil society, however, eschew this type of dangerous and extreme response. Learning the difference between what makes sense "inside oneself" and what makes sense in society is a part of moral development. Internal rationalizations do not justify or excuse poor behavior. Understanding rationalizations, however, can help a conflict manager discover what is preventing productive conflict transformation.

Conflict Behaviors Are Learned

Social learning theory posits that attitudes and behaviors are developed by observing others. Children initially learn how to behave during conflict from their parents and caregivers. Violence in the home is a prominent factor in predicting violent behavior in some children (Margolin & Gordis, 2004). Later in life, playmates, teachers, faith community, television, music lyrics, and other media gain influence (Glascock, 2003).

> ### Discussion Question 4.3
>
> What roles do family and media play in teaching aggressive behavior? What responsibility do individuals have as consumers of media violence? How involved should parents be in monitoring or curtailing their children's exposure to violent music, movies, and games?

Prime-time television is a haven for verbal aggressiveness. Comedies contain about thirty acts of verbal aggression per hour. Research indicates that exposure to media violence leads to increased aggressiveness, particularly among young males and sensation seekers (Slater, Henry, Swaim, & Anderson, 2003). Violence in music lyrics has been linked to increased aggression (Anderson, Carnagey, & Eubanks, 2003). In another study, video game violence was shown to decrease empathy for others (Funk, Baldacci, Pasold, & Baumgardner, 2004). Fortunately, the downward spiral of media influence can be countered by positive relationships with parents or mentors, constructive peer associations, and outside structured activities.

> "It's choice—not chance—that determines your destiny."
> —Founder of Weight Watchers, Jean Nidetch

Knowing that conflict behaviors are learned is important to students of conflict management for two reasons. First, learned behaviors can be changed. Changing the patterns formed early in life may not be easy, but it is possible. Second, people have choices to make during conflict. Individuals are not destined to behave in negative and aggressive ways or in positive and cooperative ways. Behaviors are a result of the choices we make.

Goal Interference Causes Conflict

Every individual has goals. A **goal** is a desired condition. Goals may be profound or simple. Goals can include behaviors like quitting smoking; outcomes like earning an "A" in a class; self-image factors like seeing yourself as a tough, independent individual who is not dependent on your parents; image-management factors like wanting others to view you as attractive or competent; or states of being like having a fulfilling relationship with an intimate partner.

Goals always are related to needs. An examination of Mayer's (2000) categories of conflict illustrates how conflict types relate to goal interference. Mayer claims there are several common types of conflict, including communication, emotion, value, and structure.

Communication conflicts arise from goal interference about information. Which information is right? What information should be used as criteria for decisions? Is communication adequate? Are we interpreting the data the same way? If a supervisor uses all CAPITALS in a memo and the employees are upset because the supervisor "yelled at them," communicative intent may have been misinterpreted. If a couple argues about how much in monthly payments they can afford for a new car and they unknowingly are using a different base for their figures, a conflict arising from different data may occur. If the same couple knows they are using different figures and argue over which number is correct, a conflict about criteria may arise.

> "Conflict frequently escalates because people act on the assumption that they have communicated accurately when they have not."
> —conflict author and consultant Mayer (2000, p. 10)

Emotions feed conflict. *Emotional conflict* centers on the experience and expression of feelings. People are not purely rational beings. Feelings matter. The supervisor who sends an e-mail critical of one employee to the entire staff may cause a variety of emotional responses—resentment from the employee who is criticized and fear of similar ridicule from the rest of the staff. The anger of parents when children stay out too late partly is a manifestation of fear that the son or daughter will be hurt. Conflict escalation is fueled by emotions.

Value conflicts pivot around deeply seated beliefs about right and wrong. One person's **values** may not match exactly with the values of a friend, neighbor, or coworker. Couples may conflict over whether to save money (a value of thrift) or go into debt to fund vacations (valuing immediate gratification). Employees may hotly contest which radio station is played in the workplace because of the values associated with particular stations—talk radio (with a conservative or liberal leaning), country western, contemporary music, or gangsta rap. Mayer identifies goal interference around values as among the most intransigent of conflicts because self-image and identity are so inextricably tied to personal values. For example, coworkers who make fun of a colleague's country western music may also be rejecting the values embedded in the music.

Discussion Question 4.4
Give an example of a conflicts that represents one of Mayer's four causal areas.

Structure conflicts relate to the external framework in which a conflict occurs. Structure includes resources, decision-making processes, time, methods of communication, and setting. The rules or methods of making decisions may be a barrier to goal attainment, or conflicts may arise about the appropriate style for organizing tasks. For example, two competing styles of meeting management may cause distress. One approach is very organized, agenda driven, and task oriented. The other approach focuses on social relationships and is free from structural constraints. Neither style inherently is better than the other, but meetings organized by someone with an opposite style may lead to power struggles over how to run a meeting.

In Chapter 1, interpersonal conflict was defined as *a struggle among a small number of interdependent people (usually two) arising from perceived interference with goal achievement.* Interpersonal conflict occurs when interference with some goal creates a disequilibrium that affects how an individual perceives or behaves toward others. At its heart, conflict is caused because one person perceives another person is interfering with reaching a desired outcome.

Just as people act in conflicts for reasons that make sense to them, people interpret goal interference in ways that make sense to them. Tony, in Case 4.1, had a self-image as a good son and a protector of his mother. The car in front of his house was perceived as interfering with his ability to be a good son. A good son takes action to protect his mother, so Tony's self-image compelled him to take an action to achieve his goal. An objective observer would note that the goal could be achieved in other ways, but people who perceive goal interference do not necessarily analyze situations objectively or see all of their choices.

TABLE 4.2   *Goals in Conflict*

Substantive goals:	Do I have control of the resources that I need?
Process goals:	Are decisions being made in the way I want? Are we communicating in ways that work for me?
Relationship goals:	What is the nature of our relationship? Am I satisfied with my role and participation in the relationship? Do we want the same type of relationship?
Face goals:	Is my self-image being maintained? Do I need to try to change your self-image?

Scholars label and organize goals in many ways. We present a fourfold division of goals in Table 4.2. An individual's goals may relate to tangible resources (*substantive goals*), how things should be done (*process goals*), who the parties are to each other (*relationship goals*), or one's sense of self (*face goals*).

Substantive Goals

Substantive goals include tangible resources or any measurable factor around which desired outcomes can be built. *Substantive issues* are the points of clash that occur when one person's substantive goals are perceived as interfering with another person's needs. These goals speak to the question: "Do I have control of the resources that I want?" Resources can be basic, such as food, clothing, and warmth. Resources also include items such as money, property, time, and access. When a customer confronts a businessperson to get a refund for a broken product, the issue is about what, if anything, should be done about the broken item. When roommates clash over what activities should occur in their apartment on Sundays, the issue is about how time and space should be used. When a family of four is given two tickets to a movie they all want to see, the issue is about what to do with two tickets that four people covet.

Resource control and access are cornerstones of substantive conflict. The conflict will be about control of an actual or perceived scarce resource. A **scarce resource** is anything that someone perceives to be in limited supply. The perception of scarcity drives the willingness to enter into conflict to control the resource. The resource can be really scarce or just perceived as scarce. Two boys were throwing an imaginary baseball back and forth while waiting in a long line. The activity kept the four- and eight-year-olds entertained until the older boy tired of the game and pantomimed putting the ball in his pocket. The younger child became quite upset and started a fight to get the pretend ball back. Fortunately, Mom found another imaginary ball in her purse. Just as the two boys fought over an imaginary ball, adults sometimes struggle for intangible resources such as self-esteem or love as if they are in limited supply. The core of sibling rivalry is the view that parental love is limited. When love is viewed as scarce, attention given to one child lessens the amount of attention available to the other child. Perceived scarce resources may overlap with relationship and/or face goals.

ILLUSTRATION 4.1   *"Zero sum means the more cake for you, the less cake for me."*

Actual scarce resources are measurably limited. A cake has only so many slices. Every piece taken away means less left for others. Cake is a **zero-sum resource**. As portions are removed, the total available will become zero when the last slice is eaten. At work, if only one promotion is available, the resource of promotional advancement is scarce. If more than one person wishes the promotion, anyone else in consideration for the advancement can be seen as hindering goal achievement. Family income is a scarce resource. If there is $100 left each month after budgeted expenses are subtracted from the family's income, then a long list of desires compete for allocation: saving for the future, a vacation, cell phones, dining out, helping with college expenses, and the list could be endless.

> ### Discussion Question 4.5
> What perceived or actual scarce resources are prominent at this juncture in your life? Do conflicts arise around these scarce resources?

Another twist on substantive issues is the tendency to cloak other goals with a substantive disguise. A process, face, or relationship goal may be expressed as a substantive goal. When a couple habitually fights about who does the laundry, one should wonder if the conflict really is about the laundry. Repeated conflicts either have not been managed successfully or are about something other than the substantive issue. Dana (2005) comments, "We are propelled into conflict by the appearance of incompatible positions on a substantive issue—I want "A" whereas you want "B." But what *appear* as substantive issues that we believe represent our differences in rational (objective) self-interests are often, in reality, mere facades concealing perceived threats to our underlying emotional needs" (p. 87). For example, in Case 4.1, Aidan and Abigail may seem to be contesting over the scarce resource of money, but the conflict probably is more about how decisions are made (process) or Abigail's self-image as a money manager (face).

Process Goals

Process goals involve how a person wishes events to unfold, how decisions are made, or how communication occurs. Process goals speak to two types of questions: "Are decisions being made in ways that I prefer?" and "Is the type of communication that is occurring what I want to happen?" When Aidan made a decision that affected Abigail and the family's future, she objected to not being included. She felt the decision was made using the wrong process—a unilateral decision rather than an equal discussion. Likewise, when managers tell employees that new procedures are being implemented, the employees may feel a better decision would have been made if their input had been solicited.

When and where to have discussions about important topics also represents process goals. A partner who brings up a money issue in front of her significant other's parents may be violating an expectation of privacy. Arguing in front of the children or believing a couple shouldn't "go to bed mad" are examples of process expectations that can cause and/or help manage conflict. One newly married couple, neither of which was a "morning person," determined after several nasty altercations before 8 A.M. that they just shouldn't talk to each other before each had a cup of coffee. Together they determined the best process for communicating—for them.

> ### Discussion Question 4.6
> Conflict managers sometimes arrange to meet in a neutral location to discuss issues. If you were having a conflict with roommates, what location would be neutral? How can location affect the process of a conflict?

Relationship Goals

Relationship goals involve who the parties want to be to each other. Relationship goals speak to these questions: "What is the nature of our relationship?" "Am I satisfied with my role and participation in the relationship?" "Do we want the same type of relationship?" *Relationship issues* arise when individuals have different goals for the relationship. For example, one may want romantic intimacy and the other wants just to be friends.

Friends may have divergent perceptions about what it means to be friends, how often friends should see each other, and what type of personal information friends should exchange. Jealousy can affect romantic relationships, friends, and family members with equal vigor. Parents and teens may develop different goals about when and how the teenager expresses autonomy and whether tattoos or piercings are good ideas. Employees may desire an equal relationship with a supervisor, whereas the supervisor prefers a more subordinate-superior relationship. The depth and shape of relationships are not automatic; they are negotiated.

Relationship goals are complex, and they may change. As children age, they struggle to define their relationship differently than before, creating boundary management issues. When a six-year-old informed his mom that "When I'm seven, I can ride my bicycle wherever I want," she disagreed. Her definition of the relationship includes being a protector of her child, which cannot be done if he's riding his bicycle miles away.

Face Goals

The concept of face links to self-concept. **Self-concept** is defined as a relatively stable set of perceptions about oneself (Adler & Proctor, 2007). Even though self-concept changes throughout life as an individual accumulates experience, at any specific moment in time self-concept is resistant to change.

"**Face** represents an individual's claimed sense of positive image in the context of social interaction and consists of three components: self, other, and mutual" (Ting-Toomey, Oetzel, & Yee-Jung, 2001, p. 89). Face can be subdivided into three areas: *Self-face* relates to one's personal image. *Other-face* relates to awareness, or lack thereof, about the other's image of himself or herself. *Mutual-face* exhibits concern for both parties' images and/or the image of the relationship.

CONFLICT KEY 4.1 **Become aware of your own goals.**	One of the assumptions of face theory is that all people are concerned about face in one way or another. Although everyone does not view the same things as problematic, embarrassment and personal attacks activate face issues. Many inter-personal conflicts begin with someone defending against a perceived attack.

Rogan and La France (2003) claim "conflict is generally deemed to be an inherently face-threatening interactional context" (p. 461).

Face goals are the affirmation, reaffirmation, saving, transformation, or subver-sion of self or other face (Table 4.3). When meeting new people, individuals *affirm* or create a public image. One might tell a joke to affirm his image as a funny guy. As rela-tionships develop, the face that one has adopted is *reaffirmed* through repeated behav-iors. Consistently making jokes reaffirms his identity as a funny guy. If one's behaviors seem outside of the desired public image or the acts of others cause embarrassment, *face saving* may need to occur. He tells an off-color joke in front of his boss, and his boss is offended. He apologizes. As individuals grow and change, *face transformation* may become desirable. He now wants to get a promotion and to be seen as a mature per-son. He quits telling jokes at work. *Subversion* of face occurs when one person acts to counter the image that another presents. Someone else who wants the promotion may remind coworkers of what a goof the other is, thereby subverting his attempts at trans-formation.

Discussion Question 4.7

Do you have the same face/self-image now as when you first started college? What type of face goals or image management kicked in when you first enrolled in higher education?

TABLE 4.3   *Face Goals*

Affirmation of face:	Creating a new self-image
Reaffirmation of face:	Consistently exhibiting a self-image
Saving face:	Acting to correct a tarnished image
Transformation of face:	Changing from one self-image to another
Subversion of face:	Acting to tarnish someone else's self-image

Image or face management is a constant part of life. Verbal aggressiveness sometimes involves attacking someone's self-concept (face) or their desired outcome on a substantive issue. Some scholars argue that face attacks occur through verbal aggressiveness because the attacker thinks he or she is not skilled enough to achieve goals through persuasion (Rogan & La France, 2003). In other words, when people fear that they won't be able to reach their substantive goals, they may shift the conversation to relationship goals or face subversion. It may be easier to call someone "stupid" than to explain one's deeper feelings.

Face is dynamic because people do not present a single, uniform identity to the outside world. An individual may enact a different aspect of self-identify at work than at home. At work, Marco may be all business, use powerful language, and demand respect. At home, Marco may defer to his partner and exhibit warm and loving mannerisms. Managing multiple identities and goals can be difficult. An account executive who has cultivated a tough, uncompromising image may be embarrassed at social events if work and home identities clash. At a dinner party, his partner may expect him to be warm and affectionate, behaviors that contradict his work image.

> ### Discussion Question 4.8
>
> What are each party's face goals in Case 4.3, "Moving Back In?"

CASE 4.3 • *Moving Back In?*

When Bob was young, he thought of himself the way his mother described him: "a good boy." Bob would try to behave to make his mother happy. Sometimes, the other kids would make fun of the clothes Bob's mother chose for him—slacks with matching button-down shirts and sweaters. Bob was a quiet and polite but not a very popular kid at school.

As Bob became a teenager, he was less interested in what his mother wanted and more interested in what his peers thought. When the family moved to a new town, Bob decided it was time to assert himself. Taking money from his savings account, Bob bought baggy trousers, trendy shirts, and an IPod. He contemplated several tattoos.

Bob's parents were shocked and disappointed. They lectured him, saying he was ruining his life. Bob was pleased that it was easier to make friends at his new school in his new "rags" and didn't pay much attention to his parents.

After graduating from high school, Bob moved out and got a job at the coffee shop near the local college. Although the shop required a dress code of all black, Bob would "forget" and wear printed T-shirts about once a week. Bob would imitate his thirty-year-old boss behind his back and call him a stupid mocha-nerd. One day, Bob came to work and his boss said, "I guess I'm not as stupid as you think I am. You're fired."

Out of work and out of money, Bob called his parents to see if he could move back home. They agreed—but only if he cleaned up his look, got a part-time job, and enrolled in college next term. Bob has a decision to make.

Perception Patterns Affect How Goals Are Interpreted

Other human behavior research findings add to the complexity of identity management and perception (Adler & Proctor, 2007; Ayoko, Callan, & Hartel, 2003).

1. **We judge ourselves more charitably than we judge others.** As stated in Chapter 2, a **self-serving bias** judges the same behavior differently in self than in others: "When *she* says something evaluative about another friend, it's because she is nasty; when *I* make critical comments, they are intended to be helpful."

2. **We attribute our behaviors to external circumstances and others' behaviors to internal character traits.** "If *I* am late to work, it is because something important held me up. If *you* are late to work it is because you are lazy and inconsiderate." Dana (2005) labels these tendencies *wrong reflexes*. Assuming the other is a "bad person" is the wrong reflex. Dana highlights the inflexibility that can result from internal attributions of the others' behavior if someone thinks the "conflict is the direct result of your incompetence, ignorance, meanness, or other defect; it can only be resolved if you recognize and correct your defects" (p. 29).

3. **We tend to favor negative impressions of others over positive ones.** We are more influenced by negative than by positive descriptions. A professor who is unkempt and disorganized, even though very knowledgeable and interesting, may be given low evaluations by students. When asked to describe this professor, students might be inclined to highlight the negative attributes over the positive ones.

4. **We are influenced by what is most obvious.** Employees who are bullied over time often lose their jobs while the bully is unaffected. The higher-ups see a loss of productivity, fire the victim, and are oblivious to the subtle harassment that led to the productivity decrease in the first place.

5. **We cling to first impressions.** On the way to meet a salesperson for lunch, an inconsiderate driver zoomed into a parking space that another driver was waiting for. When entering the restaurant, the client realized the salesperson was the parking space robber. Regardless of how pleasantly the salesperson behaves during lunch, any future relationship is tainted by the negative first impression. Likewise, the first tactics used during conflict may carry a greater impression than those developed later.

6. **We assume that others are similar to us.** When a new employee won't look a superior in the eye, the boss may infer that the employee is shifty, lying, or untrustworthy. If the new employee is from a culture where eye contact with those in a higher social position is impolite, the behavior may be intended as a sign of respect. Judging others by personal or cultural standards is common, yet extremely unfair. Intercultural conflicts sometimes are caused by differing expectations of how communication should unfold and how people should act. For many Westerners, directness is preferred as a means of communication. The act of being direct matches a self-image as decisive, efficient negotiators. In some cultures, indirectness is preferred and matches a value of maintaining harmony and preventing embarrassment (Ma, 1992).

7. **We predict the reactions of other people based on our perceptions of them.** According to **expectancy violation theory** we anticipate how people will act by looking at the relationship we share, our views of that person, and the situation. Then, how the other person reacts is interpreted and compared to expectations. When expectations are violated, negative reactions and conflict are more likely (Hullett & Tamborini, 2001). In Case 4.1, Abigail expected to be included in the decision and that her knowledge of monetary matters would carry some weight in how her spouse's retirement funds were allocated. When Aidan casually made a decision without her, expectations were violated.

Goals Are Dynamic

Although it is beneficial to categorize goals to understand and study conflict, goals may overlap and change as the conflict evolves. Conflict may begin with one cause and morph into another. There are four primary reasons why goals are dynamic: (1) The goals may have been unconscious or ill defined at the beginning, (2) individuals are opportunistic and may adapt goals to fit changing circumstances, (3) perceptions may change, and (4) goals may be recast after the conflict episode. The following example illustrates the transitory nature of goals: A woman attempts to return a sweater to the department store because it has a flaw. She does not have a receipt. Her initial goal is to take the sweater back, but she hasn't considered how she would like the reimbursement—a replacement sweater, in-store credit, or refund. Upon seeing the sign that says, "No refunds without a receipt," she determines that the policy is unfair if there is a flaw in the product. She now has the goal to get a cash refund. As she speaks with the customer service representative who is upholding the store policy, she sees him as uncaring and the store as mismanaged. She grudgingly settles for an in-store refund. After she leaves the store with her in-store credit, she writes the CEO of the company to discuss how customer service procedures could be improved, a very different goal than when she first arrived at the store with the flawed sweater. As conflicts progress, goals shift.

Table 4.4 summarizes the three phases that goals go through during a conflict: initial, in process, and retrospective. At the beginning, each individual may be aware of *initial goals* or only have a vague notion of what would be a desirable outcome. As a conflict

TABLE 4.4   *Goals Emerge and Change*

Initial goal:	I felt neglected by my girlfriend, so I tried to make her want to be with me by ignoring her.
In-process goal:	Ignoring her wasn't working, so I gave up on that and started acting normally again. I just wanted her to spend more time with me. She broke up with me.
Retrospective goal:	Looking back, I wasn't interested in a long-term relationship anyway.
New goal:	I just want a relationship with someone who will spend lots of time with me.

unfolds, goals may be modified as new information is learned or perceptions change. Goals are *in process*. After a conflict episode is completed, individuals look back and may state to self or others what Wilmot and Hocker (2007) call a **retrospective goal**—what one "says" the goal was during the conflict. At the end of one conflict episode, expectations may reset to create a new initial goal.

Face goals frequently are reshaping retrospectively. When the outcome would cause embarrassment, an individual may tell friends that "he really didn't care anyway" or that his real goal was something different. For example, Ashley and Andrew may struggle over who has to clean the bathroom because both individuals dislike the work and think it is beneath them. Their goals are to get the other to do the cleaning (initial goals). Ashley may persuade Andrew that he should do the cleaning this time. As a surprise reward, Ashley makes dinner for him. Andrew may tell his other roommates that his goal all along was to get Ashley to make him dinner (retrospective goal).

Identifying goals can be problematic due to their dynamic nature. Is it a relationship issue or a process issue when one partner doesn't consult the other about a major decision? What may begin as a substantive issue (where to live?) can become a conflict over a relationship or about each person's self-identity, depending on what type of goal interference is perceived. Goals overlap and may not fit entirely into one neat category. Substantive goals may take on face-threatening aspects or give rise to process questions. Process goals may overlap with relationship issues. The complexity of goals can be difficult to unravel.

For example, a group of friends gather on a rainy weekend afternoon and decide to play Trivial Pursuit. The initial goal is to do something together. The nature of competitive games, however, may activate other goals. One friend may have a goal of proving how smart she is to the rest of the group. Another may want to compete and win to reinforce a self-image as a worthy person. Are the goals in conflict? Perhaps. It depends on how each person pursues accomplishing an individual goal and if one set of behaviors leads another person to perceive interference with goal achievement. For instance, Ellie wants to chat and be with her friends, and she does not pay much attention to the strategy of the game. Devon and Jerome see her behavior as devaluing their goals of winning through competition. Because of the interplay between Ellie, Devon, and Jerome, Molly may decide that she now wants to win to show Devon and Jerome how petty they are. Ellie may decide that if people are going to say mean things to each other, she isn't going to play at all.

> #### *Discussion Question 4.9*
> Have you been in the middle of a conflict and realized that you don't really want what you're fighting for?

Knowing what you want is an important key to success. Unfortunately, individuals sometimes are not self-aware of goals. Determining "what is it that I am struggling to achieve?" can be slippery. People who are not aware of their goals demand things that do not really meet their needs. When others comply with those demands, everyone is confused and angry when the issue is not resolved.

Skills to Enhance Goal Analysis and Development

In conflict, one of the most important skills is becoming conscious of goals. "What do I want to achieve at the end of the conflict?" "If the conflict is settled, what would I need to meet my goals?" "What is keeping me from accomplishing the goal on my own?" Understanding feelings and the goal interference that give rise to conflict provides greater clarity. With clarity about goals, conflicting parties can work together to discover better outcomes. The analysis chapter later in this book presents more tools to discover goals.

Helping the other person understand your intentions also is a critical conflict management skill, particularly when defensive reactions occur, the conversation is tense, or the medium of communication reduces important nonverbal cues. Telephone and e-mail lack the full range of nonverbal cues that help the other party interpret the meaning of messages. A casual note dashed off on e-mail may elicit a defensive response if it is interpreted as personal criticism. **Metacommunication**, communicating about communication, can help. Television talk show host Oprah Winfrey often metacommunicates to preempt defensive comments by saying, "I don't mean this question in a bad way . . ." When comments are contextualized with a statement about intention, they are less open to misinterpretation. When a spouse asks her partner to take out the garbage, he may reply, "Sure." After waiting five minutes, she may say, "Fine, I'll take it out myself!" and remove the garbage. Each party had a different interpretation of "when" the garbage should be taken out—immediately or when he got around to it. When he says, "Sure," she might metacommunicate: "By 'sure' do you mean you'll take the garbage out immediately because it smells? When are you planning on taking it out?"

> ### *Discussion Question 4.10*
>
> The television program *Cheaters* "helps" people who think a loved one is being unfaithful by tailing the partner and videotaping any clandestine activities. A hallmark of the show is an emotional confrontation between the heartbroken client and the cheating partner and his or her paramour. Many of those caught cheating blame their partner for the infidelity, claiming the partner somehow "forced" the other into cheating. Which concepts from the chapter explain how the one committing the infidelity can blame his or her actions on the faithful partner?

Although understanding the general cause of conflict is important, conflict managers cannot dwell too long on the past. Knowledge of causes helps determine where the goal inference is located. Different strategies are used when interference is perceived but not actually occurring. For example, the perceived interference could be based on misassumption, misperceptions, or inadequate information. If actual goal interference is occurring, knowledge of causes is crucial to understanding which outcome will meet the other's needs. Focusing too much on the past, however, can be counterproductive. In general, productive conflict managers are not particularly concerned with root causes, deep historical background, or every tactical move that occurred over the duration of a conflict. Effective conflict managers need to be **future focused** and move ahead into a different and more productive future. Be aware of the past, but focus on the future.

CONFLICT KEY 4.2

Be aware of the past, but focus on the future.

TOOLBOX 4.1

Identifying Issues

Here are some questions to ask to determine what a conflict really is about.

- Have similar conflict episodes occurred with this person before? What goals were seen as incompatible during the past conflict?
- What does the other person seem to need from the conflict?

- What might the other person be afraid of losing?
- What combination of goals is the other person working to achieve?
- Are perceived or actual scarce resources a part of the conflict?
- Are other goals hiding behind substantive issues?
- Would an apology settle the issue?

Summary

Conflict topics are not the same as conflict goals. People may not consciously be aware of their goals or may conceal goals for a variety of reasons. The topic that precipitates a conflict may not be what the conflict really is about. Because of the complexity of goals, people should not jump to conclusions too quickly at the onset of a conflict; circumstances frequently are not what they appear. Similarly, becoming aware of personal goals is a powerful force and a critical skill for competent conflict managers.

Individual conflict behaviors are motivated by reasons that make sense to that person. Sense-making is how one weaves together past experience and knowledge to interpret the world. Sense-making is not a logical activity; instead it is governed by variables such as self-concept, culture, religion, and subject matter knowledge.

Although genetics, hormones, or body chemistry can influence behavior, social learning theory posits that most conflict responses are learned. Many factors influence behaviors—family, culture, media, and friends. Fortunately, conflict participants usually have a choice in how to act so behaviors are not determined solely by one's past.

The cause of conflict is a perception of goal interference, which falls into four main types: substantive, process, relationship, and face. Face can be affirmed, reaffirmed, saved, transformed, or subverted. Perceptions of goal interference are further complicated by a series of self-serving biases.

Conflict managers must realize the dynamic nature of goals. Goals change before, during, and after the conflict. Focusing on the future, being aware of one's goals, and metacommunication are key skills in the conflict manager's toolbox.

Chapter Resources

Exercises

1. In the Mastery Case for this chapter, assign the roles of Washington, Smith, and Jones. Role-play the conversation that would occur between the three roommates. Washington should start the conversation casually and then surprise Jones with the decision that Jones needs to move out. What goals emerge during the role play? Do the goals of any of the

individuals change in-process or retrospectively? Does face become an issue? How do face goals emerge during the role play?

2. In groups, discuss two conflict scenarios that recently occurred. Pick one scenario (if you can't decide on a scenario, use the topic of two roommates conflicting over who has to pay how much for the cable bill when one person ordered the movie channels without getting explicit agreement in advance from the other roommate). Role-play how the conflict scenario would play out differently depending on which type of goal (process, face, substantive, or relationship) was the primary driver for the roommate who wasn't consulted. In the cable charge example, if a process goal was evident, the conflict would be about how the decision was made; if a relationship goal were evident, the dispute focus would be on "Do we have the type of relationship where one person can make decisions for the other?" or "Who has the power to make these types of decisions?" If a substantive goal were most important, it would be all about the money; if a face goal were activated, the conflict would be about self-image and not losing esteem (or, if approached negatively, putting the other person down).

Essay Topic

1. Identify some of your most important personal goals. Goals can relate to relationships, things, processes, or self-esteem and face. Do you think the same goals will predominate throughout your life? What changes might you expect?

Research Topics

1. Explore the concept of "face" and how it is conceptualized in different cultures.

2. Review conflict research from the past two years to determine what conflict topics are experienced by workers or college students.

Mastery Case

In Mastery Case 4, "The Roommate Revolt," which concepts from this chapter best explain what is occurring?

The Roommate Revolt

Smith, Jones, and Washington are on the college soccer team and decide to be roommates their junior year. Disputes soon erupt over housework. Smith and Washington like the house to be picked up so, in their words, "it doesn't look like a pig sty." Jones isn't as concerned about clutter, as long as things are relatively clean. Smith and Washington made several direct comments to Jones like, "Hey, pick up your stuff from the living room because somebody might come over." Jones might pick up a few things, but it doesn't last. Jones rarely does the dishes or any of the "inside" chores, although Jones does take out the trash, pick up the yard, and do any repairs that are needed. Jones had a part-time job for a while but was fired and hasn't looked for another job, which means more time for Jones to hang around the house.

The issue has bubbled beneath the surface for a few weeks. Jones casually mentioned that the rent would be late this month. Washington noticed that Jones has several new CDs and is planning a ski trip over winter break. Washington and Smith decide that Jones is ducking paying the rent and has to go. They ask Jones to be sure to be home at 6 o'clock that evening so they can talk about a few things. They will demand that Jones move out.

5

Interpersonal Conflict Variables

Objectives

After reading the chapter, you should be able to:

1. Understand the purpose of social research and its importance to interpersonal conflict studies

2. List common variables in interpersonal conflict research

3. Differentiate between earned and unearned privilege

4. Critique the collectivism/individualism culture dichotomy

5. Differentiate between distributive and integrative views of power

Variables in Interpersonal Conflict

Life would be easier if conflict were predictable. Because so many factors may shape an interpersonal conflict, 100 percent predictability is impossible. However, researchers have isolated several variables that consistently affect conflict, providing insight into how conflict begins and why it persists.

A research **variable** is a specific trait, behavior, or pattern that is isolated for investigation. For example, sex is a common variable in social science research to determine if boys and girls or men and women behave in ways that are similar or different. Research is useful for many reasons. We highlight three of them.

First, research provides insight into personal behaviors. You may peruse the section on gender and conflict in this book and say, "That is exactly what my experience has been!" or "My experience is not like that at all!" Second, research is useful to understand others' behaviors. Knowledge of the range of normative behavior helps individuals understand possible responses to conflict situations and to avoid the fallacies of thinking that "everyone else must act just like me" or "I'm the only one who feels this way." Third, research—to the extent that patterns of behavior have been identified—offers a way to anticipate how others might behave during conflict. Knowing that when variable X is activated in a conflict, outcome Z has a probability of occurring provides opportunities for thoughtful choice making.

Before we begin an exploration of variables, let's clarify the limitations of research. First, social science research always is limited because of the plethora of things that are occurring simultaneously. No matter how carefully an experiment in human communication is designed, researchers cannot control what people feel and think to isolate only one variable at a time. Unlike pure laboratory experiments where a chemical can be put in one test tube but not in another to observe the reaction, humans cannot turn off their thoughts, experiences, or perceptions to isolate just one variable. In addition to the difficulties of isolating variables in human research, the choices people make in one context may be different than the choices they make elsewhere. For example, the conflict styles that are engaged at work may be routinely avoided at home. Context matters when looking at human behavior research.

Discussion Question 5.1

How can conflict research benefit you personally in your everyday interactions? Which of the reasons why research is useful is the most meaningful to you?

Second, some research outcomes represent so-called average behaviors. For example, the average age of first marriage is 24 years, with a range of age 22 to 26, representing approximately 60 percent of the population. People who married before the age of 22 or after the age of 26 (about 40 percent of the population) are not "average" in their marriage behaviors. Move far enough away from the average—marry in your late 30s—and you become an "outlier" in statistical terms. Averages become more complicated when isolating communicative behaviors. Researchers apply powerful levels of mathematics to sort through their data, move beyond averages, and determine if differences discovered in a study are statistically significant or if they might have resulted from chance.

There remains a range of human behavior in any situation that is not represented fully by average or statistical results. For example, one study found that people who are more committed to a relationship are less likely to report thinking about alternatives to the relationship and less likely to feel trapped (Stanley et al., 2002). These results suggest commitment is an important variable that may explain why individuals choose different tactics during relationship conflicts. But not all persons in the same relationship commitment category react in the same way consistently. No social science research result can have the predictive power of a chemistry experiment. Unlike chemistry, social science research provides trends and averages, not universal laws.

Third, because of convenience, research in the social sciences has been conducted primarily on university students who do not represent the full range of human experience. For example, individuals who begin a career before or immediately after high school graduation would systematically be excluded if only university students are used as subjects—as would most elderly and any other group that is underrepresented on university campuses.

> ### Discussion Question 5.2
>
> Identify any research findings presented so far in this book or in your class that speak directly to your experience. Do you think the findings apply to everyone who is in your demographic group?

A fourth limitation of research is embedded in who asks the questions that guide research. The questions for study tend to be chosen through some connection to the researcher's life experiences. When the ranks of researchers were dominated for decades by upper-middle-class white men, few questions were asked from the perspective of women, nonwhites, or the working poor. As the ranks of researchers opened to more socially and racially diverse populations, research increased about communication patterns unique to blacks, Latinos, Asians, women, and other underrepresented groups.

Regardless of its limitations, social science research is useful because it aspires to understand and predict human behavior. Research results are helpful to understand which variables are activated when a conflict evolves differently with one person than with another.

This chapter explores the known research on several relatively observable variables that affect conflict. Although numerous other variables could be explored, we focus on those variables that have received considerable attention through the years: gender, race, culture, age, and generation. Additional factors that affect how conflict is perceived also are discussed, including power, trust, climate, humor, and language. Before delving into research that uncovers the factors that make a difference in conflict according to research, one qualification statement is necessary. We do not wish to give the impression that all important research in the social sciences is variable-analytic. Other perspectives guide many critical lines of research into the understanding of human communication and human behavior.

Conflict Management Variables

Sex/Gender

Considerable research explores potential differences between how women and men experience conflict. For example, findings indicate men tend to withdraw from conflict and engage in activities that distract from relationship threats. Men engage in more overt aggression, women in more covert aggression, and men have more internal physical reactions to conflict than women (Buysse et al., 2000; Verona, Reed, Curtin, & Pole, 2007). Research on gender similarities and differences, however, is dynamic. For example, meta-analysis on the question of whether men or women disclose more information to others found that women did disclose more, but the differences were small and changed depending on whether men talked to men, women and men talked together, or women talked to women (Dindia, 2000).

Researchers generally fall into one of two camps when explaining apparent differences between men and women. One camp claims differences are based on nature: genetics, hormones, or other biological/chemical processes. The other perspective argues that differences are due to nurture: influences of upbringing and culture. Most social science research on males and females in conflict subscribes to "nurture" and social learning theories. Although the research on gender as a learned variable is compelling, some differences may have physiological components. Psychological research indicates that men and women may process conflict information differently, which might be a result of hormonal or other biological causes.

Two competing "nurture" hypotheses guide gender research (Thimm, Koch, & Schey, 2003). First, the **genderlect** hypothesis posits that women talk in measurably different ways than men and that responses to women's speech are caused by these differences. Central to the genderlect hypothesis is the assumption that a male standard of speech is the norm; women's speech was viewed as abnormal. Genderlect researchers in the 1970s discovered that women habitually used less powerful forms of speech than men—such as permitting interruptions, using qualifying words ("somewhat"), adding softeners ("maybe we should"), and appending **tag questions** ("It's a nice day, isn't it?"). More recent research suggests that although males have a wider repertoire of verbal strategies than women, powerless speech is used by both genders—depending on situations, social status, and power (Thimm et al., 2003). Genderlect researchers highlight a double bind for women who adopt powerful speech patterns. They may be perceived as acting outside the norm of their gender and labeled as pushy and not feminine. Similarly, men who show high sensitivity or speak softly are labeled as indecisive, weak, and not masculine.

Discussion Question 5.3

How is conflict managed differently at work if the group is all women, all men, or mixed?

Research subscribing to another thread of nurture theory focuses on the claim that gender is learned and part of **cultural socialization.** From this view, "girling" and "boying" of individuals begins at birth (McConnell-Ginet, 2003). Those who greet a newborn baby have difficulty knowing what to say or how to talk if they do not know the child's gender. Whether the baby is "strong and hearty" or "sweet and precious" depends on the visitor's perception of the infant's gender. Cultural socialization teaches children from birth what is expected from their sex.

Cultural socialization theories contend that socialization continues in the school system. Girls and boys historically were treated differently in elementary classrooms and portrayed differently in textbooks. Although textbooks have gradually accepted gender-balanced language and less stereotypical images, "witch" and "mother" were the primary "careers" mentioned for women in children's books before the 1990s. Research also indicated that children did not perceive the generic "he" as including females. To balance the presentation of gender in textbooks, unnecessary gender references were altered, such as writing "mail carrier" rather than "mailman." If sentence structure required a pronoun, "he or she" or the plural was used. To counter those who claimed he or she was silly and pronouns really didn't make a difference, some college textbooks were published using "she" instead of "he" throughout the text (arguing that if the pronoun really didn't matter, nobody should object if "she" was the pronoun). Grade school textbooks have moved slowly to include women and men in modern, more diverse career roles.

Different treatment of boys and girls reinforced the theory that gender—and gendered conflict management strategies—was learned. Calling out in class, being aggressive, and other behaviors accepted in boys were reprimanded in girls, giving boys advantages in receiving teacher attention. Boys also had more opportunities to use scarce science equipment and learned to take chances in order to succeed (Pipher, 1995). Differences in boy/girl or male/female behavior continue to diverge and solidify as a part of group identity creation. Hence when women in the workplace used powerful and assertive language, which was traditionally reserved for men, they were viewed more negatively. For example, a study of male and female conflict strategies in the workplace found that females used avoidance, cooperative conflict strategies, and problem solving most often, with only 6 percent of women using aggressive tactics. Men used aggression 32 percent of the time (yelling, getting loud, pressuring people), followed by problem solving, with all other strategies far behind (Thimm et al., 2003). Both males and females felt their gendered identity affected their choices of communicative strategies at work.

Research continues to uncover areas where gender affects conflict behaviors. In a bargaining experiment, Kray, Thompson, and Galinsky (2001) found that when told an experiment was to test inherent negotiation ability, women did worse on the task and men did better. The authors suggest that **stereotype confirmation** is a powerful force in bargaining: Individuals adapt their behaviors to fit the prevailing social stereotype that men are good bargainers and women are not. In a second experiment the authors found that when male and female pairs were reminded of social stereotyping, women performed better as bargainers and men performed less well. The researchers theorized that telling women that negotiation skill differences were just stereotypes motivated them to do well. Conversely, giving men the message that society expected them to be better negotiators caused stress and pressure to live up to high social expectations; or, perhaps men felt so confident that they would "let" the women gain some advantage from a chivalrous sense of fair play. The two studies indicate that the way in which a stereotype is activated—calling it an inherent trait or calling it a social stereotype—affects how individuals react. In another study, men selected control strategies and were more verbally aggressive than women; women were more concerned with relationship goals than were men (Rogan & La France, 2003).

Kolb (2004) argues that conflicts at work include a **shadow negotiation** that determines how gender and race impact communication (Table 5.1). In conflict, one party may make moves to delegitimize the other person. For example, women and minorities may be challenged more often than white men on their competence, have their ideas demeaned, receive

TABLE 5.1 *Shadow Negotiation Tactics*

Challenging Competence	"You haven't been at this very long." "Your ideas are way out of line." "When you've been around longer, you'll understand."
Demeaning Ideas	"You can't be serious." "That's a really naive suggestion."
Criticizing Style	"That's thinking like a woman." "Don't get so upset." "Why aren't you a team player?"
Threatening	"Go with me on this proposal or you'll never get anywhere in this firm."
Appealing to Sympathy/Manipulative Flattery	"I know you won't let me down." "You're so much better at this kind of project. Why don't you take care of it?" "I really need your support on this project, and I know I can trust you."

criticism for their style rather than the substance of their remarks, be labeled as "emotional" or "difficult," be the recipient of threats, or become targets of manipulative flattery.

The sum of recent research on gendered communication, however, seems to be breaking down the consensus that gender itself is a key factor that dramatically affects communication and conflict behaviors. For example, research examining men and women's instant messaging communication found that women were more expressive than men (consistent with common stereotypes and past research), but other results depended more on the message recipient's gender than the gender of the sender (Fox, Bukatko, Hallahan, & Crawford, 2007).

Thus the body of literature about gender and communication seems to indicate that sometimes gender matters and sometimes it doesn't. There is a wide mosaic of gendered behaviors, and differences may be superficial, related to status, or situational (Freed, 2004; McElhinny, 2004).

TOOLBOX 5.1

Responding to Shadow Negotiation Tactics

Ignore threats	Refrain from a defensive response and make offers to work as a team.
Avoid reactive countermoves	If labeled as "emotional" don't respond, "I am not." It only fixes the label in the listeners' minds.
Turn the tactic around	Interrupt the other in mid-rant with a change of topic or problem-solving comment: "Excuse me. Are we going to get to the problem today?"
Name the tactic	"You're just saying that to distract from the real problem."
Question the speaker's motives	"I wonder why you don't want to talk about this issue."
Correct	When a boss evaluates one's desk as "messy and disorganized," reframe the label to say, "I am busy and productive."
Divert	Shift the focus to the problem and take control of the process. "So what I suggest we do is . . ."

Race

Just as most researchers agree that gendered behaviors derive from sociocultural influences rather than from biology, communicative behaviors of racial groups are seen to arise from historical influences of culture, status, and power rather than from biological imprinting. As mentioned earlier, research in the United States used a male, white upper-class model as the "norm" and labeled all others as different from the norm. Early research tended to cast "differences" as deficits in communicative skills, rather than looking for the strengths in each group's style (Vasques-Scalera, 2002). This perspective denied the cultural identity, voice, and unique experiences of many people. Modern research, in comparison, applies a diversity standard to differences—noting differences without evaluating any one group's communicative behaviors as "inherently better" than another.

> ### Discussion Question 5.4
> In what ways are you privileged? Are your privileges earned or unearned? How are you disadvantaged by others' unearned privileges?

One interesting concept developed from gender and race research explores privileges. A **privilege** is the taking of an advantage. Some privileges are earned. Students earn the privilege to use the university library through their status as a member of the university community. The university president probably has a private parking space earned through the designation of his or her job. Other privileges are taken but are not earned. An **unearned privilege** is taken as if it is perceived as a right based on a social hierarchy. Those with inherited wealth have access to resources that were not earned: money, better credit scores, influential social networks, opportunities to attend prestigious universities, and so on. Those who falsely believe that one group inherently is better than another take privileges that are unearned. The concept of *whiteness* as an unearned privilege has garnered attention in recent years (see the research topics at the end of the chapter).

How does unearned privilege impact conflict management? To the extent that race, gender, or any other variable becomes a lens through which the other person is perceived, the variable matters. Competent conflict managers assess the extent to which their tactics and strategies are affected by the taking or giving of unearned privilege.

Culture

Culture refers to national or ethnic groups who share common assumptions, tendencies, and experiences. The term also has been applied loosely to any group that develops common experiences. For example, some argue that there are different cultures for women and men, rural and urban, suburban and inner city, young and old, snowboarders and golfers, and so forth. Culture is an important variable in conflict because cultural groups have different assumptions about how conflict should be managed.

> "Almost all peoples believe that their way of thinking about and doing things is the best way. They learn to evaluate other ways of thinking about and doing things as unusual, wrong, or inferior. . . . To question the universality of your own reality or mindset, or to acknowledge that the reality or mindset of other may fundamentally differ from your own is disorienting."
>
> —Kimmel, 2000, p. 457

Because individuals from various cultures have different perceptual filters that shape what is appropriate, intercultural communication is fertile ground for ethnocentric errors. For example, during a group project, Xing Li did not bring his concerns about the work into the open. Group members from other cultures accused Xing Li of holding out on the group and being manipulative. From Xing Li's cultural standpoint, he *was* supporting the group. When we interpret others' behaviors based on what we would expect from ourselves, we make an **ethnocentric error.** These errors invite defensiveness, create negativity, and either cause conflict or make conflict more difficult to manage.

The most popular typology for distinguishing cultures is the notion of *collectivism* (high context) and *individualism* (low context), as seen in Table 5.2. Nonverbal researcher Hall (1976) introduced the notion of high- and low-context culture in *Beyond Culture*. In **low-context cultures,** most of the meaning is in the message. Several languages are low context, and the way the language is structured implies concrete cause-and-effect relationships (e.g., in German, English, and Northern European languages). If the meaning is determined more from the context of the message than the words, then the culture is **high context.** High-context language groups use more linguistic imagery or metaphor (e.g., Japanese, Chinese, Arabic, and Mediterranean languages).

Individualist cultures value the person's needs and goals first, whereas **collectivist cultures** value the group's needs and goals first. During conflict, these preferences are believed to result in differing behaviors. Individualists work assertively and use direct communication to achieve their personal interests; collectivists use indirect communication and defer to the interests of the larger group. Individualists are more confrontational and less sensitive to the other party's needs, interests, or face during conflict; collectivists avoid public confrontation, prefer compromise, and are sensitive to the other's face needs.

TABLE 5.2 *Individualist and Collectivist Cultures*

Individualist Cultures	Collectivist Cultures
Low Context	*High Context*
United States	Japan
Australia	Russia
Germany	China
Canada	Taiwan
	Korea
	Hong Kong

Discussion Question 5.5

What are the characteristics of your root culture, according to the individualistic/ collectivist framework? Do your personal behaviors fit those predicted in the framework?

Contemporary researchers discovered that reality is considerably more complicated than the simple dichotomy offered by the individualist and collectivist culture framework. First, not all individuals from a particular geographic area integrate cultural teachings in the same manner or in the same depth. Thinking all persons in a group are alike commits the stereotype of **essentializing**, assuming just because people share some commonality, they all think or act alike and are essentially the same.

Second, cultural assumptions, even when integrated by the individual, do not always spin out in ways that seem logical. For example, individualistic cultures are assumed to be more confrontational than collectivist cultures. However, Cai and Fink (2002) found that members of individualistic cultures reported using the avoidance style more than did individuals in collectivist cultures. Also contrary to the basic tenets of the high- and low-context theory is the amount of competitive conflict tactics exhibited among Japanese or Russians. Because rank and status determine one's power and share of resources in hierarchical cultures, competitive tactics to establish one's place in the hierarchy are common (Adair et al., 2004). Contrary to the theory's predictions, collectivist cultures exhibit individualistic traits, such as Russians and Japanese exhibiting extreme competition in some situations.

A more sophisticated culture profile looks at several dimensions rather than just collectivism and individualism. France is both high and low context (a history of nuanced diplomacy and a contemporary focus on direct problem-solving processes). France is categorized as both egalitarian (through its socialist politics) and hierarchical (interested in status and rank). Russia is categorized as collectivist, yet it also exhibits a competitive "have" and "have-not" social hierarchy. Japan and Brazil are collectivist in conversation and hierarchical in organization. In negotiation studies, individuals from these countries do not behave as predicted by simple cultural categorization. Contrary to what might be expected for an individualistic culture, U.S. negotiators have in common with Brazil a strong preference to share information (where secrecy to gain advantage might be predicted). Russian and Japanese negotiators are more likely than other negotiators to use specific power negotiation strategies when the model would predict cooperative behaviors (Adair et al., 2004).

An alternate perspective on culture describes an individual's predispositions on two variables: *how disagreement is expressed* during conflict and *how emotions are expressed* during conflict. Hammer (2002) developed the Intercultural Conflict Style Inventory as a means of assessing intercultural differences. Hammer's research finds two stylistic ways that disagreements are expressed in conflicts—directly or indirectly—and two ways that emotions are managed during conflict—expressively or with restraint (Table 5.3).

TABLE 5.3 *Dimensions of Intercultural Conflict Style*

How Conflicts Are Expressed

Direct	*Indirect*
Words carry meaning	Meaning in the context
Directly state the problem	Ambiguity, stories, metaphor
Face to face	Intermediaries
Speak one's mind	Withhold to save public face
Highlight differences	Highlight commonalities
Persuade and argue	Indirect to save face
Solution focused	Relationship focused

How Emotions Are Expressed

Expressive	*Restraint*
Overtly expressed	Withheld and suppressed
Humor as a tension regulator	Avoid humor
High use of nonverbal to express feelings	Use nonverbal to hide feelings
Passionate and loud	Soft and constrained
Build trust through joint expression	Build trust through emotional control
Need emotions first; then work together	Need calmness; then work together

According to Hammer (2002), the dimensions of cultural style interact to create four distinct intercultural conflict communication styles: discussion, engagement, accommodation, and dynamic. The styles tend to align with geographic cultural areas. However, an individual within a culture could display a non-normative style. **Discussant cultural style** individuals are high in direct expression of conflict and low in showing emotion. These individuals confront conflict directly, are highly verbal, argue, and prefer to hold emotions inside (e.g., Northern Europe, Australia, and the United States). **Engagement cultural style** individuals also are high in direct expression of disagreement, but they differ in preferring more expression of emotion and may be intense, loud, or passionate (e.g., Southern Europe, Cuba, and Russia). **Accommodation cultural style** individuals prefer to express conflict indirectly and to hold emotion inside (e.g., Chinese, Japanese, Native American, Mexican, and Korean). **Dynamic cultural style** individuals prefer high expression of emotion in conflict with indirect expression of the issues. The topic of the conflict will be expressed passionately but vaguely through stories, metaphor, or other indirect strategies (e.g., Kuwait, Iraq, Egypt).

For individuals in each cultural style, the ways in which "competent" conflict management occurs are different. Some express conflict directly and some tacitly; some energetically express emotions, and some strategically withhold emotional information. These differences can be critical. When viewed through the eyes of one's culture, the behaviors of the other person will seem wrong and be open to ethnocentric errors. For

TABLE 5.4   *Levels of Cultural Awareness*

1. *Cultural chauvinists* know very little about other cultures and have little interest in them.
2. *Ethnocentric* individuals see differences caused by nationality, racial, or religious groupings as a reason to feel superior.
3. *Tolerant* people believe their own culture is best and see differences as caused by understandable differences and as a result of living in different places.
4. *Minimalists* understand differences but trivialize them, believing all people basically are alike.
5. Those who *genuinely understand* know differences are real and many times based on fundamental value differences.

Source: Adapted from Kimmel (2000).

instance, Su (2006) found Taiwanese and U.S. accounting students had different views on what constituted unethical accounting practices. Communication differences across cultures too often are misinterpreted as motivated by ill will, strategic manipulation, or the intent to do harm.

Culture may play an important role in how individuals in conflict perceive each other, how they select strategies, and the styles they prefer. The key word is *may*. When in conflict with a person from a different *root culture* (the cultural group an individual was born and raised in), a sophisticated conflict manager will be alert to the *potential* of cross-cultural variation but would never assume that the individual essentially is like all others in a cultural group. **Self-construal,** or how one views oneself, is a powerful influence in developing communicative styles and sometimes trumps general cultural identity (Gudykunst & Kim, 2003; Kim, Lee, Kim, & Hunter, 2004; Takahashi, Ohara, Antonucci, & Akiyana, 2002). Kimmel's (2000) levels of cultural awareness in Table 5.4 suggest that genuine and deep knowledge of a culture's values is superior to superficial knowledge or stereotypes (see also Kim, 2007).

Age and Generations

Generational cohorts may engage conflict management differently. A **generational cohort** is a group that is influenced by major events that affect their worldview. The experiences of different generations in Table 5.5 illustrate the influences and tendencies of the generations coexisting today. Whether these differences derive from common values of a generation cohort or from the differing goals and experiences of age groups is open to debate.

The importance of generational differences during interpersonal conflict is that what feels like the "correct" way of thinking and acting for one generation may be different from the next generation. For example, Boomers and Net Generation individuals may have different values about work and levels of loyalty to an employer. Goal achievement and self-identity tied to success at work are more likely in a Boomer than in someone just entering the workforce who may see work just as a means to achieve other goals. Xers' primary complaints about work are that management ignores their ideas and does not give them enough recognition (O'Bannon & Dennis, 2001). Xers feel they deserve quick recognition and a place at the decision-making table; Boomers assume recognition

TABLE 5.5   *The Experiences of Different Generations*

Builders/Traditionalists

Born	1901–1945
Influenced by	The Great Depression and World War II
Tendencies	Cautious about money, willing to work for the common good, disciplined
Weaknesses	May be inflexible and too cautious

Boomers

Born	1946–1965
Influenced by	Vietnam, civil rights movement, threat of nuclear war, television, the Beatles, rock and roll
Tendencies	Live the good life, self-absorbed, workaholics, confident, willing to take on causes, team sports, optimism
Weaknesses	Think they are "special," will break rules/ethics in own self-interest

X-ers

Born	1966–1977
Influenced by	Divorce, Watergate, MTV, Bill Clinton, Madonna, Beavis and Butt-Head
Tendencies	Distrust government, more open to diversity, work is just a means to an end, independent, comfortable with technology, individual sports
Weaknesses	Pessimistic, personal life trumps work; may seem unmotivated, easily bored

Y-ers

Born	1977–1986
Influenced by	AIDS, Princess Diana's death, *Challenger* explosion
Tendencies	Ability to multitask and change directions quickly, adaptable, curious, direct, willing to think outside the box
Weaknesses	Impulsive, expect to know, don't expect jobs to last forever so may leave them often, question directions, may seem impertinent or insubordinate, may be distracted easily

Net Generation (also called Millennials)

Born	1987–1997
Influenced by	Internet, political scandals, cell phones
Tendencies	Comfortable with change, expect to know details, consumer driven, nonlinear thinking, tolerant, technology savvy, generally optimistic
Weaknesses	Less comfortable in hierarchy. Expect to be informed and may not follow well

Source: Adapted from Hicks and Hicks (1999); Lancaster and Stillman (2002); Raines and Hunt (2000).

should be earned and that employees should be self-motivated. These differences create areas ripe for conflict and misunderstanding. O'Bannon & Dennis (2001) state, "If Boomers fail to recognize and acknowledge the unique issues facing Xers, the result will be a workplace fraught with miscommunication, misunderstandings and harsh feelings, resulting in higher-than-normal turnover ratios and dysfunctional supervisor-employee relationships" (p. 97).

> ### *Discussion Question 5.6*
>
> What generation do you belong to? What influences your generation that isn't listed in Table 5.5? For example, was your generation molded by the President Kennedy's assassination, the Columbine shootings, or the attacks on September 11, 2001?
>
> What generation does your supervisor or teacher belong to? Give an example of a situation in which generational differences caused conflict or made mutual understanding more difficult.

The assumptions and experiences of different generations can cause distress when parents and children, bosses and subordinates, or age-separated coworkers communicate. Not only may their assumptions and goals be different, but given what we know from attribution theory, evaluations of the other age group probably will be less than charitable. Raines and Hunt (2000) studied the perception gap in the workplace between Boomers and Xers. They argue that perceived differences across the generations necessitate three levels of response. Level 1 is acknowledging the difference and letting it go. If the issue is not important, there is little profit in using energy to engage in conflict. Level 2 is changing personal behavior. Adapt to the preferences of the other generation by changing word usage or adopting the style of communication that the other prefers. Level 3 is "using a generational template to talk it over" (p. 46). In level 3, the generational difference is brought to the surface as a point of discussion. For example, Boomers believe in working one's way up the organization and are offended by young Xers who expect fast advancement and who push their agenda forward. A manager who orchestrates a discussion among staff of what it means to work as a team can create an alternative model that all generations can follow.

Power

> "The fundamental concept in social science is power, in the same sense in which energy is the fundamental concept in physics."
>
> —Philosopher Bertrand Russell (1938)

The perception of power, or its absence, is an important variable in conflict. Those who perceive they do not have power may be motivated to reach for more power. Too often, both parties in a conflict view the other party as having the most power, leading to an out-of-control spiral of negative power-grabbing tactics.

Power is defined as the ability to have influence or bring about a desired outcome. Coleman (2000) identifies four themes in how power is treated in social science research: (1) Coercion power, or *power over,* is the ability to force someone do something they would not otherwise have done. (2) *Power with* is jointly developed, noncoercive, or partnership power. (3) *Powerlessness* or dependence is a view of the powerless that leads to rigidity, power struggles, irrationality, and violence. (4) *Empowerment, independence,* and *power to,* where individuals have enough power to achieve their goals, is the flip side of powerlessness. Students in a classroom may perceive that the professor has *power over* them and can force them to do things they would not otherwise have done, such as read books, write papers, and take tests. If a group of students feels alienated from the campus, ignored by campus leaders, and *powerless* to affect the system, protests or violence may erupt. If students feel safe in negotiating the usefulness of assignments in a class, they are *empowered*. Students who have voting seats on university promotion and tenure committees have *power with* others.

> "It is critical to bear in mind that power is typically context-dependent and that even the most powerful people are powerless under certain conditions."
>
> —Coleman, 2000, p. 124.

Traditional views of power are **distributive:** Power is seen as a fixed resource that can be wielded to gain concessions from others. If the instructor has 95 percent of the power in a class; the students can only have up to 5 percent. Within this perspective, power is zero sum, meaning its parts add up to 100 percent, and taking any of the power pie results in less for others. As portions of a zero-sum item are taken away, eventually none remains. In a distributive world, one must scramble for a share of the power pie.

Power typologies describe sources of power. French's (1956) typology (see Table 5.6) asserted there are five traditional sources of interpersonal power: reward, coercive, legitimate, expert, and referent (Raven & Rubin, 2001). Employers who give performance raises, parents who give or deny praise when their children succeed, or friends who celebrate success with a night out all are exerting **reward power.** In a traditional sense, the person desiring the reward has less power than the individual who controls the giving of the reward. To "earn" the reward, one must comply with the powerful person's wishes.

Bosses who threaten to fire an employee, parents who admonish children for family infractions, police who take drunk drivers into custody, or teachers who threaten to give pop quizzes if students do not read their assignments are applying **coercive power.** Coercive power threatens retribution if the desired behavior is not forthcoming.

A formal title, rank, or office in an organization bestows **legitimate power.** Legitimate power derives from the respect given to the office and the right of officials to lead others. Professors, judges, police, and government officials all have the power of positions awarded to them that create a legitimate power base.

Having specialized knowledge, skill, or expertise is the source of **expert power.** Skilled professionals, such as plumbers, protect the exclusivity of their craft by requiring specific training. Across generations, children may have expertise that parents and grandparents lack when it comes to using computers or cell phone technology.

Finally, **referent power** arises from valued personality traits. Movie stars and athletes demand high salaries when making commercials because the public admires them. Advertisers ride along with the star's referent power and hope that the admiration for the star is associated with their product.

TABLE 5.6 *Five Sources of Traditional Power*

Reward power	Control of material or psychological resources that can be given
Coercive power	Use of fear and punishment to control behavior
Legitimate power	Position within a hierarchy
Expert power	Knowledge and specialized skills
Referent power	Admiration of the individual or his or her association with positive traits

Individuals in conflict make judgments about the other person's power. These judgments are influenced by cultural norms about power. Powerful people are perceived as having more control of resources. Perceptions of power are made based on power indicators such as the kind of car driven, clothes worn, or technology used. On campus, a student saw a woman he was working with on a group project driving into the parking garage in her Lexus convertible. He walked over to her and said, "Wow, is *that* your car?" You could almost see his perception of the Lexus driver changing based on an attribution of status and wealth. An impressive job title, a large office, expensive jewelry, and an address in an exclusive area are perceived as indicators of power and status.

Power, however, is not innate or automatically attached to those with property, titles, or status. Power is based on the connections among the individuals that motivate one individual to *give* precedence to another. Because the student in the example just cited valued an expensive car, he granted his classmate higher status and power. If one values and respects a title, then power is given to the person who holds the title. Because students respect the title "doctor of philosophy" and the university gives the teacher the authority to award grades, professors are granted legitimate, expert, and reward power. Each of these sources of power, however, can be removed. Students can remove a teacher's power by refusing to comply with instructions during class time or deciding that they no longer care about their final grade. The influence of a manager can be undercut if the CEO ridicules his or her work. The power of the person who owns the only car in a friendship group is diminished when another friend purchases a vehicle.

Discussion Question 5.7

What are your sources of potential power (see Table 5.7)? Do you have a tendency to rely on just one or two sources? Do you use different power sources in different contexts (home or work)?

The changeability of power based on the connection among individuals and their perceptions of each other is the basis of the **integrative power model.** Contrary to the self-focused applications of distributive power, integrative power models hold that power always is based on a line of connection between individuals. Emerson (1962) theorized that *the power of person A with person B is equal to how much B is dependent on A. Likewise, the power of B with A is equal to how much A is dependent on B*. For Emerson, the most important linkage between individuals was dependency on another person to reach a goal.

French's typology can be expanded to include many nontraditional sources of power that better fit a power integration model. For example, referent power can encompass networking and who one knows. The expanded typology suggests that there are many potential sources of power. In this sense, power can be perceived like a *currency*. A currency is only powerful if it is valued by the other person.

In a traditional distributive view, power is limited. Modern **power currency** perspectives attempt to break the boundary of their distributive roots to offer an expansive view of power. If one's sources of power are weak in a specific relationship, changing to another power source that is more valued by the other party can develop power. For example, during times of economic downturns, employees may not receive raises or additional financial compensation for their work. They may even be asked to pay more for health care or to take

TABLE 5.7   *Power Currencies*

Traditional View
Property
Money
Designated authority through titles, position, or legal judgments
Expert knowledge
Resource control
Networking
Information

Expanded View
Cooperation
Links to community
Endurance and a reputation for doing what one agrees to do
Cultural traditions
Listening
Networking
Integrity
Patience
Attractiveness
Nuisance ability
Persistence
Public speaking and verbal skills
Languages
Traditional logic and organization ability
People skills
Dependability
Self-esteem
Emotional stability
Ethical sense
Spirituality
Personal self-worth

a pay cut. In these instances, bosses no longer have the traditional pay raise reward power at their disposal. Lower-level supervisors need other sources of power to motivate their employees, perhaps creatively using travel monies, training opportunities, special assignments, praise, or other nonmonetary resources as rewards.

The expanded view of power currencies and the interactive power model suggest there are many ways to cultivate power, all based on the interaction between specific individuals. Related to the concept of cultivating power is **power management.** When one or both individuals perceive power as too unbalanced, a redistribution of power may be necessary to set the stage for conflict management. Folger et al. (2005) conclude, "there is widespread agreement among scholars of conflict that any significant imbalance of power poses a serious threat to constructive conflict resolution" (p. 127). When an employee feels that management holds all the power and will not listen, there is little incentive to enter into negotiations. When difficulties arise, an employee may simply quit or rebel through passive-aggressive tactics. If the employer wants to reduce dissatisfaction and turnover, steps may be taken to empower the employees, perhaps by creating feedback systems or problem-solving mechanisms that help employees and supervisors work together. When one partner believes the other has all the power, there is little incentive to work on the relationship. If both want the relationship to continue, the perceptions about power must be adjusted to create an environment where conflicts can be managed productively.

Without power management, power struggles can lead to inefficient workplace behaviors, decreasing interpersonal relationships, and a tendency to choose destructive tactics. When power struggles erupt, individuals may attempt to gain or exert more power through coalition building, aggressive tactics, emotional distancing, starting rumors, using intentionally annoying behaviors, avoiding the other person, or personal attacks.

When power differences exist, power management strategies can be implemented. The goal of power management is *not* to make power exactly equal, but to manage the perception of power in a range where the lower power person no longer feels helpless. Power management strategies by the more powerful individual include the following:

- Allowing the other to be included in decision making
- Listening
- Restraining from power-grabbing moves
- Remaining silent until the other has a chance to express his or her ideas
- Sharing information
- Increasing statements about the connection between the two individuals
- Highlighting the value of the other in the relationship
- Validating the other's concerns or experiences

Leaders who sincerely want to know their worker's ideas have learned to ask for input before expressing their thoughts. Once the powerful individual speaks, others may be unwilling to indicate disagreement or feel that decisions already have been made so why bother with more discussion. Making statements about the commonalities that both parties share enhances the sense of positive interdependence among the parties.

Power management strategies of the less powerful individual also can be addressed. Those who feel powerless are vulnerable to defeatist strategies that reinforce weakness and may lead to an acceptance of extreme measures or violence as the only solution. Positive power management can be undertaken by the less powerful individuals in these ways:

- Making commonality statements to enhance positive interdependence
- Developing other power currencies
- Asking nonthreatening questions
- Suggesting creative problem-solving techniques such as brainstorming as a way of getting many ideas on the table
- Staying engaged rather than withdrawing
- Using calm persistence (Wilmot & Hocker, 2007)

"Trust is the glue that holds relationships together."
—Researchers Lewicki and Wiethoff, 2000

Trust

Trust is defined as "an individual's belief in, and willingness to act on the basis of, the words, actions, and decisions of another" (Lewicki & Wiethoff, 2000, p. 87). Trust is related to whether intentions are attributed positively or negatively. When trust is high, behaviors are perceived as stemming from good intentions. When trust is lacking or has been broken, the same behaviors are attributed as manipulative, self-centered, or motivated by ill will. Lewicki and Weithoff conclude that individuals decide how much to trust based on a personality predisposition to see good or evil in others, psychological orientation, reputation, stereotypes, and actual experiences over time.

In new relationships, trust is constructed from small bricks into a solid structure. To create trust, individuals can spend time on shared activities, cultivate common interests, find common goals, comment on reactions to similar situation, and build on areas where both stand for the same values (Lewicki & Wiethoff, 2000). When trust is lost, the reconstruction process can be lengthy and difficult.

Discussion Question 5.8

Have you been in a relationship where trust was lacking or broken? How was communicating with that person different from the communication with someone you did trust?

Humor

Humor might seem the same regardless of when it is used or who uses it. Researchers disagree. Humor during conflict typically is intended to decrease tension, anxiety, or

---

TOOLBOX 5.2

Are You Trustworthy

1. Do you behave consistently and appropriately?
2. Are you reliable?
3. Do you meet deadlines?
4. Do you follow through as promised?
5. Do you set upfront commitments and deadlines for others and consequences if they are not met?
6. Do you seek agreement on procedures to evaluate the actions of self and others?
7. If distrust occurs, do you cultivate other ways to exhibit trustworthiness?
8. Do you discuss expectations to increase common awareness rather than assuming everyone has the same expectations?
9. Can you admit your errors?
10. Do you take responsibility for your choices and their outcomes?

aggression—motives that would seem productive. People who use humor may be trying to lighten the situation. When humor works, it can be a useful communication device.

Research on humor (Bippus, 2003) discovered interesting effects that can be explained using attribution theory. Generally, people do not credit a well-intended humor user with good intentions. Furthermore, identical humor attempts can be perceived in many different ways by individual listeners. If the humor is perceived as funny, then the recipient might go along with the tension-relieving intention. If the recipient perceived that the humor was made for mood improvement or to establish common ground, then it was viewed as productive (an attribution that the humor was used for the benefit of both parties). If the receiver of the humor perceived that the humorist used a joke because of a lack of argumentative skills, it also could be perceived as productive (an attribution that the speaker was self-oriented but not negative). If the receiver perceived that the others used humor because of their hostile nature, to change the topic to their advantage, or to make the receiver look bad, then a negative attribution occurred and the conflict typically escalated.

Although humor can be a tension reliever, it also is known as an aggressive tactic. Humor can be used to cloak a personal attack. When confronted about a negative criticism, the speaker may say, "Just kidding," as if to rewrite the history of the remark. Aggressive humor can attack by making someone the butt of a joke, or humor can be an avoidance tactic to turn attention away from an unwanted topic. Humor can be used to point out social norm breaking or to gain compliance through shaming. Instead of asking a late coworker to get to work on time, a colleague may comment in a joking fashion, "Oh, look who's decided to grace us with her royal presence."

> ### Discussion Question 5.9
> Are there other variables that you believe impact conflict behaviors than those discussed in this chapter? What other factors might make a difference in how people behave during conflict?

Sources of Conflict Patterns

Where do the patterns discussed in this chapter come from? What forces move entire groups of people to act in similar ways? Many social scientists point to social learning for the answer. Partly, we play out scripts written for us by external forces—culture, television, customs, and rituals. We are taught how to behave as a parent, male, female, subordinate, and so forth. Social roles create expectations and provide an easy model for behavior whether the behavior is sensible and productive during conflict or not. Coleman (2000) comments, "These social norms establish shared expectations among members of a system, which in most cases came into existence long before the individuals who now respond to them. It argues that we largely act out these preexisting scripts in our institutions and organizations, and that it is these roles, these shared norms and scripts, that dictate our experiences, our expectations, and our responses" (pp. 119–120).

Perceptions of other individuals affect what one expects and how one behaves. In many situations, none of the variables discussed in this chapter may seem to matter. In other situations, one or more variables are somehow activated and become crucial. The competent conflict manager is aware of variables that impact how the process of conflict plays out and how the individuals in conflict are perceived.

Summary

Variables are specific traits, behaviors, or patterns isolated in social science research. Knowledge of common patterns of behavior is useful during conflict to isolate problem areas or to make predictions about potential behavior. However, social science research is limited by its ability to isolate communicative behaviors and there are cautions when making predictions about human behaviors.

Genderlect and cultural socialization theories underpin research on gender. Genderlect focuses on language differences, and social culturalization explores how individuals learn socially appropriate gendered behaviors. Culture refers to national or ethnic groups who share common assumptions, tendencies, and experiences. A common typology of cultural behavior contrasts individualistic groups (low context) with collectivist groups (high context). A weakness of this typology is essentializing: treating all members of a group as if they are the same. An alternative cultural typology examines two dimensions (how disagreement is expressed and how emotions are expressed) to create four intercultural conflict styles (discussant, engagement, accommodating, and dynamic).

Another variable appearing in much research is age. Generational cohorts perceive events differently enough to create sources of conflict. Conceptions about work, in particular, seem to vary across age groups.

Power is the ability to have influence or bring about a desired outcome. It can be perceived as power over others, power with others, powerlessness, or empowerment. In a competitive view, power is perceived as a fixed resource (distributive). In a cooperative view, power is seen as flexible (integrative). French and Raven identified five sources of power: reward, coercion, legitimate, expert, and referent. Power also can be viewed as a currency exchange.

Trust is a willingness to act based on another person's words or actions. Behaviors during conflict are perceived differently when trust is high than when trust is low. Similarly, humor is judged differently depending on perception of the speaker's intent.

The existence of patterns of behavior is interesting to conflict researchers and has strong implications for competent conflict managers. Isolating characteristics and variables that give rise to certain outcomes or conflict behaviors offers insights into possible entry points for transforming personal conflicts.

Chapter Resources _____

Exercises

1. A group of coworkers are moving into a newly renovated building. The supervisor says it doesn't matter who gets which office and that the group should decide over lunch. The supervisor is called away just before the meeting starts. Based on the variables discussed

in the chapter, how might the discussion play out if some of the workers want the same office and

A. All of the workers are female (or male).
B. One female and one male both want the same large office with a window.
C. All of the workers but one is from the Boomer generation.
D. One worker is more verbal and argumentative than the rest of the employees.
E. One worker consistently is a top sales earner and another has more seniority but is less productive.

2. Which of these definitions of power are more distributive and which are more integrative?

A. "Power is the ability to get things done, to mobilize resources, to get and use whatever it is that a person needs for the goals he or she is attempting to meet" (Rosabeth Moss Kanter).
B. "Power is the ability to act to meet ones personal needs or a group's objectives" (Donald Klein).
C. "Power is the ability to cause or prevent change. It may be a moving force or a blocking force" (Rollo May).
D. "The processes of power are persuasive, complex and often disguised in our society" (John French and Bertram Raven).

3. In a culturally diverse class, each individual will report on how and when the New Year is celebrated in their homelands. How do these differences/similarities show reflections of what is important in a culture? (adapted from Gerritsen & Verckens, 2006).

4. List all of the counties of origin represented in the class. Reference each country on Hofstede's cultural index (http://www.geert-hofstede.com/) and create charts for each culture pair. For example, if the countries of origin were United States, Mexico, Japan, and Nigeria, the pairs created on the Hofstede index would be: U.S with Mexico, U.S. with Japan, U.S. with Nigeria, Mexico with Japan, Mexico with Nigeria, and Japan with Nigeria. Discuss the communication challenges that each paired group might experience.

5. For one week, keep a log of "ethnic encounters" where you interact with someone from another culture/ethnicity. Include the day, time, context, age of both parties, and any communicative elements that may have affected the conversation. Examine the log to speculate if race or ethnicity is a dominant factor that affected the encounter (vs. age, sex, context. etc.) (adapted from Harris, 2004).

Research Topics

1. Examine conflict research conducted in the last two years in communication and psychology journals. Do gender, race, or class appear as variables in the research studies? If so, what was discovered? What other variables are used in the studies?

2. Review several resources on trust. How is trust built, broken, and rebuilt?

3. Investigate the research on "whiteness" and racial identity construction. How does the construction of racial identity impact conflict in particular areas, such as sports, media, sports mascots, politics, or the music industry? Suggested beginning resources in your research journey include the following:

Suggested Readings

Acker, J. (2006). Inequality regimes: Gender, class, and race in organizations. *Gender & Society, 20*(4), 441–464.

Farough, S. D. (2006). Believing is seeing: The matrix of vision and white masculinities. *Journal of Contemporary Ethnography, 35*(1), 51–83.

Hunter, M. L. (2002). "If you're light you're alright": Light skin color as social capital for women of color. *Gender & Society, 16*(2), 175–193.

Kusz, K. W. (2007). From NASCAR Nation to Pat Tillman: Notes on sport and the politics of white cultural nationalism in post-911 America. *Journal of Sport & Social Issues, 31*(1), 77–88.

Staurowsky, E. J. (2007). "You know we are all Indian": Exploring white power and privilege in reactions to the NCAA Native American mascot policy. *Journal of Sport & Social Issues, 31*(1), 61–76.

Mastery Case

Analyze Mastery Case 5, "John's Brief Internship." Which concepts from the chapter best explain what is occurring in the case?

John's Brief Internship

John, a twenty-year-old college junior, was excited to start an internship at the library. John grew up in the town and had been in and out of the library as a patron since he first learned to read. John started his internship full of ideas on how to make the library better.

One of the supervisors, Mrs. Bean, has worked at the library for twenty years. Although Mrs. Bean has lots of experience, she tells others what to do more than doing the work herself. She calls John "The Intern" and doesn't seem to know what his name is even after two weeks on the job.

She often makes snippy remarks to John and to patrons when they ask questions, implying that if they were intelligent, they wouldn't need to bother her with questions.

John is tempted to fight for his rights as an employee, but after listening to other workers, it seems like her behavior has been going on for years. Complaints have been filed, but nothing ever seems to happen. Mrs. Bean knows many of the movers and shakers in town and chats with them about plays that are at the performing arts center. John knows it would take lots of energy to fight a battle against Mrs. Bean. John's friends have remarked that he is usually angry when he meets them after work. John finally couldn't take it anymore and approached his supervisor to ask for a different internship placement.

Conflict Management Skills

Section II presents essential skills in a conflict manager's toolkit. Most people enter conflict with some fears, hopes, and skills learned through experience. Unfortunately, much of our learning about conflict comes from the adversarial and sometimes cruel world of the grade school playground, the middle school quest for identity, and questionable media programs. Some individuals seem to have learned their conflict coping skills from the television cartoon character Bart Simpson's school of social graces—full of withering sarcasm and hurtful indifference. The competent conflict manager must understand how to restructure unproductive communication.

Training and increasing skills can have a positive impact. A study of doctors and medical personnel found five positive long-term effects of conflict training: (1) A new spin or view of the potential positive aspects of conflict was built, (2) knowing how to analyze conflicts encouraged time to reflect before automatically responding, (3) discovering cooperative and interest-based ways of approaching difficulties was an eye-opener, (4) self-awareness and knowing one's hot buttons built confidence, and (5) learning it's better to listen than to be smart helped reduce tension and allow problem solving (Zweibel et al., 2008). Chapter 6 presents the most basic skills that competent conflict managers must master: listening, defusing emotions, reframing, and asking questions. With these basics, individuals are prepared to respond skillfully to a variety of conflict situations.

Chapter 7 examines conflict management styles. Knowledge of conflict styles—one's own and the styles of others—helps the conflict manager adapt to different situations and people. Moving away from seeing some conflicts as a clash of personalities and toward viewing them as stylistic differences allows more strategic options for conflict transformation.

Chapter 8 teaches negotiation skills. Productive skills for competitive negotiation are revealed. Methods for interest-based bargaining are presented.

Finally, Chapter 9 delves into a deeper understanding of conflict through sophisticated methods for analyzing conflict. Successful analysis provides conflict managers tools to determine optimal strategies.

6

Listening and Seeking Information

Objectives _____

After reading the chapter, you should be able to:

1. Explain the disadvantages of poor listening in competitive and cooperative conflict
2. Contrast the six types of listening and explain which are most useful to conflict managers
3. Apply techniques to defuse emotion and reframe positional statements

Listening is the primary way to discover what is happening during interpersonal conflict. Contrary to popular opinion, listening is not automatic. **Hearing** is an automatic, physiological event that occurs for anyone with fully functioning ears. **Listening** requires mental effort to process the stimuli garnered through hearing. It begins with the perception process of attending to a message, organizing the stimuli into something that makes sense, and evaluating its meaning.

For conflict managers, focused listening is essential. First, listening is a way of gathering information. Knowledge of the other party's goals and needs is a prerequisite to productive conflict management. For example, discernment of the other party's

CASE 6.1 • *The Mistake*

Gerald was sad to see his last assistant, Marcie, take a promotion within the hospital. She had worked for him for more than ten years, and they had a great synchronicity that made their small unit very efficient and able to serve the needs of their patients. Sometimes it was almost as if they had telepathy. He would ask about a task and she would just smile and say, "Already done." Marcie often would work late to be sure that orders were ready for the next day.

Because Gerald was a senior unit manager in the technical field of medical imaging, he conducted the interviews to fill Marcie's vacant position. He selected Paulo, who was a young graduate fresh from school.

Gerald spent extra time in the unit during the first week to be sure that Paulo had the routine down: Schedule the patients; confirm their insurance will pay; let everyone on the team know when patients are coming for the next two days; and order the supplies to do the imaging tests. Sure, there were some nuances to the details of getting things done, but Marcie always sorted things out, so it was assumed that Paulo would figure everything out.

It had been a rough week with training added on top of regular duties, and they had stayed a little late on two days. Gerald stayed particularly late on Thursday to catch up on his weekly reports so he could play golf on Friday afternoon. About 4 P.M. he dropped over to Paulo's station and asked if everything was going well. Paulo said, "No problems."

"Great," said Gerald, "I'm taking off, and I'll see you next week." Paulo, because he had worked overtime on two days that week, left shortly after Gerald.

Gerald arrived as usual on Monday morning ready to work with their typical fifteen to twenty patients a day. He was shocked to see that patients filled the lobby instead of being in the ready room. As soon as he sat down in his small office, three of the technicians crowded into the room, very angry that their equipment wasn't ready and the lobby was full of patients who weren't going to get their tests. It turns out that Paulo, who isn't scheduled to arrive for another fifteen minutes, left Friday without picking up the supplies for the Monday morning tests. It was going to be a rough day.

latitude in bargaining is helpful when engaging in competitive conflict, and knowing the other's needs is critical to an interest-based approach. Second, listening is an essential skill because demonstrating empathy creates a connection among individuals. When the conflict partner is seen as a responsible individual rather than an evil opponent, a less caustic range of tactics and strategies is more likely to be chosen. Finally, listening is critical because it develops power. Having information and knowledge is a basis of power.

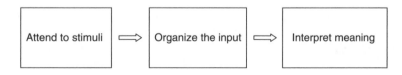

FIGURE 6.1 *The Listening Process*

> "A wise old owl sat in an oak. The more he heard, the less he spoke. The less he spoke, the more he heard. Why can't we all be like that bird?"
>
> —Children's nursery rhyme

An Introduction to Listening

The Nature of the Listening Process

Listening can go wrong in numerous ways. The three-step listening process itself contains traps for the unwary. The *attending step* requires that attention be blurred or focused so the mind is not overwhelmed with data, yet can still collect important information. While reading this chapter, several things may compete for your attention: People may be talking in the next room, you may be listening to music, a car alarm may begin to blare, or thoughts about upcoming plans for the weekend may intrude. To comprehend what is being read, you must tune out extraneous stimuli so they recede into the background. If the conversation in the next room turns to a topic of interest, attention may wander from reading to eavesdropping. If the word "apartment" appears in one of the cases, it could trigger some internal turmoil if you just broken up with a significant other and need to find a new place to live. Physical pain, hunger, discomfort, and other internal states also are distracters vying for your attention.

> **Discussion Question 6.1**
>
> What challenges do you face in attending and organizing messages while sitting in class, talking to your friends, or at work?

Without constant vigilance, attention may drift during important encounters. Paying attention takes energy and effort. *Multitasking*, doing more than one thing at a time, seems to be omnipresent in modern life. Some U.S. states have banned cell phones while driving because attending to a phone conversation takes attention away from driving a car safely. When conversing with a friend on the phone, there may be a tap-tap-tap sound in the background (the person on the other end of the line probably is e-mailing or playing a game). Multitasking requires dividing attention between tasks, and some portion of the message is filtered out.

Listening also can be sidetracked in the next step of the perception process. In the *organizing step*, the mind takes the incoming data and makes sense of it. The mind compares current information to past knowledge. Perceptually, people tend to see and hear what they expect to see and hear. Our past experiences create filters through which we perceive the world. When a stranger speaks loudly and with intensity, the veracity of the message is filtered by comparison to one's past experiences with loud and intense people. The message then is categorized as coming from someone who is _____ (fill in the blank with an impression: angry, frustrated, from a different culture, etc.). Because the perception process means we organize data based on what we already know about the world, we rely on prejudgments or stereotypes to categorize data.

KEY 6.1

Listening is the quintessential mark of a competent conflict manager.

After organizing and categorizing the incoming message, the listener then *interprets* it and chooses how to respond. Is the message good or bad? Is someone ignoring me or really didn't hear me ask a question? In the interpretation step, the message is put into context and decisions are made on how to respond. The meaning of any message lies in the interpretation of the receiver of that message. What goes into our interpretations (cultural biases, past experiences, relational history, beliefs, values, and much more) affects our ability to listen effectively.

The three parts of the listening process work together to create understanding or to distort reality. A tragic example occurred several years ago near Los Angeles when a deaf woman was killed by members of a gang, reportedly for using a sign language gesture they misinterpreted as meaning a rival gang (Lee, 1991). They attended to the message by observing her use of sign language, organized the gesture through their past experiences as belonging in the category of "rival gang sign," and interpreted her use as showing a lack of respect. The consequences were fatal.

Effective conflict managers challenge themselves to be aware of how they are attending, what is influencing their categorization of information, and how interpretations influence their responses. The effectiveness of the listening process requires constant awareness of each of the three elements: attending, organizing, and interpreting.

> "The average person suffers from three delusions: (1) that he is a good driver, (2) that he has a good sense of humor, and (3) that he is a good listener."
> —Former president, University of Southern California, Steven Sample

Barriers to Effective Listening

A significant barrier to good listening is created by the listener's attitudes. One attitude stems from the assumption that listening requires no special effort. Thinking no effort is required deters skill development. Acknowledging that listening can be improved is a necessary first step. A myth about listening states that not talking is being a good listener. Unfortunately, being trained to "be quiet" when someone else is speaking does not necessarily mean the silent person is attending to what is said. Teachers know that a good percentage of students who smile and nod during a lecture are thinking about something other than the topic of the moment. Table 6.1 summarizes common listening barriers.

> **Discussion Question 6.2**
> What did you learn about being a good listener as you grew up? Did listening equate to silence? Who taught you about listening? Describe the behaviors of a good listener according to your family.

Pretending to listen, called *pseudo-listening*, also does not qualify as listening. One commercial illustrates the trap of pretending to listen. The scene starts with the husband reading the newspaper. His wife comes into the room and says, "Does this dress make me look fat?" From behind the paper he replies from habit, "You bet." She is not amused. Pretending to listen and giving fake feedback can be disastrous.

TABLE 6.1   *Listening Barriers*

Internal Listening Barriers

Internal preoccupation:	Using the gap between speaking (125–250 words per minute) and comprehending (500 words per minute) to think about other things.
Self-involvement:	Focusing on personal needs and ignoring the interests of the other party.
Selective attention:	Focusing only on part of the message and ignoring everything else.
Listening with an agenda:	Listening for facts that will fit preconceived ideas about the conflict or its outcome.
Ambushing:	Listening for points to attack the speaker or his or her ideas.
Physiological turmoil:	Experiencing pain, hunger, coldness, or other physical conditions.
Emotional turmoil:	Feeling anger, euphoria, sadness, confusion, or other strong emotions.
Multitasking:	Attempting to perform multiple tasks or thinking about multiple topics simultaneously.
Stereotyping:	Assuming someone will think or behave in particular ways because of generalized expectations about the group he or she is perceived to be a part of.
Preconceptions:	Letting past interactions or first impressions contaminate how a current message is interpreted.

External Listening Barriers

External distractions:	Attending to background noise, setting, or other distractions.
Communication style:	Focusing on the accent, grammar, or other stylistic features of speech instead of the speaker's meaning and intentions.
Message overload:	Being bombarded with too much information all at once.
Message difficulty:	Receiving messages with complex or technical meaning that require additional time to process and understand.

We learn an array of bad listening behaviors, such as *pseudo-listening*, listening selectively, or multitasking while listening. Unfortunately, these are not the only detractors from effective listening. Perception traps awaits the listener as messages are assessed, organized, and interpreted. **Selective perception** is the filtering of available stimuli and choosing the bits that match one's attitudes. An **attitude** is a relatively stable predisposition to act or believe in specific ways. If one's attitude is that another person is untrustworthy, then the behaviors that verify the belief will stick out, and those that do not will recede into the background. For example, if you think a friend is ethical and has good character, you will tend to notice when he loans other friends his truck to help them move to a new apartment and not notice that he sneaks a box of steaks home from the restaurant where he works.

Where there are gaps in information, people seek closure and fill in the gaps to complete the picture, often with unfounded speculation and attribution errors. For instance, two friends at a party are looking in your direction and laughing. What is going on? Depending on one's attitudes, you might believe (a) They are just talking about a something funny, or (b) they are talking about you in an unflattering way. Lacking solid facts about what really happened rarely inhibits people from inferring a story and attributing motives.

People may find working on their part of conflict difficult when hurt feelings, anger, or other emotions block the ability to listen. They may reject outcomes that are in their best interest when mired in hurt feelings. Listening and being listened to offers the opportunity to move beyond the hurt feelings into a zone where productive conflict management can occur. Van Slyke (1999) says, "The problem in conflict, however, is not whether the other party listens to us, but rather whether we listen to and understand the other party's perspective. Only after we have listened to the other party will that party want to listen to us. Only after the other party feels understood will he or she want to understand and be influenced by us" (p. ix).

> ### Discussion Question 6.3
> What are the possible consequences to pseudo-listening? Think about two conversations you've had today. Where would you fall in each conversation on the continuum of listening effectiveness in Table 6.2?

Listening in Competitive and Cooperative Modes

Both competitive and cooperative conflict require skillful listening. Competitors in particular may fall prey to misassumptions about listening. First, competitors may assume that talking is powerful and listening is weak, believing power and control comes from doing most or all of the talking. Second, competitors may assume that listening is the same as agreement. They think, "If someone listens without interrupting, the person must agree with what is being said." Conversely, if the other person does not agree, it must be because he or she did not listen. These assumptions not only are false, but they may be disadvantageous in competitive bargaining.

Listening is necessary to understand what is being said. After understanding the situation and the facts, one can make an enlightened decision about whether agreement or disagreement is the right response. A final misassumption is that competitors should use listening as a tactic to amass information for future counterattacks. Listening solely for

TABLE 6.2   *The Continuum of Listening Effectiveness*

	Ineffective Listening ↑
Pretending to listen	
Looking for key places to interrupt and to change the topic	
Attending to selective content for later rebuttal	
Trying to remember everything exactly as it was said	
Giving full attention and listening for main points	
Giving full attention to emotions and content	
	↓ **Effective Listening**

opportunities to raise disagreement twists the process in negative ways. All of these assumptions arise from the win-lose perspective and hinder an ability to uncover issues, maximize options, and discover optimal solutions.

> ### *Discussion Question 6.4*
> What barriers to listening challenge you the most? Think of examples when specific listening barriers inhibited your ability to listen well.

Cooperative conflict managers also prosper through effective listening. They need well-honed listening skills to move efficiently through the early stages of conflict so problem solving can be accomplished. Although listening purely to understand or to show empathy are noble endeavors, conflict managers apply empathetic listening techniques strategically toward the goal of managing a problem. Effective listening may seem to take too much effort. In reality, taking the time to listen is efficient because it avoids the time lost in leaping to erroneous conclusions based on assumptions.

Types of Listening

Hargie and Dickson (2004) list six types of listening: discriminative, comprehensive, evaluative, appreciative, empathetic, and dialogic. **Discriminative listening** is attending primarily for particular signals. When waiting for a call, the faintest tune from a cell phone can be picked out from among other louder noises. The ability to discriminate while listening can be advantageous, such as when listening for the "word of the day" on a radio station to call in to win a prize or when parents pick out their child's call of distress from the raucous noise of dozens of children at play. On the down side, discriminative listening can mask the larger picture if someone listens just for particular words or phrases.

Comprehensive listening fosters an understanding of the overall message. The listener attends to the main idea or general theme. When in conflict, listening to grasp the main topic or issue before responding is crucial. Comprehensive listening is effective when the general theme of a message is enough. However, it is less effective when understanding specific details is important or when implicit emotional or relationship messages dominate the exchange. A variation of comprehensive listening is pure content listening. *Pure content listening* ignores the emotional subtext and picks out specific details in a message.

Evaluative, or **critical listening**, judges the value of a message and gauges the speaker's intentions. The message is critiqued for logic, spin, accuracy, and truthfulness. Evaluative listening is useful in situations where manipulation is anticipated. Competitors need to evaluate the worth of settlement offers. Citizens should apply evaluative listening to political and product advertisements rather than accepting them at face value or viewing persuasive messages as entertainment. Too much evaluation too soon, however, may bypass a comprehensive understanding of the speaker's intent or create defensiveness.

Appreciative listening focuses on the artfulness or aesthetics of a message. For example, relaxing with one's favorite music illustrates appreciative listening. Appreciative listening can foster renewal and reenergize the weary, or it can detract from understanding. One of the authors once was told at a conference that a listener was so struck by her presentational style that he didn't really pay attention to what was said. Appreciative listening removes attention from most of the substance of a message, and therefore it is not an essential skill in interpersonal conflict management.

Empathetic listening gives the other person unconditional space to vent or speak without evaluation or criticism. It is effective when helping someone think through difficulties by talking with a trusted friend. Empathetic listening is essential to conflict managers who are working to moderate emotion or to build rapport. When responses are necessary or problems await resolution, empathetic listening alone is not enough. Relied on too much, empathetic listening can move the conversation in unproductive directions.

Dialogic, or **relational, listening** involves going back and forth between a speaker and a listener role in an effort to understand. In practice, it means joining with the other person to search for an agreeable outcome. Relational listening is closest to the activities involved in mutual gains bargaining where conflicting individuals actively look for common goals in an effort to reach a mutually beneficial solution.

> ### *Discussion Question 6.5*
> What might happen if someone is expecting one type of listening and gets another type (e.g., expecting empathy and getting evaluation)? Has this happened to you?

Effective Listening Skills for Conflict Managers

Which type of listening is the best? The competent conflict manager uses several listening skills depending on the situation.

Effective listening means discriminating when to focus on the verbal content, when to focus on the relationship implied in a message, and when to focus on the overall emotional tone. For example, if a person agrees to a solution, but crosses her arms, glares, and sounds surly when saying "yes," the nonverbal message contradicts the verbal message. A supervisor who considers employees "friends" gives a different message when he speaks while sitting behind a desk than if he is standing in a relaxed pose. Listening uses more senses than the ears and involves more than silent assessment. In the next section, we present the eight steps for effective listening listed in Table 6.3.

Mentally Prepare

Listening starts with self-awareness and the right attitude. One reason for interrupting others is the attitude that "What I have to say is more important than what you have to say." Listening requires discipline and concentration. Preparing for listening means putting aside

TABLE 6.3   *Steps for Effective Listening During Interpersonal Conflict*

1. Mentally prepare to prevent missteps
2. Give the other person your momentary full attention
3. Evaluate which type of listening best fits the situation at the moment
4. Deal with emotions, if necessary, before dealing with content
5. Elicit more information
6. Give information the other needs to know
7. Reframe the problem into an issue where agreement is possible
8. Check for mutual understanding

other tasks, thoughts, and distractions. Listening requires self-control, the strength to remain quiet, and a willingness to let another person express his or her ideas and feelings. Preparation can focus a listener on the goal of understanding before evaluating, criticizing, or responding. If engaging in conflict with a reticent person, preparation includes leaving empty space in a conversation to allow the other time to think and respond.

Wood (2006) labels the mental state of an effective listener as **mindfulness**. She concludes, "Being mindful is a choice we make. It is not a talent that some people have and others don't. Instead, mindfulness is a personal commitment to attend fully and without diversion to another person. No amount of skill will make you a good listener if you do not choose to attend mindfully to others. Thus, one's choice of whether to be mindful is the foundation of how one listens—or fail to" (p. 176).

In addition to the right mental state, preparation sometimes involves thoughtful anticipation of useful questions. A list of possible questions is helpful to elicit information from the other person without causing defensiveness. If confronted with a surprise conflict, preparation may simply mean putting the brake on defensive reactions. Once a receptive state of mind is achieved, the conflict manager can apply the techniques provided in this chapter more effectively.

Discussion Question 6.6

While preparing to listen, what does it mean to give someone your momentary full attention? What other activities would cease? What does "giving someone your full attention" look like?

Give the Other Momentary Full Attention

Full attention is required for two reasons. First, attending to the other person during interpersonal conflict shows that the issue is taken seriously. The other party no longer must struggle to get attention. Turn off the cell phone! Find a private space to talk. Put down the remote control and turn off the television. Turn toward the other person and pay attention. If you are perceived as taking other people seriously, they are more likely to show similar respect in return. Second, full attention for a moment is more efficient than making mistakes while paying half attention. Attending to the other person has implications for how the conflict will unfold.

Evaluate Which Type of Listening Is Necessary

Sometimes one party to an interpersonal conflict calmly and logically presents facts about goal interference and asks the other party to participate in problem solving. For example, a coworker might observe that the work relationship seems to be deteriorating and ask, "Is there something the two of us should discuss?" Other times someone may state a position aggressively and make demands. For example, the coworker might say, "You aren't getting me the information I need on time anymore. I need you to get me the data every day by 1 o'clock." Sometimes the conflict partner talks around the real issue while expressing anger, sadness, or despair. For example, the coworker might talk about how overwhelmed he or she has been lately.

Not all conflicts start with the disputing parties in the same mental state. Depending on the state the other party is in, the competent conflict manager will respond with empathetic, analytical, or evaluative listening skills. Van Slyke (1999) comments on the outcome of not evaluating which response is necessary:

> The first step we often take toward resolution is to offer additional information intended to demonstrate the logic and reasoning that supports our view of a fair solution. When the parties remain unconvinced, we typically provide further amplification of the position already rejected by those in dissension. When this fails, we persuade, cajole, argue, manipulate, sulk, bully, stamp our feet, arbitrate, or withdraw from the interaction. (p. ix)

Discussion Question 6.7
What is your greatest challenge as a listener when in conflict with a good friend or significant other?

Deal with Emotions First When They Are Present

When someone criticizes, judges, speaks loudly, or expresses anger, the temptation to respond in kind may be strong. When someone is sad, cries, or expresses emotions the listener finds awkward, the impulse may be to ignore or downplay the emotion. Responding in kind to negative emotions or simply pretending emotions don't exist are unproductive strategies that often make conflict worse. Telling someone, "Don't be so emotional" rarely helps. Devaluing others creates face issues as the conflict becomes more personal and emotions run higher. Generally, a more productive response is to moderate emotions as they emerge through techniques such as empathy.

One of the functions of empathetic listening during conflict is to manage affective events. An **affective event** is any emotional spike. Managing emotions enables the work of conflict management to go forward. When emotions are present, it generally is useful to manage them before confronting substantive issues. Attempting problem solving during an emotionally charged moment is an exercise in frustration. It is difficult for someone awash with emotion to function as a creative problem solver. The emotional mind, as opposed to the rational mind, makes rapid decisions based on associations and perception of facts—and is often wrong (Van Slyke, 1999). A good solution offered to a person in the midst of strong emotions probably will be ignored or misjudged. Specialized listening skills help conflict managers transcend these difficulties. Defusing emotions is one skill that should reside in every conflict manager's toolbox. When individuals are highly emotional, they generally are unable to get past their personal feelings and move toward resolutions. Empathizing with a highly charged person can lead to a calmer interaction, once the other feels heard and understood.

Toolbox 6.1, "Defusing Emotions," is a method to moderate affective events during conflict. Four qualifications about the skill are necessary. First, the defusing of emotion skill is designed for use while the affective event is occurring. Waiting until the expression stops before applying the skill makes it seem, and be, contrived. Second, using the skill when the other is calm and speaking about facts rather than feelings is inappropriate. Third, conflict managers must realize that in conflicts about face or relationship issues, feelings may be the issue. Although moderating emotional display to be able to discuss the issue is important, it is unreasonable to expect feelings to evaporate completely after one skill application. Finally, display of emotion also is a variable of personal and/or cultural style. Expressive individuals display emotion as a part of their process. Nonexpressive individuals incorrectly tend to interpret such expressions as anger, belligerence, or irrationality. Attempting

---

TOOLBOX 6.1

Defusing High Emotions Through the Emotional Paraphrase

1. Prepare to listen.
2. Give your momentary full attention.
3. When the other is emotional or showing high intensity, speak over the top while the other is still talking.
4. Create a three- to six-word phrase from this equation and then stop speaking.

The Emotional Paraphrase Equation
Lead-in phrase + feeling word

Pick the lead-in phrase that you can say +	*Feeling word that fits situation*
"Sounds like you're . . ."	Angry/mad/sad/upset
	Concerned/troubled/worried
"That must be . . ."	Difficult/disturbing/troubling
"That sounds . . ."	Maddening/upsetting
"You're feeling . . ."	Frustrated/ignored/angry

This technique works best when the person visibly is emotional and you say the three- to six-word emotional paraphrase at the same time as the other vents. If the other is not visibly upset, there is no reason to defuse, but you may use the equation with mild feeling words like "troubled," "frustrated," or "concerned" to show empathy without interruption or overtalking.

to stop the expression of stylistically or culturally based emotion is not productive. Mirroring the energy level in the emotion of people from expressive cultures is a better choice in some cases. For example, some Russians are more direct and enthusiastic than North Americans. Telling someone with a direct and emotive style to "calm down" generally has the opposite effect. Likewise, being overly calm is open to misinterpretation from an emotive person who might think that you don't care. Instead, mirroring the volume and tone might demonstrate "listening" from the other person's cultural perspective.

Validating identifies the emotion the other is expressing. For example, "You're upset because I was late." Validating at any point during a conflict may be helpful in moving someone from an emotional reaction toward problem solving. Identifying what someone is feeling acknowledges the other's value. Even though we discuss defusing emotions as an early step within the conflict process, simple validation of the other's concerns and feelings can be useful at any stage.

KEY 6.2
Manage emotions before moving to problem solving.

Elicit More Information

Once initial barriers to productive problem solving have been moderated, both parties benefit if the basic facts that drive the conflict are put on the table. The primary skill for eliciting information is asking questions.

Generally, conflict managers start with broad, open-ended questions. **Open-ended questions** do not have a "right" answer. For example, a coworker being given the cold shoulder by a former friend may say, "I've noticed our relationship isn't as good as it used to be. Where did things go wrong for us?" The answer is not "Yes," "No," or a predetermined fact. Asking broad open-ended questions at the outset allows the other to tell his or her story without feeling interrogated or herded in a particular direction. Starting with closed-ended or probing questions may cause defensiveness or miss giving the other person a chance to express important issues.

Closed-ended questions have a specific concrete answer. "Did you take the money out of my drawer?" is answerable by "Yes" or "No." Specific questions such as "What do you want me to do?" or "Why don't you just . . ." leap ahead in the process to problem solving before the real issues in the conflict have been determined.

People who are good problem solvers are vulnerable to stepping over the information-gathering stage, relying on closed-ended questions, and moving instantly to offering solutions. Too often, the quick solution has little to do with the real issues. A supervisor may notice a worker is less productive than usual and assume the equipment is inefficient and give the worker a new computer. In reality, the issue could be a conflict with a coworker that is not resolvable by buying a new computer. The supervisor who doesn't take the time to gather information will be disappointed when productivity doesn't go back up after supposedly solving the problem. Leaping ahead in the process often wastes time and resources.

Once the arena of the conflict is determined (values, data, process, etc.) through general and open-ended questions, then probing questions are used. **Probing questions**

TOOLBOX 6.2

Asking Questions

Each type of question has its time and place during conflict management.

1. **Open-ended questions** allow an expansive response with no exact right answer.
   "How do you like your work?"
   "Please describe how you see the situation."
   "What has it been like for you being a worker at _____?"
   "How will this decision affect you personally?"
   "What else has been going on for you?"

2. **Closed-ended questions** have a specific, factual answer.
   "Are you still living in the same place?"
   "Have you ever talked to _____ about this difficulty?"
   Close-ended questions check your understanding of the facts or agreements reached.
   "So, you used to enjoy working with _____?"
   "So, you haven't talked to him directly?"
   "So, you come to work at 6 A.M. and need to use the Internet hookup exactly at 10?"

3. **Probing questions** seek more detail within a topic area.
   "What exactly happened to you that day?"
   "What is it that keeps you from doing your work?"
   "What did you do when you realized this was occurring?"
   "How is your house/shop/room/workstation located in relationship to [the other party]?"

4. **Detailing questions** make the agreement concrete and specific.
   "When would you be able to [do the agreed-upon task]?"
   "How exactly will you tell _____ that the off-color joke is not welcomed?"
   "How or where will the two of you talk together about problems in the future?"
   "In what form will you get the money to _____ (cash, check, etc.), and how and when exactly will that occur?"

elicit details. "What specifically about how we are working together is a problem?" or "What do you want from me to turn this situation around?" or, "So, how do you feel about me taking the kids over winter holiday break and you taking them at Thanksgiving and spring break?" Probing questions might make abstract terms less vague. "When you say we need to spend more time together, what do you have in mind?"

Give Information

Asking questions to elicit information from the other party is not sufficient. Information also must be volunteered if it is critical to the issue. Withholding information may allow someone to feel powerful, but it often is an unproductive strategy in the long run. Two general types of information can be given: personal information and factual information.

Personal relationships are developed by symmetry in levels of disclosure. A disclosure from the other about feelings and previously unknown facts should be matched with similar information—if appropriate to your relationship. If the other party relates that he or

INSERT 6.1

Putting Facts on the Table . . . Culturally

Not all cultures discuss conflict issues in the same way. North American and many Northern European cultures teach individuals to lay the facts on the table and directly confront the other person. Hammer (2002) relates that many individuals from indirect cultures (e.g., some Asian cultures) feel that confrontation and open discussion cause too much social disturbance and loss of face. For individuals with this cultural orientation, problems must be discussed indirectly, metaphorically, or through intermediaries. Open-ended questions at the beginning of an interpersonal conflict episode may create too much social stress for members of indirect cultures. Instead, asking background questions and approaching the problem indirectly is a better strategy. Instead of first asking an open-ended question such as, "What is the problem with your workgroup?" one might begin with close-ended questions to set the context. "You've been with the group for how long?" "You work with several teams in the company?" "There have been some difficulties with the work?" Ask probing questions after trust and a relationship has been established. Using this approach, the issues probably will emerge in a series rather than all at once. Asking, "What else do I need to know for the good of the group?" will elicit the beginning of the next issue. The explanation that follows may be indirect, through a metaphor or a story.

Likewise, if a friend from an indirect culture suddenly starts telling you stories or using a specific metaphor, he or she may be engaging in conflict management behavior. A story about a past friend who was always there to help may be an indirect request for assistance. Listening through the ears of direct culture will miss these overtures and frustrate both parties.

Understanding intercultural conflict style is complex. We encourage readers to research the cultural conflict styles of groups that are prevalent in their geographic area.

> ### Discussion Question 6.8
> Do you interact regularly with a person from another culture? How is good listening the same or different in that person's culture? How can you become a better listener when interacting with that person?

she feels overwhelmed at work and that nobody will help, sharing a similar story of when you were the new employee or giving information about how to ask for training may be appropriate. If a wife discloses that she feels angry, it is appropriate for her partner to disclose feelings as well.

Giving factual information also is important. A library patron may be angry about fines for late books. While he is venting, the librarian may realize the patron lacks information about how these matters are handled at the library. In this case, it is appropriate to give factual information about the library's policy.

Reframing

Reframing moves an issue from a narrow frame offered by one party into a larger frame where cooperation can occur and solutions may be found. A reframed statement moves the focus from positions to more general interests. It is not unusual during conflict for the other party to make a positional demand: "You have to . . ." The instinctive reaction is defensiveness: "No, I don't," or "No, *you* have to . . ." As long as the conflict is framed in a way that gives one party an advantage over the other, a cooperative approach is unlikely. A way of escaping this dilemma is to reframe the issue into a larger and more general frame.

Joel may threaten his roommate by saying, "You have to pick up my part of the rent this month, or I'll move out tomorrow." The frame is set to pressure compliance. Before the underlying issues can be discovered and the conflict discussed, the frame must be altered. A reframed response ignores the threat or positional statement, takes away the attempt to gain an advantage, and instead makes the issue larger to seek a common ground where problem solving might occur. The roommate might respond, "So there's some problem with the rent payment?"

Check Mutual Understanding

Although it is important in the early stages of a conflict to avoid content paraphrasing while fishing for the issues and defusing emotional barriers, content paraphrasing is essential during later stages. **Content paraphrasing** verifies facts and checks for mutual understanding.

Highlighting the content of a message can be beneficial in this step to check the accuracy of information or to pull out important points. For example, a customer comes into the store with a complaint about a refrigerator he purchased. He comments, "The fridge has been making a whirring sound that seems to be coming from the back and the food is not cold." The shop owner may provide a content paraphrase to make sure the important message has been understood. "So the temperature seems to fluctuate and not chill as much as it used to, and there is a buzzing sound coming from the back?" The customer could agree that the owner understood or could offer more explanation such as, "No, it's more of a whirring sound, not a buzz. Kind of like a bad fan."

Content paraphrasing is a good skill but one that can be misunderstood, overused, or applied too early. If one partner says to the other, "I've got a busy schedule and I won't be home until after dinner, so I need you to pick up the dry cleaning," a reply phrased as a content paraphrase may come across as sarcastic or demeaning. "You won't be home until late, and I have to pick up the dry cleaning." Of course, the interpretation of a message is up to the receiver. Those using this technique should recognize that content paraphrasing runs the risk of sounding canned ("So what I hear you saying is . . .") or insincere. If used when the other person is emotional, a content paraphrase ignores an important component of the conflict. If used too early, content paraphrasing can fix the topic of conversation in an area that skirts the real issue.

Summarizing is a tool to recognize the primary issues raised by the other person. Summaries indicate that someone's concerns have been heard and understood. For example, "You're upset with not getting your reports on time and need a workable system in place for storing data." "You're concerned about all the bills that are piling up and want a plan for managing our budget." "You need some quiet time in the house to study every weekday, are concerned about who buys the food that we share, and want to keep expenses lower in our rental house."

Once an agreement is reached, one person should paraphrase what has been agreed to check that the other party has the same understanding. "So we agree that we will use the

Thompson report in the future to get our productivity statistics, is that right?" or "So we've agreed that you will come home early, meaning before 11 P.M., right?" Or, put as a question, "So we've agreed that you'll be home early. What do you mean by early?"

If mutual understanding is not checked, both parties may leave thinking the conflict is managed but have quite different pictures in their heads of exactly what the decision meant. An example is the boss who gives an employee vague feedback about not meeting the company image. The employee may vow to do better and will try harder by wearing a tie to work. Unfortunately, the boss wanted the employee to proofread his reports more carefully. The boss will be disappointed and angry that work has not improved. The employee will feel betrayed and lied to when reprimanded again. A simple check of the exact understanding between the parties and careful attention to possible points of misunderstanding can prevent future conflict.

Summary

Beyond the contribution of listening to a civil society, listening is a primary way to understand the causes of and possible solutions to interpersonal conflict. Without listening, individuals work from a one-sided and limited knowledge base that is fraught with misassumptions, factual inaccuracies, and self-serving biases.

Listening, unlike hearing, is a learned skill that requires effort to master. The listening process includes attending, organizing, and interpreting data. In each of these steps, a listener can falter. Numerous internal and external barriers to listening distract from concentrating on the other person's message. Several types of listening are possible, including discriminative, comprehensive, evaluative, appreciative, empathetic, and dialogic. There are benefits to listening for both competitive and cooperative situations. Eight listening steps are the hallmark of effective listeners during interpersonal conflict: (1) mentally preparing, (2) giving momentary full attention, (3) selecting the right type of listening, (4) dealing with emotions first when they are present, (5) eliciting information through questions, (6) giving information, (7) reframing issues, and (8) checking mutual understanding.

Listening is the quintessential skill of an effective conflict manager. Unfortunately, many people carry poor listening habits into their conflicts. Fortunately, listening abilities can improve with awareness, knowledge, and practice.

Chapter Resources

Exercises

1. Reframe the following positional statements (i.e., remove the positional demand and restate the general concern).
   A. "The only way we're ever going to finish the project and get a good grade is if we get the teacher to throw Erika out of the group."
   B. "This is the way it's going to be. I'm going fishing so I can finally get some peace and quiet."
   C. "Dr. Reyes, you have to let me retake the test or I'll get a C in your class and won't be able to get into graduate school."

3. Use Toolbox 6.1 skills to defuse the emotion in the following examples.
   A. A client says, "Your staff is so incompetent. They couldn't even get a simple order right even when I held their hand through the whole process!"
   B. A coworker says, "I hate these new policies. How am I supposed to get my work done with all this paperwork I have to process!"
   C. A student in your project group says, "I'm really worried about the project. Everybody else is fooling around and I'm stuck here trying to find the information before the deadline."
   D. Your best friend has been acting oddly lately. She calls and says, "I hate it when you treat me the way you do. You don't really like me at all. I don't know if I want to hang out with you anymore."
   E. Create your own example.

4. Consider Maureen's listening challenges in the Mastery Case when she returns the call from Danielle. Using the eight steps of listening as a guide, what could Maureen do?

Essay Topic

1. Are you a good listener? What skills do you possess or need to develop? How does your listening skill level affect those around you?

Research Topics

1. Research other tools to improve listening. Write a report on at least three recommendations for improving listening that were not included in this chapter.

2. Look for studies that explore listening in a particular context (e.g., workplace, family, or classroom). Report on three different listening studies and the similarities and differences in their findings.

Mastery Case

Analyze Mastery Case 6, "The Car Conflict." Which concept from the chapter best explains what is occurring in the case?

The Car Conflict

The National Public Radio show *Car Talk* in July 2005 received a call from Maureen, who described this experience. Maureen's friend, Danielle, owned a truck that she inherited from her father's estate. It was old and had lots of problems, but she was attached to it because it had belonged to her father. Danielle was very generous in loaning the truck to friends when they needed one. Maureen and her partner Jeremy asked to borrow the truck. Danielle said that would be fine, but they would have to jump-start the truck because the battery was low.

Jeremy, an electrician, and Maureen tried to jump-start the truck. Jeremy previously had a car where the battery ran down so he had all the cables and was experienced with the procedure. The truck wouldn't start. Maureen called Danielle and told her about the problem and said that Jeremy could charge the battery overnight in his garage. Danielle said, great, thanks, go ahead. After charging the battery, Jeremy put it back into the truck and nothing happened—not even any clicking or whirring. After consulting with Danielle, they had the truck towed to Danielle's neighborhood mechanic.

The next week, Danielle called and left a message for Maureen demanding $1,400 because she and Jeremy had ruined the battery and the entire electrical system in the truck. Her mechanic said they must have charged the battery backward, and he had to make $1400 in repairs and put in a new battery.

7

Styles and Behavior Patterns

Objectives

After reading this chapter you should be able to:

1. Explain how style differences cause and/or exacerbate interpersonal conflict
2. Differentiate among personality styles and other types of styles
3. Explain how conflict styles differ across cultures
4. Recognize the advantages of identifying style differences and their impact on conflict

When you have problems with a friend or colleagues at work, would you confront them? Try to smooth things over? Work with them until you find and fix what is wrong? Just let the others have their way? Remove yourself from the situation? Do you feel comfortable politely raising issues, or does even thinking about it create a knot in your stomach? The answers to these questions reveal matters of style. People have different preferred ways of communicating and different behavior patterns. In this chapter, we examine how style differences can be at the root of some conflicts.

    A working knowledge of communication style is important for two primary reasons. First, people who are aware of their styles and can learn style adaptation have a greater

CASE 7.1 • *"Yellow"*

When I was a teenager—in that stage when my parents could do no right—I was really bothered by something that my father did. When he answered the phone he said, "Yellow." Not "Hello" but "Yellow." It sounded just like he was identifying the color of our neighbor's house: It's yellow. It drove me crazy.

No matter how eloquent my suggestions of alternatives, he would never change—not because he was right and not because he didn't "know better." He didn't change because he liked answering the phone that way. It was his style. He enjoyed it. He thought it was funny. And his style really annoyed me.

It was all right, though, because we were tied together with the bindings of love. Then one day, when I was older, I finally realized *he* wasn't the one who had the problem.

chance of managing conflict productively. In contrast, people who can only see "differences" and "wrongness" in how others communicate probably will find their lives in constant turmoil.

Second, differences in style can create an expectancy violation. *Expectancy violation theory* suggests that people have preconceived ideas about how others should behave, based on perceptions of that individual, the relationship, and the situation. When expectations are violated, we view the other person negatively (Hullett & Tamborini, 2001). Different styles themselves do not cause conflict. However, style differences do lead to feelings of being obstructed in how communication should occur or how people should behave (goal differences). It is the perception of goal obstruction that leads to conflict.

Style differences can precipitate mistaken assumptions that the other person is intentionally being obstructive. In Case 7.1, the father's verbal style clashed with the daughter's expectations and perceptions of the right way to answer a phone call. Because they were family, the annoyance wasn't a big problem. Unfortunately, in our everyday work lives, we do not have built-in forgiveness factors to mitigate the effects of those who annoy us or the grace of time to "grow up." So we must have something else, some other skill for dealing with style differences. Otherwise, style annoyances risk becoming conflicts that rob us of happiness in our relationships and the ability to do our jobs well.

"You really don't understand what I said, because if you did, you would agree with me." (Turner, 2003)

What Is Style?

A **style** is a person's habitual way of communicating: It is what feels natural and right. Styles arise from personality characteristics and become patterned ways of behaving. It is too simple to say that each person has only one style that never changes. As individuals mature, they learn that what feels natural to one person may be offensive to another. Most people find that different styles may be necessary in different contexts. In other words, how one reacts at home, at school, with friends, and on the job may require moving from a preferred style to a style that is effective in a specific situation.

For example, someone who is shy who moves into management may need to adopt a more forceful leadership style.

For example, Suzanne has a very organized, analytical style. Over the years, she has learned that a direct style offends people in some situations. Many years ago, a student finishing her master's degree brought in a copy of her thesis to show it off. She was proud of her hard work and accomplishment. After looking at the document, this was Suzanne's first comment: "Your margins are wrong." This comment, although sensible within a direct and analytic style, showed a lack of social sensitivity. Teachers who prefer analytical-critical approaches might feel it is efficient to mark only errors on student papers. Through experience, the analytic teacher may discover that, for many students, learning is enhanced when criticism is paired with positive comments.

"Very rarely are conflicts true personality issues. Usually they are issues of style, information needs, or focus." (Jourdain, 2004, p. 23)

There are many ways to view style and behavioral patterns. Each viewpoint offers insights into how styles affect behaviors. With knowledge of styles and how styles can clash, conflict managers can make more purposeful choices and not remain trapped in the narrow confines of personal styles.

"One of the most common framings of conflict is the ubiquitous 'personality conflict.' " (Furlong, 2005)

Personality Styles

A **personality style** is a relatively stable pattern of thinking and processing information that suggests certain types of behaviors. Personality tests abound and are useful in understanding how one's impulses are similar or different from others. If prepared for personality style differences, the behaviors during conflict are less likely to be attributed as intentional interference. Many unnecessary conflicts arise from differences in personality styles. We discuss several personality style typologies to provide insight into how style might confound issues when engaging in conflict.

The Myers-Briggs Type Indicator

The **Myers-Briggs Type Indicator** is a popular test to determine personality styles. Based on Jungian theory, the test categorizes preferred behavior patterns into four paired groups (Table 7.1) (for more information, visit www.myersbriggs.org).

TABLE 7.1   *Myers-Briggs Paired Personality Traits*

Extrovert (E)	or	Introvert (I)
Sensing (S)	or	Intuitive (N)
Thinking (T)	or	Feeling (F)
Judging (J)	or	Perceiving (P)

The Extrovert/Introvert (E/I) dimension specifies whether energy and excitement lies with the outer world of social contact or the inner world of ideas. Extroverts tend to be verbally expressive, enjoy interacting in larger groups of people, act first and think through critical details later, and enjoy a variety of people and relationships. In contrast, introverts tend to be private, enjoy quiet reflection alone, think first and act later, and prefer one-to-one interactions.

The Sensing/Intuiting (S/N) pairing describes how individuals process information. Sensing individuals relate to external stimuli such as sounds and smells. They mentally focus on the present, have a commonsense approach, remember specific details about the past, prefer known facts, and like clear and concrete data. Intuiters relate to possibilities and potentials. They focus mentally on the future, are imaginative, remember patterns, work from theories or idealism, and are comfortable with change or with projecting from incomplete data.

The Thinking/Feeling (T/F) dichotomy describes how one prefers to make decisions. Thinkers analyze, use objective facts, are task oriented, can be critical, make decisions based on criteria, see conflict as a way of making choices, may observe more than participate, and take a long-term view. In contrast, people with a feeling personality act on emotions or instinct, are sensitive to others' needs, seek consensus, are sympathetic, make subjective decisions, understand events through participating in them, make decisions based on values, and may be uncomfortable with conflict or disagreement.

The final pairing, Judging/Perceiving (J/P), describes how one views other people and the outside world. Are life decisions structured and organized around a plan or discovered as one goes along? Judgers have plans, are task oriented, like orderly sequences, complete work before deadlines, and are organized. Perceivers make up the plan as they go, like to multitask, work best just before a deadline, meander toward objectives, and avoid structures that inhibit flexibility.

Those firmly entrenched on one side of a pair of the Myers-Briggs terms may clash with the other side if they are not prepared to see the value of the opposite trait. If one person is trying to organize work into discrete segments and the other just wants to get started on the project and see where it goes, a process conflict may emerge about "how to get the job done." Without awareness of style preferences, the differences often are attributed as intentional goal interference or as a personality deficiency.

For more detailed information about specific personality styles, the preferred behavior from each pair in the Myers-Briggs Inventory can be combined (see Table 7.2). For example, one can be an ENFP (extrovert, intuiter, feeler, and perceiver). The Myers-Briggs test is proprietary and can be taken in paper-and-pencil form or online for a fee. Millions of employees in

> ### *Discussion Question 7.2*
> What's Your Myers-Briggs orientation? Based on the description in this chapter, or you could find a test on the Internet, select the item from each pair that best describes your preferred way of behaving. Are there people with whom you are close that would fit in different categories? How might this affect a relationship if not addressed?
>
> Extrovert (E) __×__   Introvert (I) _____
> Sensing (S) __×__   Intuiting (N) _____
> Thinking (T) __×__   Feeling (F) _____
> Judging (J) __×__   Perceiving (P) _____

the United States and abroad have taken the test to understand how styles differ in workgroups. Some have gone so far as to put colored dots on each employee's nameplate representing his or her Myers-Briggs combination, so others know what to expect based on personality style.

The purpose of understanding personality style differences for corporations is so people can begin to notice when style differences are causing problems. After style difference enters conscious awareness, someone can point out that the individuals struggling to work together have different styles. For example, instead of the extroverts assuming that anyone who wants to go to lunch will just invite himself or herself along, they will think to invite their silent, introverted coworkers who may be feeling left out. Sensors can appreciate that intuiters have good ideas but arrive at their conclusions in a different way. Thinkers will better appreciate that feelers will raise issues about how clients will react to a new policy that would never have occurred to them. Companies with employees who have different styles can reduce conflict through style awareness training, and companies with homogeneous styles in their workforce can identify potential areas of weakness. For example, one study found all students majoring in computer information science had a "thinker" style (McPherson & Mensch, 2007). A one-style workforce might develop habits or blind spots that could harm their effectiveness.

The Gregorc Styles Model

Although the Myers-Briggs Inventory is very popular, other style perspectives are useful to gather different insights into human behavior. The **Gregorc Styles model** places people on a continuum between the perceptual preferences of *abstract* or *concrete* and the ordering preferences of *sequential* and *random*. Abstract individuals are very comfortable living in the world of ideas and concepts, looking at many possibilities, and playing with the "what ifs" in decision making. Concretes, in contrast, want ideas backed by facts and experience and prefer to know rather than to speculate. The Sequential versus Random dimension contrasts how people approach tasks, see time, and organize their world. A Sequential proceeds step by step, has a desire to complete one project before starting another, makes lists, and sees time as fixed. Randoms come at decisions from many different directions, enjoy multitasking, easily move from project to project, handle interruptions well, work from crisis to crisis, and see time as fluid (Gregorc, 2006).

TABLE 7.2   *Sixteen Personality Types*

ESTJ: Energy comes from interaction with others. Prefers facts, makes logical decisions, is organized and somewhat impersonal, detail oriented.

INFP: Energy comes from inside. Likes patterns, possibilities, dealing with people, flexibility, is adaptable, and creative. Prefers work with a meaningful purpose.

ESFP: Energy from the outside and spoken words. Prefers facts and takes them at face value. Is present oriented, yet impulsive and friendly. Makes friends easily and likes troubleshooting.

INTJ: Energy comes from the world of ideas. Prefers possibilities about the future, makes decision based on impersonal analysis, is organized, has goals, is skeptical and critical, has a strong intellect, and can deal with details that are relevant.

ESFJ: Energy comes from the outer world of action and ideas. Prefers facts, makes value-based decisions, people, harmony, values friendships, dislikes conflict or criticism, and is very loyal.

INTP: Energy comes from inner thoughts. Prefers dealing with patterns, makes logical decisions, is flexible, quiet, detached, somewhat adaptable, may make a stand on principle, hates routines, and is good with complex problems.

ENFP: Energy comes from the world of action and the spoken word. Prefers patterns, people, value-based decisions, flexibility, new ideas, creativity, uses insight, seeks new ideas, might neglect details or planning, and works toward general goals.

ISTJ: Energy comes from the world of thought. Prefers facts, analytical decisions, organization, logic, quiet, seriousness, preparation, observing, practical, efficiency, and might not express ideas to others.

ESTP: Energy comes from action and the spoken word. Prefers facts, objectivity, logically based decisions, flexibility, action oriented, practical organization, impulsive, troubleshooting work, problem solving, but might neglect follow through.

INFJ: Energy from the inner world of thought and emotions. Prefers people-focused possibilities, value-based decisions, organized around people, private sense of purpose, quiet concern for people, likes to help people, has good insights about people that often are not shared.

ENFJ: Energy comes from the outside world and the spoken word. Prefers possibilities for people, value-based decisions, seeks to maintain stable relationships, actively promotes personal growth, highly sociable, expressive, finds conflict and criticism difficult, and works best in a team.

ISTP: Energy comes from the inner world of thought. Prefers facts, logically based decisions, flexibility, new information, quiet, detachment, somewhat adaptable, thinking through problems and solving them, curious about how things work, impulsive, and sometimes unpredictable.

ENTJ: Energy comes from the outer world of action and words. Prefers possibilities, making thoughtful decisions, logical approach to personal decisions, control, organizing people to complete tasks, being a director, businesslike approaches, and may be intolerant of others who don't seem to be competent.

ISFP: Energy comes from the inner world of thought and emotions. Prefers facts, people, value-based decisions, somewhat adaptable, quiet, friendly, enjoys people in small numbers, is sensitive and caring, helps others, dislikes confrontation, and is a supportive team member.

ENTP: Energy comes from the outer world and spoken words. Prefers patterns and logically based decisions, is adaptable, likes new ideas, works to increase personal competence, an ingenious problem solver, tries new ideas, enjoys a good argument, and likes change.

ISFJ: Energy comes from the inner world of thought and emotion. Prefers facts, people, value-based decisions, organizes life around personal relationships, quiet, observer, conscientious, loyal, wants to be of service to people, perceptive of others' feelings, and dislikes conflict.

In a local business, two partners found themselves constantly at odds. One issue surrounded the morning meetings that the two had agreed to have twice a week on Tuesdays and Thursdays at 8 A.M. Lee was a Concrete-Sequential and always showed up to the meeting promptly at 7:55 with an agenda for discussion. Stella was an Abstract-Random. She'd come into the office at 7:30 and stop to chat with her employees. She believed contact early in the day was crucial for efficiency. She often helped employees problem-solve situations that could not wait due to customer needs. Stella generally arrived at the meeting with Lee around 8 o'clock or a little after. Lee saw this behavior as unprepared and lazy.

> ### Discussion Question 7.3
> What is your style according to the Gregorc model? Do your coworkers/friends have similar or different styles?

Conflict habitually arose at the beginning of Lee and Stella's meetings. Lee would be irritated that Stella wasn't prepared to meet. Stella was confused by the formality of the meeting. Stella wanted her employees to know that she was available if needed and that they should interrupt her if they had a problem. Lee considered these meetings to be sacred and believed they should be protected from interruptions.

Lee and Stella became so conflicted that they required third-party intervention. A consultant helped them see each other's behavior as coming from different styles—Stella's A/R versus Lee's C/S. After exploring the benefits of each style to their business, they worked out an agreement for their meetings. They built in a fifteen-minute buffer to accommodate Stella's possible crisis fixing. During that fifteen minutes Lee would do something else until Stella indicated she was ready. The day before, Lee sent Stella an agenda that Stella could add to. They agreed to tell employees not to interrupt during these meetings. In sum, they became aware of the other's style and worked out a plan that took both styles into account.

Social Style Model

Another style perspective, the **social style model,** uses direct observation by a trained observer to assess a person's behavior. Unlike the Myers-Briggs assessment where individuals rate themselves, the social style model is designed to be more objective. Two basic dimensions create the style: assertiveness and responsiveness.

Assertiveness describes whether a person "asks" or "tells" while interacting with others. Those who are direct and forceful in their communication, speak faster or louder, and have direct eye contact with forceful gestures are called *tell assertive*. Those who are reserved and speak less, slower, or softer while keeping their thoughts to themselves are labeled *ask assertive*.

Responsiveness measures how much emotion is displayed. *Controlled* individuals are more distant, formal, and do not express much emotion. Those who *emote* display feelings openly and are more animated.

Four dimensions are created from the ask-tell and control-emote pairings: High control and high assertive individuals are labeled *driving*—independent, task and results oriented, decisive, fast paced, and dominating. Low control and high assertive individuals are *analytical*—prudent, task oriented, careful, logical, and low key. Low assertive

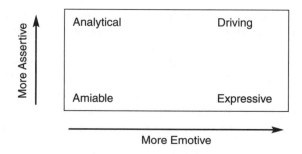

FIGURE 7.1   *Social Style Model*

and low emotive are *amiable*—dependable, relationship oriented, supportive, open, pliable, and conflict averse. High emotive and low assertive are *expressive*—visionary, animated, flamboyant, fast paced, impulsive, and opinionated (Furlong, 2005).

For example, Jamey ordered a hamburger, and the order wasn't exactly what she wanted. If Jamey quickly and forcefully told the waitress who delivered the meal that she doesn't like onions on her burger and ordered her to take them off while simulating gagging to show her disgust, she is assertive and emotive. If she waits until the waitress leaves and takes the onions off, she exhibits an assertive and controlled style.

Social styles, like personality styles, are useful to identify areas where miscommunication can lead to conflict. For example, equally competent coworkers with different styles might experience mutual frustration. One seems eager to please but not task oriented (amiable), whereas the other seems cold, heartless, and only interested in getting the job done (driver). The amiable person might withdraw or perceive the driver as a bully. The driver might perceive the amiable colleague as unskilled and slow. Bringing style differences to light could increase mutual respect and productivity.

Conflict Management Styles

A **conflict management style** is a patterned response to conflict situations. Conflict management styles are influenced by culture and social expectations. Each individual is believed to feel more comfortable with some conflict styles than with others but can, with time and effort, learn to adopt new styles. When they are used strategically rather than habitually, styles create more options for responding to conflict.

The Five Styles of Conflict Management

The most popular conflict management style perspective is a five style approach adapted from Blake and Mouton's 1964 notion that styles exist at the intersection

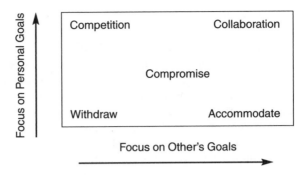

FIGURE 7.2   *The Five-Style Conflict Management Grid*

of one's *concern for personal goal achievement* (assertiveness) and one's *concern for the other party's goal achievement* (cooperativeness) (Hammer, 2005; Holt & DeVore, 2005).

Low concern for self and other leads to **withdrawing** or avoidance of the conflict. Low concern for self and high concern for the other results in **accommodation** of the other's wishes. High concern for self and low concern for the other person leads to **competition.** High concern for self and other manifests in **collaboration** where the needs of both parties are met. Moderate concern for self and other tends toward **compromise** so each person gives a little to gain a little.

Withdrawing/Avoiding   Withdrawing can be advantageous when the conflict is not yet ripe for settlement, the issue isn't very important, there will be little future contact between the individuals, or the situation might be dangerous.

In some families, avoiding certain topics is the only way to spend time together. For the sake of harmony, all family members avoid the areas of potential conflict (e.g., Don't ask CeCe about the tattoo; don't make comments about how Aunt Emily got revenge on her ex; and don't mention Rafe's weight!).

> **Discussion Question 7.4**
>
> What experiences have you had with gunnysacking or the withdraw-complain cycle?

Disadvantages of avoidance include never engaging issues that need to be confronted. When conflict is suppressed, it typically bursts out in some other form. Several dysfunctional variations of avoidance occur. In the **withdraw-complain cycle,** the avoider withdraws from communicating with the other person in the conflict but complains to friends and family about it. For example, when asked by Cara if anything is wrong, Paula may say everything is fine (withdraw) and then complain to all of her friends about the problem with Cara. Instead of confronting the conflict, she talks about the other person behind her back. Another dysfunctional practice, called *gunnysacking,* is withdrawing from

conflicts as they arise but keeping mental track of the grievances. When too many grievances accumulate, one's gunnysack is full to bursting—and that is what happens. All of the
issues are let out in one dramatic explosion.

Habitual avoidance can lead to a gradual erosion of relationships because avoidance
can lead to more avoidance. The longer an issue is avoided, the harder it becomes to discuss
it. In the long term, unexpressed conflict becomes a weight dragging on the relationship. In
frustration, one party may create a crisis—typically through an outburst, verbal aggressiveness, or some extreme measure. The negative encounter leads to less incentive to engage
the issue, and both draw even further apart. At some point, it may seem easier to end the
relationship than to face the accumulation of conflict.

In contrast, temporary avoidance, or *postponement* of a conflict encounter to a specific
time, can be helpful. Because Steve knows that he gets too hot when surprised with a conflict,
he learned to postpone discussion on new topics for at least an hour to give him time to adjust.
When Mary blurts out that she made reservations at an expensive restaurant for Friday so they
can go out and have a good time, Steve will say, "Let's talk about this in an hour so I'm not
distracted," instead of his old pattern, yelling about spending too much money.

Discussion Question 7.5

When would avoidance be an effective strategy? What possible disadvantages
to avoidance do you see?

When avoidance is strategic and intended to avoid a negative consequence or to not
engage a trivial concern, it takes three forms: (1) Choose not to confront the other person
and withhold comments; (2) if engagement starts, use tactics to prevent more discussion;
(3) if more discussion continues, move to have the topic declared taboo (Afifi & Guerrero,
2000; Roloff & Ifert, 2000). Generally, however, avoidance does not get rid of the issue. If
the issue is important, it will reemerge.

Competition   Competition can be advantageous when there are genuine scarce resources,
time is short, it occurs for fun, or achieving a goal is more important than the relationship.
If competition is not advanced through tactics that humiliate and destroy others, it can be
effective and appropriate. However, one danger of competition is that the loser gains a
powerful motivation for retaliation and destructive power struggles may ensue.

Disadvantages to competition occur when relationships are harmed or the other party
feels humiliated. For example, a couple conflicting over which movie to see may result in
one person winning. Both will go to the winning person's movie, but the loser can use
passive-aggressive tactics to ensure that the "winner" does not have a good time, such as
delaying departure so part of the movie is missed or talking during the movie. In some
cases, the price of winning may be too high.

Discussion Question 7.6

Has your use of competition ever backfired and led to a worse outcome? When is
competition appropriate?

Compromise   Compromise can be advantageous because neither party wins or loses everything: Both give a little so nobody loses face. Compromise is quicker than collaboration and a natural fallback position to avoid destructive competition. It also can be used to entice avoiders and accommodators to engage a conflict. A meta-analysis of past studies indicated that in individualistic cultures, females use compromising styles more than males (Holt & DeVore, 2005).

The major disadvantage to compromise is that it sometimes produces a mediocre outcome. Even though compromise is valued as a quick way to settle an issue (let's split the difference), neither party has complete goal attainment. Moving too quickly to compromise doesn't allow for creativity that might mutually benefit everyone. For example, Kasi and Jake broke up after several years together and were preparing to move to new apartments. They had several items that they purchased together. A compromise might be to sell everything and split the money. With more time to explore their needs, however, the couple could determine that because Jake commuted and Kasi was moving near a bus line, the old car should go to Jake. Kasi was more into music, so she should take the sound system. She also really wanted the leather couch. Kasi had a refrigerator in her new apartment; Jake didn't, so Jake took the refrigerator. Both parties wanted the computer. Because Jake took the car, which was more expensive, they decided that Kasi should get the computer and Jake would buy a new one. Yes, selling everything and splitting the cash would have worked, but ultimately collaboration got the parties more of what each needed.

Accommodation   Accommodation, like avoidance, is advantageous when the one giving sway has little interest in the outcome, is minimizing a loss, does not want to rock the boat, is atoning for a wrong, or has high or low commitment in the relationship. In cases in which accommodation occurs where there is high relationship commitment, the relationship is so valued that its maintenance may take priority over achieving other goals. In the workplace, the employee may give in because the commitment to, or need for, the job is more important than the issue at hand. Conversely, if the employee has a low commitment, he or she may feel that taking the effort to engage in conflict isn't worth the trouble. Stuart made a comment to his date about a very large man urinating against a wall while waiting in line to get into a club. The obviously drunk man overheard and aggressively came at Stuart saying, "Who do you think you are? Are you trying to be smart?" Stuart replied, "No, I really am stupid." The drunk, confused that he'd won so easily, said, "All right, then," and a fight was avoided. In this case, avoidance showed a high concern for self-preservation.

Disadvantages of accommodation include allowing power to become unbalanced, lack of personal goal achievement, and relationship lethargy. Like avoidance, accommodation can be chosen strategically if the cost of confrontation might be too high. An overbearing and hypercritical roommate may be accommodated because the other roommate determines that the cash coming in is more important than ending the current living situation.

Discussion Question 7.7

Have you ever used accommodation strategically? What damage could occur to someone who always accommodates?

Collaboration   Collaboration sometimes is presented as the best conflict management style. This style encourages the parties to communicate their interests and to work together to find the best alternative. Advantages include maximizing both parties' goal achievement, engaging in creative problem solving, and gaining commitment to the solution.

However, collaboration is a laborious process. Disadvantages include the length of time it takes, the amount of energy needed to collaborate, and the potential manipulation of the process by clever competitors. If one or both of the collaborators also are perfectionists, trying to get the outcome to be "perfect" may hinder the process. Conflict managers need to determine if the effort that will be expended to collaborate is in the best interests of the parties. Sometimes a quick resolution through competition, accommodation, compromise, or even avoidance may be the optimal strategy. Case 7.2 compares the five styles in action.

Discussion Question 7.8

What types of situations call for a collaborative style? In what situations would collaboration be ill advised?

Most style frameworks have limits. For example, the five styles of interpersonal conflict are based on only two characteristics—concern for personal goals and concern for the other's goal achievement. Whenever just two choices (self or other concern) are available, limitations occur. Do individuals who withdraw in potentially violent

CASE 7.2 • *The Five Styles in Action*

Julia and Latesha are assigned as roommates their freshman year. From different backgrounds, they have little in common. Soon their differences begin to surface, and conflict is inevitable. Julia asks if she can borrow a scarf from Latesha, who agrees. Soon Julia is borrowing shirts, coats, and whatever else she wants without asking.

If Latesha is an avoider, she will suffer silently, think bad thoughts about Julia, and probably complain to friends. If Julia asks what is wrong, Latesha will say she has to go study in the library and leave the room.

If Latesha is an accommodator, she will say she doesn't mind that Julia borrows things. If Latesha has a competitive style, she will confront Julia and demand that all her clothes be washed and never borrowed again.

If Latesha uses a compromiser style, she will raise the issue of borrowing clothes with Julia. Then some middle ground will be sought. For example, the clothes can be borrowed if Julia asks every time in advance and washes and irons the clothes when returning them.

If Latesha is a collaborator, she will ask Julia to sit down with her to discuss the roommate situation. She will frame the issue in a comprehensive way, asking what it means to be roommates and discussing each of their expectations. At some point, borrowing clothes will be discussed as part of the bigger picture.

situations or when they have little investment in the relationship really show a low concern for self? When a person accommodates a loved one to maintain social harmony, doesn't that indicate a high concern for a goal to create a satisfactory home life? Does all competition have to be win/lose in a negative way? If collaboration takes too long, is it really advancing each party's goals? Although the five conflict styles are a convenient way to view conflict, a superficial application of them may overvalue collaboration and undervalue the strategic advantages of avoidance, competition, compromise, or accommodation.

Three Conflict Management Styles

The five-styles approach seems intuitive and is helpful in understanding different tactical approaches to conflict, but researchers are beginning to support the idea that there really are only three conflict management styles: avoidance, distributive engagement, and integrative engagement. **Avoidance** attempts to minimize the conflict. A **distributive engagement style** is direct, competitive, and may include persistent attempts to wrest concessions from the other side. The **integrative engagement style** is direct, cooperative, and seeks a mutually satisfactory outcome (Kuhn & Poole, 2000). Accommodation might manifest as a type of avoidance of conflict or as a result when one loses a distributive engagement. Compromise is seen as a tactic in distributive engagement (splitting the difference) or the fallback position when integrative engagement fails.

KEY 7.1

Competent conflict managers are comfortable with many conflict and communication styles.

Styles Across Cultures

Additional difficulties arise with categorizing conflict styles when culture is considered. European Americans, whose culture favors openness and direct speech, are comfortable with the five-styles approach to interpersonal conflict. However, Kim and Leung (2000) observe that the application of the five-styles grid across cultures creates a problem. For example, people in some cultures think conflict avoidance is ideal. It "can help the individual to control emotion, and may at times also allow the passive expressive of discontentment without the dangers of a direct challenge . . . Avoidance (or withdrawal) strategies can be seen as positive or negative by members of different cultural orientations" (Kim & Leung, 2000, p. 241; see also Brew & Cairns, 2004). In the collectivist cultures (discussed in Chapter 5), avoiding is a positive response that shows high concern for the other's face goals.

Different style preferences also exist within geographic areas. For example, African Americans, as well as other ethnic groups in the United States, do not necessarily embrace European American styles (Holt & DeVore, 2005). Walker (2004) observes that 517 American Indian tribes use conflict management styles based on a different worldview from European Americans. The Tsalagi (Cherokee) Talking Circle, Hawaiian Ho'oponopono, the Haudenosaunee (Iroquois) Great Law of Peace, and the Navajo Justice and Harmony Ceremony, for example, all stem from a focus on involving everyone in a community, using ceremony as a balancing and healing process, bringing authentic emotions and apologies into the process, and building past lessons into the discussion of current conflicts.

Learning how to engage with others from another culture is a lifelong activity. A European American communication expert was asked to facilitate a high-conflict meeting at a hospital on a local Indian reservation. Her Euro-American bias about conflict caused her to rush the narrations that individuals were relating in an attempt to move the process along. After realizing that her approach was not working, she apologized and used a different style of facilitation that was more culturally appropriate. Cultural lessons should be collected over the course of a lifetime and are considered valuable assets for conflict managers.

As research on cross-cultural conflict styles develops, new models will emerge, such as Hammer's (2005) **Intercultural Conflict Style Inventory.** As introduced in Chapter 5, Hammer examines two dimensions: how conflict is expressed and how emotions are expressed (see Table 5.3).

> **Discussion Question 7.9**
>
> What is the intercultural conflict style in your culture of origin? Does your personal style match your culture of origin?

Knowledge of intercultural conflict styles is critical in the modern workplace. As Brew and Cairns (2004) state, workplace conflict across cultural groups "are due to differing needs, conflict management styles, assumptions and expectations, and stress related to today's fast-paced business environment" (p. 28). Knowledge of intercultural styles can prevent some conflicts and assist in the management of others.

Communication Behaviors That Affect Conflict Management

In addition to personality and conflict management styles, individuals also develop personal communication habits. These communicative habits impact how conflicts develop and how they are managed. This section discusses rhetorical sensitivity, general communication style, escalators versus fractionators, and conversational style.

Rhetorical Sensitivity

Adapting to another's style is a style choice in and of itself. People who adapt to another's style (whether in an accommodating fashion or as a strategic move) are called *Rhetorical Reflectors* (Hart & Burks, 1972). Reflectors generally put other peoples' needs before their own and let others determine the tone of conversations. People who maintain a habitual style, regardless of the situation, are deemed *Noble Selves*. Noble Selves believe that their style is right and other people should adapt to them. The *Rhetorical Reflector* recognizes that different contexts and different players require people to adapt their style. Rhetorical Reflectors assess the situation and make style choices that fit the moment. Some people use one communication style at work and a different style with loved ones. At home, a very competitive businessperson might be more accommodating and considerate of the feelings of family members.

General Communication Style

Folger et al. (2005) conclude that communicative behaviors related to disclosiveness, empowerment, activeness, and flexibility form styles that impact the perception of conflict behaviors. Hiding or disclosing information about one's goals and strategies is called *disclosiveness. Empowerment* assesses whether power is shared or hoarded. The intensity of involvement in managing a conflict when it first arises is a measure of *activeness.* Finally, *flexibility* addresses how much one is willing to give to manage a conflict. Difficulties arising from general communication style can impact conflict. For example, individuals who are nondisclosive may have trouble talking about personal goals, which is necessary for collaboration.

> ### Discussion Question 7.10
> Identify examples that illustrate disclosiveness, empowerment, activeness, or flexibility. Explain how those behaviors might affect a conflict interaction.

Escalators and Fractionators

Those who see conflict as a crisis and become very excited have a style of **escalation.** What feels natural to an escalator is making a conflict bigger. At their extreme, escalators add other conflicts to the mix to create a crisis. In contrast, **fractionators** feel it is natural to become calm and go straight to problem solving.

There are obvious areas where escalator and fractionator styles clash. First, they are pulling in opposite directions: One wants drama and the other wants calm. Second, because the behaviors are going in opposite directions, misunderstanding likely will occur. While the escalator is venting, the fractionator may make comments like this: "If you weren't so emotional, we could work this out." Such reactions probably are perceived as judgmental and as indicating the other doesn't care about the problem. More escalation may result. Fractionators probably see escalators as too excitable and out of control. Ironically, the differences can precipitate a conflict around how to behave during conflict as each person tries to push the other into behaving "correctly." During conflict, fractionators can adapt by withholding the impulse to leap to problem solving and allowing the escalator time to explore the size of the issue emotionally.

In the film *A League of Their Own,* the manager of a 1940s World War II era women's baseball team used an aggressive escalation style. When an error occurred that allowed the other team to score, he responded by yelling and exaggerating the importance of the mistake (escalation)—resulting in some players crying, to which he would exclaim, "There is no crying in baseball!" Toward the end of the film, the manager confronted a player who missed an outfield throw. Visibly shaking with rage, he controlled his natural response and calmly said, "Try to practice the cutoff throw over the winter." The manager had learned to moderate his style.

Conversational Style

With so many options, how can we determine the most effective way to interact with others? **Conversational style** refers to speech and vocal habits—for example, how fast to talk, how long to pause between speakers, and whether to interrupt or overlap while another person is speaking (Beaumont & Wagner, 2004). Individual conversational styles can inflame or subdue a conflict. For example, how long should the pause be between when one person finishes speaking and the other begins? Depending on what was learned while growing up, the pause could be several beats—before or after the other finishes speaking. Those with quicker styles may perceive those with longer pauses to be slow or uninvolved. At times, it can be difficult for those with a slower response speed to enter a conversation: Faster people take every pause as an opportunity to capture the conversational lead.

Some linguists (Tannen, 1994) advance the notion that there are two basic European American conversational styles: report and rapport. **Report talk** is a style focused on keeping the floor while talking, so the speaker learns many facts, figures, and stories, and gathers techniques for interrupting and capturing the topic from other speakers. For two individuals within this style, a conversation is like the child's game of King of the Hill. Each individual attempts to push the other's topics aside, wrestle for topic control, and gain the conversational high ground. In **rapport talk,** the individuals work together to build a conversation by nodding, making verbal sounds indicating one is listening ("Uh huh"), and telling short stories on the same theme. Then the two switch roles (Tannen, 1994).

Difficulties arise when a report person converses with a rapport person because of *style clash*. Each will follow the rules for his or her conversational style and each will encounter unsatisfactory results. The report person will do most of the talking while the rapport person plays the supportive role and patiently waits for a turn. When the floor is not relinquished, the rapport individual perceives the report talker as uncaring, egotistical, and rude. The report person views the rapport talker as uninteresting, uninformed, and less powerful for not joining in the fray. If the other person had anything important to say, it should be said without prompting or turn taking. These attributions about the other are a direct reaction to style clash.

Even regional dialect or vocal inflection can cause attribution errors. A coworker may speak quite differently from most of the group and lead to stereotypes that become the basis for an interpersonal conflict. A group of professionals in training were practicing a model in which two individuals worked together while mediating a dispute. After the first half hour, one mediator, with a fast New York City style of speaking would make a comment and the other mediator and disputants would ignore him. A few moments later, the other mediator, from Denver, would make the same comment, and the disputants, also from the West, would respond positively. What was happening in this situation? Because of stereotypes of a New Yorker's verbal style as aggressive and uncaring, the others in the room discounted the content of that mediator's remarks. Frustrated at being ignored, it would be easy for the New Yorker to attack the group verbally and precipitate a conflict. At minimum, unconscious attributions about the New Yorker led to some social exclusion.

Conversational styles are important because "research by social psychologists has confirmed that speakers who use similar speech styles rate each other as more likeable, warm, trustworthy and friendly than those who use different speech styles" (Beaumont & Wagner, 2004, p. 340). Similarly, the negative feelings that arise when styles clash can be perceived as goal interference and precipitate conflict. For example, research indicates that adolescents tend to use a *high-involvement conversational style* with frequent interruptions and overlapping speech. Parents tend to exhibit a *low-involvement conversational style* with few overlaps or successful interruptions. This means that parents expect children will not interrupt with excuses while being lectured. According to one study, this difference in style caused frustration on both sides and resulted in higher perceptions of conflict (Beaumont & Wagner, 2004).

Discussion Question 7.11

What's your style?

Place an X on the continuum to mark your conversational preference at work. What problems might arise when working with someone with an opposite preference?

Just business _____ ✓ Social talk OK

Ask for your help ✗_____ Tell you what to do

Single tasker ✗_____ Multitasker

Polite talk ✗_____ Blunt talk

Emotional Intelligence

As discussed earlier in the book, emotional intelligence is an increasingly popular way of thinking about social skills. **Emotional intelligence** (EI or EQ) was crafted as a counterpart to intellectual intelligence (IQ). Current EI tests emerged from the European American worldview and are indexed to Western values.

Hughes, Patterson, and Terrell (2005) explain that emotions are what we feel, with fear and desire among the most powerful primary emotions. Emotions are processed automatically, based on past experiences "without having to consider them rationally" (p. 13). The brain then orders hormone or chemical reactions that produce physical and mood reactions such as stress, the elation of love, or the excitement of fear. The significance for conflict management is that the desire to win competitively or to feel rewarded through cooperation might also become an automatic program. Changing the program requires self-awareness, desire, and emotional intelligence.

EQ is measured through many copyrighted instruments. After analyzing all the EQ tests, Hughes et al. (2005) found fifteen key competencies that cut across all the tests (see Table 7.3).

TABLE 7.3   *Fifteen Key Emotional Intelligence Competencies*

- Self-regard
- Emotional self-awareness
- Assertiveness
- Independence
- Self-actualization
- Empathy
- Social responsibility
- Interpersonal relationships
- Stress tolerance
- Impulse control
- Reality testing
- Flexibility
- Problem solving
- Optimism
- Happiness

The fifteen competencies are important to conflict management in numerous ways. A better *self-regard,* or positive view of oneself, enables self-confidence and less fear of failure during conflict, allowing new tactics and styles to be developed. EQ researchers find self-regard one of the highest predictors of competent behavior.

Self-awareness is the ability to understand what is being felt—"it enables us to connect with our underlying beliefs, assumptions, and values and to know what drives us" (Hughes et al., 2005, p. 45). Individuals often feel that "something is wrong" or "this is the right thing to do" without consciously knowing why. A higher self-awareness brings the causes of these feelings to the surface. The counterpart to self-awareness is awareness of others' feelings, or *empathy.* Self-awareness helps conflict managers keep their goals in the forefront and not be sidetracked during conflict.

Assertiveness is the ability to express oneself and advocate for goals without being verbally aggressive. Assertiveness is a hallmark of the emotionally intelligent person. Assertive individuals garner the respect of others because they can be depended on to state what is important in ways that don't demean others. When individuals in conflict know that someone is assertive, rather than avoidant or aggressive, trust can be developed.

Someone who is not overly influenced by a group and can process ideas by himself or herself exhibits *independence.* The opposite of independence might be *codependence,* where a person is so fixated on another individual that he or she can't make decisions without knowing that person's view. Although a degree of independence is required to know one's goals in life, too much independence may be damaging during conflict with significant others. Too much independence can be perceived as selfishness. Competent conflict managers aim to balance independence with *social responsibility,* indicating a concern for the welfare of others.

Self-actualization involves becoming the best person one can be—to climb to the top of Maslow's hierarchy of needs. Self-actualized individuals have attained basic survival

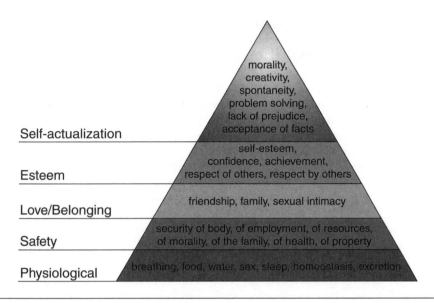

FIGURE 7.1   *Maslow's Hierarchy*

resources: food and shelter (physiological needs), feel safe (security needs), have people to be affectionate with and give affection to (belonging needs), and have self-respect and are respected by others (esteem needs). With the bottom of Maslow's pyramid of needs mastered, they can work on self-actualization, the last step. Many conflicts occur at the lower levels in Maslow's hierarchy—contesting for scarce resources needed to survive, to feel secure, or to gain esteem and affection. By establishing meaningful and mutually satisfying relationships with others, emotional maturity is developed and unearned sarcasm is less hurtful. Much of the bickering and sarcasm that people find so hurtful are attacks on self-esteem. Self-actualization should be balanced with *interpersonal relationships* because it is difficult to know oneself without interacting with others.

Stress tolerance allows an overall higher quality of life without emotional or physical overstimulation and negative health effects. Individuals who can tolerate general stress also can tolerate more uncertainty about the outcome of a conflict while collaborative strategies are developed. Those who can manage stress have more options available during conflict. Controlling stress relates to *impulse control*. "Impulses are urges that compel action" (Hughes et al., 2005, p. 87). Although some impulses may be good, such as hugging someone who is sad, many other impulses are unproductive, such as punching a hole in a wall in anger. Conflict managers who think before they act can control the impulse to say hurtful things or to use destructive tactics and will become better conflict managers.

Reality testing means viewing the world as it is rather than how one might wish it to be. It enables a clear view of the real consequences of actions. Hopes and dreams may be comforting, but competent conflict managers can cut through the fog of wishful thinking to see the real world.

Rigidity inhibits the creativity that is necessary for competent conflict management. *Flexibility* in how goals are achieved allows variability in approach, processes used, or the shape of the exact outcome. Flexibility does not mean giving in to the desires of others at the cost of personal goals. Paired with flexibility is *problem solving*. Having the skills necessary to define, research, develop creative ideas, and evaluate which proposal is the best solution is an asset for the conflict manager.

The final two skills of emotional intelligence are *optimism* and *happiness*. Those who believe that problems can be overcome are more likely to work to overcome them. Although it may seem strange to phrase it this way, those who allow themselves to be happy will be more effective conflict managers than those whose self-concept is built on sustaining an image of personal tragedy.

Emotional intelligence provides skill sets and characteristics that make people better conflict managers. People with high emotional intelligence may be more successful in their personal and professional lives than those who are low EI.

Functional versus Dysfunctional Styles

This chapter offers many opportunities to speculate about individual style and behavior patterns along a number of dimensions—personality, conflict management, emotional, social style, among others. It is important to know how a style interacts with others and whether the style one currently uses works productively or causes more distress.

With awareness, the conflict manager can bring differences in style to a conscious level. Sometimes just verbalizing that someone has a different style can transform the negative attributions being made. Saying, "I've noticed that we have different ways of approaching this problem" or "I've noticed that you're better at the detail work and I'm better at the long-range vision" may be helpful. At a board meeting two individuals were in conflict over whether to hire an executive director. One advocate passionately focused on the vision of making the organization bigger and more successful and was confident that the details could be worked out if the plan was adopted. Another board member argued against the plan because details were lacking, like who would fill out the forms to deduct payroll taxes or what deliverables the executive director would have for each month. When a third board member observed that the two individuals had different styles—one being a visionary and one being detail oriented—and that both styles were necessary for any plan to work, the entire nature of the discussion changed from competitive to collaborative. Awareness of styles affords the opportunity to transform dysfunctional conflict into more productive possibilities (see Table 7.4).

TABLE 7.4 *Lessons Learned About Style*

- Style explains how good people can see the same thing in opposite ways.
- Gut reactions coming from style aren't automatically superior.
- We can't change somebody else's basic style.
- Styles can mesh together if we are aware of our strengths and weaknesses.
- Relationships are stronger when people give each other grace about style differences.
- Strong teams lean into each other's strengths and prop up each other's weaknesses.
- With time and effort, new styles can be learned.

Summary

Styles are patterns of behavior that influence the way individuals communicate. Awareness of differing styles can help us recognize style clashes when they arise and provide options for adapting personal styles to be more effective. Many problems attributed to "personality conflicts" can be understood as differences in style.

Personality styles are a popular way to understand how people approach conflict differently. The Myers-Briggs Type Indicator categorizes people along four distinct pairs: extrovert/introvert, thinking/intuitive, feeling/perceiving, and judging/perceiving. The Gregorc styles model identifies people as abstracts, concretes, randoms, or sequentials. Gregorc style indicates how people see time, deal with details, and organize thoughts. The social style model uses direct observation to assess assertiveness and responsiveness.

The five styles of conflict management typology has been widely used, modified, and adapted since 1964. It includes avoidance, accommodation, competitiveness, compromise, and collaboration. Much of the style research is based in Western culture, and its usefulness breaks down when applied to non-Western cultures. Avoidance and accommodation may be seen as more ideal strategies in collectivist cultures than in individualistic cultures. Communication styles are key in assessing the effectiveness of a conflict manager. The approach to conflict we take includes whether we hide or disclose information, if we empower others or attempt to keep power to ourselves, and our levels of activeness and flexibility. Other communication styles that affect conflict management are degrees of rhetorical sensitivity and whether individuals escalate or fractionate conflict. Even conversational styles can affect outcomes. Learning to adapt a communication style to the situation is possible with awareness, desire, and training.

Finally, emotional intelligence offers a way to evaluate our skills in social situations. Individuals who demonstrate high emotional intelligence make more effective conflict managers than those who do not.

The styles we adopt can be functional or dysfunctional. Functional styles effectively work with others to manage conflict. Dysfunctional styles seek to undermine others' goals and are often selfish.

Chapter Resources

Exercises

1. Do an Internet or journal search for a free personality style inventory. Take and self-score the test. Think about how you engage in conflict in a specific relationship that is important to you. Take the test a second time thinking about a different context—perhaps how you engage in conflict at work with your supervisor, at home with a significant other, or with a college roommate. In a group, compare and discuss your scores. Are you surprised by the outcome? Did your score change? Discuss with your group why styles might be different in these two situations. What are the advantages and disadvantages of your style during interpersonal conflict? (Suggested source: Conerly & Tripathi, 2004.)

2. In small groups, observe your classmates to guess their social style. Check to see if your observations match their self-perceptions. How might each social style be an advantage or a disadvantage during interpersonal conflict?

3. Ancient Greeks and Romans categorized four temperaments based on types of fluids in the body: sanguine (cheerful, optimistic, vain, unpredictable), phlegmatic (cool, persevering, needing direction), melancholic (soft-hearted, does things for others, slow to respond), and choleric (stubborn, domineering, opinionated, self-confident). How different or similar are these typologies from modern personality theories?

4. What role does culture or subculture play in your development of a personal style? How do cultural styles affect conflict management between people from different cultures? What are your biggest challenges when in conflict with others?

5. Make a list of tactics that people use to avoid engaging in conflict. When are these tactics productive and when are they unproductive?

Essay Topics

1. Use the social style model while observing a boss, roommate, or friend for one week. Write your observations in a journal. Using your insights as evidence, write an essay that explains the other person's social style. What difficulties might arise for the two of you during conflict because of his or her social style?

2. Write an essay about your intercultural conflict management style. Using Hammer's four intercultural styles, identify the style of your root cultural group. Do your conflict behaviors match those of your cultural group, or do you fit more comfortably in one of the other categories? What challenges will you face when engaging in conflict with persons from other cultural groups?

Mastery Case

Examine Mastery Case 7, "The Doggie Discontent." What styles are evident in the case?

The Doggie Discontent

Before Tess and Molly became roommates, Tess made sure that Molly would be fine with her lovable little dog Gretel, a five-year-old schnauzer. After about two months, Molly met Tess at the door, obviously upset:

Molly: "We need to talk. I hate living here! I can't stand your dog anymore. She jumps on me and the house smells like a dog. I like some animals, but I hate your dog!"

Tess: (Shocked). "You knew about Gretel when we moved in. She's a schnauzer for God's sake—they love everybody. It's not like she's a pit bull and going to attack you. What did you expect?"

Molly: "I was hoping the apartment wouldn't allow dogs."

Tess: "I wouldn't have moved in with you then. I could never live without Gretel."

Molly: "I think you should get rid of her."

Tess: "That is not going to happen! You knew I had a dog. And I don't have the money to move. You got yourself into this situation, so you figure a way out of it."

Molly left the apartment and slammed the door. Gretel, sensing something was wrong, walked over to comfort Tess.

8

Negotiation

Objectives

After reading the chapter, you should be able to:

1. Recognize the underlying assumptions of competitive and cooperative bargaining
2. Differentiate between appropriate tactics in competitive and collaborative negotiation situations
3. Develop a strategy to move competitive negotiators toward more collaborative processes

> "They always say time changes things, but you actually have to change them yourself."
> —Artist Andy Warhol

Negotiation is a common endeavor, and most people negotiate every day. Merging in traffic, choosing where to eat with a friend, and determining topics for conversation all involve some negotiation. In the broadest sense, a mother's stern glance at her daughter can be a condensed negotiation they engage in every weeknight, with a stern look serving as the winning argument.

Mother:	"Get off the phone and do your homework."
Daughter:	"Can't I have any privacy to talk to my friends!? You always nag me when I'm on my cell. I don't have that much homework anyway."
Mother:	"Do your homework first and then you can talk on the phone. If you don't have that much, it won't take very long."
Daughter:	"Just fifteen more minutes."
Mother:	"Two minutes or I'm taking your phone."
Daughter:	"Mom, that's so unfair!"
Mother:	[Looks sternly at daughter.]
Daughter:	"All right, all right, I'm hanging up!"

As people enter a subway car, one seat is left. The individual who put her bag on the seat may pick it up voluntarily to allow someone to sit or a nonverbal negotiation may occur. A passenger who has no seat may gesture at the seat as if to say, "Mind if I sit?" Friends negotiate where to go to for coffee or when to gather at the local club on Friday night. Couples negotiate where to go on vacation. Students negotiate due dates of assignments with their professors. A common cause of conflict among college roommates is not specifically negotiating expectations and boundaries when they move into an apartment. Who will do the dishes? How often is the house cleaned? What does "clean" mean? Who does what cleaning? Can we have overnight guests? Are there times when the house should be quiet for studying? Upfront negotiation can preserve relationships and make expectations known.

Negotiation, or bargaining, occurs when one person (or group) engages in conversation with another person (or group) to pursue goals. Fisher, Ury, and Patton (1993) more simply define negotiation as the "ability to persuade someone to do something" (p. 4). There are contrasting approaches to the pursuit of goals: acting persuasively, coercively, entirely egocentrically, or with consideration of the other party. This chapter differentiates between two basic approaches to negotiation—competitive and cooperative—and the tactical choices inherent in each approach.

For negotiation to succeed, several conditions must be met (Table 8.1). First, the individuals need some meaningful connection or common interests. Without an apparent connection, there may be no incentive to negotiate. Second, the outcome of the negotiation is unpredictable. If one party is confident that her or his goals will be met

---

TABLE 8.1 *The Conditions for Negotiation*

- The people involved must have some type of interconnection.
- The outcome must be unpredictable to some degree.
- The difference must be about negotiable issues.
- The people must be willing to communicate.

with 100 percent certainty, there will be little or no drive to negotiate with the other party. Third, the issue to be negotiated must include more than a clash of values. **Values** are deeply rooted feelings about right and wrong and generally are not negotiable. For example, people are unlikely to negotiate away their cherished feelings of patriotism toward a country or devout adherence to a religion. However, parties may be willing to negotiate issues such as what behaviors are appropriate when expressing patriotism. Finally, if one person is unwilling to communicate or engage in negotiation, little progress can be made. Negotiation by its nature involves communication as parties attempt to meet their needs.

Discussion Question 8.1

Explore the necessity of the four conditions needed for successful negotiation. How important is it for parties to feel interconnected to negotiate effectively? How does uncertainty affect negotiations? Can values be negotiated? What options exist when one person in a negotiation is unwilling to communicate?

Because the likelihood of a successful negotiation is affected by the presence of the four conditions just described, sometimes a party will need to help set those conditions in place before negotiation. For instance, Esther is a supervisor over several employees. In the day-to-day operations, she is not required to negotiate with employees. She has the authority to order employees to do their work in specific ways and can refuse to listen to their requests. When dealing with a high-power person who is uncommunicative or unwilling to negotiate, those in low-power positions must persuade the other person to enter into negotiation. Esther's employees could bring her to the negotiation table in a number of ways. They could convince her that negotiating will serve her interests (demonstrate interconnection) or explain to her that if she does not negotiate with them she will have no say in how the conflict will unfold and ultimately be resolved (establish unpredictability). The employees could appeal to a higher authority, the company's owner, to require Esther to negotiate (force communication). Using any of these tactics with a person of higher power, however, does have inherent risks.

KEY 8.1

Appealing to interests can transform an uncooperative negotiator into a cooperative negotiation partner.

Ideally, appealing to someone's interests is the most collaborative way to bring an uncooperative negotiator to the table. Jamilla wants to change her scheduled shift at the bar where she works. From past experience, she knows that her boss, Ramon, will say "No" if she directly asks for a change in shift. He has the power to say "No" and does not see anything in it for him if he negotiates. Jamilla analyzes the situation to create a strategy that will engage Ramon's self-interest and persuade him to negotiate. She chooses to say, "Ramon, I know that you have difficulty filling the schedule during the holidays, and I was thinking that if I took some time off now when no one else has anything going on, then next month I could work the two weekend shifts when everyone will want that time off." By focusing on a need that Ramon already recognizes (filling hard spots in the holiday schedule), Jamilla engages his interest. By not giving too much information at the outset about the specifics of her goal (getting the next two Saturdays off), Jamilla has a better chance of avoiding Ramon's automatic "No" response.

The Worlds of Negotiation

Negotiation strategies and tactics align with the two views of conflict presented in Chapter 3: competition and cooperation. Framing a negotiation as a competition (win/lose) would naturally lead to competitive (power-based) negotiation strategies; conversely a cooperative framework would promote collaborative or mutual gains negotiation techniques (needs based).

Competitive bargainers place a higher priority on achieving personal goals over meeting the needs of others. Competitors work to control the allocation of perceived scarce resources (**distributive negotiation**). Control is a primary strategy of a competitive negotiator. Commonly, competitive negotiators engage in tactics to manipulate the negotiation process and how issues are framed, and they work to rig the criteria applied to attain an outcome that will achieve their self-interest. If one party is able to maintain control of the process, the other party's bargaining options are reduced significantly. In competition, winning is defined by getting the best outcome for oneself.

The other approach to negotiation, cooperative, also is called **mutual gains, collaborative negotiation,** or **integrative negotiation.** Cooperative approaches are designed to keep personal goals clearly in mind while simultaneously considering the interests of the other. Cooperative negotiators explore mutually beneficial options and seek outcomes allowing maximum goal achievement for both parties. Winning is defined as what is best for all concerned, instead of what is best for only one side.

> ### Discussion Question 8.2
> How does the framing of a negotiation as either competitive or cooperative affect the relationship of the parties? Are you more comfortable negotiating competitively or cooperatively? What influences your preference for one approach over another?

Competitive Negotiation

Competition is driven by a desire to win but can involve a wide array of techniques—healthy or destructive. Competitors may engage in tactics distinguished by cordial assertiveness, polite dialogue, and appropriate positioning. They also can use manipulation, outrageous demands, dirty tricks, and destructive aggressiveness to gain the upper hand in negotiations. In an organization where there is one promotion available and the hiring choice will be made from an internal pool of candidates, competitive negotiation can be appropriate and effective if everyone puts forward their best efforts and uses nondestructive tactics. However, the competition can be perilous (to the parties, as well as to the long-term success of the organization) if employees undercut each other, spread rumors, and try to destroy the other applicants in an effort to gain an edge. Although circumstances may call for competition, *how* one engages in competition is a choice. Recognizing the options available within the realm of competitive negotiation is what distinguishes skilled and ethical competitors from those who leave paths of destruction in their bargaining wake.

Negative Competition

At the heart of competition is the power to influence the other to achieve a desired outcome. Some competitors may exhibit one or more unhealthy or destructive approaches in order to win. First, competitors may lose sight of tangible goals and make the outcome of the competition personal. A divorcing couple may be negotiating the division of property, but when one party feels particularly slighted or hurt the goal changes to "making sure he doesn't get a dime!" Competition can become particularly fierce when power, self-esteem, and saving face come into play. Competitors can be convinced of the uncompromising value of their proposals and feel offended when others don't immediately comply. Dad tells his son to mow the lawn. The son says he has plans to visit a friend, but will do it when he gets back in a couple of hours. Dad sees this response as a threat to his authority and provides an ultimatum to mow the lawn now before he goes to his friend's house. "Arguers almost always enter a negotiation with the goal of persuading their opponent of the worth of their stance, especially at the beginning of a negotiation. They believe that their position is better and more valid than their opponent's position" (Stein & Albro, 2001, p. 114). Sometimes people enter into negotiation "to determine who will be the more dominant person in a relationship" and that may explain "much of the seemingly irrational behavior that occurs in arguments" (Stein & Albro, 2001, p. 114). Sometimes negotiation becomes more about self-identity than about a substantive issue.

A second outcome of negative competition occurs when competitive negotiators fall victim to the winner's curse. The **winner's curse** occurs when someone is victorious in the negotiation but isn't happy with the results. For example, people caught up on the competition of an auction may pay ridiculous prices for mundane objects (Bazerman & Samuelson, 1983). For example, an eBay auction is exciting, but one may lose sight of the goal of getting a good deal and become invested in beating the other bidders. Logically, making a purchase should be simple: Research the value of the item, set a limit, and enter the bargaining arena to get the best price. However, it may not turn out that way. People pay too much for a variety of reasons, including lack of research, poor bargaining skills, fear of losing, emotional involvement with the idea of owning the object, or craving the thrill of victory.

The winner's curse can be understood by looking at what the actual, and often unintended, cost was to the winner. For example, a roommate may win compliance from his housemates about who pays for a scratch on the paint of his car, but the cost of winning is that a once congenial friendship now is marred by resentment. A worker may win the most preferred schedule over other coworkers but lose their respect and help in the future. The winner's curse ultimately is caused by either unfocused goals or a lack of thought about the consequences that winning might incur.

Discussion Question 8.3

Describe a time when competition over a tangible resource changed to a competition over self-esteem, power, or identity. Can you identify the point where the conflict goal switched? How can we avoid the winner's curse in negotiations with others?

A third outcome of a negative competition could occur when the critical issue is left unsolved. Competitors may turn a negotiation into a quest for a personal victory rather than solving a problem. They may ignore a good solution offered by the other party ("If it is your idea, it must be bad for me") and judge the success of the negotiation by how much the other person suffers ("If you are really unhappy, the outcome must be good for me"). People involved in this cycle may assume that the best personal outcome is achieved through winning at all costs, but they may not consider that the other's loss translates into more headaches for the winner. Thompson and Nadler (2000) found that losers in a win/lose situation convert the outcome to a lose/lose situation in about 20 percent of negotiations. In *lose/lose outcomes,* the party whose goals are not met may sabotage the system so the "winning" person's goals cannot be achieved. For example, a one person may "win" a promotion at work but find that those she beat to get the job are working to limit her chances of success by withholding needed information, building coalitions, or ruining her reputation in the organization. Thompson and Nadler continue, "Our psychological immune system is so efficient that we do not even realize our judgments are tainted with self-interest" (p. 219). That blind spot may lead competitors to select tactics not in their long-term self-interest.

Engaging in destructive competition may prove to be more damaging than if the competitor did nothing. Destruction to relationships, unintended consequences, and an unhealthy communication climate can make winning an empty victory.

> ### *Discussion Question 8.4*
> One negotiation philosophy contends, "What is good for you and doesn't harm me is good for both of us." How might managers or parents put this philosophy into practice?

Productive Competition

Although the very nature of competition is about setting parties in opposition to one another, this quality is not inherently negative. Competitive negotiation can be effective and appropriate in a variety of contexts: when resources genuinely are scarce (only one promotion is available), time is limited (we want the kids to clean their rooms before Grandma visits), the topic is deeply valued (we take a stand on drilling for oil in pristine wilderness areas), and/or moderate tactics are chosen (whoever has the highest sales numbers this month gets a gift card for 50 gallons of gasoline).

Competition can be motivating, fun, productive, effective, and result in high morale. Some families and social groups include friendly competitive games as part of valued time together, and many organizations have competitions designed to increase sales or production. To maximize the possibility of productive outcomes, competition should operate in an environment of trust, commitment to fair and equitable treatment, access to information that will affect the competition, and delineated clear criteria for what constitutes a "win."

Competitive Negotiation Tactics

Competitive negotiators have a variety of tactics to choose from as they work toward goal achievement. In this section, we highlight the tactics presented in Table 8.2. Depending on how the tactics are implemented, they exist on a continuum from benign to destructive.

TABLE 8.2   *Competitive Negotiation Tactics*

Verbal aggressiveness
Hypothetical offers
Splitting the difference
Force the other to make the first reasonable offer
Manipulate the bargaining range
Offer the other the deal they offer you
Doing your homework
Use humor to devalue the other's position
Boulwarism
Threats
Promises
Obnoxious persistence
Coalitions
Frame the issue favorably to your side
Ask for concessions
Enumerate complaints
Manipulate pity, guilt, or other emotions
Lie
Call in debts
Quid pro quo
Ask questions
Tit for tat

Although not a requirement of competition, verbal aggressiveness is a characteristic often associated with hard-line negotiators. **Verbal aggressiveness** is expressed in countless ways—for example, attacking through name-calling, mudslinging, angry tones, loud volume, demeaning personal attacks, criticism, and hostile body posturing. As a tactic, verbal aggressiveness may be successful but is strongly related to destructive conflict, physical violence, and relationship deterioration (Rogan & La France, 2003). Negotiators give more concessions to angry people but dislike them more (Van Kleef, De Dreu, Pietroni, & Manstead, 2006). The alternative to aggressive competition is **assertive negotiation.** Assertive competitors advance their interests through persuasion and engage in direct and pointed dialogue to promote their needs without personal attacks.

A competitive negotiator may use **hypothetical offers** to gauge an opponent's willingness to change positions. "What would you be willing to do for me if I agree to go with you to visit your mother?" "What extra work can I expect from you if I let you use my car this weekend?" "If I were to offer to sell you both the truck and the boat for $10,000, would you be interested?" The strategic nature of hypothetical offers emerges when an offer is not one the negotiator really would make. After discovering the buyer has $10,000 that he would be willing to give for the truck and boat, the offer can be withdrawn—it was just hypothetical—and the seller can try to get a higher price for just the truck. Bringing in another negotiator who must review any offer is a common tactic at this point, as in, "I'll have to talk to my husband about whether he really wants to sell the boat, but I know the truck is worth quite a bit."

S*plitting the difference* is a familiar strategy used when a negotiation stalls. When trying to buy a used car, the deal may deadlock with the seller wanting $8,000 and the buyer not wanting to pay more than $7,500. Typically, one party will say, "Let's just split the difference," and a bargain is struck at $7,750. A variation of splitting the difference involves *contingency agreements.* If the real future value of the agreement is unknown, the compromise can be contingent—open to renegotiation if particular events happen (Kray, Thompson, & Lind, 2005). For example, heirs settling an estate can decide to split the profits from the deceased parent's home, but only if it sells for more than $200,000. If it sells for less, the agreement would be renegotiated.

There sometimes is an advantage to *letting the other person make an offer first.* With one offer on the table, the second person has an option to respond, ignore the offer, or argue against it (Garcia, 2000). A negotiator might seek to have the other make the first offer simply by saying, "What do you think we should do?" or "What do you think is a fair outcome?" When negotiating a fixed-price item, such as a used car, the one who makes a serious offer first is at a strategic disadvantage because that offer becomes the **anchor point.** The second person can adjust his or her response, knowing that the final price probably will be somewhere in the middle of the first two serious offers. If a seller originally sets a price of the car at $10,000, a buyer can come in with a price of $7,000. The age-old negotiation dance calls for the seller to inch the price downward ($9,500 then $9,250, then $9000) and the buyer to inch up the offer ($7,500 then $7,750 then $8,000). The bargainers approach the midpoint until impasse is reached or a bargain is made (often by splitting the difference). An important consideration in this type of negotiation is the setting of the anchor point, in this example $10,000. However, a high anchor point may be used strategically to give the seller room to negotiate.

Negotiators generally have a range of acceptable settlement figures in mind. For instance, the buyer would like to buy a car for $7,500 but is willing to pay as much as $8,500. The seller will take no less than $8,000 but would like to receive as much as a buyer will pay and sets the price at $10,000. When the seller sets the first offer close to what he thinks is a fair value, it leaves room for the buyer to manipulate the **bargaining range.** By decreasing the first offer to $7,000, the buyer creates a midpoint (between $7,000 and $10,000), and the final agreement likely will be around $8,500. If the seller's first offer was $9,000, the midpoint changes to around $8,000.

Any purchase offers an opportunity for competitive bargaining. The familiar dance of competitive bargaining is used to get a better deal from naive bargainers. Buyers use competitive bargaining to get better purchase prices through assertive tactics: laughing at the car salesperson's first offer to downplay it, pitting one dealership against another, doing research to know reasonable pricing, and knowing one's consumer rights. Buyers sometimes can gain a better price in a store simply by asking for one. The magic words, "Is this your best price?" said to a store owner or manager can result in a discount. For example, Melanie was at a shop getting her car fixed. The mechanic quoted a price, including labor. Melanie asked, "Can you knock something off the price because I come in here whenever my car needs work?" The price came down $75. Individuals with good credit ratings can obtain lower interest rates on credit

---

TOOLBOX 8.1

Negotiating for a Car

Getting Ready

- The Internet contains information on models, pricing, and so on. Do your homework.
- The sticker price is not a realistic offer. Don't let the sticker price be an anchor.
- Don't give away your trade-in! Negotiate just as hard on the price of the trade-in.
- Work a package deal to your advantage. Make each agreement contingent on the entire deal.
- Get financing in advance. Then negotiate an even better deal with the seller.
- Don't buy a vehicle just because it has a nice sound system or color.
- Don't pay for extras you don't want like rust proofing, fabric protection, paint protection, dealer paperwork fees, or window etching.
- Always be willing to walk away from a deal. If you fall in love with a car, your negotiation posture is weak.

Specific Tactics to Buy a Car

- Bring a friend along to point out negative features of the car and say things like, "That price is too high." "That's a terrible color."

- Ask for items that you don't need to be taken off the price. "I don't care about custom wheels, so take those off or reduce the price."
- When the seller goes to "talk to the manager," use the office phone to call other dealers. Call someone for advice. Use the salesperson's phone to call another dealer to see what they have on their lot. (Be aware of the strategy of them taking your keys to show your trade-in to the mechanics. The longer they get you to stay, the more invested in time you are to the deal. You can give them a time limit or have them set an appointment to see your car.)
- Don't share with the dealer your love of the car. Make it seem that you might be willing to settle for it, but you wished there was something better available.
- Have a friend call you on your cell phone and walk outside to take the call. Communicate that buying a car is only one of the many important things you have going on, and the dealer needs to keep your interest.
- Don't buy on your first visit; ideally, the seller will call you back.

---

card balances or loans simply by calling and asking for them. Those who avoid competition pay the asking price.

Offering the other the deal they offer you is an interesting competitive strategy that could be useful when the other party refuses to move from an unreasonable demand. Jacey and Darla have shared an apartment for two years but are now moving into separate homes. Darla argues that she should get to keep all the furniture and not have to do any cleaning; in exchange Jacey could keep all of the $500 deposit money. This is a good deal for Darla if it would cost more than $250 to replace the furniture, the cleaning is extensive, or getting a deposit refund is in doubt. The deal is not very good for Jacey, however. In response, Jacey could ask Darla if she thinks it is fair for one person to take all the furniture and not have to do any cleaning. If Darla says, yes, then Jacey could say, "OK, I'll take *that* deal. *I'll* take all the furniture; *you* do all the cleaning, and you can keep the deposit."

CASE 8.1 • *The Dance of Competitive Negotiation*

Applicant:	"I really need a starting salary of $50,000."
Interviewer:	"That's a bit out of our range."
Applicant:	"What figure did you have in mind?"
Interviewer:	"We were thinking in the range of the low $40s."
Applicant:	"That really is not enough for my qualification level. I couldn't consider anything less than $49,000."
Interviewer:	"We started our last applicant at $45,000."
Applicant:	"Wasn't that last year? My qualifications plus changes in the market really make this position at least a $48,000 starting rate."
Interviewer:	"Why don't we split the difference and start you at $46,500?"
Applicant:	"That's acceptable to me."

Applicant	Interviewer
$50,000	Low $40s
$49,000	$45,000
$48,000	$46,500

"You aren't paid what you're worth; you're paid what you can negotiate."

—Anonymous

Humor can be used to move the other from a fixed position. The humor can be minimal, such as laughing with a salesperson at a car's inflated sticker price. Humor also can be aggressive and mean-spirited, such as snickering at someone who stutters or laughing while challenging someone's credibility: "What would a college-kid like you know about business?" Humor can work to move parties to more reasonable offers, or humor can function to undermine someone's credibility and confidence. The ethics of purposefully hurting someone must be considered. However, regardless of how wrong it is, such attacks can be effective.

In negotiation, information is power. The side that has the most knowledge has an edge in competitive bargaining. *Doing your homework* may involve research on the Internet about competitive salaries, finding out about someone's financial position from friends, gleaning information from the other while not revealing much about yourself or your position, or knowing the organization's policies better than one's boss.

Boulwarism, named after former GE vice president Lemuel R. Boulware, announces a firm opening offer and the policy of refusing to bargain. Essentially, the Boulware strategy starts the negotiation with a take-it-or-leave-it offer. The other side has no opportunity to develop a negotiation strategy. An add-on to the Boulware strategy is *diminishing offers.* If the other party attempts to bargain after the take-it-or-leave-it statement is declared, the negotiator takes part of what was offered back off the table. A parent might say: "You can go out if you are back by midnight—take it or leave it!"

TABLE 8.3 *The Economic Impact of Gender Differences in Negotiation*

- "Women entrepreneurs launch at least 40 percent of new businesses, but get less than 10 percent of total investment dollars to work with" (Riley, 2001).
- "Women who negotiate for someone else will ask for 22 percent more than when they negotiate on their own behalf" (Riley, 2001).
- "Up to one-third of the differences in men and women's salaries result from men negotiating for more when first hired and women taking the initial salary offer" (Barron, 2003).
- "Those who negotiate salary receive an average of $1,500 more than those who don't" (O'Shea & Bush, 2002).
- "Seventy percent of men and 30 percent of women feel they are entitled to more salary than their peers" (Barron, 2003).

If the daughter tries to negotiate for 12:30 A.M., the mother's timetable would shrink. "OK, now the time is 11:45." Raiffa, Richardson, and Metcalfe (2002) comment, "The Boulware strategy of making a reasonable opening and holding firm works sometimes, but more often than not it antagonizes the other party" (p. 127). Assuming the daughter continues to try to negotiate the midnight curfew, Mom's winning the battle through Boulwarism may not be worth the increased anger and rancor that the thwarted teen brings to future family dynamics.

Threats and promises are overused in competitive bargaining. A *threat* is a statement that a negative sanction will occur if the other party does not comply. The manager may threaten that if production goals aren't met this week there will be no bonuses this month. To be credible, a threat must be within the power of the individual, the individual must be viewed as willing to carry through with the threat, and the threatened consequence must be seen as undesirable. A *warning* is a threat that the speaker does not have control over: "If you don't buy this car today, you'll regret it for the rest of your life." A *promise* is a statement that a positive reward will occur if the other party complies. "If you meet all your performance targets this year, you'll get a 20 percent salary bonus."

A common strategy of competitors is *acting obnoxiously persistent.* The strategy is to wear someone down by being persistent enough that the negotiator will give in just to get the offensive person to go away. A colleague once lost her airplane ticket. After asking two agents in the terminal for help, she was referred to the main check-in area, where she discovered a long line waiting for assistance. If she stood in line, her plane would leave without her. So she went to the middle of the crowded airport check-in area and loudly repeated over and over: "I've lost my tickets and nobody will help me. I'm going to miss my plane. Why won't anybody help me?" Soon an agent came over and took her aside to get her replacement ticket, and she made her flight.

> ### Discussion Question 8.5
> Identify examples when competitive negotiation is appropriate.

Coalitions occur when individuals join together to reach a goal that one person does not have enough resources or power to achieve. One student may talk so much that it fills class time with his or her personal questions and comments. When other students try to contribute, they may be unsuccessful in taking attention away from the student who is dominating the discussion. If several students join forces to complain to the professor, to support each other's comments, or to keep the stage-hogging student from doing all the talking, they are more likely to reach their goal. On a larger scale, unions are coalitions created to gain power and engage in collective bargaining.

Competitors seek to *frame the issue favorably to their side.* By controlling how the topic is phrased, a competitive advantage is acquired. If Sergio wants to have a party at the house, he can ask his roommates, "Who should we invite to a party Friday?" The frame assumes that they will host a party without asking his roommates for permission or agreement.

> "The inadequacies of traditional negotiations first surface in the preparation phase, which resembles a mobilization for war. Differences are accentuated, villains identified, weapons honed, war paint generously applied. The parties then arrive at the bargaining table in full battle dress. The focus tends to be on separate, or what are assumed to be, competing interests. The negotiations process resembles strategic retreat from exaggerated positions."
>
> —Stepp and Sweeney, 1998, paragraph 2

Competitors may make an offer and then demand concessions or enumerate several complaints in one session. If bargaining with someone with an avoidance or accommodating style, simply *demanding concessions* can be successful. Some competitors simply take resources as entitlements, as if they are socially superior and deserve more than anyone else. For example, an employee may demand a larger office because she's been at the company longer than anyone else. Related to demanding concession is the tactic of *downplaying what the other has to offer.* Even though you may like the color of a used car or covet the multiple CD changer, competitive-minded car buyers will claim to dislike the color or not care about the CD player and demand concessions on that basis saying, "The CD player is not a big deal to me so I'm not going to pay extra just because it's there."

Enumerating several complaints may make the negotiator's stance seem stronger than it really is. Related to enumeration is the tactic of gunnysacking, discussed briefly in Chapter 7. *Gunnysacking* occurs when someone avoids direct conflict but secretly keeps a list of grudges. At some point, the grievances become more than the person can bear, and all of the complaints are dumped on the other party in one giant heap. Strategic gunnysacking can be used as a basis to demand concessions.

Manipulation of pity, guilt, or flattery are used to persuade others to comply. **Compliance gaining** is the communication of tactics designed to induce the other to do one's will (see Table 8.4). "Won't you make me a grilled cheese sandwich? You make the best grilled cheese sandwiches." These requests apply flattery to cajole someone into performing a personal service. Teens commonly complain that parents attempt to gain compliance by making them feel guilty. "Your grandparents drove all this way to see you and you would rather go out with your friends tonight?" To get one's partner to quit watching TV and clean the house, saying, "Don't mind me. I've worked all day but I can clean up the kitchen, take out the garbage, and finish the laundry by myself" may induce the other to chip in. However, it could be met with attempt to create pity in return with a

TABLE 8.4 *Compliance-Gaining Strategies*

1. Actor responsibility: Stating a willingness to help others or work on the request personally. *"Can I help you finish the painting?"* *"Don't worry about cleaning the garage, I'll just do it."*
2. Altruism: Appealing to the other's basic goodness of heart. *"Please send money to help the victims of the tsunami."*
3. Altercasting (positive or negative): Claiming compliance will make the party a good person or noncompliance will make one a bad person. *"Helping your grandfather with the garden is what a loving grandchild would do."* *"Only a bully would threaten someone like that."*
4. Authority appeal: Using a power position as the basis for the request or demand. *"I'm the mother, that's why."*
5. Adverse stimulation: Continuing an undesired behavior until they comply. *"Dad, can I get the new Lego set? Please? Please? Can I? Huh? Come on. We can go to the store right now, can't we? Dad, pleeeease?"*
6. Challenge: Goading others into accepting the dare. *"I bet you can't drink two beers in three minutes."*
7. Criticize: Attacking the other personally. *"You're so cheap. You never take me anywhere."*
8. Debasement: Attacking one's own self-worth to encourage compliance out of pity. *"I'm just so stupid when it comes to math. I'm surprised they let me out of sixth grade. Could you help me with this problem?"*
9. Debt: calling in a favor or something owed. *"Remember when I covered your shift when you got sick? I'm just asking for you to step in for three hours on Saturday for me."*
10. Demanding: Commanding the other to act. *"Clean up your mess!"*
11. Disclaimer: Dismissing rules or constraints, downplaying the task, or dismissing the cost of compliance. *"I see the 'No Public Bathrooms' sign, but this is an emergency."* *"It's not that hot outside, so go mow the lawn."* *"You're not working today, so could you drive me to the mall?"*
12. Duty: Seeking compliance by reminding someone of their responsibilities. *"As a parent you need to watch your children more closely and not let them play in someone else's yard."*
13. Esteem (positive or negative): Seeking compliance by claiming they will be seen more positively/negatively if they comply. *"If you pay your bills on time, others will see you as a good credit risk; if you don't, you'll be seen as a deadbeat."*
14. Invoke norm: Seeking compliance by suggesting that they will be out of step with what everyone is doing if they don't comply. *"Nobody else has asked for a travel budget; why should you get one?"*
15. Logical empirical: Seeking compliance by appealing to reason or facts. *"The lease has only our names on it, so we can't let your friend move in."*
16. Moral appeal: Seeking compliance by claiming the action is the right/ethical thing to do. *"Don't use plastic bags because it is bad for the environment; get a cloth bag and reuse it."*
17. My concern for you: Seeking compliance by claiming one is looking out for their best interests. *"I'm worried that you're not making friends here, and we can't hang out together all the time. Join a club or something."*
18. Pregiving: Seeking compliance by giving a gift or positive action in advance. *"Enclosed in this letter you will find personalized mailing labels for you to use. Please consider sending us a donation."*
19. Promise: Seeking compliance by offering a later reward. *"If you give me the money for the movie, I'll wash your car when I get home."*
20. Self-feeling (positive or negative): Seeking compliance by claiming they will feel good/bad about themselves. *"I know you're tired, but you'll be happy that you went to the gym with me later."* *"You'll feel guilty if you don't call your sister on her birthday."*
21. Surveillance: Getting others to comply by informing them they are being or will be watched. *"Don't cheat. I've caught some of the best in my time."*
22. Threat: Seeking compliance by indicating a punishment awaits them if they don't comply. *"If you are late one more time, you will be fired."*

(continued)

TABLE 8.4   Continued

23. Warning: Seeking compliance by suggesting a negative consequence will occur if they don't comply. *"If you go out with a guy like that, he'll end up breaking your heart."*

24. Welfare (others): Seeking compliance by claiming others will be harmed otherwise. *"You'll hurt Grandma's feelings if you don't show up for Thanksgiving." "Your gift of only pennies a day makes it possible for children like Sophia to survive."*

25. Why not?: Seeking compliance by requiring them to justify not complying. *"Because you two are so committed to one another, why don't you just get married instead of live together?"*

26. Your concern for me: Seeking compliance by appealing to the other's regard for the person asking the request. *"If you really care about me and my future, you will quit smoking."*

Source: Adapted from Kellermann and Cole (1994).

reply of, "Sounds fair because I spent the whole afternoon cleaning the garage, and moving those boxes was exhausting." Table 8.4 summarizes several compliance-gaining strategies.

> "Liars share with those they deceive the desire not to be deceived. . . their choice to lie is one which they would like to reserve for themselves while insisting that others be honest."
>
> —Bok, 2004

> ### Discussion Question 8.6
>
> Are all lies created morally or ethically equal? Is it ethical to withhold certain information or offer only part of the picture when negotiating? Can any of the types of lies identified by Lewicki and Robinson be considered ethical? If so, under what circumstances?

Lies—whether by omission or outright deception—may be considered part of the game by some competitive negotiators. Lewicki and Robinson (2004) identified five clusters of lying during negotiation: misrepresentation of a position to an opponent, bluffing, falsification of information, deception, and selective disclosure. In their survey of MBA students, most lying tactics were considered unethical by the respondents. However, deceptive tactics considered acceptable during negotiation included asking around to gain information about the other's strategy, making an opening demand far greater than one expects to receive, hiding the real bottom line, and conveying a false impression that time is not an issue.

Competitors may manipulate the perception of concessions to build up future credit. If both participants perceive that a credit exists, one party can *call in the debt* during the next negotiation. The phrase "OK, but you owe me one" indicates that current goal achievement has been traded for an unknown future favor. If you accept a loan from a friend, the monetary debt may be leveraged to gain all sorts of other favors—lending your car, taking books back to the library, or doing the dishes more often. **Quid pro quo** literally means "something for something." If you help me; I'll help you. The negotiators trade items to reach a decision where both feel they have gained and lost equal value.

Asking questions without giving reciprocal information is another competitive tactic. Competitors may ask questions to discover information that will provide an advantage without sharing information that might help the opponent. A real estate agent may ask many questions to know how to appeal to a prospective buyer's emotions and needs: "How long do you plan to live in the area?" "Do you have pets?" "Do you like to cook or entertain?" "What ages are your children?" "Is this your first home purchase?" Later, the agent can appear to be your friend while using the information or highlighting certain aspects of various homes. If you have a young family, an agent can highlight nearby schools and bike paths. If you like entertaining, homes with large kitchens and decks are shown. A manipulative agent may say that homes are going fast, show several overpriced and problematic homes, and then take clients to the house that she wants to sell saying, "This one will probably be gone by this afternoon, so if you are interested in it, you'd better put in an offer today."

A final commonly used tactic is *tit for tat*. Negotiators do what is done to them—incremental move for incremental move, ridicule for ridicule, and so forth. The danger of tit for tat is creating a series of negative and dysfunctional tactics that spiral down into a hopeless deadlock. Two boys were arguing over Legos. When the biggest boy just grabbed the desired piece, the smaller boy took another ten pieces out of the larger boy's pile. Mutual name-calling and snatching of each other's stash ensued. The conflict escalated into mutual destruction of both building projects.

> ### Discussion Question 8.7
> Which competitive negotiation tactics are you most comfortable using? Which are you least comfortable using? Are there any you consider to be wholly unethical?

Cooperative Negotiation

The potential for negative impact of competitive negotiation on relationships and the probability that "losers" will not follow through enthusiastically with their agreements leads some competitors to search for alternatives. Cooperative negotiation, often called **mutual gains bargaining**, starts with the premise that it is possible for both parties to "win" most of what they need if the parties work together. A cooperative approach affords each person the opportunity to disclose real needs and to gain assistance in moving toward goals. Instead of automatically attempting to thwart the other's goal achievement, mutual gains negotiators look for ways for both to prosper. Cooperative strategies, however, are not without drawbacks. Unbridled cooperativeness could result in being taken advantage of by sneaky competitors. The competitor might encourage the naive cooperator to create better outcomes (add value) and then capture the majority of what was on the table (take value) (see Foo, Elfenbein, & Aik, 2004).

The Collaborative Mindset

Because competitive bargaining is so entrenched in European American culture, it may take some preparation and thoughtfulness to engage in cooperative bargaining. *Physical and psychological space* affects how people feel and how they behave. Sitting across from each other at a formal table invites debate, argument, and competition. Creating a more relaxed physical space may invite a more relaxed negotiation style. Symbolic gestures of engaging in some conversation before jumping into negotiation (called *schmoozing* in the business world) may thaw a tense situation. A family who bakes some cookies and then sits down to discuss vacation plans with all the electronic devices turned off may have more success than the family who broaches the subject while riding in their car. Bargainers who schmooze and engage in social chitchat sometimes reach superior solutions, in part because they discover social cues that more task-oriented negotiators miss and develop interpersonal linkages that make discovering the other's interests possible.

Mutual gains negotiators understand the difference between *interests* (underlying needs) and *positions* (demands that conceal needs). By focusing on interests, all parties might have their needs met. At the grocery store a cashier repeatedly propped open a door to avoid the overpowering smell from a scented product placed by her checkout stand. The clerk at the customer service desk, seeing the door open, repeatedly closed the door because she was cold. The conflict, however, was expressed through positions: "I want the door open," and "I want the door closed." Because the underlying needs were not disclosed (avoiding the smell and being warm), creative or mutually satisfactory solutions never had a chance to emerge.

To negotiate collaboratively, two basic elements must occur: The negotiator must consider the other person's needs and give up the notion that personal ideas automatically are the best. As Cooley (2005) states, "The need to be right all the time is the greatest barrier to new ideas" (p. 11). Therefore, collaboration must start with a suspension of judgment about what the exact outcome will be. Collaborative negotiators must live with some uncertainty and ambiguity while searching for a mutually satisfactory outcome.

Instead of the "my way" versus "your way" tussle of competitive negotiation, collaborators join together against a mutual problem. A competitor might say, "You drive the car to work most days, so I get it today." A collaborator might frame the negotiation opening differently and say, "I need to go to the bank this afternoon and you need to get to work. How can we work this out when we only have one car?" The problem to be solved is separated from the individuals in the negotiation, and psychologically, the other person is not forced to defend a position.

KEY 8.2

The initial framing of the negotiation can create either a competitive or a cooperative climate.

Preparing for Collaborative Negotiation

When possible, mutual gains negotiators prepare for negotiation in advance, including analyzing each person's interests. Toolbox 8.2 presents the steps in mutual gains negotiation preparation. Selecting a time and place that is private and comfortable for both individuals may encourage more mutual gains thinking. After studying the needs of both parties and the emotions or fears that might hinder the negotiation, the negotiator considers how to begin. Sometimes, a comment that both could benefit if they worked together on a solution will help create a cooperative frame and establish an overarching goal. A couple who begins a discussion about finances with an affirmation of their commitment to each other and to making decisions based on what's best for "the team" may find the discussion of money goes more smoothly.

TOOLBOX 8.2

Preparing to Negotiate Cooperatively

1. Research the facts and the situation: Do your homework!
2. Analyze both parties (goals, needs, and fears).
3. Consider strategically how to frame the negotiation.
4. Consider introducing mutual gains bargaining to the other party.
5. Listen and validate the other's needs and fears (as necessary).
6. Ask open-ended questions, particularly those designed to uncover interests.
7. Comment about commonalities.
8. Reframe the issue as something both parties share.
9. Look creatively for mutually beneficial outcomes that meet each party's interests.

Instead of starting the negotiation competitively with a demand, the negotiation might be framed at the beginning with a question. Students who anticipate conflict while negotiating a group project topic might start with the question: "What do we all want to get out of doing this group project?" As each person answers, underlying interests and expectations will emerge. Asking questions and listening to each other's answers provides information. Several may only be interested in a good grade. One may want to do something that might lead to an internship placement. Another may just want it not to take up much time or have the project cost any money. With an awareness of everyone's interests, the group is more likely to choose a mutually beneficial topic than if they fought over whose favorite topic would win selection. If someone is distraught at the slightest chance of receiving a mediocre grade on the project, another group member can highlight the interest by saying, "So the grade is the most important thing for you," letting the person know that the concern has been heard and giving voice to that concern for the rest of the group to hear.

One published account itemizes how even a trained conflict manager went astray during negotiations when preparation was not sufficient. A professional mediator confronted a neighbor about his barking dogs.

> My first step, prior to the actual conversations with my neighbor, was defining my interests. In retrospect, this stage of the negotiation was woefully inadequate. I had focused solely on my need for a quieter atmosphere, and though I intended to use a friendly tone in our conversation, I chose a strategy of honesty and openness, even bluntness if necessary. . . . In so doing, I failed to consider the prominence of my other main interest, that of having friendly ongoing relations with my neighbors. As a result of choosing a competitive, rather than collaborative, approach to our negotiations, my ability to preserve the relationship was compromised. (Stringer, 2006, p. 35)

By forgetting his neighbor's fears and interests, he bypassed the critical other half of the conversation and turned what could have been a cooperative discussion into a competitive interaction. The negotiation was engaged by knocking on his neighbor's door and demanding that a new fence be built to stop the barking. Surprising the neighbor with the issue was confrontational, and the opening frame of the negotiation set a competitive tone. By beginning the negotiation with his own preferred solution (position) for the barking dogs, the neighbor was denied a chance to think about the problem and to be drawn into the negotiation or motivated to look for a long-term solution. The dog owner was, unsurprisingly, defensive and angry. The bottom line: Planning matters.

KEY 8.3

Advanced planning improves negotiation.

Cooperative Negotiation Tactics

Several collaborative tactics flow from earlier discussions: searching for interests, preparing a physical and psychological space, and listening. This section focuses on the tactics in Table 8.5.

Identifying commonalities is helpful, if not crucial, during mutual gains negotiation. A **commonality** is any trait, attitude, goal, need, or fear shared by the negotiators. Identifying and verbalizing commonalities helps the parties see their similarities instead of allowing differences to shape the negotiation. After talking about what each person's goals are for a group project, one member may summarize, "We all need to have something to turn in on the due date, and all of us are concerned about our grade."

Reframing is useful during negotiation to keep the discussion on productive problem solving. If one person jumps ahead in the process and advances a position, "So let's host a poker tournament and give the proceeds to the Red Cross," another group member might reframe: "Let's look for an event for our project that best meets all of our needs." Reframing also can focus on issues instead of attacks. For example, if a group member responds to the suggestion of critiquing a movie with, "I'm not doing another lame project where we analyze some movie and wind up with a bad grade," another student might reframe away from the attack and toward a central issue: "The project needs to be significant enough to warrant a really high grade."

TABLE 8.5   *Collaborative Negotiation Tactics*

Identifying commonalities and interests
Reframing
Suspending judgment
Applying creativity
Brainstorming
Challenging the status quo
Dueling lists
Magic wand
Asking questions
Giving information
Putting more than one option on the table at a time
Something now for something later
Changing the size of the issue
Focusing on the future
Patience

Mutual gains negotiators must learn to *suspend judgment.* They must accept some uncertainty about the exact outcome. They then frame the issue as a mutual problem; that is, they phrase the problem in a way that everyone can join together in finding a mutually beneficial solution. Case 8.2 illustrates some cooperative strategies for a salary negotiation.

Another key to collaboration is bringing some *creativity* to the situation. If conflict managers and negotiators think there is only one best solution (obviously the one that "I" thought of), then there is no need for creativity. Once the possibility of other ideas enters the scene, creativity is needed to discover other potential solutions. *Brainstorming* is a technique to spur creativity and generate ideas that might solve the issue while meeting each party's needs. The cooperative negotiator may need to teach the basic format for brainstorming to the other party (see Toolbox 8.3).

Other creative techniques include challenging the status quo, dueling list creation, and magic wand questions. During conflicts, starting from the current situation and assuming that what was done in the past should be done in the future is the easiest route, but is it the best path? Just because one partner always has taken the car in the past doesn't mean that it might not make sense for both individuals to take the subway to work and leave the car at home. Just because a family always has taken a one-week vacation in the summer with the negotiation centering on where to go doesn't mean that other creative options might not be more desirable—if allowed into the conversation. Maybe three long weekend vacations would better meet their needs. Asking questions about assumptions is a powerful negotiation tactic in *challenging the status quo.*

The *dueling lists technique* has each individual make a long list of possible solutions. For example, a couple can each create a list of places to go on vacation. Then the two examine the lists to find common ideas that might lead to a mutual solution. If one lists Cancún and the other Mazatlán, they can talk about their common interest in going to a warm place with a beach and lots of parties.

To use the *magic wand technique,* ask, "What would you really need if you could wave a magic wand and get the outcome that would make you the happiest?" Then state your own magic wand outcome. It sometimes is easier to discuss basic needs and to gain a greater understanding of each other through an idealized viewpoint (Creo, 2005). Questions are asked such as: "What is your idea of a good neighbor?" "What type of communication with coworkers is ideal for you?"

In some respect, mutual gains bargainers rely on two key skills: *asking questions* and *giving information.* Questions are asked to elicit information. If one party has key information

---

TOOLBOX 8.3

Introducing Brainstorming

"Let's see if we can generate some other ideas using brainstorming. What we do is make a list of all the ideas we can think of, even wild and crazy ones. To keep the creative juices flowing, we need to help each other keep from criticizing ideas as they come out; we can do that later. Do you want to try this for five minutes to see what happens?"

CASE 8.2 • *The Creativity of Cooperative Negotiation*

Applicant:	"I really need a starting salary of $50,000."
Interviewer:	"That's a bit out of our range."
Applicant:	"What figure did you have in mind?"
Interviewer:	"We were thinking in the range of the low $40's."
Applicant:	"That really is not enough for my qualification level. I couldn't consider anything less than $49,000."
Interviewer:	"I don't have that much in my budget."
Applicant:	"What other incentives do you have to offer?"
Interviewer:	"Well, we could start you at $45,000 with a review for your first pay increase after six months."
Applicant:	"That sounds promising. How about $46,000, add a onetime signing bonus of $5,000, and pay for my moving expenses?"
Interviewer:	"We could offer $2,000 in dedicated training or travel funds but not as a cash signing bonus. We could pay moving expenses up to $2,000. I also could put you in an office that faces the river."
Applicant:	"I can see that you have some budget restraints, but this is a workable package for me."

Applicant	*Interviewer*
$50,000	Low $40s
$49,000	$45,000 with 6-month review
$46,000 with 6-month review	$46,000 with 6-month review
$5,000 signing bonus	$2,000 in training and travel
Moving expenses	$2,000 Moving expenses
	Office with a view

that the other lacks, the information is shared so a better solution can be crafted. Questions can be asked about assumptions and traditions to see if there are good reasons for them.

Asking a question about tradition can start a conversation about how individuals, groups, or organizations change over time: "Does the way we've always done this task still meet all of our needs today?" Rather than attacking the ways things are, such as "That's a stupid way to write an agenda," ask, "How does this agenda format help organize our meeting?" By keeping the question focused on interests (the agenda) instead of on people ("your stupid agenda"), face goals are less likely to be threatened.

Discussion Question 8.8

Which collaborative tactics are you the most/least comfortable using? Identify examples when cooperative negotiation is appropriate. What cooperative negotiation tactics would be the most effective in each example?

Meiners and Miller (2004) identify *sharing information* as one of the key characteristics of cooperative negotiation between supervisors and subordinates. They identify three types of information sharing: elaboration, directness, and mutual concessions. The amount of information that is shared is called *elaboration*. The more information is exchanged, the greater the possibility of creative solutions. *Directness* refers to the clearness and openness of the negotiators about their goals and interests. *Mutual concessions,* or a give-and-take exchange, indicates flexibility. Mutual concessions work best when several issues are negotiated at the same time. In the same study, employed undergraduate college students found cooperative negotiation was more likely to occur when the situation was formal than in spontaneous situations—indicating a need to prepare for negotiations in advance if one wishes to use cooperative tactics. Similarly, students using a casual and friendly tone were more successful at integrative negotiation than those using a more impersonal approach.

Another tactic of mutual gains negotiation is to *put more than one option on the table at a time.* Typically, several negotiation steps are involved in buying a car: the new car price, the trade-in value, warranty extension, interest rates, car features, or extras. The savvy purchaser makes each section of the negotiation contingent on the outcome of the other items. Once you state you will buy the new car at an agreed-upon price, the incentive to cooperate in good faith on the other negotiation items is lessened for the seller. By keeping the final purchase decision open, the incentive to think creatively about the next negotiation item is maintained. Because the price of the car was higher than anticipated, the buyer may expect more on the trade-in, a lower interest rate, and/or items added to sweeten the deal— for example, a radio upgrade or free oil changes for a year. Having several items in play at the same time also allows for the option of trading across items.

Mutual gains negotiators can bring time into the negotiation. *Something now for something later trades* can be advantageous. Instead of fighting competitively to control which movie is seen tonight, a couple can widen the frame of the negotiation and decide what choices will be made over the next three or four times they go out. An employee negotiating for a raise may request for more frequent evaluations (quarterly instead of yearly) to increase opportunities for raises when denied a big raise immediately.

If negotiations falter, consider *changing the size of the issue.* If the issue seems too overwhelming, **fractionate** it by breaking it down into smaller parts. If negotiation about the house not being clean becomes defensive, focus on smaller parts of the larger issue: Which roommate will do the dishes, who will sweep the floor, and who will do the laundry? If two roommates gang up on a third about not picking up the house, enlarge the issue to overall workload in taking care of the house so everyone's duties are put on the table for consideration and each person's responsibilities become clear.

A trademark tactic of mutual gains negotiation is *focusing on the future*—how to get out of the conflict—more than on the past causes of the situation. Simply stating that one is more interested in how two parties will act toward each other in the future than on past grievances sometimes can change the frame of a negotiation from defensive to more cooperative. Neighbors who have had a tense relationship may both desire more congeniality in the future. The goal to get along helps frame the negotiations in the present and the future rather than in the past. For example, a neighbor might say, "Chances are we're going to be living next door to each other for years. Let's try to figure out a way that we can have a good relationship and move beyond our past differences."

A final, important tactical consideration for mutual gains negotiators is *patience*. Working with someone takes longer than making decisions like a dictator. Finding about others' needs and bringing creativity to a situation takes thought and energy. Living with

---

TOOLBOX 8.4

Negotiation Worksheet

Issue: _____

Where am I coming from on this negotiation?

    Needs: _____

        Fears: _____

Where is the other negotiator coming from?

    Needs: _____

        Fears: _____

What are the obstacles to working out a solution?

    My obstacles _____

        The other's obstacles _____

---

some ambiguity about the final outcome can be stressful. Controlling impatience is necessary for mutual gains bargaining to have time to work.

Negotiators have a philosophical and tactical choice about the process of negotiation. Where competitive bargainers focus on difference, mutual gains bargainers focus on similarity. Competitive negotiators fight for their share in a world of scarcity, whereas mutual gains bargainers live in a world of potential abundance. The way the negotiation tactics function in competitive and cooperative perspectives is quite different, as are the consequences to continuing relationships.

> **Discussion Question 8.9**
>
> As you turn in your first short essay in a class, you realize that the second essay is due the next week. You probably won't get the first paper back before the second paper is due and would like to renegotiate the due date. Because the instructor has the power to say "No" to the request, how can you phrase the issue to appeal to the instructor's interests and move toward cooperative negotiation?

Moving from Competitive to Collaborative

Collaborative bargaining is not easy. Kolb and Williams (2003) comment, "Bargainers don't naturally trust each other. They worry that in revealing too much they will give the other person an edge . . . It takes work to change the perceptions that people bring to negotiation and to cultivate a climate of openness and mutual respect. It takes work to keep a dialogue going when the other party's only inclination is to put demands on the table and press for a deal. It takes work to get everyone to own his or her part of the problem" (pp. 236–237). Although collaboration is more labor intensive, the payoffs for improved outcomes makes the effort worthwhile in many cases.

A negotiator may, in good faith, attempt cooperative tactics, only to be rebuffed by a competitive negotiator. Some research suggests that individual disposition and style directly relate to a party's willingness to use nonconfrontational problem-solving strategies and to avoid verbal aggression (Rogan & La France, 2003), but scholars do not believe that style or disposition automatically determine what will occur. People can opt to make other choices, and, with time and effort, they can change their approach.

> "The clever thing to do is not to let the negotiation drift toward two mutually exclusive alternatives—your way or my way."
>
> —Management expert Mary Parker Follett

To make a transition from competitive to a more mutual gains approach, a negotiator must have some degree of trust. He or she must believe cooperation can lead to goal achievement. Table 8.6 summarizes specific tactics useful in persuading a competitive individual to try mutual gains negotiation.

Tactics to Move Competitors to Collaboration

Some techniques to move toward mutual gains were discussed in the cooperative section: highlighting commonalities and focusing on interests. Collaborative techniques of recognizing positions and asking questions to uncover the underlying interest are key in creating cooperative interactions. For example, "You've said that you'd like to be the leader on this project. What is it about the leadership position that attracts you?" Some competitors, once they understand that more than one person's goals can be achieved simultaneously, may no longer feel compelled to seek a decisive personal victory.

TABLE 8.6 *Moving from Competition to Cooperative Bargaining*

Selecting the right channel of communication
Metacommunicating
Reality checking
Bringing the relationship into the decision
Reformed sinner
Mirroring
Rewriting the past
Apologizing
Fogging
Common fact finding
Postponing
Setting criteria
Adding humor
Asking for help
Engaging in negotiation judo

One method of moving toward collaboration involves *selecting the right channel of communication.* Written channels, such as e-mail or text messaging, are less personal than telephone conversations; phone conversations are less personal than face-to-face interaction. The less personal the channel, the easier it is to compete. One option when seeking to change the style of negotiation is to move to a more personal channel.

Metacommunication—talking about negotiation process, styles, and tactics—can be useful. Metacommunication acknowledges that individuals disagree. For example, when a competitor continues to repeat a position over and over with increasing frustration, the other might say, "I know sometimes people keep repeating the same thing because they think the other person doesn't understand what they are saying. I think I do understand what you are saying but simply don't think we are limited to that option. What I understand your concern to be is _____. Is that what you are saying?"

For some diehard competitors, more direct techniques may be necessary to persuade them to give mutual gains a try. A *reality check* probes the value of winning what the competitor has demanded. For example, "It sounds like the path we are on now would result in both of us not getting what we really want. Is there a way we can work around that and find a solution that better meets both our needs?" "If we give you what you want and you become the leader of the group, are you willing to do all the planning, organizing, and work that is required in the position?" "Do you still want to buy a new plasma TV knowing that it will put our ability to pay for school next semester at risk?" If it is an important relationship, a partner or friend may be more willing to consider other options once the reality of the *impact on the relationship* is brought to the surface. "I know you want your sister to stay with us, but you know she disapproves of my religion and comments on it often, causing a lot of tension between us. Perhaps you can encourage her to stay in a hotel when she visits for the weekend if we pay for part of it?"

Another tactic to move a competitor toward cooperative bargaining is called the **reformed sinner** strategy. In this technique, initially one competes, then switches to cooperation—showing that he or she could compete and win if desired (Folger et al., 2005). Sometimes proving that one won't give in is necessary. Ingrid heard through the company grapevine that her counterpart, Fred, in another division was a hard bargainer and ran over people he thought weak, particularly women. When Ingrid and Fred met to work out details on a project, Ingrid chose to start with hard competitive tactics and demanded that Fred's crew meet her schedule. Fred responded with his usual competitive style. Ingrid continued to use competitive tactics and restated her demands. Once an impasse was reached, she used a common goals statement and reality checking to move toward collaboration: "Well, we're both stuck, and at this rate neither one of us will get our projects done. We're both professionals; let's find a compromise where neither of us gets hurt too badly."

Stating a willingness to fight may motivate the other to consider collaboration as a way of getting a beneficial outcome. A colleague used this technique to get a manager to renegotiate a decision by saying, "Look, I don't want to go through the hassle of filing a grievance—that wouldn't be good for our continued relationship or the department, but this is important. I'm confident we can work this out between us." By mentioning a possible grievance, the manager was aware that the employee knew the system and was willing to bump the issue to the next level. Ultimately the two negotiated a mutually acceptable agreement. If a degree of trust exists, this tactic can lead to more creative negotiation. If it is perceived as a threat, competition may ensue.

Mirroring tactics can demonstrate that a negotiator understands competition and won't give in if the other insists on hard bargaining. Until the negotiator shows the ability to win competitively, the diehard competitor may persist in the mistaken assumption that the one who prefers mutual gains will eventually just wear down and give in. When Fred and Ingrid met, he spoke loudly and pounded on the table. If she used mirroring, Ingrid would also speak more forcefully and likewise pound on the table to demonstrate her point. After both parties briefly demonstrated their mastery of competitive skills, they were able to move toward more collaborative processes. Both know that there would not be an easy victory over the other.

If there are hard feelings from the past, *rewriting the past* may be necessary. One negotiator would express regret about past behaviors and a desire to find a better way (Reese & McCorkle, 2005). Offering an apology for past behavior can be a powerful negotiation technique. If hurt feelings were blocking the negotiation, an apology may lead to a significant concessions from the other negotiator or allow a relationship to be rebuilt. If Ingrid unsuccessfully tried competitive tactics with Fred, she might use rewriting and apology tactics to get through the resulting impasse. "Fred, I'm sorry we got off on the wrong foot in our meeting. I've been so focused on my own unit's needs that I've missed some opportunities for us to work together on this. If I had it do over again, I would have spent some time learning more about your department's needs. Can we start over?"

> ### Discussion Question 8.10
> Which tactics to transition to mutual gains would you be most/least likely to use?

Fogging is a technique to take some of the steam out of a competitor's words and create opportunities for change. For example, if the other negotiator uses negative criticism, sort through the comments for items that are true but irrelevant. If the criticism is true but not relevant, simply agree with it. Next, reframe the issue to a problem-solving frame. If an angry student accuses a group member of just caring about taking notes on everything, the accused could refuse to take the bait or to become defensive. The criticized student might agree with what is true and ignore the negative implications: "True, I am very thorough in keeping a good record for the group. What challenges do we all see in getting the project done?"

If the conflict centers around whose facts are correct, instead of deadlocking on an "is so/is not" argument, suggest looking up the facts together. *Common fact finding* clears the air—in a cooperative way—and may help build a better relationship. Jerry and Raoul differ on which topic to pick for a group project. Jerry is convinced that his idea for a poker tournament to raise money for a charity would work; Raoul is sure that state laws prohibit gambling, even for charity. Instead of just disagreeing more and more loudly, Raoul could suggest they use a speakerphone together and call the state attorney general's office and find out if their plan is legal.

Postponement, or time-outs, are effective to let one or both parties cool down when tempers are hot. It might be advisable to say, "I think we will both have a better outcome we take a few minutes off before we say something we'll both regret later." This strategy is effective only if there is trust that the parties actually will return to the negotiation table. Setting a time to return to the discussion can make this option more attractive to someone who doesn't want to quit for fear of being ignored. Saying, "Let's plan to come back at 1 o'clock, after lunch, so we can think about how we want to proceed" can assure the other that the issue will be discussed further after a time-out.

Focusing on criteria that any good outcome would have for both people creates a more cooperative frame. If the other party probably will come to the table with a competitive demand, start the discussion by saying, "I know we both have specific ideas that we think will work, but I'd like us to start by thinking about what an outcome might look like that would be good for both of us." Continue to ignore positional statements that might creep into the discussion until mutually agreeable criteria are created. Melanie put an ad in the paper to sell her car for $7,200. The prospective buyer offered $6,500. Rather than focus on the price, which would engage the dance of competitive negotiation, Melanie focused on criteria. When the buyer made the lower offer, Melanie asked, "How did you come up with that amount?" The buyer replied, "It seemed about right." Melanie responded, "Well, we are both looking for a fair deal at the right price. Why don't I show you how I came up with $7,200, and you can decide if what I'm asking is fair." After looking at her comparables and data, the buyer paid the asking price because she felt that the criteria of a fair outcome were met.

For some, *humor* is a technique to overcome competitiveness. A few people nonverbally stiffen their posture and puff up before making a particularly outrageous demand. Among friends who recognize the pattern and metacommunicate about it in advance, laughing may be the best reaction during the puffing-up stage before the outrageous demand reaches the air. Other demands can be treated humorously instead of seriously to keep the competitive tone from taking command of the situation. When supervisors are negotiating their share of budget increases, one may demand 100 percent of the increase. A colleague could reply with good-humored laugh and say, "That would be great, wouldn't it! No, really, what are your department's expectations for your share of the increase?" Shared humor builds commonality. Mistaken humor, however, causes more divisiveness. Humor requires extreme social sensitivity and can be dangerous if not done well. Laughing with people is different than laughing at them.

Asking for help may seem like an odd tactic to persuade someone toward mutual gains negotiation. The request is an attempt to engage the other person and build mutual ownership of the problem. If used at the outset, a request for help in solving the problem may be seen as a sign of weakness or bargaining inadequacy. If used after some trust is established, the tactic may meet with more success. In determining departmental budgets, one manager may say to the other, "Help me out with some advice. How much do you allot for travel in your budget?" Asking for help can change the other person's view of their role in the conversation from opponent to adviser.

Finally, *negotiation judo* can build a better climate by ignoring criticism, attacks, and outrageous demands. When occasional criticism or negative comments occur (if not outside the boundaries of acceptance), the negotiator does not respond. Instead of becoming defensive, focus is maintained on the issue. Techniques such as emotional paraphrasing or reframing can be used. Thomas Crum's 1987 book, *The Magic of Conflict,* explains how conflict management is like the martial art of aikido: If someone is centered and has good self-esteem, other people's attacks do not hurt as much, and in fact, their negative energy can be channeled into more productive paths. For example, during a heated discussion Jessie slams her notebook down in frustration. Curtis can use that energy and say, "The frustration in here is high and that is because we are both passionate about doing what's best for our departments. What a boring place this would be if neither of us cared, wouldn't it?" Turning high frustration into positive energy can move parties to more positive interactions.

Summary

People negotiate every day. Negotiation is communication in pursuit of goal achievement. Four conditions are necessary for negotiation to occur: a meaningful connection, outcome unpredictability, issues other than values, and a willingness to communicate.

Negotiation can be categorized as either competitive or cooperative. Competitive negotiation can be destructive if it degenerates to face issues, the winner's curse occurs, or personal victory is sought at all costs. Of the numerous competitive bargaining tactics, some are more constructive than others.

Cooperative negotiators search for a mutually satisfactory outcome for all. Focusing on interests instead of positions is a key skill. Preparing for collaborative negotiation entails several steps and consideration of a different set of tactics. Moving a negotiation partner from competition to cooperation can be difficult, but it is possible through the use of several specialized tactics.

Chapter Resources

Exercises

1. In the following cases, consider the steps in preparing to negotiate competitively versus preparing to negotiate cooperatively.

Case One

You have been concerned that one of your work team members, "Travis/Teressa," is not carrying his or her weight on projects. Travis/Teressa has been late in getting the data to you that you need and has started avoiding you. You need the data each week by Wednesday noon if you are to be able to submit your report to the director by Friday noon.

Case Two

You need to have every Friday afternoon off to take your child to music lessons. You have asked your boss to alter your schedule, but he or she just laughed and said "No" before you had a chance to give your reasons.

Case Three

You can't stand that your colleague in the next office "holds court" every morning for an hour with other coworkers and the administrative assistants. They review everyone's personal life and their favorite cable programs. You are planning to do something about the situation and will talk to your coworker tomorrow.

Case Four

You have several tests on the same day. You want to ask your instructor to allow you to take the test in this class at a different time.

2. Use the Negotiation Worksheet (Toolbox 8.4) to speculate about each person's interests in the cases in exercise 1.

3. Discuss the lessons you learned or messages you received about negotiation from your family as you were growing up. Were the lessons and messages you received more competitive or cooperative?

4. As a group, select a televised drama program. Record an episode of your chosen program and analyze the specific negotiation tactics that are used by the characters. Are most of the tactics more competitive or cooperative?

5. Compare Cases 8.1 and 8.2. What specific tactics are used in each case?

Journal/Essay Topics

1. Create and implement a plan for one of the situations provided. Write a one-page report on your "plan" and its effectiveness.
    A. If your credit is good, call your credit card company and ask that your interest rate be lowered on any outstanding balance.
    B. If you have been employed at the same place for over a year without a raise and your work record is good, ask your boss for a raise.
    C. If purchasing a product over $50 at a small store or market, negotiate the price.

2. Reflect on a specific past negotiation that was markedly successful or unsuccessful. What tactics did you employ?

Research Topic

Review the published research that highlights the differences in negotiation by two specific cultures or subcultures. What advice would you give to individuals entering negotiation with either of those cultures?

Mastery Case

Analyze Mastery Case 8, "The Self-Mediated Divorce." Which concept from this chapter best explains what is happening in the case?

The Self-Mediated Divorce

Gabrielle and Jacques were married for over twenty years when, after too many fights and other circumstances, they decided to divorce. Believing they could work out the details without attorneys, they decided to negotiate the divorce themselves. Jacques was a successful business-man who owned a construction company, and Gabrielle was a retail manager for a department store. Jacques moved into a new apartment leaving Gabrielle the house.

It was clear to Gabrielle from the beginning that these conversations were going to be difficult. Jacques was a practiced negotiator. Gabrielle was adept at collaborative interactions and determined to make these negotiations inter-est based.

Over several months, Jacques became more locked in extreme positions, and Gabrielle kept trying to meet her needs while moving closer to his demands. It seemed the more information she shared, the more that Jacques used that information to make demands that met his goals instead of hers.

Finally, after a particularly frustrating con-versation, Gabrielle exclaimed loudly, "Look. I'm at the point where I'm ready to hire a bulldog attorney to get everything I can get. I've even got a some names that my friends have given me. I've been trying to meet you halfway and you keep moving the mark closer to you. I'm at the point that if I lose more by going to court, I'm OK with that. It beats talking to you about it."

Jacques, surprised by Gabriele's willing-ness to play hardball, backed off from using extreme tactics. Negotiations were still difficult, but they did come to a resolution together that met their needs.

9

Conflict Assessment

Vocabulary

Clusters of Conflict tool	Conflict Road Map	Metaphor
Comprehensive Conflict	Critical choice points	Mulling
Checklist	Imagined interaction	Negotiation Analysis Grid
Conflict assessment	Interactive Conflict Map	

Objectives

After reading the chapter, you should be able to:

1. Explain the usefulness of conflict analysis
2. Understand the focus of different conflict analysis tools
3. Apply a conflict analysis tool to a personal conflict

Understanding Conflict from the Inside Out

Conflict involves many factors: the relationship of the parties to each other, the context of the conflict, precipitating events, personal styles, power resources, personal histories, and much more. People find themselves in conflict and wonder, "How did I get here?" "What is really going on?" and "How can we move forward?"

The ability to analyze conflict allows insights that may escape the participants in the heat of an interaction. **Conflict assessment** involves taking a step back to evaluate the many factors that led to this moment. Through analysis, conflict managers can make informed decisions and purposeful moves to foster a goal of productively managing the conflict situation.

The basic building blocks to understand conflict are interests and goals. In many ways, analysis of interpersonal conflict is all about self- and other-awareness. Self-awareness requires the courage to ask tough questions and to give honest answers.

CASE 9.1 • *Dress Codes*

Kaitlin and William dated for months before recently moving in together. Sometimes William is uncomfortable when other men look at Kaitlin because she likes to wear low-cut blouses and tight jeans. William has asked Kaitlin to tone down her wardrobe. She said she understood, but she needed to be herself. One day, William confronted Kaitlin when she dressed for their night out.

William: "You've got to be kidding. You're not wearing *that*."

Kaitlin: "What do you mean?"

William: "You look like a cheap hooker."

Kaitlin: "A hooker? Are you kidding me?"

William: "I thought you said you'd tone down your clothes. What were you thinking when you put that on? Do you want everyone to stare at your chest all night?"

Kaitlin: "I thought I would wear what I wanted and I don't care what other people think. You used to like this outfit when we first met. I can't believe you are so judgmental and mean!"

William: "Hey, I'm just telling you what everybody is thinking. You look like a hooker."

Kaitlin: "So you want me to change and that will shut you up?"

William: "Hey, I don't really care. I'm just not going out with you looking like that."

Kaitlin: "You're assuming that I still want to go with you."

The tandem requirement is an ability to move beyond self-centered attributions about the other person's motives by making informed inferences. The level of awareness, maturity, and desire of the parties involved is critical in the successful analysis of a conflict episode. This is not an easy task. Successful analysis requires both experiencing the conflict and stepping outside of it while it is happening. Using a model of conflict interaction requires parties to coordinate their discussion, moderate their emotions, and channel energies into purposeful and goal-focused interactions. However, although difficult to do, conflict assessment can bring about greater clarification, improved interactions, and relational growth. In short, the effort is worth the work.

Analyzing current conflicts can help determine the best strategies to meet the goals of the parties. However, it is useful to scrutinize a past conflict to learn from personal history as a route to escape destructive patterns in the future. The benefits of conflict analysis include: an opportunity to build a better understanding of a conflict, to learn from past mistakes, and to reflect on productive choices rather than responses from habit.

This chapter discusses some ways to analyze and learn from the past so future conflicts can be managed more productively. It also presents several choices to guide conflict analysis (Table 9.1). First-level tools are easier to apply and include the Clusters of Conflict tool and Mapping. The next section presents tools for more comprehensive analysis: The Comprehensive Conflict Checklist, the Conflict Road Map, and Interactive Conflict Analysis. A third section presents analysis tools based on specific concepts, including Metaphor Analysis, The Negotiation Grid, and the Imagined Interaction. Finally, we encourage you to create your own tools for conflict analysis.

Conflict Assessment: First Level Tools

Clusters of Conflict

Mayer's Wheel of Conflict is the basis of the first assessment tool discussed in this chapter (adapted from Furlong, 2005; Moore, 2003). According to Mayer (2000), one or more of five clusters cause conflict: communication, emotions, values, structure, and history. Which cluster a conflict primarily resides in matters because, according to Mayer, the initial actions taken to change a conflict differ for each cluster. The questions in Toolbox 9.1 help identify where a conflict resides.

The strategies to transform the conflict from destructive to productive vary depending on the cause of the conflict. If the conflict is about one person having different information than the other (communication), then conflict transformation starts with a focus on information: who has it, is it different, how can the individuals reach agreement about which information to use? If the conflict falls mainly into the value area, such as whether unmarried couples should live together, then more information probably won't be helpful. Strategies to bring shared values to the surface, to create commonality, or to agree to disagree are paths to conflict transformation.

For William and Kaitlin, the parties in Case 9.1, the heart of the conflict could reside in several portions of the Wheel of Conflict. Conflict located in the *communication* section centers around the negotiation of meaning and creating a common framework for discussion.

> ### Discussion Question 9.1
> In Case 9.1, what parts of their communication are open to interpretation? For example, what does it mean to "tone down" wardrobe choices?

Kaitlin and William most certainly have strong emotions associated with this conflict interaction. Conflict arising from the *emotion* area is focused on the feelings each participant has and how they react to hurt or embarrassment.

> ### Discussion Question 9.2
> How did William feel about Kaitlin's attire at different points in their relationship? What emotions become apparent for each of them as their relationship progressed?

Value conflicts are the most difficult to resolve because they require the exploration of underlying beliefs, cultural influences, and deeply seated views of how the world should operate. Values may come into play as each person determines what "appropriate" means. Because values are so ingrained in our sense of what is right and what is wrong, values may never be agreed on in a conflict. At times the best we can hope for is to respect the differences and agree to disagree.

> ### Discussion Question 9.3
> Identify possible value differences between Kaitlin and William. What do you think the likelihood is that one or the other of them will modify their values? How else might they manage their value conflict?

Structure concerns the framing of the relationship and any rules that govern how decisions are made or how events unfold. What topics are open for discussion? Who has the right to tell the other what to do? Structure concerns the "how" of the communication event.

TOOLBOX 9.1

Clusters of Conflict Assessment Tool

Answer each question to analyze a conflict. Where does the conflict reside most strongly? Although an issue may incorporate more than one area, generally what sustains a conflict cluster in one main category.

Communication

1. How is communication in the conflict being expressed?
2. What assumptions have I made that I have not verified?
3. What assumptions is the other party making about me that may not be true?
4. Are language, culture, age, or other differences inhibiting effective communication?
5. Do the parties have different styles of communication?
6. Did either party leap to problem solving before isolating the real problem?

Emotions

7. What emotions are driving the conflict for each party?
8. How are emotions being expressed in the conflict?
9. Are there style or cultural differences in how emotions are/should be expressed in this conflict?
10. Are emotions being vented appropriately?
11. Would it be helpful to share feelings with the other party?
12. Are there emotions that I could validate for the other to show my understanding?

Values

13. Are values different in the conflict?
14. What values do both parties share that might be used for commonalities?

15. Is the conflict being described as "right" and "wrong" behavior?
16. Where have we learned these values, and are these factors still influential for us?

Structure

17. What is the setting of the conflict?
18. Are there rules (formal or informal) or procedures for conducting conflict in this situation?
19. How are decisions made? Are there differences among the parties on how decisions ought to be made?
20. Are there time constraints built into the situation that affect the parties' actions?
21. Are there resource limitations in the situation that are a part of the structure?
22. What access to information do the parties have?
23. Are there legal issues as a part of the conflict?
24. Do the parties interact face to face frequently, rarely, or not at all?

History

25. What background does each party bring to the situation?
26. What customs are built into the system about how conflict occurs?
27. Are there previous interactions that affect this conflict?
28. How did the parties learn their approaches to conflict?
29. Does this conflict have precipitating events or interactions that have fed the situation?

Because they are newly together, *history* is not as much at play in the conflict as it might be if this conversation occurred years into Kaitlin and William's relationship. Conflicts located in the history cluster concern past interactions, past hurts, past resolutions, and past emotional reactions to each other. But history can also include one's personal history apart from the other. If Kaitlin chose her personal style as a reaction to a very conservative and demanding parent, her history may be a factor in this conflict.

Of course history, values, structure, emotions, and communication are not mutually exclusive of one another. Values are partly determined as a result of embracing or rejecting early teachings in one's family. However, a Conflict Cluster analysis provides the basis for insight into which parts of the conflict are more important than others at that moment. In this case, emotions and values predominate for Kaitlin and William and must be addressed to reach a mutually acceptable conclusion.

Mapping

A more visual representation of conflict can be created through mapping. The Australian Conflict Resolution Network suggests listing in writing each person's fears and needs about an issue. With that knowledge, one can understand how actions precipitate fearful reactions. Important in this process is understanding the difference between what someone "wants" (positions) and what he or she "needs" (interests). Mapping forces attention on the interests that underlie positions. Someone may *want* an apology (position) but *need* to have some recognition of how she was affected by the other's actions (interest).

A second aspect that the mapping tool highlights is fear. Personal fears are identified, as well as the probable fears of the other person. According to the mapping model, understanding needs and fears keeps the focus on the essentials during conflict and builds empathy toward the other party.

After the incident in Case 9.1, William and Kaitlin didn't go out, and a rift was created between them. William decided to analyze what was going on because he feared that the two of them were on the verge of breaking up. Using the mapping worksheet (Toolbox 9.2) William laid out what he thought was going on. He posited that Kaitlin probably feared losing autonomy while he feared the disapproval of his parents, as well as losing her (which manifested in jealousy of other men). Yet this did not provide enough explanation of how their conflict developed. Although mapping was helpful, William needed a more detailed tool to help him think about the conflict.

Conflict Assessment: Comprehensive Analysis Tools

When a simple analysis is not revealing, a more complex method of viewing the conflict becomes necessary. By following the steps and answering the questions in a comprehensive tool, the entire dynamic of a conflict is laid bare. Comprehensive tools are useful when it is not obvious at first glance what is driving the conflict or what may be motivating the other person. Several comprehensive tools are discussed in this section: The Comprehensive Conflict Checklist, the Conflict Roadmap, and the Interactive Conflict Map.

TOOLBOX 9.2

Mapping Worksheet

Party 1: _____

Needs (Interests): _____

Fears (Barriers to Settlement): _____

```
┌─────────────────────────────────┐
│                                 │
│                                 │
│          The Issue              │
│                                 │
│                                 │
│                                 │
│                                 │
└─────────────────────────────────┘
```

Party 2: _____

Needs (Interests): _____

Fears (Barriers to Settlement): _____

Source: Adapted from the Australian Conflict Resolution Network.

Comprehensive Conflict Checklist

A companion to mapping, also developed by the Conflict Resolution Network, is the foundation of the first tool discussed in this section. The **Comprehensive Conflict Checklist** in Toolbox 9.3 asks a series of questions that reveal an expansive view of the conflict.

William completed the Comprehensive Conflict Checklist to help him better understand his conflict with Kaitlin (Toolbox 9.3). He answered all thirty questions, representing Kaitlin's viewpoint as honestly as he could without her input. He gained insights in the *need* and *cooperation potential* areas, and he determined that each of them only thought of their personal interests and never talked about the situation in ways that permit mutual interests to emerge. He discovered in the *empathy* area that he previously didn't think about her perspective very much and that either of them could have *framed* the conflict better—perhaps like this: How can Kaitlin have independence and individuality in the way

TOOLBOX 9.3

Comprehensive Conflict Checklist

Needs

1. What is my real need?
2. What is his or her real need?
3. What do I want as an outcome for both of us?

Cooperation Potential

4. Are our needs mutually exclusive? If so, can the scope of the issue be expanded to find an area of mutual benefit?

Empathy

5. What is it like to be in his or her shoes?
6. What is the other trying to communicate?
7. Have I really listened? Do I need to paraphrase or validate so the other person knows I'm listening?

Framing

8. How can I state what I need without blaming or attacking the other person?
9. How can I state the problem so we both can be involved in finding the solution?

Power

10. How am I using power?
11. How is he or she using power?
12. Is either party using power inappropriately?
13. Is either party trying to gain more power out of a feeling of powerlessness or of being attacked? How can I allay those fears?
14. Is power too imbalanced? If so, what can I do to manage power?

Emotions

15. What am I feeling? What emotions are driving my actions or holding me back?

16. What is the other person probably feeling? What emotions are driving him or her or holding the other back? What fears underlie any anger that is being expressed?
17. Will telling the other how I feel help the situation?
18. Am I acting from a desire for revenge or to punish the other? Is that what I want to do?
19. How can I manage my feelings?

Willingness to Resolve

20. Do I really want the conflict to be managed?
21. Does the conflict serve some other function for our relationship?

Negotiation

22. How can I make this a fair deal for both parties?
23. What do I think the other wants to achieve? How can I find out if my perception is correct?
24. What does the other have that I want?
25. What do I have that the other wants?

Face

26. Has either of us invested our personality or face into the conflict?
27. How can I help the other save face?
28. What can I do to help save my face?

Aftermath

29. What do I want our relationship to be like in the future?
30. What should we do if problems arise in the future?

Source: Adapted, in part, from the Australian Conflict Resolution Network.

she dresses and at the same time William feel less jealous or concerned about other people's reactions? Other areas of the comprehensive analysis revealed more about the dynamic nature of their conflict.

After answering all the questions, William decided which areas were the most critical and offered the most opportunity to manage the conflict more productively. For example, given a different framing, Kaitlin might have been less defensive and able to talk the issue through. Armed with this knowledge, William felt better prepared to enter a conversation with Kaitlin that would be less hostile and more productive.

> **Discussion Question 9.4**
>
> How could William approach Kaitlin more productively? What do you think would have to happen to make Kaitlin receptive to working on this issue?

Conflict Road Map

Wehr (1998) recommends answering a series of questions to create a road map of the conflict. Although Wehr's tool was developed for group or international conflicts, we adapted it to form the basis of a road map to analyze interpersonal conflict. One or both individuals create the map to seek insights about the conflict. When possible, both parties compare maps or work together to form a mutual map—and thereby create a common view of information, goals, and communication processes.

After the fight, Kaitlin looked back at the episode in Case 9.1 using the Conflict Road Map. She wrote her recollections in each of the eight areas of the road map. In the *parties* area, she recorded that the conflict was driven, in part, by William's relationship with his parents. Under *contrasting beliefs*, she listed the influence of William's church on his perceptions of appropriate dress. She noted her easygoing attitude from her California "valley" upbringing, as well as the rebellion she felt in reaction to her own father's conservatism. In the *dynamic* section she itemized the types of name-calling and mirroring tactics that led them to hurt each other's feelings. After gaining insight from each area of the Conflict Road Map, she retrospectively assessed which areas were most important to the conflict at the time and which behaviors might be altered to manage conflict productively in the future. Using the Conflict Road Map, Kaitlin concluded that because they didn't directly confront their different values and beliefs, the conflict likely would grow and that the tactics each one currently used might create a destructive spiral of negativity.

Awareness Wheel

The conflict analysis tools just discussed can be accomplished by just one person. Another approach is for parties to work through a conflict analysis together.

Miller, Miller, Nunally, and Wackman (1991) created a model of conflict analysis called the Awareness Wheel in which the listener and the speaker have specific responsibilities. Two people alternate the speaker and listener roles. Using this model, Kaitlin, as the first speaker, starts the process by giving her *observation of data*, presenting a picture of what she has noticed in nonjudgmental terms. The other person takes the listener role. The listener's job is to *attend to the message* fully. The listener may *acknowledge* the speaker verbally or nonverbally

---

TOOLBOX 9.4

Conflict Road Map

Conflict context	Gather information about the conflict history and context. Conflicts do not exist in a vacuum.
Parties	Draw the primary parties who have a stake in the outcome and who are opposing each other in a circle. In an outer circle, place the secondary parties and/or allies who have a stake in the outcome but may not be directly involved in the interaction. Put any mediators or other third parties who try to intervene off to the side.
Causes and consequences	List what seems to be driving the conflict (the goal interference) and the consequences of the conflict (hostility, defensiveness, etc.).
Contrasting beliefs	In two columns, list any contrasting beliefs or values held by the parties.
Goals and interests	In two columns list what the parties say they want (positions). What interests seem to be beneath the positions?
Dynamics	What is the historical flow of the conflict? Has it escalated? Are the parties polarized? Is each person mirroring the negative tactics of the other?
Functions	Does the conflict have a purpose? What does maintaining the conflict do for each person?
Regulation potential	What is keeping the conflict from getting bigger (self-restraint, rules, laws)? Are there forces that limit the conflict or could help to manage it?

Source: Adapted from Wehr (1998).

---

but not give an opinion during this stage. Kaitlin could say to William, "William, I've noticed since we've moved in together that you have commented on my outfits more often than before we moved in together." Next, the speaker presents an *interpretation* of the event. This is an opinion of what the observed behavior means. Kaitlin may say, "I think that you are ashamed of me or really jealous." Presenting how she feels about the situation is the next step. She might say, "I feel confused because I thought you liked how I dressed. I'm feeling hurt when I think I'm being judged." Throughout this process, William's job is to continue listening and indicate his attention through verbal or nonverbal acknowledgments. If he's confused by something, he can ask for more information, being careful not to take the floor from the designated speaker by judging or offering an opinion.

Kaitlin's next step is voicing her wants: for herself, for William, and for the two of them together. She could say, "I want for me to be able to express who I am through my clothing choices without feeling judged. I want for you to be comfortable being seen with me and confident that I am not looking for another guy. I want for us to be able to talk without being mean to each other and to work through this and other problems that might arise." Finally, Kaitlin would indicate what actions she is willing to take. She might say, "I am willing to listen to your concerns about clothes and may be willing to make modifications if I see them as reasonable."

In summary, the Awareness Wheel has the speaker address five areas: (1) what I sense, (2) what I think, (3) what I feel, (4) what I want for me, you, and the relationship, and (5) what I will do. Once Kaitlin completes the wheel and she feels confident that William is aware of her views, they switch roles so the listener role is assumed by Kaitlin and William becomes the speaker. The new speaker works through the five areas of the model while the partner listens.

> ### Discussion Question 9.5
> Discuss the benefits/disadvantages of one party speaking at length while the other listens, as suggested in the Awareness Wheel.

Interactive Conflict Analysis

Talking for a long time while the other is relegated to a listening role may not work for everyone. Interactive Conflict Analysis provides a chance for parties to create a shared understanding of the conflict as they work through a three-step model. Interactive Conflict Analysis is divided into three focus points: the Past, the Present, and the Future. Each party has a chance to speak within each focus area.

The Past focus area asks, What behaviors led to where you are now? One person starts the process by making *Observations of Fact.* Key to this part of the process is to present an observation that is *behavioral* without interpreting what you think the behavior means. Kaitlin would not say, "I noticed that you got all mad at me [an interpretation] when you saw what I was wearing." Instead she would focus on the behavior she noted, "When I came out wearing this outfit, you said, 'You're not wearing *that.*'" A good way to test if the observation is judgment free would be to determine if the statement is arguable. If it is so factual that the statement could not be argued with, it is probably not an interpretation. For example, if Kaitlin offered, "You yelled at me," William could argue that she interpreted his tone incorrectly and argue, "I didn't yell."

William's role would be to *Clarify* and *Summarize* what Kaitlin observed without defending himself. He might ask for more information about what she observed ("When did that happen?"). He then summarizes his understanding: "You came out and I said, 'You're not going to wear that.'" Once she agrees that he presented her past observation accurately, he offers his Past Observation. He says, "You came out wearing your red miniskirt and low-cut black Lycra shirt." She would clarify the message, if necessary, and then summarize.

The next step is *Past Interpretation* of the situation. Interpretations can include how one feels about the situation and what one thinks it might mean. Kaitlin might say, "I felt judged by your comment. I thought you liked the outfit and now you seem ashamed of me." William would summarize her interpretation. Once she agrees that he has represented her interpretation accurately, it is his turn. He could say, "I was shocked when I saw you. I mean, I like how you look, but I don't want everyone looking at you like that. My mom and dad are going to be at the restaurant." William and Kaitlin must work hard to keep inflammatory language out of the process. Kaitlin would then summarize William's Past Interpretation.

TABLE 9.1 *Conflict Assessment Tools*

Tool	Analysis Level	Best Use	Individual or Mutual	Source
Clusters of conflict	First	Locating general causes	Individual	Mayer's Wheel of Conflict; Moore's Circle of Conflict
Mapping	First	Visualizing interests and barriers to settlement	Individual	Australian Conflict Resolution Network Worksheet
Comprehensive Conflict Checklist	Second	Total overview of the conflict	Individual	Australian Conflict Resolution Network
Conflict Road Map	Second	Total overview of the conflict; larger issues or multiparty	Individual	Wehr
Awareness Wheel	Second	Mutual analysis and understanding of a conflict	Mutual	Miller, Miller, Nunally & Wackman
Interactive Conflict Analysis	Second	Mutual analysis and understanding of a conflict	Mutual	Reese
Metaphor Analysis	Concept-Based	Comparative analysis of how the conflict is perceived	Individual	McCorkle & Mills
Negotiation Analysis	Concept-Based	Pre-negotiation strategy	Individual	Slaikeu's Negotiation Grid
Imagined Interaction	Concept-Based	Rethinking past conflict strategies; choice points	Individual	Honeycutt & Ford

The *Present Focus* includes exploration, validation, clarification, and acknowledgment. Parties take turns exploring how the event is affecting them now—along with possible causes, concerns, fears, and needs. The partner in the process validates emotions and asks clarifying questions to gain a better understanding. Exploring causes of his behavior, William might acknowledge that he really wants his mom to like Kaitlin; he's worried that she won't. He could explain that his mom is pretty conservative, and he's seen her judge people negatively in the past for what they wear. Kaitlin would summarize William's concerns and provide her concerns for William to validate and acknowledge. Next they would state their fears if the conflict is not resolved. Kaitlin could share that she worries that she will lose her individuality and autonomy if she changes just to please other people. William would validate, acknowledge, and clarify if necessary. During William's turn he might say, "I'm afraid that if we don't work this out, we're going to break up." Kaitlin would validate his feelings and concerns.

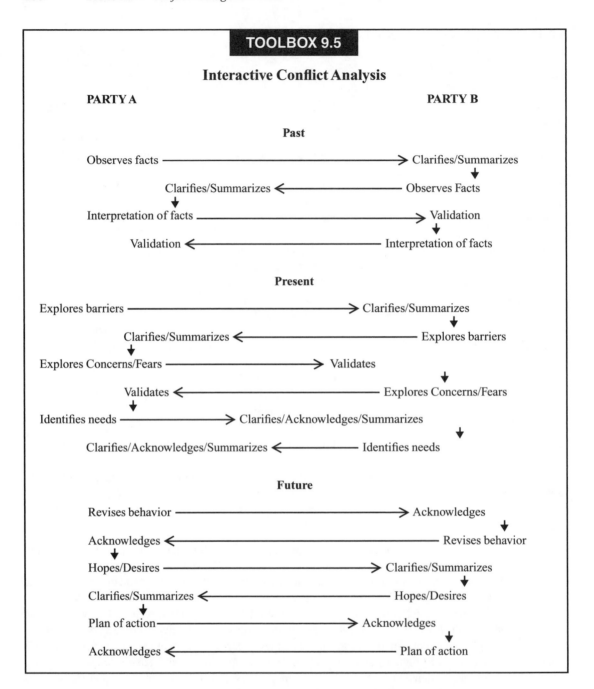

TOOLBOX 9.5

Interactive Conflict Analysis

PARTY A   PARTY B

Past

Observes facts ──────────────────────→ Clarifies/Summarizes

Clarifies/Summarizes ←────────── Observes Facts

Interpretation of facts ──────────────→ Validation

Validation ←────────── Interpretation of facts

Present

Explores barriers ──────────────────→ Clarifies/Summarizes

Clarifies/Summarizes ←────────── Explores barriers

Explores Concerns/Fears ──────────→ Validates

Validates ←────────── Explores Concerns/Fears

Identifies needs ──────────→ Clarifies/Acknowledges/Summarizes

Clarifies/Acknowledges/Summarizes ←────────── Identifies needs

Future

Revises behavior ──────────────────→ Acknowledges

Acknowledges ←────────── Revises behavior

Hopes/Desires ──────────────────→ Clarifies/Summarizes

Clarifies/Summarizes ←────────── Hopes/Desires

Plan of action ──────────────────→ Acknowledges

Acknowledges ←────────── Plan of action

The last step in the Present Focus asks the parties to express their needs to the other person. Kaitlin might say, "I need to know that you respect me and stop calling me names." William might say, "I need to know that you understand my concerns." They both might express a need to keep the relationship together.

Once the parties are ready to move forward, they acknowledge that everything up until this point is considered the Past. During the *Future Focus*, they can choose to share what they would have preferred to do differently if they could start over. They talk about how they will act in the future in similar situations. William might say, "I wish that I hadn't compared you to a hooker. That was rude, and I wish I had just told you why I was upset rather than call you names." Kaitlin might say, "I know that you have expressed concerns about my clothes in the past and that this dinner is important to you. I could have included you by asking your opinion about what to wear."

During the Future Focus segment, the parties agree to look toward the future rather than dwell on the past. They present their hopes and specific plans of how to build a different future together. William could say, "I hope that we can work out this difference. If I am unhappy with something, I agree to present my concerns without name calling or an angry tone." Kaitlin may agree that she will take William's concerns into account as she makes clothing choices. If the event is something very important to William, she agrees to include him in deciding what she will wear.

> ### Discussion Question 9.6
> How should parties determine who goes first and second in the Interactive Conflict Analysis? Should they switch off or maintain the same pattern throughout the model? Does it make a difference?

The benefit of the Interactive Conflict Analysis is that both parties continuously are involved in presenting their stories. A second benefit is that the model requires listening and validation before responding. A final benefit is that the model clearly distinguishes what has happened in the past from what parties plan to do in the future. It helps focus on the important task of moving forward together along a less confrontational path.

Concept-Based Analysis Tools

Metaphors

Although elaborate metaphors are not used by all individuals or in all conflicts, metaphors are significant when they appear. "Metaphors can help individuals to explain their reality through language without literally having to define the experience" (Pawlowski, Thilborger, & Cieloha-Meekins, 2001, p. 180). If someone describes a conflict with a partner as "talking to the wall," a sense of frustration and lack of authentic communication is clear.

Recognizing metaphors that describe a conflict is useful at several levels. First, metaphors can be positive or negative—although almost all metaphors used to describe conflict are negative (McCorkle & Gayle, 2003). Second, use of a strong metaphor ("I have to go to war over every little thing") may be a clue that the conflict is important—that someone is feeling interference with a critical personal goal. Third, an extended analysis of metaphors can reveal important details about the conflict.

People use a variety of metaphors to describe conflict. Conflict can be like being in "a rowboat in a hurricane" (a natural world metaphor) or like "being in a prison" (a physical and mental state metaphor). Depending on a conflict's importance, different types of metaphors may emerge. Individuals who rate their conflicts as not very important may select physical/mental states metaphors ("I'm going crazy"), and those who rate their conflicts of moderate importance tend to use machine/object metaphors ("I'm being pulled into a blender"). Those who rate conflict as highly important used warlike metaphors ("bringing in the heavy artillery" or "planting bombs all over the place") (McCorkle & Gayle, 2003).

Metaphors are built by comparing one thing to another. Conceptually, scholars believe the implied world of a metaphor—nature, war, sports, animals—carry with it rules and associations about how conflict should be conducted. For example, in a war metaphor, knowledge about war influences how one thinks about the conflict and how the conflict should be conducted. Wars are serious situations. People in wars may harm others to protect themselves. Drastic tactics may seem more acceptable. People need to be on the defense all the time. If these warlike thoughts shape how an interpersonal conflict is perceived, it certainly will result in different behavior than if the individuals describe their conflict like "two chefs in a small kitchen."

McCorkle and Mills (1992) recommend a five-point assessment to reveal the importance of conflict metaphors (Toolbox 9.6). In the metaphor, "I was talking to a brick wall," the nature of the process is *one-way communication*. The person using the metaphor is expressing that he or she is trying to work on the conflict, but nothing is being reciprocated. The role of the person using the metaphor is positive but frustrated. The role of the other person is to be the wall—the one blocking progress. Power probably is viewed as in the hands of the person portrayed as the wall—as long as the wall stands, nothing can change. When an unclimbable wall is in the way, several strategies and tactics seem obvious: give up, go around, climb over, or get a big hammer to smash the wall. In conflict, those who use the "talking to a brick wall" metaphor may give up in frustration or escalate to get a response. Identifying and understanding a metaphor is important to realize how language may be affecting perception and choice of tactics.

TOOLBOX 9.6

Metaphor Analysis

1. What is conflict like within the metaphor? Is it like a game, a war, a rough and windy road, a raging river?
2. Inside the metaphor, what is the role of the person who uses the metaphor? Is the person a player, a general, a director, a victim?
3. Inside the metaphor, what is the role of the other person in the conflict?
4. Who (or what) has power within the metaphor?
5. What strategies and tactics are implied within the metaphor? Do we need a better strategy, a safe shelter, a parachute, a river guide?

> ### *Discussion Question 9.7*
> Choose two metaphors that people use in conflict, one negative and one neutral or positive. Provide a list of choices for handling the conflict that are implicit in each metaphor.

Metaphors can be adapted linguistically to alter perceptions, but only if one is aware of their creeping influence. The brick wall metaphor can be altered by looking for ways to transcend the communication barrier or to encourage the other to be more cooperative—perhaps talking about getting a tall ladder to peek over the wall. If one's partner in conflict is using war metaphors such as "we're going to battle over this," neutral or positive metaphors can be substituted. For example, "Can't we skip the war and go straight to the peace table?" Battle, war, or aggressive metaphors are particularly concerning because they may suggest a willingness to use extreme negative tactics.

Negotiation Analysis

A method to analyze negotiation situations was created from Slaikeu's (1996) conflict grid. The names of the negotiators are placed on the top of the grid. Along the side are the points of analysis: interests, hot buttons, facts, best alternative to a negotiated agreement (BATNA), and possible solutions. Information about each negotiator is placed in the squares. To evaluate the situation, several questions are asked: "What are the underlying needs (interests) of each person?" "What types of tactics or words are *hot buttons* that might aggravate the other person?" "What are the facts about the conflict and the general situation?" "What is each person's BATNA?" and, "What is the range of possible solutions that would meet each person's needs?"

KEY 9.1

Knowledge, through analysis, creates opportunities to transform conflict.

The Negotiation Analysis Grid is designed to create awareness of the triggers of negative conflict and focus parties on the process toward creating a workable outcome. For example, with an awareness of what might set them into a negative spiral and a focus on mutually satisfying outcomes, Kaitlin and

---

TOOLBOX 9.7

Negotiation Analysis Grid

	Name	*Name*
Interests		
Hot buttons		
Background facts		
BATNA		
Possible outcomes for mutual gains		

Source: Adapted from Slaikeu (1996).

TOOLBOX 9.8

The Imagined Interaction

1. Write a dialogue that was typical during the conflict.
2. What was your goal?
3. What was the other person's goal?
4. What goal interference occurred?

5. What comment or nonverbal behavior precipitated the conflict?
6. Rewrite the dialogue at the point that the conflict emerged to imagine the conversation going in a more productive direction.

William may be able to have a constructive conversation about the emotional and value-laden issue of appropriate attire.

The Imagined Interaction

When approaching an interview, a job candidate "buys the right suit, reads the right books, conducts the right company research, and prepares herself for the questions that the potential employer may propose. In preparing herself for those questions, she develops a mental picture of the situation, including likely dialogue. She imagines the questions the interviewer may propose while also developing possible answers she may offer" (Honeycutt & Ford, 2001, p. 315). While preparing meticulously for a job interview seems natural, people rarely prepare with the same level of detail for difficult or conflict-laden encounters. Mentally anticipating what will occur during an interaction is called

---

CASE 9.2 • *The Grand Old Opry: Part I*

Jackson (excited and happy): "Good news, baby! I've got hotel reservations this weekend in Atlantic City and we're going to see a Grand Old Opry Review show."

Betina (happy at the first part of the news, and then the emotion changes to scorn): "Grand Old Opry Review? I'm not going to any lame country western show while we are in Atlantic City. I want to have some fun!"

Jackson (crushed): "I'm trying to set up something nice. You probably want to lie around the pool all day and then drink in some hip-hop bar all night."

Betina: "That's right. The pool, the casino, some great music, and dancing. There's not going to be any hokey country western thing. It's like I should have that big Dolly Parton hair and wear a funky little cowgirl hat. No way."

Jackson (getting mad): "Fine. We'll just stay here and I'll watch the games all weekend with my friends."

Betina: "Now don't get all sulky and mad."

Jackson leaves, slamming the door.

the **imagined interaction.** They are different from **mulling,** where one obsessively replays a past negative encounter. They also are different from *fantasy*, which is based on wishful or fanciful thinking.

The imagined interaction can be an important tool for developing new scripts to use in the future. The imagined interaction also can be adapted as a tool for analyzing past conflicts. Case 9.2 illustrates a past conflict episode written like a small short story or play, with dialogue and context.

If Betina applied the imagined interaction tool, she would analyze the conversation retrospectively to determine her goal, Jackson's probable goal, any goal interference that occurred during the interaction, and the point in the episode where the conflict emerged. After understanding the conflict through the initial analysis, Betina then rewrites the dialogue to what she wished would have happened (Case 9.3).

By rewriting the dialogue, Betina forms a new mental script that is available when similar conflicts begin in the future. Instead of just reliving the conflict in her mind, which keeps the conflict alive, she changes the scenario. She can identify the point in a conflict where her comments provoked defensiveness. With a new script and new tactics in mind, she has more choices. Imagined interactions are mental rehearsals in preparation for the next conflict encounter.

A final way that Betina could use this analysis tool is to share what she wished she had said to Jackson by reading him her imagined script. This action has the benefit of showing Jackson that she is willing to consider his views and his efforts. The process of introducing the imagined interaction into the conversation allows the parties to reenter negotiations on a positive note.

CASE 9.3 • *The Grand Old Opry: Part II*

Jackson (excited and happy): "Good news, baby! I've got hotel reservations this weekend in Atlantic City. and we're going to see a Grand Old Opry Review show."

Betina (happy about the surprise weekend away): "Atlantic City! That's fabulous! What a great idea to get out of town together this weekend."

Jackson (happy and proud of himself): "Yeah, I've been planning this special weekend for a couple weeks. It's been hard not telling you, but I wanted it to be a surprise."

Betina (still praising Jackson): "That's so nice. What about this Old Opry thing? You know I'm not crazy about that twangy country music."

Jackson (cautiously; he knows this might set Betina off): "I know. I know. You like that hip-hop gangsta music. But this is so special. The hotel is amazing with an inside atrium. The show has the stars from that talent contest program that you're addicted to. You love that show, so I was thinking we could go and see something that I like for a change, and it shouldn't be *too* painful for you. It's only a couple of hours, and we can do something else afterward if you want."

Betina (thoughtfully): "You're right that I can't stand that country western stuff, but it'd be fun to see some of those contestants. As long as I don't have to wear one of those cowgirl hats. Maybe I'll get some earplugs or take my iPod. And casinos are open all night, right?"

Creating an Analysis Tool

Sometimes the tools created by others to analyze conflicts aren't exactly right for a specific conflict. Feel free to create a conflict analysis tool from the concepts elsewhere in the book. For example, some conflicts seem to erupt simply because two people have different styles and one can't stand how the other person behaves. If a style difference is the basis of a conflict, the tools described in this chapter are less useful. Instead, use the style chapter to create your own method of analysis.

To create a style analysis tool, select one of the style approaches in Chapter 7, for example, escalators and fractionators. Put your name and the other's name in two columns on a sheet of paper, and then list the behaviors and style characteristics each person exhibits. Draw a line at the bottom of the characteristic section. Then list how each person perceives the other's style. Betina might analyze her interactions and discover that she has an escalatory style that relies on exaggeration and sarcasm, whereas Jackson has a more fractionator style—but will become defensive and blow up when he feels rejected. Knowing that these style differences exist, Betina can choose to ask questions instead of escalating the conflict through sarcasm. By understanding **critical choice points** in the conflict, a different path can be selected.

A specific concept within any of the chapters may bring just the right insights to a conflict. Be creative and invent new analytical tools.

Transformation Is the Key

Conflict assessment can assist in understanding past conflicts, be a guide to transforming a current situation, or provide a road map for future interactions. Without knowledge, choices seem limited and negative patterns are more likely to be repeated. Without understanding how individuals fall into conflict, it is difficult to work one's way out of conflict or prevent destructive interactions. With knowledge, choice multiplies.

To alter the shape of a conflict, some aspect of it must be transformed. Because the strategy of persuading the other person to change his or her behavior rarely works, the possibility of change is in the hands of the student of conflict management. Now that you know more about conflict, you are the one who can make a move to keep relationships from becoming crippled by dysfunction.

Assessment will determine the critical pattern or behavior that turns an exchange dysfunctional or keeps a conflict alive. An unexamined conflict is like a ball of string where everything is tangled together. People must find the end of a thread to pull and release the tangle. Pulling the string without planning can make the knots more difficult to untie. Conflict assessment identifies the specific thread of a conflict that might unravel the complex mass.

After assessing the conflict, one can create a plan for transformation. Change in any one aspect of a conflict may affect the entire dynamic. Some aspects that might be transformed include changing: perception of the other person's motives, expectations, goals, information shared, communication styles, structural barriers, how decisions are made, moving relationally closer or further away, boundaries, power management, tactics, cultural differences, face concerns, and/or common values.

Summary

Conflict analysis is a beneficial method to develop self-awareness and options for future conflict management. The Clusters of Conflict tool locates a conflict as primarily residing in communication, emotion, value, structure, or history. The Australian Mapping tool presents a simple analysis of the needs and fears driving an issue. The Comprehensive Conflict Checklist and the Conflict Road Map are comprehensive tools to analyze a conflict systematically. The Awareness Wheel provides speaker and listener roles and responsibilities to help parties navigate through a discussion of a conflict. Interactive Conflict Analysis asks parties to create a story together, taking turns to present their understanding of the past, the present, and plans for the future. Negotiation analysis helps prepare the way for mutual-gains bargaining. Metaphor analysis can reveal the inner thinking of conflict participants and how language affects tactical choices. The Imagined Interaction is helpful to locate the behaviors that turn a conflict toward the unproductive side and allows individuals to rehearse conversational strategies that might transform a conflict.

When existing methods of analyzing conflicts are not suitable to a specific circumstance, other concepts from the book can be made into an analytical framework for analysis. The key to conflict management is transformation of some element of the conflict. Analysis uncovers the critical place to focus transformative action.

Chapter Resources

Exercises

1. Describe a recent conflict by comparing it to something else. For example, was the conflict like "walking on broken glass" or "walking on air"? What metaphor best describes the conflict? Analyze the metaphor you created using Toolbox 9.6. Are the metaphors positive or negative in tone? Do the metaphors fit into any of the categories mentioned in the chapter?

2. Select a case from another chapter in this book and choose a tool from this chapter to analyze the case.

Journal/Essay Topic

1. Describe a conflict from your personal history. Apply one of the tools in this chapter to that past conflict. After analyzing the conflict, identify what was sustaining the conflict and critical choice points where you could have used a different tactic or made a different choice to transform the outcome.

Research/Analysis Topics

1. Record an episode of any situation comedy. Choose one of the tools in this chapter to analyze the conflict in the episode. (Hint: If you take out the humor, what would the episode be about?)

2. Review the literature on metaphor and conflict. What other types or clusters of conflict management metaphors emerge from past research?

Mastery Case

Which concepts from the chapter best help explain Mastery Case 9, "Roadblocks at the Bank"?

Roadblocks at the Bank

After discovering that her bank was changing a fee of $25 per year on each of her Roth IRA accounts (which was more than she was earning in interest), Dana wanted to move her account to a bank that didn't charge fees. The new bank filed the paperwork three times to make the transfer and the old bank either ignored the requests or found some minor error each time. They didn't notify anyone of the errors, so months would go by before Dana discovered the money hadn't been transferred.

She called the toll-free number on her account and was told that she had to visit the local branch. After arriving at the local branch she was told that they couldn't do anything, and she should call the national toll-free number. Dana explained that she had called the number and was told to come to the branch. The information clerk called the number and heard the instructions and then consulted with branch managers in her office. The clerk returned to say that they couldn't do anything and the new bank should just send in a request. Dana said, "They have sent three requests already. Are you saying you don't have the authority to do anything or that you are choosing not to do anything?" The clerk replied, "We can't do anything." Dana repeated her question and the clerk repeated her answer, becoming red in the face. Dana explained that she wanted to know if the lack of action was a policy or an internal decision. The clerk left and returned with the branch manager. Dana repeated her question. The branch manager explained that they couldn't get into the retirement accounts with their computers and had no control over them. Dana expressed frustration that the national number sent her to the local branch when they don't have the authority to do anything, and she left.

Beyond the Basics

Dealing with difficult behaviors saps our energy and can make life miserable. People who are normally rational, under stressful situations, can become difficult. There also are people who seem to relish wielding their power who become bullies. Bullying in the workplace is a common experience that only has recently emerged into our consciousness. Regardless of the causes or motivations of people who exhibit difficult behaviors, conflict managers need practical strategies to respond because the standard rules of engagement may not apply in these special circumstances. Chapter 10 answers the questions: What makes a difficult person difficult? What behaviors may make difficult people escalate conflict? How prevalent is bullying? What can be done about bullying? Chapter 11 examines what happens when individuals no longer can manage their conflicts and others are called in to assist, with special attention to mediation. Chapter 12 looks beyond the obvious to determine the effects of strong emotion on conflict, as well as the role of apology, forgiveness, and reconciliation.

10

Difficult People and Bullies

Vocabulary

Bullying
Bystanders
Cyberbullies
Griefers

Happy slapping
Mobbing
Outing/Trickery
Psychological terror

Unearned criticism
Workplace bullying

Objectives

After reading the chapter, you should be able to:

1. Understand the error of attributing motives to difficult behaviors

2. Explain the critical lessons about difficult encounters

3. Explain how bullying differs from other difficult encounters or incivility

4. Discuss the prevalence of bullying in schools and workplaces

5. Contrast the three theories about what causes bullying

If life were easy, all conflicts would be about simple issues, people would treat each other with courtesy, and everyone would have compatible communication styles. Sadly, we occasionally meet and work with people who seem difficult to get along with. This chapter examines the general nature of these difficult people and some common contexts where difficult encounters occur. Although we recognize the danger of labeling someone "difficult," we are starting from the viewpoint of the recipient of problematic behavior. It is the perception of difficulty that produces feelings of goal interference and hence conflict.

These are the first questions often asked after a difficult encounter: "What did I do to deserve that treatment?" or "Why can't I make the other person treat me better?" The truth is that those who suffer the brunt of annoying or difficult behaviors may or may not have provoked the episode. Sometimes people have personal problems or extreme skill deficiencies. But, as we discussed in Chapter 6, personal behaviors, such as a superior tone or evaluative comments,

CASE 10.1 • *You Can't Park There*

Melinda rode her scooter to the mall and pulled her bike into a parking spot. There were three parking spots in front of the entrance, two of which were clearly marked for patrons with disabilities by an upright sign and a wheelchair painted on the asphalt. Melinda pulled into the empty spot without a handicapped insignia nestled between the two handicap spots.

A large older sedan was parked way over the line into the space on her left, and a large van with an extended wheelchair ramp parked on her right. Melinda pulled into the middle of the spot, careful to leave room for the ramp. She was taking off her helmet when the owner of the poorly parked sedan came out of the store with her friend.

The two elderly women walked to the sedan's passenger side. The passenger required assistance to get into the car, but if the large door of the sedan were opened it would have hit the scooter. The sedan's driver turned to Melinda and said curtly and loudly, "You need to move out of the way, you parked too close to us."

Melinda said, "Sure, I can move my bike over, but I need to give the van plenty of room, too."

After moving her bike, the driver of the sedan said, "It's rude and illegal to park in a handicapped spot if you don't need it."

Melinda's gut reaction was to meet the woman's snide remark with a good dose of sarcasm about her sloppy parking job. However, instead she said calmly, "I can see how you would think this is a handicapped spot, but it isn't." The woman retorted as she helped the other woman into her seat, "Yes it is; and you're breaking the law. You should be ashamed!"

Melinda held her tongue again and said in a matter-of-fact and pleasant tone, "With the two handicapped spots on either side, I'd agree it is odd that this one is not a handicapped spot. But notice that there is no sign like the others and no markings on the asphalt."

The woman and her passenger looked for a sign and saw none. Without talking or even looking at Melinda, the driver went to her side and got into her car. As they pulled out of their spot, the passenger rolled down her window and sincerely apologized for her driver's rudeness. She wished Melinda a good afternoon as they drove away.

---

sometimes *do* provoke defensiveness in others. Sometimes the styles of the two people grate across each other's sensibilities. In Chapter 7 we reviewed various communicative styles. We noted that polar opposite styles might give rise to a perception of goal interference based entirely on personal preference. Whatever the cause, the effective conflict manager is responsible for trying to diffuse difficult situations and work toward more productive outcomes.

An Overview of Difficult Encounters

> ### *Discussion Question 10.1*
> Describe the behaviors of a difficult person you've encountered. How might that person rationalize his/her behavior?

Just as there are many contexts and variables of interpersonal conflict, there are many complexities of difficult encounters (Duck, Kirkpatrick, & Foley, 2006). What makes these encounters "difficult" is that the conversation does not unfold as expected and customary communication strategies don't work. The anticipated give-and-take of conversation in an office may not occur because one employee does all the talking or aggressively steps in to tell everyone else what to do. A financial aid counselor's comment that a student's parking tickets must be cleared before a check could be awarded may be met with extreme anger and personal attacks. Attempts to get a group member on a class project to do her share of the work may be met with belligerent defensiveness and a retort that the leader always picks on her. Asking a sincere question to clarify a policy may be met with personal attacks about how the questioner is a presumptuous troublemaker.

Once we can recognize difficult behaviors, the next step is to think about why customers, family members, coworkers, friends, or acquaintances might behave in these strange ways. What might motivate difficult person behaviors? Table 10.1 lists the possible motives of people during difficult encounters.

When experiencing a difficult situation, it is tempting to attribute negative motives or a defective personality to the other person. For example, if a coworker speaks loudly when giving instructions, one might attribute that he needs to control the situation because he thinks he is superior. We tend to combine our past experiences, some speculation, and a few facts to create a story: He is trying to push me around. We then act in response to the "story" we created, based on a guess about why that person is behaving as he is.

A discussion with a group of librarians elicited an encounter that evidently repeats almost daily in the library. The patron arrives with an overdue fine grasped in his fist. The patron approaches the desk in a huff and angrily states, "You people don't keep very good records here. I am sure I returned this book and it is probably on the shelf right now." The librarian feels attacked, thinks the patron is an ogre, and wants to respond with something like "Too bad! Pay the fine or get out." If the difficult encounter is managed poorly, the librarian will suffer more verbal abuse, the library misses its end goal of serving the public and getting the book back, and the patron will still have an unpaid bill—leaving all parties unsatisfied. Is the patron really an ogre, or could the difficult behavior be masking something else?

One of the critical questions in learning to deal with difficult people is to ask, "How can we tell which motive matches which behavior?" The simple answer: We can't. Unless you have telepathy, you cannot know what motivates a person's behaviors at any given moment in time. What one person interprets as snobbish or superiority may be motivated by something else entirely: insecurity, cultural upbringing, or even poor hearing. Because we can't read people's minds, we must rely on communication skills, experience, patience, and lessons learned from research to guide our responses.

TABLE 10.1 *Possible Motives of Difficult People*

A desire to control the situation

A need to exert power

A cover for embarrassment

Fear of loss of self-esteem or loss of "face"

Fear of economic loss

Need to be recognized

Low self-esteem

Cultural habits

Need to feel superior

Critical Lessons About Difficult Encounters

The First Critical Lesson

The first lesson in dealing with difficult encounters is to distrust first impulses—often to attack or defend—and to withhold judgment until more information is obtained. Often, as in the case of the patron with the library fine, the difficult behavior is masking a real need—to avoiding paying a bill for a mistake or to be able to use the library even if she has no money to pay the fine. Unfortunately, some people have not learned how to state their needs gracefully or how to ask for help. They fear being taken advantage of by "the system" or in starting off in a weak negotiating posture. Instead of reasonableness, they become belligerent, exaggerate their claims, and even conceal the real problem behind a show of anger, whining, or misdirection.

> **Discussion Question 10.2**
>
> In Case 10.1, suppose that Melinda reacted with her first impulse to the elderly woman who confronted her. How would the scene have played out differently? What are your first reactions when someone criticizes you or makes cutting sarcastic comments?

One of the underlying factors exacerbating difficult encounters is poor communication skills. Some people lack the skills to be assertive without being aggressive. Some people use extreme tactics because they are afraid of appearing weak. Others simply continue to use the tactics they know or that have worked for them in the past. Mirroring these behaviors with equal aggressiveness can cause a difficult situation to spiral out of control. Learning to withhold gut reactions and to take a moment before responding helps set the stage for a more satisfactory resolution.

The Second Critical Lesson

The second critical lesson is that if the relationship is important to you, you must be the one to look for the real issue behind the difficulty. Typically, the person who is acting in a difficult manner will not change unless provided good reasons to do so. By developing skills to discover the real issue underlying the difficult behavior, the situation can be made less difficult, relationships can be strengthened, and negative patterns can be transformed.

> **Discussion Question 10.3**
>
> What do you think Melinda's goal was during the interaction with the elderly driver of the sedan in Case 10.1? Did she achieve it?

A Third Critical Lesson

The third critical lesson is the value of self-awareness, which is important during difficult encounters on two levels. First, becoming aware of personal reactions when entering a

TABLE 10.2   *Behaviors That Make Matters Worse*

A superior tone of voice (implying "I am better than you")
Giving deceitful or wrong information
Appearing not to care about other people or their possessions
Putting personal needs in front of everything else ("me first")
Threats
Comparing someone to a negative example ("You're just like your father!")
Personal attacks
Negative comments

difficult encounter creates a position of strength. Understanding the types of comments that you find the most distressing can insulate you against them. These are the types of behaviors that, for you, might provoke an unproductive response. For example, if being called a particular name really pushes your buttons, having a plan for how you'll respond when and if it happens puts you in control. Second, self-awareness requires an honest look at where *you* might be being difficult. Sarcasm, biting retorts, or superior tones of voice are unproductive habits for a conflict manager. Table 10.2 lists some behaviors that many people find offensive. Where we might think we're being "funny" and trying to lighten the mood, others might find us difficult or caustic. Many of the items in Table 10.2 provoke the difficult person because the behavior can be perceived as an attack on the other's worth, self-esteem, and face.

The Fourth Critical Lesson

The fourth critical lesson is to discover hidden needs. In every difficult situation the other person wants something. They could want a specific service, have a need to feel important, or harbor any one of thousands of motivations. The effective conflict manager is adept at using questioning and listening tools to discover what the other needs. Using the listening skills in Chapter 6 and looking for interests behind the difficult behavior refocuses energy into productive communication.

Difficult people expect your attention. For some individuals, simply listening to them is the essential step to transform difficult encounters. In business, clients may be afraid of the faceless bureaucracy when they reach for the telephone, so they attack the voice on the other end of the line. Acknowledging feelings or difficulties, even without agreeing with them, opens doors to find the underlying problem. In a very real sense, businesses run on relationships. Thirty seconds of active listening can save considerable time later when customers become calmer and clearer in what they need and want. As a problem solver and conflict manager, you can use this technique to encourage others through their "difficult" stage quickly so you can respond to the real need. The skills for moving difficult people past their aggressiveness or anger are feeling paraphrases and validation statements (see Chapter 6). Likewise, many difficult encounters with family or friends are better met with validation, feeling paraphrases, or questions than with a mirroring of the negative behavior.

Specific Difficult Encounters

Bookstores are filled with advice for dealing with difficult people in a variety of contexts. For example, Solomon (2002) suggests that with the *belligerent bully* boss, employees must respect themselves enough to respond without belligerence or servility. For *revenge seekers*, we should clear up misconceptions and give honest and more frequent recognition. For *backstabbers*, we're told we must report what we heard them say and give them a graceful way out (now that they know we know).

Formulaic Feedback

People who continuously interrupt, argue, or give endless excuses when you are trying to give feedback are a special type of difficult encounter. In these cases, memorize what you want to say in advance using a specific formula for giving feedback (see Toolbox 10.1). The *formulaic feedback technique* helps the speaker stay on track and avoid being distracted by interruptions or excuses. If a messy roommate has excuses, politely listen and then go back to the top and restate all the steps. Step 4 is important to test agreement and the other's willingness to comply. If the answer is a surly "Yeah, sure," you may wish to test the depth of the commitment. "It sounds like you're not really interested. Is there something else that's going on that I need to know about? Maybe you have some other ideas on how we can work this out?"

The Interrupter

Several different techniques are useful in responding to people who constantly interrupt. Four suggestions are provided for those who need a more assertive approach. First, an assertive statement of understanding without agreement may help, such as "I understand your perspective. You think _____. Now I'd like you to understand my perspective.

TOOLBOX 10.1

Giving Feedback

Step 1: Focus on One Specific, Recent Event
"Today, I noticed that you left your books all over the living room and kitchen table."

Step 2: State a Consequence
"As a result, I was embarrassed when my parents arrived. They had no place to sit and I had to clean the kitchen table off before we could eat."

Step 3: State the Desired Reformed Behavior
"When you say you are going to clean up the house, I really need to know I can depend on you."

Step 4: Ask for Agreement or Input
"Can you do that?" or "What do you think we can do to avoid this in the future?"

Please listen for a moment." A second technique is to refuse to follow their lead to another topic. For example, after being interrupted, simply go back to your original topic and flow of thought: "Now, as I was saying . . ." A third, more assertive technique is to interrupt the interruption: "Excuse me, I am not finished." A fourth technique, useful with people who change the subject to avoid conflict, is to agree with their subject change but postpone the new topic. For example, "I'd be glad to discuss that after we finish this topic" or "We seem to be off track. Let me recap where we started . . ." Be aware that all of these techniques can be blueprints for being difficult, so be sure to check your motivations as you use these tools.

Unearned Criticism

Dealing with unearned criticism is another type of difficult encounter. **Unearned criticism** occurs when you are accused unjustly of generic faults such as being a barrier to success, inefficient, a troublemaker, always late, or not helpful. Three techniques can be used to reply to unearned criticism. First, ask for specific information about the criticism. If the boss says you are "inefficient" and you sincerely don't know what is being referenced, say, "Can you give me a specific example of when I was inefficient? I want to be sure I know what you mean by that." The second technique is to agree at some level. If you are unfairly accused of not holding up your end of the work on a group project, reply in principle that "Yes, I agree that reports should be timely" or "Yes, the group's performance concerns me too." Agreeing in principle allows some validation of the speaker and may open the channel

---

TOOLBOX 10.2

Responding to Yelling

What are the risks and benefits of each of these strategies when a manager yells at an employee? The employee says,

A. Say, "Wait. I don't think everyone heard you yelling. Bob, Ann, Mark, come here. Jean has something to say to me."

B. Apologize for something you didn't do and quietly stew about the unfairness of the situation.

C. Wait until the manager is out of earshot and say to the group, "Someone is wound a bit tight."

D. Worry that everyone thinks you are incompetent.

E. Acknowledge the error and get back to work.

F. Say to the manager, "I won't be yelled at. If you have something to say, act professionally, and then I'll listen to you. It's okay; I'll wait."

G. Attempt to diffuse with humor, "Dang. I lost that $5. I bet someone that I wouldn't get yelled at before noon!"

H. Plan how to get revenge by writing a scathing evaluation of the manager.

I. Wait until the manager is out of earshot and make some offhand comment such as, "Well, wasn't that pleasant?" and then go back to work.

J. Quit on the spot.

K. Do an impersonation of the manager as soon as she leaves for those who missed the show.

L. Ask the manager to explain the unfair criticisms.

M. Educate the manager by demonstrating how the same concerns could have been stated better.

CASE 10.2 • *The Delayed Evaluation*

Denny and his principal Christine both started this year at Tavis Elementary. Denny, a fifth-grade teacher, came from another district and had an outstanding record of service for over fifteen years. Even with his experience, he was on a three-year probationary period because of the new district's policy for all teachers. Christine had been a principal for eleven years, and she was three years away from retirement when she was moved to Denny's school. Denny and Christine seemed to get along fine, often trading good-natured banter. After a few weeks, Denny noticed that Christine made critical comments about other teachers behind their backs and mocked parents. He'd heard that she didn't leave her last school on good terms with many of the teachers.

Principal Christine was a go-getter, worked very hard, and had an expectation that the teachers would work as hard as she did. She was irritated when she looked around at 4:30 P.M. and saw most of her staff was gone. Single and without family obligations, she stayed until 7 P.M. or later most nights. Christine was scheduled to provide Denny with an initial evaluation by October, but she was too busy to do it. Denny assumed that all was fine because Christine and he were on such good terms and he'd been helping with the district's new computer software.

Finally, in March, Christine scheduled Denny's evaluation. Denny had no more than sat down when Christine pulled out a list of complaints—mostly about his lack of commitment, his cluttered room, a couple of incidents where parents talked to her about their concerns with the curriculum (over which Denny had no control), and a barrage of personal criticisms about his lackadaisical attitude. Denny was too shocked to react and was still reeling when he left her office. This evaluation could derail his career in the district!

for joint problem solving. A final technique is to beat the other to the punch with a solution to a general criticism. For example, "I couldn't agree more that the group needs to increase its performance, and I have some ideas on what we might do."

Discussion Question 10.4

How could Denny respond to Christine's negative evaluation in Case 10.2? How can he turn this around so he can be proactive and regain some power in the situation? What mistakes must he avoid?

Bullying and Violence

Bullying is an extreme example of difficult behavior that occurs in a variety of settings, such as schools, work, faith communities, family, and friendship circles. Few people can say they have never experienced bullying, as a victim, perpetrator, or observer. **Bullying** involves the oppression of an individual through a series of negative behaviors that range from purposeful humiliation to sabotage, destruction, isolation, manipulation, coercion, and control, and sometimes even violence.

In the United States, bullying garnered little attention until it was related to high-profile workplace violence and school murders. Although no single factor could explain the tragedy, a shooting rampage by two Columbine High School students in Littleton, Colorado, led to intense scrutiny of the link between school violence and bullying (Chapell et al., 2004; Fried & Fried, 2003). More recently the thirty-two murders and the suicide at Virginia Technical Institute illustrated how violence can become a response when someone who is psychological imbalanced meets social isolation, bullying, or adversity. Sadly, examples of societal violence are plentiful. Given the prevalence of bullying in U.S. society, we may be fortunate that so few targets seek retribution.

School Bullying

Information on school bullying has become robust since the year 2000. A Kaiser Foundation study found that three quarters of preteens identified bullying as a regular occurrence at school, and 86 percent of children twelve to fifteen were teased or bullied (Coloroso, 2003). One study found 13 percent of sixth to tenth graders bullied others regularly (Chapell et al., 2004). Children stay home from school because they are afraid of what will happen on the bus, in the locker room, or on the playground. Bullying creates an environment of fear, where it is difficult to concentrate on learning.

Some studies report that most primary school bullying occurs during recess and that student peer mediation programs significantly reduced physical aggression in schools (Cunningham et al.,1998; Heydenberk, Heydenberk, & Tzenova, 2006). A newer form of bullying occurs on cell phones, websites, and message boards. **Cyberbullies** mass-mail hurtful text messages or instant messages to or about the target; post derogatory comments on discussion boards; secretly take unflattering pictures and post them on websites; go for the emotional jugular on blogs, Facebook, or MySpace pages; or send the target's e-mail address to porn sites.

National news followed the case of thirteen-year-old Megan Meier, who after a falling out with a girlfriend, allegedly was victimized by her ex-friend's mother in a bizarre cyberbullying attack (Welch, 2008). Stories said the friend's mother, posing as a boy interested in the victim, flirted and established an online relationship with Megan. Once

CASE 10.3 • *Being the Bully*

Everyone has something that they wish they could take back—something that was so bad you want to be able to rewind that moment and record over it. Back in junior high school, my friends and I would always make fun of a certain kid just because he was different. He wasn't the "typical cool" person and didn't fit into any of the cliques. He would try to play sports, but we would give him a hard time because he always came in last place. We made fun of him just because he had red hair. If he hadn't had red hair, we would have found something else to taunt him about.

I know that this was in junior high and we were very immature at the time, but I still feel bad for giving him such a hard time. I don't know where he is today because he went to a different high school. I hope that he realizes how young we were and that I feel bad about the way we treated him. I think we acted that way because we could. We thought that it was fun to make fun of someone else to make us feel better about ourselves. Junior high is tough enough, so I can't imagine what it must have been like for him to have us on him day after day. It must take a lot of courage to show up for school every day and take the verbal and mental beatings he took.

Megan's trust had been won, the messages changed. The "boy" then broke up with Megan in a series of humiliating e-mails, the final message from "him" saying, "The world would be a better place without you." The case only came to light after the distraught girl committed suicide. The mother/bogus boyfriend has been indicted in the case ("Missouri Mom Indicted," 2008). Children are reluctant to disclose this torment to adults because of a fear that a parent will take away their technology access (Snider & Borel, 2004).

Variations of cyber abuse that may or may not fit the technical definitions of bullying include griefers, outing/trickery, online ostracism, and happy slapping. **Griefers** deliberately offend or disrupt others in online games or worlds such as Second Life. **Outing/trickery** occurs when embarrassing information about someone is revealed in a video, blog, or through messaging—sometimes by tricking the victim into thinking the other person is a friend to get to the hidden information. *Online ostracism* might include blocking a specific individual from a website, list, or blog.

Happy slapping, a disturbing trend first reported in England, is an illegal assault. The happy slapper walks up to a stranger and slaps him or her in the face while a friend takes a camera shot of the victim's expression. The photo is posted on the web (Kowalski, Limber, & Agatston, 2008). In the United States and elsewhere, happy slapping has been linked as a precursor to more serious violence, such as cases of unprovoked and increasingly more violent physical beatings and random murders ("Stark Warnings," 2008).

Although stories of school bullies are considered common, raising the issue of adult or workplace bullying may lead to snickers—as if bullying is just an occasional lunch box theft during primary school or a problem only for the young. During one *Today Show* episode, guest anchor Campbell Brown laughed while introducing a story on workplace bullying, whereas regular host Matt Lauer replied that it was a serious problem for people who were afraid of coworkers and who went to work everyday with "sweaty palms" (*Today Show*, 2004). Even though few U.S. scholars are studying it, bullying in the workplace looms as an enormous problem. As one author noted, playground bullies can take your lunch money, but bully bosses can take your livelihood (Glendinning, 2001).

Although only recently gaining attention in the United States, **workplace bullying** is a well-studied phenomenon in Europe. In 2001, the European Union Parliament passed a resolution against workplace bullying, and many European countries have specific anti-bullying legislation (Seward & Faby, 2003). The British were so frustrated by the behaviors of neighbors, coworkers, and bosses who, in the words of then Prime Minister Tony Blair "make life absolute hell," that they passed an Anti-Social Behavior law that can ban individuals from swearing or making sarcastic remarks in cases of ongoing bully behaviors (Lawless, 2004). Bullying goes beyond incivility to a concerted effort at making a specific person's life miserable.

In the United States, eyes are slowly opening to the human and business costs of bullies (Tracy, Lutgen-Sandvik, & Alberts, 2006). It's estimated the country loses $180 million of productivity time per year from bullying—a number that is startlingly low because Britain places their estimate at $1.6 billion ("Bullying at Work," 2005–2006; Farrell, 2002). Managers and supervisors already spend at least 20 percent of their time managing conflicts among employees; bullying only makes their jobs more difficult.

"All of us are difficult on occasion. Bullies are difficult on purpose."
—Bullying expert Sam Horn, 2003

Defining Bullying

Bullying research began in Europe, where it sometimes is called **mobbing** or **psychological terror** (Sheehan, Barker, & Rayner, 1999; Stein, 2001; Zapf & Wolfgang, 1999). Bullying is distinguished from other antisocial behaviors by five key characteristics: (1) The harassment is frequent; (2) it involves a pattern over time; (3) it does harm; (4) it begins with or results in a power disparity between the bully and his or her victim; and (5) recipients perceive themselves to be the specific target of the bully (Tracy et al., 2005). Zapf and Gross (2001) provide a definition specific to workplace bullying:

> Bullying occurs, if somebody is harassed, offended, socially excluded, or has to carry out humiliating tasks and if the person concerned is in an inferior position. To call something bullying, it must occur repeatedly (e.g., at least once a week) and for a long time (e.g., at least 6 months). It is not bullying if it is a single event. It is also not bullying if two equally strong parties are in conflict. (p. 498)

According to research by the Workplace Bullying and Trauma Institute (2003), the most popular bully tactics used against those who reported being the targets of bullies include falsely accusing someone of errors (71 percent); staring, glaring, nonverbal intimidation (68 percent); discounting the person's thoughts in meetings (64 percent); and silent treatment or icing out the victim from coworkers (64 percent). Table 10.3 lists common verbal and nonverbal bully behaviors.

Bully behaviors fall into five basic types: (1) Attacks on self-expression and the way communication happens (interruptions, yelling, criticism, threats); (2) attacks on social relations (isolation, invisible treatment); (3) attacks on reputation (rumors, ridicule, accused of being mentally ill, name calling); (4) attacks on career (no special tasks are given, given meaningless work, tasks given below one's ability to affect self-esteem or above ability to question competence, supervisors sabotage the work area); and (5) direct attacks on health (physically strenuous work, threats of physical violence, physical violence, physical or sexual abuse)

TABLE 10.3 *Bully Behaviors*

Nonverbal Bullying	*Verbal Bullying*
Aggressive eye contact	Convincing lies
Staring	Angry outbursts
Dirty looks	Yelling
Snubbing	Put downs
Ignoring/the silent treatment	Malicious rumors
Rude gestures	Public humiliation
Invasion of physical space	Threats
Finger pointing	Name-calling
Slamming/ throwing objects	Unfounded criticism/blaming
Sarcasm	Unreasonable job demands
Rolling eyes	Stealing credit
Exclusion/social isolation	

TABLE 10.4   *Facts About Workplace Bullies and Their Targets*

Men and women are equally likely to be bullies

Women are targets in 84 percent of cases

Men target women in 69 percent of cases

Eighty-one percent of bullies ranked higher in work status than their target

Fourteen percent had the same rank as targets

Five percent of bullies targeted higher-ups

Bullies are everywhere: corporate, government, small business, family business, and nonprofits

Sixty-three percent of targets had college experience, 17 percent had graduate degrees, and 4 percent were PhDs, MDs, or lawyers

Sixty-seven percent of targets reported they had never been bullied at work previously

In 77 percent of cases there was no protected class status for the target

Over 77 percent indicated that there was more than one target of bullying (88% for government workers)

Approximately 35 to 50 percent of U.S. workers experience one negative bullying act a week

Average time of bullying: 17 months for nearly half of targets (men, 18 months; women, 15)

Source: Compiled from Field (1996); Horn (2002); Lutgen-Sandvik, Tracy, and Alberts (2007); Namie and Namie (2003).

(Blase & Blase, 2003). Of course, any single instance of these behaviors might be reprehensible, but it does not constitute bullying. Bullying is the persistent repetition of abuse over time. Table 10.4 presents facts about workplace bullies.

Workplace Bullies

The Workplace Bullying and Trauma Institute claims one sixth of employees experience bullying (*Today Show*, 2004). Fifteen percent of all violent crimes in the United States occur in the workplace, and murder was the third largest cause of workplace death. See Toolboxes 10.3 and 10.4 for tactics in how to respond to some types of violent threats in the workplace.

The Society for Human Resource Management estimated in 1994 that aggression in the workplace "caused some 500,000 employees to miss 1,751,000 days of work annually, or 3.5 days per incident" (quoted in Randall, 1997). One in four employees who witness or experience bullying leave their jobs (Ayoko et al., 2003). The statistics on those who experience workplace bullying vary from study to study (partly due to differences in definition)—from 38 percent of employees to 90 percent (Glendinning, 2001).

Bullying affects the bully, the victim, and the organization. In the workplace, the effect of bullying on the organization includes both opportunity lost and direct costs. Bullying takes time and leads to supervisor intervention, which also takes time. Productive employees who are bullied take more sick leave and are more likely to leave, causing increasing hiring and training costs due to a hiring-bullying-resignation cycle (the bully remains and the productive employees leave). Bystanders of bullying may fear retaliation or being selected as the next victim.

TOOLBOX 10.3

When Someone Threatens Violence, Don't . . .

- Use styles of communication that generate hostility such as apathy, the brushoff, coldness, condescension. Don't go strictly by the rules or give the runaround.
- Reject all demands from the start.
- Pose in challenging stances, such as standing directly opposite someone, hands on hips, or crossing your arms. Avoid any physical contact, finger-pointing, or long periods of fixed eye contact.
- Make sudden movements, which can be seen as threatening. Notice the tone, volume, and rate of your speech.
- Challenge, threaten, or dare the individual. Never belittle the person or make him or her feel foolish.

- Criticize or act impatiently toward the agitated individual.
- Attempt to bargain with a threatening individual.
- Try to make the situation seem less serious than it is.
- Make false statements or promises you cannot keep.
- Try to impart a lot of technical or complicated information when emotions are high.
- Take sides or agree with distortions.
- Invade the individual's personal space. Make sure there is a space of 3 to 6 feet between you and the person.

Source: This list was adapted in part from a violence crisis response training at the University of Nebraska, Lincoln and Department of Labor, OSHA website. See the OSHA website and your college's safety office for current recommendations.

Bully Meets Victim

Coloroso (2003) commented, "Bullies come in all different sizes and shapes: some are big, some are small; some bright and some not so bright; some attractive and some not so attractive; some popular and some absolutely disliked by almost everybody. You can't always identify bullies by what they *look* like, but you can pick them out by what they *act* like" (p.11). Victims of bullies, whether children or adults, are selected for a reason. The reason, however, may have little to do with the target's physical, social, or mental characteristics. Fried and Fried (2003) tell the story of one child who was selected as a target merely because she was the first to get on the bus and the last to leave. Workplace victims may be selected because they are unusual, popular, competent, or perceived to threaten the bully's "place" in the organization (Workplace Bullying and Trauma Institute, 2003). The research on causes of bullying center on three elements: the target, the bully, and culture.

One view holds that bullying is the target's fault: The target somehow invites bad behavior from others. Some research indicates targets may be less assertive, have less developed conflict management skills, and/or are less socially adept than other workers (Zapf & Wolfgang, 1999). However, contradictions abound in the research about what a typical target of bullying looks like.

TOOLBOX 10.4

When Someone Threatens Violence, Do . . .

- Project calmness: move and speak slowly, quietly, and confidently.
- Be an empathetic listener; encourage the person to talk and listen patiently.
- Focus your attention on the other person to demonstrate you are interested.
- Maintain a relaxed yet attentive posture and position yourself at a right angle rather than directly in front of the other person.
- Acknowledge the person's feelings. Indicate that you can see he or she is upset.
- Establish ground rules if unreasonable behavior persists. Calmly describe the consequences of any violent behavior.

- Use delaying tactics, which will give the person time to calm down. For example, offer a drink of water (in a disposable cup).
- Be reassuring and point out choices. Break big problems into smaller, more manageable problems.
- Accept criticism in a positive way. When a complaint might be true, use statements like "You're probably right" or "It was my fault." If the criticism seems unwarranted, ask clarifying questions.
- Ask for recommendations. Repeat back what you feel he or she is requesting.
- Arrange yourself so your route to the exit is not blocked.

Source: This list was adapted in part from a violence crisis response training at the University of Nebraska, Lincoln and Department of Labor, OSHA website. See the OSHA website and your college's safety office for current recommendations.

A second view proposes that bullying is a personality fault of the bully. Bullies have unusual perspectives in areas like feelings of entitlement, intolerance toward difference, disrespect of others, liking to dominate others, using others, single focus on personal needs and pleasures, hurting others when there are no consequences, viewing weaker people as prey, blaming others to explain shortcomings, lack of responsibility for actions, or a craving for attention (see Coloroso, 2003; Randall, 1997). Smugness, self-centeredness, narcissism, power mongering, prejudice, or elitism may drive bullies (Fried & Fried, 2003). Some experts view bullying primarily as a manifestation of power—either the bully covets power or has power and behaves badly because he or she can (Simpson & Cohen, 2004).

A third explanation is that culture causes bullying by permitting it (Freiberg, 1998; Porhola, Karhunen, & Rainivaara, 2006; Simpson & Cohen, 2004). For example, a culture of bullying could be created if popular students are allowed by teachers to make fun of less popular students. Supervisors who bully their employees model bad behavior for other workers, which may, in turn, induce more bullying.

The Bullying Process

Bullying typically builds gradually. There are four phases of workplace bullying: (1) An incident occurs that triggers the bully's attention; (2) over time, the bully wears down the victim and separates him or her from other employees; (3) management notices the victim's loss of productivity; and (4) someone gets reprimanded or fired, usually the victim. A key feature of the bullying process is that it is incremental. Small successes lead to more extreme bullying. For example, Davis mentions to his coworker, Miranda, that the two of them might improve their work output by adopting his suggestions. The comment, although well intended, is threatening to Miranda. She begins a rumor campaign to alienate other workers from Davis. Davis is confused and hurt, but mostly he ignores Miranda's behavior. Seeing no repercussions to her behavior, Miranda makes fun of Davis and, if he complains, tells everyone he "doesn't have a sense of humor." Davis finally complains and is labeled as a troublemaker. Gradually, coworkers begin to avoid Davis. Davis's work suffers. Miranda sabotages his work area, lies about his work, and encourages others not to help or share information with him. Management begins to notice a drop in productivity within the unit. When management asks what is going on, everyone points to Davis. He receives a reprimand. Research predicts a high likelihood that Davis either will leave voluntarily or eventually be fired. Table 10.5 lists some responses bullies use to mask their aggression.

The Bystander Effect

"Evil prospers when good men do nothing."
—American Revolution patriot Thomas Paine

Bullies do not work in isolation. Many of the behaviors of bullies involve **bystanders** who witness or participate in the process. A survey of abusive workplaces found that 77 percent of bullies enlist the help of others (Workplace Bullying and Trauma Institute, 2003). Bystanders can be supervisors, friends, or those who are supposed to prevent bullying, such as human resource departments or teachers.

One study found that 60 percent of college students had observed a student bullying another student, and 44 percent had seen an instructor bully a student (Chapell et al., 2004). In other studies of faculty-to-faculty bullying, male faculty were much less likely to claim they had witnessed bullying than female faculty, suggesting that when bullying is not perceived, bystander intervention is unlikely (Simpson & Cohen, 2004; Twale & De Luca, 2008). Table 10.6 lists the types of bystanders.

Discussion Question 10.5
Have you noticed bullying in the college classroom or in the workplace? Who was involved? What type of bystanders did you observe? What behaviors might have changed the bullying patterns?

TABLE 10.5   *The Bully's Favorite Responses and Excuses*

"I was just kidding."
"Why are you so sensitive?"
"You need to lighten up."
"You need to learn to take a joke."
"What's the matter? A little joke going to make you cry?"
"I'm just hot tempered."
"That's just the way I am—get used to it."
"If I didn't act like this nothing would get done."

Source: See MacIntosh (2006).

TABLE 10.6 *Bully Bystanders*

Angry witness:	May be annoyed at the target for creating the situation
Fearful witness:	Thinks about intervening but are afraid the bully will turn on her or him
Voyeur:	Gets some pleasure from watching
Accomplice:	Laughs at the bully's putdowns and becomes an active audience
Helpful witness:	Challenges the bully
Inactive witness:	Tries to avoid the situation

Source: Fried and Fried (2003).

Strategies for Victims

Most experts agree it is best to stop bullying in its larval stage (Glendinning, 2001; Horn, 2002). As previously noted, most bullying is incremental, starting with an equal power situation that gradually is eroded, particularly if the victim lacks assertiveness and conflict management skills. Even though many individuals prefer to avoid all conflict, accommodation and avoidance will be ineffective with bullies: Once bullying begins, it rarely will simply go away. People who successfully cope with bullying actively engage the behavior and respond with emotional intelligence. They find ways to maintain a strong sense of self and feelings of competence.

Conflict managers must separate early and late stages of bullying. In the early stages, bystanders, supervisors, or targets may be able to change the situation using conflict management skills. In the late stages, the life cycle of bullying reduces the target's power, resources, and his or her ability to manage the situation proactively. Intervention from a powerful source such as a teacher or manager is required in the late stages of bullying.

> ### Discussion Question 10.6
> What messages did you receive growing up about how to deal with bullies?

At the early stages of bullying, a target's assertiveness may help. Assertiveness empowers targets to change the communication patterns and behaviors that may attract bullies (Randall, 1997). Setting boundaries with a bully may stop the gradual worsening of bully behaviors. For example, when a bully demeans or is sarcastic, wait until the person is calm and tell him or her how the comment affected you. One might also respond in a good-natured way, saying, "I don't appreciate that kind of humor." If that does not help, instead of avoiding or becoming defensive, the target could say, "Excuse me?

TABLE 10.7 *Bullying Web Resources*

The Workplace Bullying and Trauma Institute	http://bullyinginstitute.org
KickBullies	http://www.kickbully.com
British Workplace Bullying	http://www.workplacebullying.com/

What did you say?" to highlight the inappropriate comment or begin to record all the bully's behaviors. Say to the bully, "Let me write that down. You said . . ." One formula for setting boundaries is the following statement: "If you continue to _____, I will need to _____." For example, "If you continue to withhold the information I need to do my reports in a timely fashion, I will need to take this list of documented occurrences and witnesses to the next level." If the offending behavior does not stop, the target must be willing to act. Unrealized threats are clear signs of weakness. Because power is part of the bullying dynamic, targets can benefit from analyzing their sources of power and developing new options (see Table 5.7).

> Workplace bullying is "a constant drumbeat, a relentless picking away at what they do, what they say, how they look, how they sound, and how they work."
> —Communication scholars Tracy, Lutgen-Sandvik, and Albert, 2005

MacIntosh (2006) found three levels of dealing with bullies: formal, informal, and general. Each of the three levels uses different strategies to reclaim power from a bully. *Formal strategies* involve using work or community resources, such as an employee assistance program (EAP), union, or legal assistance office. *Informal strategies* involve educating oneself about the company's rules, policies, and grievance procedures; keeping a written record of all incidents in a safe place away from work; saving messages, memos, or e-mails; requesting that discussions or reprimands take place in open public spaces; following up verbal agreements with e-mail confirmation, asking for copies of any reprimands in writing; tape-recording conversations; carefully increasing other workers' awareness of the bully's behavior; taking another employee or witness to meetings; and directly letting the bully know how his or her behavior impacts others. *General strategies* require working hard to maintain mental and physical health during

KEY 10.1

Stop the bullying early in the process.

the stressful situation and finding a support network at work or away from work. Lutgen-Sandvik (2007) recommends three tactics: (1) formal or informal complaints, (2) precise written documentation of bullying, and (3) using experts or providing expert research about bullying to management.

The best response to bullying is institutional support, unbreakable self-confidence, and communication competence. Field (1996) recommends individual responses be "firm, resolute and assertive" (p. 203). Have a clear and small goal in mind such as stopping teasing. Use only assertive behavior rather than becoming aggressive or accommodating. Be positively entrenched and persistent. Ignore provocation or threats. These strategies serve to gain power back from the bully and put a stop to the unpleasant behavior. Knowledge of the behaviors of bullies can stop bullying before it poisons the workplace. Early intervention, boundary establishment, application of conflict management skills, and/or the intervention of appropriate third parties may halt most bullying. The strategies and tactics in the first part of this chapter on dealing with difficult people also may be helpful during the initial stages of bullying.

TOOLBOX 10.5

Should I Take on the Bully?

Assess Your Circumstances

- Is my human resources department effective or ineffective?
- What evidence of the bullying do I have if I go to my supervisor or human resources?
- Will higher-ups or other employees side with the bully?
- Do I have any support (network, union, family, friends, boss)?
- Am I or is the bully in a protected class (sex, age, religion, national origin, race, color, disability)?

Assess Your Communication Skills

- Can I assert myself verbally when the bullying happens?
- Do I have a strategy for how to respond?
- Do I know my boundaries, and can I express them?

Assess Your Options

- Am I tied to this job emotionally, professionally, and financially? Can I leave if I have or want to?
- Can I separate my home life from my work life?
- Can I put in for a transfer?

Assess the Possible Costs

- What will it cost me to challenge the bully? What will it cost me to take the abuse? How much am I willing to risk?
- Can my family absorb the cost (either the financial cost or the emotional costs) if I leave my job?
- Will I make life difficult for others at work if I fight or if I do nothing?
- What is the cost emotionally and physically if I do nothing?
- Can I put up with this without it killing my spirit?

Assess Your Goals

- Do I want to change the organization and how it treats employees?
- Do I want to get coworkers to join me in objecting to the bully?
- Am I willing to be more assertive and change my behaviors?
- Can I change my boundaries, my limits, and/or my reaction?
- Do I just want better working conditions for myself?

Summary

Like conflict itself, encounters with difficult people seem inevitable. Difficult encounters occur in many contexts, and determining the motives of difficult people is problematic. Four critical lessons guide responses to difficult people. First, control the impulse to label motives and reactions based on attributions. Second, change the situation to require the recipient of the unwelcome behavior to take positive action. Third, engage in two types of self-awareness: awareness of comments from others that cause an emotional reaction and comments to others that cause defensiveness. Fourth, develop listening and questioning skills necessary to discover the interests behind the difficult behavior. Specific difficult encounters include giving critical feedback, responding to interruptions, and unearned criticism.

Bullying is a growing concern in society, particularly in schools and the workplace. Bullying is the harassment of someone over time that results in or comes from unequal power. Few people have not experienced or observed bullying in educational and/or work settings. Three explanations for bullying are that it is provoked by the target, it is a personality flaw in the perpetrator, and it is encouraged by culture. In the early stages of bullying, targets can respond using the conflict management skills discussed in this book. In the later stages of bullying after the victim has lost power and become stigmatized, only positive management intervention will help.

Chapter Resources

Exercises

1. Visit one of the national anti-bullying websites listed in Table 10.7. Find a tactic for responding to bullies that is different from the ones in this chapter and bring it to class. Be prepared to present your tactic to the class and discuss whether you personally could use the tactic.

2. Discuss the following case and decide as a group how to respond.

   You have been with a company for a long time. You know your job well and the jobs of those around you. You are transferred to another site where you are now working for a newly instituted manager, Carmen, who has little experience in the company. You get along well with others and with Carmen. You shared your insights about the company and top management with Carmen. Fast-forward one year. You are in line for a promotion, and Carmen has started telling others that you are unhappy with the company. In addition, you seem to be in trouble with Carmen all the time now—called on the carpet for minor, even meaningless, infractions. You suspect that she is trying to keep you down because you may surpass her. You overheard her talking to another staff member about you. What do you do?

3. Discuss the following case and decide as a group how to respond.

   You've worked for XYZ Company for three years; you have a colleague, Xavier, who just doesn't seem to like you. You need to have data from this person by the third week of the month so that you can compile a report to send "upstairs" by the fourth week. Consistently you receive this data late, and only then after several requests. On two occasions, you have not delivered your report upstairs by the deadline and were spoken to about it by upper management. You have tried talking to Xavier, but he responds, "If you worked harder, you could get it done." Xavier is a good friend of your immediate supervisor, and your supervisor backs him. Xavier gossips about you at the office and you are noticing that coworkers are less friendly than usual. You think that you do quality work and Xavier is instigating this anti-You public relations campaign to get you to quit or be fired.

4. For the cases in questions 2 and 3, explore if your perception of the bully changes if you change the sex of the bully. Would age affect your perception of the bully? Ethnicity? Are we more likely to excuse some behavior based on what group the target or the bully comes from?

Journal/Essay Topics

1. After reading Case 10.3, write an essay where you portray yourself in the role of the bully. Put yourself into the context of junior high school. What made someone a target? What would your objective have been? What would need to change to stop your bullying ways?

2. After reading Case 10.3, write an essay in which you portray the role of the target. What do you think would make you the target of the bully? What are bystanders in this situation likely to do? Would you tell others about the bully? What if anything could you do to stop the bullying?

Research Topics

1. Find up-to-date statistics on school or workplace bullying. Write a summary that illustrates trends in bullying research.

2. Conduct research and/or interviews to determine if your college/university has anti-bullying policies. If so, analyze the policies and state if you think they are effective. If there is no policy, explore the pros and cons of formal anti-bullying policies.

Mastery Case

Examine Mastery Case 10, "Micah's Internship." Which concepts from the chapter help explain the behavior patterns in the case of both the bully and the target? What strategies might help Micah?

Micah's Internship

Micah signs on to a marketing firm for his senior internship that, he hopes, will result in a job offer. Micah's field supervisor, Samuel, has been with the firm for a long time and has a reputation as a difficult person. Micah is energetic and popular with the younger workers at the firm. At first, Samuel seems to want friendship and is very helpful in training Micah on his job duties.

Micah confides in Samuel that he is having a conflict with his fiancé and second thoughts about marriage. Soon, Micah notices that others stop talking when he enters a room and aren't available to go to lunch as they were in the past.

A coworker finally admits that Samuel has been telling everyone that Micah's work is no good because he spends all his time in bars and "having fun" with lots of different women. Micah is shocked. He confronts Samuel with the rumor; Samuel denies saying anything to others and calls Micah paranoid.

In the next group meeting, Samuel spends forty-five minutes tearing apart Micah's last report, yelling at him for being incompetent, and predicts that he will never get a job in advertising. Micah tries to do better, even though he is now unsure about what is expected. Samuel gives him last-minute assignments that are beyond his training and publicly humiliates him when he does a poor job. Samuel contacts his university supervisor and reports that Micah has sexual addiction problem and isn't mature enough to be employed anywhere. He recommends a "D" for Micah's final grade.

11

Moving Beyond Self-Help

Adjudication
Alternative dispute resolution
   (ADR)
Arbitration
Balanced Model of Mediation
Close-ended/Open-ended question
Closure

Commonalities
Conflict coaching
Directiveness
Impartiality
Intrusiveness
Issues
Mediation

Neutrality
Positions
Problem-solving mediation
Reality testing
Reframing
Settlement range
Validation

Objectives

After reading the chapter, you should be able to:

1. Differentiate among types of third-party processes
2. Explain the phases in the Balanced Mediation Model
3. Differentiate between interests and positions
4. Recognize key communication strategies of effective mediators

There are many ways to respond to conflict: We can avoid it, escalate it, work on it directly with the other person, or attempt to change ourselves and hope we transform the other. Because of its complex nature, people sometimes find they are unable to manage conflict effectively without assistance. Thus far, we have focused on the main theme of this book: personal conflict management. However, competent conflict managers know that sometimes a conflict goes beyond the point where personal management is effective and the help of others is beneficial. This chapter explores some of the ways that third parties can assist with conflict management, with a special focus on the process of mediation.

CASE 11.1 • *We're Still Parents*

Jack and I (Lola) were married for eight years, and we now have two girls ages seven and three. We were too young, too broke, and too selfish to make it work at the time. Of course, I thought it was all Jack's fault—if he had been more understanding, kinder, or patient it might have worked. I'm sure he thought, "Lola made this mess." He used to say I was the one who changed. When we finally decided to divorce, we were so angry at each other. We had failed our marriage and our children. We couldn't talk about anything together without it turning into a huge yelling match.

The court required us to go to mediation to work out child custody arrangements, and I dreaded being in the same room with Jack. But the mediator helped us break down our problems into manageable bits, and I felt that I was heard. When Jack was talking to the mediator, he even said he felt bad about the marriage's failure. The mediator taught us that while we're divorced, we're still parents and that won't change for our entire lives. We needed to decide what kind of role models we wanted to be for our girls. The mediator made us focus on the issues rather than fall into our old patterns of bickering and blaming. The mediator made it safe to listen to each other and work on the problem together. I have hope we'll be good parents, even though we're divorced.

Approaches to Solving Conflict

The philosophical approach to conflict an individual takes dramatically affects the type of third-party intervention process that is selected. Generally, third-party resolution strategies involve one of three approaches: a focus on power, a focus on rights, or a focus on interests (Table 11.1).

Power-Based Intervention

Resolving conflict through *power* is competitive. In competition, whoever has the most ability to influence—whether through physical might, use of resources like money, knowledge, communication skill, or connections—is favored to win.

> "Power concedes nothing without a demand. It never has and it never will."
> —Nineteenth-century abolitionist, Frederick Douglass

In Western society, where competition is the standard negotiation approach, the English language is riddled with references to the quest for and necessity of power: "Might makes right," "She's power hungry," "Knowledge is power." "Money is power." Don't forget to wear a "power suit" when interviewing for that "high-powered position." Power frequently is seen as a negative yet necessary evil. However, while we are warned that power corrupts and absolute power corrupts absolutely, we're also told that power can be good if used wisely and with "great power comes great responsibility." We are encouraged to empower ourselves and others and to balance power to create more even playing fields. Despite these popular adages, power in and of itself is not bad or good. It is a resource to cultivate and exists in all relationships.

Power in conflict resolution is about having enough influence to gain compliance, or at minimum, power to assert oneself into the decision-making process.

Those with less power may see resolution by power as inherently unfair. In a power-driven universe, the big corporation has more resources to win against the employee, the bully rules the home or workplace, and big government overwhelms the individual citizen. In Case 11.1, "We're Still Parents," the physically stronger parent who assumes a power focus may be able to intimidate the other parent by way of threats, or the one with the most money can seek advantage over the other by hiring the better attorney. If we do not possess enough power individually to win, our goal in a competitive system is to find someone to fight on our side—somebody bigger (stronger, smarter, richer, better connected) than the other side.

Although we cannot deny the critical role that power plays in conflict resolution, civil society has aimed to move beyond awarding victory to the side with the most power. One alternative system stems from the science of rights.

Rights-Based Intervention

Western society has a well-defined, yet evolving process for resolving conflicts through the promotion and protection of individual rights. The court system adjudicates using a *rights-based intervention* for resolving conflicts. The goal in **adjudication,** or litigation, is to balance power so everyone will have their case decided by legal precedent, not brute power. The employee who is fired because he is considered too old can have recourse through legal rights stemming from federal age discrimination laws to triumph over a big corporation. The courts can intervene if one parent wants to deny the other parent access to their children. Of course, there are flaws within the legal precedence system because more money can buy better representation or lobbyists could influence what laws are enacted, but the cornerstone philosophy is that legal rights should prevail regardless of influence.

Unfortunately, the development of a rights-based system has been established through historical precedents and complicated legal interpretations of complex written declarations of rights (such as the U.S. Constitution). Knowledge of the rights-based system requires extensive training. Individuals seeking justice through the rights-based system may find it prudent to have trained experts advocating on their behalf (attorneys) in making arguments and appeals to the decision makers—typically judges or juries.

In the rights-based system, the locus of control over the decision generally lies outside of those experiencing the conflict. The issue, or case, is determined by a judge who will rule in favor of either the defendant or the plaintiff. Although decisions can be appealed, once the case enters the system, the outcome no longer is in the sole purview of those directly involved in the conflict. In other words, someone else makes the decision and not the disputants.

Interest-Based Intervention

Both power- and rights-based processes tend to be driven by an individual's desire to win—to have one's way at the expense of others' needs or to protect individual rights against unwanted intrusions. A focus on *interests* takes a different approach. As discussed earlier, *interests* are the underlying needs that drive a conflict. An *interest-based approach* focuses

TABLE 11.1 *Three Perspectives on Resolving Disputes*

Type of Approach	*Benefits*	*Disadvantages*
Power-based	Clear winner and loser Often expedient Violence can be avoided by threats Power resources usually easy to identify	Negative peace Lack of satisfaction by one party May lead to violence Little room for positive expression of concerns Power is tenuous and constantly under threat of being thwarted People with low power resources use what power resources they do have to be heard
Rights-based	Clear rules for engagement Specific requirements for evidence The law is the same for everyone People can be represented by attorneys Process is usually open to public scrutiny Precedents are set	Many emotional issues and interests are not allowed credence Usually expensive Usually very time consuming May require representation by attorneys Decisions are made by judges or juries Laws may prohibit creative solutions Decision making removed from the parties
Interest-based	Open to exploring emotions of parties Solutions can be unique to the parties Not limited to precedence or conventional approaches Structurally flexible as decision making stays with the parties May be more expedient than litigation May be less costly than litigation	May have little or no public scrutiny Private justice instead of public, therefore open to bias and malpractice by mediators Some may not be able to negotiate effectively and may be better served by representation No precedent set Lack of consistency in practice May deter the establishment of important precedents

Source: Reprinted with permission from *Mediation Theory and Practice (2005)*, Allyn & Bacon, p. 9.

on meeting individual needs and at the same time meeting the other's needs as much as possible. An interest-based approach has a dual focus that can consider other criteria in addition to who has the law on their side. Those with an interest focus can consider issues of fairness or other criteria that are important to each party but that may not be resolved in a rights-based system.

In Case 11.1, the rights-based system is well prepared to determine how much child support should be paid or how Lola and Jack's property would be divided. But what about how Jack feels when Lola remarries and wants the kids to call her new husband "Dad"? The court system is not designed to explore the nature of feelings of hurt, abandonment, distrust, or fear. Unless it is a legal issue, it generally is not an included in a rights-based system.

Mediation, discussed later in this chapter, offers a third-party intervention from an interest-based perspective.

> ### *Discussion Question 11.1*
> Compare the probable impact on the relationship if the couple in Case 11.1 had their case settled in a court. How does an interest-based approach help parties focus on the emotional and relationship needs they may have?

Conflict Coaching

The interest-based practice of an expert helping one person (or sometimes both) in a conflict through private coaching emerged in the United States in 1996 as one of the services offered at Temple University's conflict management center and grew into a bedrock service of many conflict centers. **Conflict coaching** "is the process in which a coach and disputant communicate one-on-one for the purpose of developing the disputant's conflict related understanding, interaction strategies, and interaction skills" (Brinkert, 2006, p. 518).

Brinkert (2006) proposed a five-stage model for conflict coaching that leads an individual through a first telling of the story/conflict, the building of multiple perspectives about the conflict, developing a view of a successful outcome, developing skills to transform the story, and systematically reviewing the entire conflict analysis. Through these five stages, a professional conflict manager can assist individuals with the perspective, strategies, and skills to transform their conflict.

Third-Party Resolution Processes

Many interest-based processes fall within the term **alternative dispute resolution (ADR).** ADR delineates those conflict management systems that are alternatives to a court of law. Although some conflicts must be handled in litigation, many do not. The overburdened court system has been active in seeking strategies to reduce its workload.

Arbitration is one form of ADR where a neutral third party or panel (typically a judge or experts in a particular field) is empowered to make a decision for the conflicting parties. When parties decide in advance to accept the decision of the arbitrator as final, it is called *binding arbitration.* If you have a cellular phone or rent movies, you probably agreed to arbitration when you signed your contract. You agreed to put your facts in a dispute to the third party designated in the contract and to be bound by that arbitrator's decision. Arbitration is a standard means of resolving many retail/consumer disputes because it is a quicker and less expensive alternative to adjudication.

Another increasingly common ADR method is mediation. **Mediation** is "the process whereby a mutually acceptable third party, who is neutral and impartial, facilitates an interest-based communicative process, enabling disputing parties to explore concerns and to create their own outcomes" (McCorkle & Reese, 2005b, pp. 14–15). In many jurisdictions, mediation is one of the ADR processes instituted to handle a multitude of issues outside of the courtroom.

In European American models, the mediator typically has no prior relationship with either party and does not favor one person more than the other (**neutrality**). The mediator also has no stake in the outcome of the dispute (**impartiality**). Where a child custody decision may be handled through the courts in terms of the *rights* of each parent and the children, during mediation a third party helps the parents negotiate their view of what options are best for the children. The mediator controls the process to help the parents arrive at a solution that can be tailored to the needs of the individuals involved.

The mediator brings specialized techniques to the conflict negotiation to help the parties find personalized solutions, see each other's needs, and understand each other's feelings and perspectives. For example, Lola and Jack (Case 11.1) went to mediation prior to submitting a parenting plan to a judge. As decision makers, they knew their work schedules and family situations and determined, with the help of a mediator, that it was best for their girls to be with Lola on major holidays and with Jack during school breaks and birthdays. A judge, who may not have the time to find out about each parent's life, might have made a dramatically different decision.

In sum, the differences in the interventions of adjudication, arbitration, and mediation generally are based in the focus on rights versus interests. However the biggest difference between mediation and the other types of intervention is where control of the decision is located. In a courtroom, and usually in arbitration, the decision is the responsibility of the judge or arbitrator. The parties present their cases (or have their attorneys present their cases), and the judge/arbitrator renders a decision. In mediation, the decision lies with the parties. A mediator serves as a facilitator of communication and process, but the outcome is the responsibility of the parties.

Mediation is an accessible and affordable third-party intervention usable in a variety of conflict areas. Many universities have mediation programs designed to resolve conflicts between faculty, students, roommates, and university employees. Community mediation centers provide alternative dispute resolution services to neighbors, homeowner associations, and various organizations. Mediators in private practice handle environmental disputes, divorce and child custody cases, civil complaints, contract disagreements, real estate disputes, and numerous other types of conflicts. The growth of mediation makes it likely that you will be involved in mediation at some point in your work or personal life. The next section examines the mediation process and reveals some of the techniques that mediators use.

KEY 11.1

When you've exhausted your personal options or reached an impasse, seek third-party solutions.

Mediation

Why Mediate?

The reasons that people come to mediation are as varied as the issues to be resolved. Sometimes parties find that they just can't seem to work out issues themselves because of the emotional nature of the subject. Sometimes their personalities or styles get in the way of solving a problem without rancor. Juvenile justice programs may require victim-offender mediation before seeing a judge. Mediation may be required by a judge to see if parties can work out their concerns before taking up the court's time and having a judgment forced on them. Some small claims courts have diversion programs where parties must meet with a mediator prior to seeing the judge. Mediation may be pursued as an option for disputes that don't qualify as a legal issue but need to be addressed. Some businesses require mediation for employee disputes. Many communities offer dispute resolution services for cases such as barking dogs, property line disputes, parking, or landlord-tenant problems. Your campus may have a student mediation program. The thread that runs among all types of mediation is the philosophy that the locus of control over decisions belongs to the parties.

Benefits and Disadvantages of Mediation

The benefits of mediation lie primarily in its flexibility, speed, moderate cost, and confidentiality. Although the legal system works well for a resolution based on the rights of the individuals, other issues may be at stake for the disputants. Mediation is ideal in cases when the parties have a continuing relationship that needs to be repaired.

Another benefit to mediation is its response time compared to the court system. Cases may have to wait months or even years to be resolved through the courts. Mediation usually can be scheduled and completed relatively quickly. Although some individuals seeking mediation also have the additional costs of legal counsel, generally the expense of mediation is a fraction of the cost of litigation. Federal agencies report saving billions of dollars between fiscal years 2002 and 2003 in attorney fees from contract disputes that were mediated instead of litigated (Brodnax & Mazur, 2008).

A final benefit to mediation is confidentiality. When the process is private, no public record is created as occurs with adjudication. When looking at the reasons a piece of property went to a sheriff's auction, Suzanne went to the county courthouse and read the court documents on the case. In the process, she learned all about a local celebrity's financial troubles and unflattering comments made by the opposing attorney in the case (who called the defendant a spoiled rich banker's son). What is said during mediation is not open to the general public, and mediators pledge to keep the details confidential.

Mediation, however, is not without disadvantages. Privacy and the dependence of parties to negotiate on their own behalf are two possible downsides to mediation. Although privacy has advantages for the individuals involved, it may be detrimental to the public. The private nature of mediation may allow for abuse or neglect of individual rights. For example, an undertrained mediator may not recognize a spouse's willingness to agree quickly as a possible symptom of spousal abuse. Additionally, a decision rendered in mediation would not establish a legal precedence. Imagine the delay in social justice that might have incurred if civil rights pioneer Rosa Parks had mediated with the Montgomery Bus Company instead of going to court. Her public defiance of the rules that relegated her to the back of the bus opened the door for legal action to overturn unjust and discriminatory practices and spurred a wave of civil rights actions. Mediation, however, may have resulted in only Parks being allowed to sit at the front of the bus in Montgomery, Alabama, and one of the sparks that ignited the modern civil rights movement quietly would have been extinguished.

> ### *Discussion Question 11.2*
> What factors can we use to determine when mediation is appropriate and when mediation would be inappropriate?

Another concern about mediation lies in its dependency on the abilities of the parties. Disputants who are skilled negotiators may have an unfair advantage over those who are less adept. Generally disputants must express their needs—with encouragement, reframing, and synthesizing by the mediator. In a court of law, the unskilled negotiator would have an advocate presenting the case. Conversely, in mediation individuals are responsible for making their interests known. Although part of a mediator's job is to ensure that the parties' needs are discussed and they are making informed choices, there is a risk for individuals who are not savvy about what information is necessary, are reticent, or who don't know what rights are involved. Furthermore, just like any other industry, there are good mediators and those who are not so good. However, unlike in a public court system, mediators who are less skilled may go undetected because of the private nature of the events they facilitate.

> ### Discussion Question 11.3
>
> What advice would you give someone who wanted to hire a mediator? How could you determine a good mediator from one who wasn't?

Mediator Responsibilities

The mediator serves many roles during the mediation process. Table 11.2 summarizes some of what a mediator does. Mediators must have a clear understanding of conflict management techniques, listening skills, factors that affect conflict interactions, and the dynamics of interpersonal conflict. They must be able simultaneously to chart the mediation process and to

TABLE 11.2 *Mediator Responsibilities*

Facilitator and process controller:	The mediator moves the process forward and ensures participation by both parties.
Coach and trainer:	The mediator is a role model demonstrating how to communicate effectively and appropriately. The mediator may meet privately with disputants to coach them on how to raise their concerns in a joint session.
Impartial and neutral third party:	The mediator has no stake in the decisions of the parties nor is he or she biased toward or against either party.
Legitimizer:	The mediator helps parties bring issues important to them to the table and validates their concerns.
Face manager:	The mediator redirects negative comments to reduce embarrassment and helps parties find ways to move from past grievances and positions.
Power manager:	When the parties have inequitable power or abilities, the mediator ensures that the less powerful has a chance to engage the process equitably.
Resource expander:	The mediator ensures that all parties have access to necessary information and are aware of available resources both in the mediation and in the community.
Agent of reality:	The mediator helps parties assess the workability of decisions and aids in the recognition of unrealistic goals or problematic plans of action.

Source: Adapted from McCorkle and Reese (2005b).

make strategic decisions that will move the process forward while at the same time ensuring the parties are well served. Mediators must be strong at synthesizing complex information and tracking multiple stories and details while validating both parties and appearing not to favor one individual over the other. The multitude of roles and tasks may seem daunting. Beginning mediators typically receive at least 40 hours of in-depth training, and some states require much more to be certified. During their training, mediators develop the ability to fulfill their roles as facilitators, coaches, power balancers, agents of reality, and the rest of their responsibilities.

Mediator Approaches

The decision to choose mediation in lieu of other resolution techniques should include consideration of its benefits and disadvantages. Mediation is an alternative to other resolution process but not a replacement. Just as there are options for the type of interventions available, there are different types of philosophical approaches to mediation. Conciliatory and problem-solving mediation are two such approaches.

Conciliation

Bush and Folger (1994) advocate for the conciliation or transformative approach in their book *The Promise of Mediation*. The goal of *conciliation* mediation is to transform parties from adversaries into individuals who see the value of the other and their relationship. Once transformed, the parties have the basis to create long-lasting and meaningful solutions. The transformative mediator thinks a focus on solutions is too limiting.

Problem Solving

In contrast, the goal of **problem-solving mediation** is to help the parties work through issues and find a resolution to their problems. The problem-solving approach to mediation generally follows prescribed phases designed to move parties toward agreement. Mediation, from this approach, focuses primarily on substantive issues (e.g., money, distribution of resources, or procedures).

The Balanced Model of Mediation

The **Balanced Model of Mediation** (McCorkle & Reese, 2005b) is an approach that contains elements of transformation and of problem solving but endeavors to deliver what the disputants need. The Balanced Model contains phases that deal with the parties' emotional or relationship issues, when necessary, and then walks the parties through a problem-solving process. If the parties have no strong emotions that are blocking their ability to problem-solve, the mediator minimizes that phase. Because the mediator is cross-trained with problem-solving and transformative skills, he or she can better meet the needs of the parties by creating understanding between them, helping them negotiate their own decisions, or providing assistance in all phases. Table 11.3 presents the six

TABLE 11.3 *Phases in the Balanced Model of Mediation*

Opening Statement
Storytelling
Agenda
Problem Solving
Testing and Writing the Agreement
Closure

Source: Adapted from McCorkle and Reese (2005b).

phases of the Balanced Model: opening statement, storytelling, agenda building, problem solving, testing and writing the agreement, and closure.

> **Discussion Question 11.4**
>
> In the Balanced Mediation Model, the mediator is required to be a neutral and impartial third party. How could mediation be impacted if the mediator is not neutral or impartial? Are there times or cultures when it is better to have a mediator who is known to the parties rather than a stranger?

The Opening Statement

Most mediation models open with the mediator giving an overview of the mediation process and laying out expectations. The opening phase includes a statement about the mediator's commitment to *confidentiality*, which is a pledge that the mediator will not divulge the details of the negotiation unless required by law. In the opening statement, the mediator also discusses what will occur during the session and sets ground rules for behavior. The importance of the opening statement is to set the stage, both structurally and psychologically, for the mediation to unfold.

Storytelling

At the heart of the mediation event is the opportunity for each party to feel heard and understood. The mediator starts this phase by probing what brought the parties to the table. Each party is offered sufficient time to express his or her concerns, perceptions, and view of the situation. The mediator is responsible for listening actively to the story, validating the storyteller's emotions, and making sure that each party has an opportunity to learn new facts and viewpoints.

The mediator employs a variety of communication skills to encourage storytelling. Early in the mediation, the feeling paraphrase may be common. *Feeling paraphrases*, sometimes called validation, identify probable emotions underlying a speaker's statement. One person may wave his arms in the air in frustration and say, "I just don't understand her. She wants me to be more involved, but then she won't talk to me when I come over." The mediator could attempt to identify the emotion of the speaker, even though the speaker didn't verbally label his emotions. The mediator could state, "You're confused by what you see as mixed-messages." A feeling paraphrase serves to validate the speaker (and must contain a feeling word, such as "confused"). If the feeling paraphrase was an accurate identification of the disputant's feeling, the speaker might respond, "Yes, it is very confusing and I just want to get this figured out." If the mediator does not select an appropriate feeling paraphrase, the speaker might say, "No, I'm not really confused. I am irritated that she doesn't seem to know what she wants." Either response from the speaker is productive because the emotional issue has been brought to the surface and clarified.

Once the disputants begin to talk about the more substantive issues, content paraphrasing may come into play. *Content paraphrasing* is a tool that the mediator uses to capture and rephrase a comment for the purpose of clarification, emphasis, and or validation. For example, an individual might say, "The only time we talk to each other, we seem to yell, and that can't be good for the girls to see from their parents." The mediator could provide a content paraphrase by focusing on the heart of the message: "The girls see you arguing and that's not an example you want to set for them." Other actions child custody mediators might take are in Table 11.4.

Effective mediators are curious and desire to get a picture of the situation. Mediators ask questions to clarify and uncover details so all parties have access to the same information. **Close-ended questions** (those that can be answered with a yes, no, or limited response) are used sparingly in mediation, particularly during the early phases. More helpful and common are **open-ended questions** that invite fuller responses. Open-ended questions are the mediator's stock and trade. Common open-ended questions include "How did that affect you?" or "What was the situation like before this happened?" "What do you do on an average day in your job?" Open-ended questions help the parties tell their stories and provide the mediator with information to keep the process moving forward. Statements that encourage detailed responses serve the same purpose as open-ended questions. "Give me some examples of how holidays were handled in the past." "I need you to explain that more fully to me so I understand." The goal of these approaches is to flesh out the story to get at necessary details.

Reframing is a skill that mediators use to take an existing message from a speaker and reconstruct it in a way that benefits the mediation. If a landlord makes an offensive statement about a tenant such as, "He is just scum. You should have seen the way he trashed the apartment," the mediator works to reframe that statement to keep the important issue the speaker identified while discarding the insult. A reframing of the landlord's statement could be, "I can see you are very upset [feeling paraphrase], and you want to have your property taken care of [an issue highlighted]. Please tell me what you found when you entered the apartment he vacated" [getting the speaker back to the issue].

A major goal of the storytelling phase is to help parties separate positions from interests. Parties are likely to enter into mediation knowing the solutions they want to see implemented or the **positions** they hold. Common positions are "I demand an apology." "I want a raise." "I want full custody of the kids." "I expect to receive that property immediately." The mediator's job is to look behind those positional statements and identify the *interests* that the parties need to have addressed. For example, behind "I demand an apology" may be an interest of needing acknowledgment of hurt feelings. Behind "I want a raise" may be an interest of wanting recognition. Expectation may be driven by interests of fairness or desires for compensation. Once identified, needs sometimes can be met in other ways than one side's initial opening position.

Part of a mediator's skill is the ability to multitask. At the same time the mediator is listening to the party's story, he or she is uncovering the issues. **Issues** are the topics of the mediation that will become the focus of negotiation. The parties arrive with a general idea of the main issue they want to discuss (division of property, settling Mom's estate, child custody). The mediator ensures that all the necessary issues are put on the table for negotiation and interests are uncovered.

> ### Discussion Question 11.5
> What is the likely outcome of a mediation where the mediator let positional statements stand and didn't identify underlying interests?

In a court of law, if an issue is not a legal issue, the legal system is not designed to deal with it. Communication and trust are common bones of contention in mediations where there is a continued relationship between parties. Family conflict offer rich sources for communication and trust concerns. For example, how are kids to talk with parents? How can teens demonstrate that they are trustworthy and therefore responsible enough for

TABLE 11.4 *What Child Custody Mediators Might Do*

1. Assume that the conflict among the parents will not go away but that it is possible to cooperate for the sake of the children.
2. Assume that both parents love the children.
3. Assume that the children need both parents.
4. State that the mediator is the advocate for the child.
5. Explain the negative effects on children when parents denigrate each other to the child.
6. Explain the ways that children may attempt to play one parent against the other.
7. Explain that better parenting will occur if each parent has alone time with the child.
8. Educate that children will have changing parenting needs as they age and that in the future the parenting plan may need to be altered.
9. Inform parents of children's propensity to want parents to reunite.
10. Educate parents that each child will have unique and different needs after the divorce.
11. Educate parents to think about "co-parenting" after divorce rather than custody as a "possession" or right.
12. Educate the parents on strategies to protect them and their children from psychological harm.
13. Prepare parents for their own stages of emotion during the divorce process.
14. Strategize ways to introduce new partners to children.
15. Explain the threshold level and proof requirements if one parent claims drug and alcohol use as cause for not allowing a parent to fulfill his or her parenting responsibilities.
16. Educate parents of various types of shared parenting and parental custody models.
17. Screen for domestic violence.

Source: Saposnek (1998), pp. 101–111.

later curfews? Will one divorcing parent turn a child against the other? Is it appropriate for the ex-husband to still be friends with his ex-wife's family, and what will that look like if she remarries? Issues such as these can be explored in mediation. Once identified, issues become the road map for the mediator to help the disputants negotiate.

The final multitasking job for the mediator during this phase is to discover and highlight commonalities. **Commonalities** are traits, experiences, or feelings that the parties share. Two people in an office both may want a respectful and productive work environment. Divorcing parents both want their children to be safe and secure. Roommates who disagree about what portion of a phone bill is each person's responsibility may still want to preserve the friendship. Neighbors with different views of what makes for a nice yard may both want to live harmoniously next to one another. Highlighting commonalities allows the parties to see the problem as the issue to be solved, not the other party as the enemy.

> ### Discussion Question 11.6
> Provide an example of a conflict either you have experienced or is currently in the news involving at least two parties. Identify the issue(s) in contention, and provide at least one commonality the parties share.

Agenda Building

The issues identified in the previous phase become the agenda to be negotiated. Mediators are savvy about phrasing agendas to be as neutral as possible. For example, Margot would feel at a disadvantage if an agenda item were phrased this way: "One item on the agenda is to make sure that Margot pays her fair share of the utilities." Instead, the mediator would say, "One item is to discuss each party's share of responsibility for the utilities." As the mediator hears issues, he or she places them on a list that is revealed at the beginning of the agenda phase.

For experienced mediators, the session may flow easily from storytelling to negotiation without a formal agenda. In all cases, however, the mediator is responsible to ensure that issues that were important to the parties are put on the negotiation table.

Problem Solving

Mediation models vary in how involved the mediator will be during the negotiation and problem-solving phase. In most mediation models, the parties are responsible for decision making. Mediators who offer suggestions are using **intrusiveness.** Disputants may think these suggestions are the "best" solution because an authority figure made them. When the parties do not come up with the ideas that become the solution, they often are less committed to following through with their agreements. Subsequently, most mediation models discourage or outright forbid mediators from offering solutions.

Directiveness relates to the amount of control a mediator exerts over the mediation process. "A high-directive mediator might lead the disputants through several problem-solving exercises to help them assess their options and to generate possible solutions. . . . A low-directive mediator will lean back and let the disputants talk their way through the negotiation—acting only when the disputants become too emotional or become deadlocked" (McCorkle & Reese, 2005b, pp. 145–146). How directive a mediator is depends on how cooperative the disputants are and how comfortable the mediator is relinquishing some control over the process.

Mediators bring many skills to the table to help parties negotiate. We only discuss two skills in this chapter: brainstorming and determining the bargaining range. *Brainstorming* is a popular technique to get parties to think outside the box. As mentioned previously, parties typically enter negotiations with a solution already in mind. Brainstorming prompts them to get that solution out on the table, but it also encourages them to consider it only as one option among many possible solutions. A mediator might open a brainstorming session by stating the rules of brainstorming, saying, "Let's make a list of as many possible solutions that you two can come up with for this issue. We won't bother with whether the solutions will work right now or evaluate them because the goal is to come up with as many options as possible in the next two minutes. Feel free to be as creative as you can be." The mediator then serves as recorder—if necessary, reminding parties not to evaluate solutions (yet).

In distributive conflicts, such as those about money, mediators help determine if there is a positive or negative **settlement range.** For example, Julio repaired Jesse's car and billed him $650 for it. The mediator has a private conversation with Julio and asks a series of questions about what his needs are. Because Julio is tired of waiting for his money and knows that Jesse doesn't have much cash, he is willing to settle the debt for $570. In a private session with Jesse, the mediator discovers that Jesse has offered to settle the debt for $520 for the car but can go as high as $590 if payments are allowed. The settlement range would look like this:

Julio	$570 --------------- $650	
Jesse	$520 --------------- $590	

The *positive settlement range* is between $570 and $590: the overlap in the amounts they are willing to pay and to receive. However, if Julio wasn't willing to go below $600 for the debt, there would be a *negative settlement range*—no overlap in their offers. In a negative settlement range, the parties must negotiate ways put other value on the table if they are going to settle. For instance, Julio may agree to take $500 in cash today, and he accepts two tickets to a Minnesota Vikings football game for the balance of the debt.

Testing and Writing the Settlement Agreement

Once the parties have determined a course of action, the mediator has the responsibility to make sure the agreement is strong. Strong agreements are specific, workable, represent parties fairly, and fit the parties' reality.

Disputants may come up with agreements that state their goodwill but are vague. Two employees who have been fighting in the workplace may agree to "respect" each other. After securing that agreement, the mediator's job is to delve into what "respect" means by making it *specific* in behavioral terms. When parties agree to notify each other if a dog is barking too loudly, the mediator helps the parties make the agreement more specific: How will the contact occur? What might the notification sound like? Likewise, strong agreements are *workable*. To test the workability of an agreement, mediators **reality test** it to see if it meets the needs expressed earlier in the session and if the parties can actually do what they've agreed to do. If someone of low income agrees to make $400 a month payments on a debt, the mediator should probe to see if that is realistic.

Reality testing may require the mediator to look back to the interests that each party expressed. If Carmella agrees to give up her dog as part of an agreement with her neighbor, the mediator might compare this decision with an interest that Carmella stated earlier. The mediator could say, "Carmella, earlier you said that you got the dog so you would feel safe living in your apartment alone. Now you are agreeing to give up the dog. Could you talk to me a bit about how your need for safety will be met?" The mediator is not trying to talk Carmella out of her decision to give up the dog but is instead reality testing the agreement to make sure it will hold up once the parties leave the mediation table. The best agreements are the ones that meet both parties' needs. In this case, Carmella may inform the mediator that she's decided to take the money she'll save not buying dog food and invest in a burglar alarm system. Her brother wants the dog anyway.

Closure

Depending on the type of mediation and the needs of the parties, solidifying the agreement can be formal or informal. Some mediations end with handshakes; other require a written agreement signed by both parties for closure to occur. Some mediations may end without the parties coming to a resolution at all. In all circumstances, bringing **closure**, or a sense of finality, is an important responsibility of the mediator.

When the mediation is done, mediators should acknowledge the hard work and commitment that the parties brought to the session. Congratulations on agreements are appropriate. When mediations do not end in a settlement, the mediator's responsibility is to help the parties realize that even though they are not walking away with an agreement, they now have a better understanding of their issues and greater awareness of how the other party sees the situation. Mediators may engage disputants in identifying next steps or other resources available in their community.

The bottom line of any mediation is that the parties feel they have been heard and understood, at least by the mediator, if not by the other party. If this has been accomplished, then the mediation can be deemed successful whether it ends in agreement or not.

Summary

Individuals assume one of three approaches when seeking third-party intervention: power, rights, or interests. Power-based approaches focus on gaining an edge that allow one party to influence the other. Adjudication through the courts uses a rights-based focus. An interest-based approach focuses on meeting both parties' underlying needs and permits discussion of issues of fairness. Mediation is a prime example of an interest-based intervention.

The term *alternative dispute resolution* encompasses many third-party processes, including arbitration and mediation. In arbitration, the third party renders a decision that the parties have agreed beforehand to be binding or nonbinding. Mediators are neutral and impartial third parties who help the disputants reach a decision rather than determine the outcome for them. Mediation occurs in child custody, business, personnel, and many other contexts.

The benefits of mediation are flexibility, speed, and confidentiality. Disadvantages of mediation include its privacy and possible weaknesses of the parties. Mediators fulfill many roles to help the disputants reach a decision, including power balancing, facilitating, coaching, and acting as an agent of reality.

Mediators philosophically implement conciliation, problem solving, or a model that uses both conciliation and problem solving. Conciliation mediators try to transform the inner states of the conflicting parties. Problem-solving mediators focus on helping the parties make decisions. The Balanced Model of Mediation contains elements of conciliation and problem solving that are emphasized according to the needs of each individual case. The six phases in the Balanced Model of Mediation are opening statement; storytelling; agenda building; problem solving; testing and writing the agreement; and closure. Generally, mediators pledge to be confidential and not disclose the details of the case unless required by law.

Mediators employ skills such as feeling paraphrases, content paraphrases, closed- and open-ended questions, reframing, brainstorming, and determining settlement ranges. Mediators separate positions from interests and focus the negotiation phase on meeting the underlying needs of each individual. The mediator uncovers the issues that become the topics of negotiation and highlights commonalities between the disputants.

Mediators who make specific outcome suggestions are intrusive, which many models discourage. Those who keep firm control over the process are directive. Regardless of which mediation style is used, the bottom line is that disputants should feel they have been heard and understood. Successful mediations are not gauged solely by the agreement reached. If parties have greater understanding, clarity on key issues, and an awareness of the other's perspective, the mediation was successful.

Chapter Resources

Exercises

1. Examine one of the cases earlier in the book. For each person in the case, explain the story from his or her perspective. Make a list of any positions each person may have. What do you think are each person's underlying interests? What commonalities do they share? Think of at least three possible solutions that might meet the interests of both parties. If the parties deadlocked in that case, which process would be the best next step: mediation, arbitration, or adjudication?

2. Does your college or university offer mediation services to students? If so, interview a campus mediator to discover how he or she was trained and what kinds of cases come to mediation.

3. Explore the qualifications to become a mediator in your state. Is there a statewide mediation organization in your area? Explore their standards of practice. What are their rules for neutrality? Confidentiality? Training? Conflict of Interests? Membership?

Journal/Essay Topics

1. Choose a conflict in your local community. What were the positions and interests of the parties? How might third-party intervention change the outcome of the conflict?

2. Many states require child custody cases to go to mediation before coming to the courts. What do you think the reasoning is behind this practice? Can you foresee any problems that this practice might bring?

Research Topics

1. Research one of the following contexts of mediation and write a position paper describing what type of cases are handled and how mediators approach their task differently in that context than in other mediation contexts: domestic violence, juvenile victim/offender, divorce and family, or small claims court.

2. What ethics are mediators required to uphold? Review journal articles or codes of mediator conduct. Are items like confidentiality, neutrality, and impartiality treated the same in all codes of conduct?

Mastery Case

Analyze Mastery Case 11, "My Space." What type of dispute resolution processes are suitable for this case?

My Space

Tanya and I are best friends. So, of course, when she asked for the password for my blog, I gave it to her. Weeks later, I started getting funny looks from some of the other kids at school. I started getting a lot of weird pornographic e-mail. One of my so-called friends finally told me that somebody had hacked into my blog about a week before, posted these awful pictures of me, and started writing all this sexual stuff like I was some kind of super slut. Well, I know who must have done it. Just because I started dating Tanya's old boyfriend is no reason for her to do something like that. I know just what to do to get back at her.

12

Managing the Aftermath: Anger, Apology, Forgiveness, and Reconciliation

Vocabulary

Compensational forgiveness
Cool posing
Expectational forgiveness
Fake apologies
Genuine forgiveness
Grievance story
Group forgiveness
Hollow forgiveness

Impulse control
Interpersonal forgiveness
Interpersonal reconciliation
Lawful expectational forgiveness
Positive intentions
Restitutional forgiveness
Restorative justice
Semi-apologies

Silent forgiveness
Sincere apologies
Social harmony forgiveness
State anger
State forgiveness
Trait anger
Trait forgiveness
Unforgiveness

Objectives

After reading the chapter, you should be able to:

1. Differentiate among state and trait conditions
2. Differentiate between forgiveness and reconciliation
3. Explain what forgiveness is and is not

Moments of anger, hurt, disappointment, and/or tragedy shade every person's life. The events that cause hurt can be dramatic—such as abuse, violence, and betrayal—or subtle, such as not getting an expected promotion or an unreturned phone call. Spitzberg and Cupach (1998) explore and itemize interpersonal harms and human failings in their book *The Dark Side of Close Relationships,* including betrayal, jealousy, envy, gossip, codependence, obsession, abuse, and abandonment.

CASE 12.1 • *Winning the Lottery*

JJ and Trini met about six months ago and just became engaged. They plan to be married June 14. Trini is a longtime lottery player and faithfully buys her tickets each week. JJ makes fun of her, saying she is wasting her money. Trini started buying the tickets when JJ wasn't around to avoid his ribbing.

JJ teased her about it—until today. Trini's numbers hit a $75,000 jackpot! She was so excited when she told him that she didn't even hear when he said, "Wow. We can really get a great start in our marriage now." When Trini told her parents the good news, they were happy for her. When she told them she was going to surprise JJ with a trip to Austria for their honeymoon, they replied, "Hey, slow down. You need that money to finish your last year in college so you don't have to work. That's what JJ would want, too."

She told JJ that her parents were being funny about the money and wanting her to spend it all on school. JJ got angry: "I thought we were going to decide together about the money." Trini didn't say anything, but she thought, "This from the guy who always said the lottery was a stupid waste of money? It is my money."

JJ's parents were pressuring him to be sure the money was used for a down payment on a house—and to pick up their share of the wedding expenses. His uncle was starting a new business and wanted them to invest, saying it could really pay off down the road.

Trini's friends started saying to blow off JJ and have a last bit of fun before she got married. They were lobbying for that bright red BMW convertible that Trini always yearns over and maybe taking a trip to Vegas.

One morning, JJ mentioned that maybe they could go down to the lottery office and pick up the check next week, after the publicity frenzy died down. Instead Trini went to pick up the check that afternoon. She opted for the lump sum payment, and after the taxes were taken out, the check was for $42,500. She went to a different bank than where they opened a joint checking account and opened a new account. She then made two stops: She traded in her old car for a $20,000 used convertible, thinking she would compromise rather than get the new BMW that she really wanted. That left about $23,000. Her second stop was to a travel agent where she booked and prepaid ($13,000) for a two-week honeymoon in Austria and Hungary.

When Trini arrived at JJ's house in her convertible, he threw a fit. Trini just said, "Hey, even though we're not married, I saved over $10,000 from the lottery money that we will decide about together. They both fumed for a while but quickly made up and started to joke about the "lucky" car. He seemed pleasantly surprised at the reception after taking their vows when she handed over tickets for a two-week honeymoon.

Trini's parents were happy that they didn't have to help pay for a honeymoon, but in the years that followed they often told Trini that she wasted her biggest opportunity to finish college early. Additionally, JJ's family took every opportunity to admonish Trini for her "wastefulness" and "selfishness." It actually became a family ritual to mull over the old lottery situation right before the couple arrived at family gatherings. The family never completely warmed up to Trini. Whenever JJ doesn't like something Trini does, he still brings up the car and the honeymoon.

Interpersonal conflict may carry pain or disillusionment as part of its baggage. Even after a conflict is managed, the bad feelings may continue. In Case 12.1, the issue of what to do with the lottery money was settled by Trini's unilateral actions. The hurt JJ and his family felt, however, was nurtured and sustained for years. Trini may think the situation is over and forgotten, but because JJ and his family did not find satisfaction and harbored hurt feelings, the conflict may never be over. As long as JJ holds a grudge and his family mulls over the past grievance, the ugly side effects of the conflict may live on, prosper, and grow stronger.

The role of anger, the value of apologies, the nature of forgiveness, and the possibilities of reconciliation are the themes of this chapter. These four areas of study emerged in the last twenty-five years as important components of effective conflict management. Prior to then, forgiveness and reconciliation were considered in the realm of religious studies or counseling/psychiatry. Psychiatrists and physicians investigated these issues to help patients who experienced mental and physical illnesses. Although few research studies from a pure conflict management perspective test the value of reducing anger, giving or accepting apologies, forgiveness, or reconciliation, we can learn much from research done in the medical and counseling community and apply those findings to interpersonal conflict management.

Anger

Proponents of emotional intelligence (Chapter 7) identify primary emotions as including fear and desire. Masking primary emotions, such as fear, are a number of secondary emotions, including anger. Angry behavior often is driven by fear: fear of embarrassment, loss of control, losing face, losing a relationship, or losing power. Both primary and secondary emotions play significant roles in conflict.

The idea of defensive-provoking communication and face were introduced earlier in the book (Chapters 3 and 4). For some, anger is a consequence of defensiveness and fear of loss of face. Researchers studying how emotions affect negotiation ability discovered that words used to label a person negatively or to tell someone what to do were the most frequent catalysts of anger and frustration (Schroth, Bain-Chekal, & Caldwell, 2005). Examples of negative labeling included judgmental phrases like, "You are a bunch of liars," or "It was your fault," and words like *unfair, silly,* and *stupid.* Telling someone what to do was illustrated through phrases such as "You need to give me a better deal" or words such as *can't, must, no way, have to, never,* or *ought to.* For conflict managers, insight into words and behaviors that provoke anger is important because anger affects the quality of communication encounters—usually for the worse.

> "If you kick a stone in anger, you will hurt your own foot."
>
> —Korean proverb

Anger and Strong Emotions

Anger can be expressed or hidden through coping mechanisms such as **cool posing,** which are adaptations to keep from expressing anger when it would be unproductive. Stevenson (2002) directly related cool poses, such as pretending apathy and resisting demonstrations of power, to personal face—particularly among groups processing historic institutionalized oppression such as young African American males. **Impulse control,** being able to forestall impulsive negative behavior, is one hallmark of the emotionally intelligent person (Hughes et al., 2005). However, controlling the anger response through cool posing, impulse control, or simply denying it becomes problematic when the control substitutes for work on one's emotions.

> ### *Discussion Question 12.1*
> Have you ever sent an e-mail or text message when you were really angry? Were there negative consequences to your message? What advice would you give to others who are about to send an e-mail or text message while consumed with anger?

Researchers separate trait and state anger. **State anger** is momentary and caused by occasional events. Conversely, **trait anger** is a relatively stable personality characteristic distinguished by a predisposition to react to events with angry outbursts. For example, a man observed stomping and cursing as he walked alone through a home improvement store would be exhibiting state anger if his behavior was unusual for him and brought on by the convergence of a broken toilet, a flat tire, and losing his wallet—all in one afternoon. If aggression and cursing were typical behaviors for almost any minor adversity that happened, from losing a choice parking spot to having to use another entry door than his first choice, he would be exhibiting signs of trait anger.

Research on date and spousal abuse provide insights into how anger is linked to violence. Parrott and Zeichner's (2003) review of partner abuse research found that two million U.S. women are assaulted by their partners each year, with 40 percent of undergraduate women in premarital relationships having experienced date or partner abuse. Parrott and Zeichner found that men's trait anger itself did not predict violence against women. Rather, those with trait anger combined with misogynistic attitudes (e.g., believing women to be stupid, greedy, irritating, irrational, selfish, spiteful, and vindictive beings who should be put in their place) seemed to produce most of the violence toward women.

INSERT 12.1

Jealousy

Both romantic jealousy and friendship jealousy are common sources of conflict. Romantic jealousy can be defined as "the cognitions, emotions, and behaviors that follow a loss or threat to self-esteem and/or existence or quality of a romantic relationship" from a real or imaginary third party (Bevan & Samter, 2004, p. 14). Jealousy can arise from fear that a romantic partner will engage in sexual intimacy with someone else, but it also stems from numerous other causes, such as loss of trust, seeing a friend share time with new people, or fear of losing a friendship.

Most interestingly, jealousy emerges in friendships with greater frequency than in romantic situations. Bevan and Samter (2004) found some people experience jealousy over the romantic partner of a friend, seeing a friend enjoy other friends and doing activities with others, or a friend withholding personal information that was shared with others. They even found it possible to be jealous of a computer when a friend or partner spends time surfing the net or playing online poker.

The paradox of jealousy is that it frequently leads people to act in ways that do not endear them to the object of their desire and may in fact drive the other away. Anger, threats, physical abuse, and murder of "loved ones" unfortunately can, and do, occur (Leary, Koch, & Hechenbleikner, 2001).

Research into anger among at-risk youth showed promise for the success of anger management programs. Prompted by a growing number of school shootings in the United States and statistics showing about half of all violent crimes are committed by young males, some schools adopted violence and anger reduction programs. Herrmann and McWhirter (2003) tested the Student Created Aggression Replacement Education program (SCARE) and found at-risk youth who completed the anger reduction program felt more able to respond productively toward those exhibiting anger toward them, as well as personally exhibiting less trait and state anger. Booster training, however, was necessary to sustain the reduction of anger over time.

> "Nothing external can make us suffer . . . we suffer only when we want things to be different from what they are."
>
> —Epictetus, first century

Other training programs aim to redirect irrational or defective thinking that result in anger. Levinson (2006) identified several irrational beliefs that lead to anger (Table 12.1). The training goal is to replace each irrational belief with a rational one. For example, even though we would like everyone to love and approve of us, the reality is, they won't. Instead of dwelling on rejection and becoming angry or depressed, the training goal is to focus on how one can be happy, even after being rejected. Feeling happy is better than letting others' lack of approval lead to misery. Ultimately, happiness is a choice. Rational responses include expecting some things to be difficult, for life to be uncertain, that we will make mistakes, and that revenge will not make hurt disappear. Internalizing rational thought translates to positive and productive behaviors in conflict.

> "You must live your life from beginning to end: No one else can do it for you."
>
> —Hopi proverb

TABLE 12.1 *Irrational Beliefs Leading to Anger*

Belief	Response
Things should be quick and easy (or I become angry).	Most things are not quick and easy. Delay reacting to let logical thought come to the surface.
People should love and approve of me (or I become angry).	Rejection is inevitable. Self-acceptance is much more important than the acceptance of others
Other people make me angry.	We choose to become angry. There are other choices.
I must have certainty in life.	Certainty is not the norm; uncertainty is more common.
I must do well in everything I try.	Trying is more important than being the best at everything. Most people are not really good at everything. The expectation is too high.
I must seek revenge for past harms.	Revenge will not change the past. The hurt feelings or embarrassment will still exist and probably increase through a cycle of mutual retaliation.

Source: Levinson (2006).

TABLE 12.2   *The OFTEN Strategy*

Observe	Make an objective and descriptive observation of what occurred to yourself (or in some cases, to the other person).
Feel	Use an "I" statement about how the behavior makes you feel.
Think	Speculate on what has been going on with the other person.
Expectations	Discuss what each person expects about the situation.
Negotiation	Brainstorm how to meet those expectations.

The Recipient of Anger or Strong Emotions

Being on the receiving end of anger is not fun. At minimum, the situation is unpleasant; at its worst, anger may be a precursor to physical violence. Successful strategies used to manage the anger of others have been identified and used effectively in a variety of contexts. Table 12.2 summarizes the OFTEN strategy (Welch, 2001). This model requires conflict managers to respond to anger by: (1) observing and describing what occurred, (2) identifying the feeling being experienced, (3) thinking about how the other person is experiencing their world, (4) exploring expectations we may have for the situation, and (5) negotiating the best ways to meet expectations. The following example illustrates the OFTEN strategy.

Lyle had a conversation during which one of his coworkers became very angry and yelled at him. Lyle didn't appreciate being yelled at and wanted to make sure the yelling didn't become a pattern. (1) Lyle inwardly reviewed what occurred—"I was just finishing the inventory job when Arnold came up and started yelling at me about the orders we had to fill next week." (2) Lyle identified how he felt: "I felt attacked for no reason and a little afraid." (3) He then speculated on what might be going on: "Maybe something happened to Arnold somewhere else and I just happened to be handy or maybe I did something wrong." (4) With that preparation, Lyle had a conversation with Arnold. Lyle said, "Arnold, this morning I was working then you came up and raised your voice to me regarding some new orders. I was concerned about that and felt attacked for no reason. Maybe there is something going on that I don't know about or should know about." (5) Moving into negotiation, Lyle added, "If there is a problem, I'd like to talk about how we can have these conversations in the future without us having to yell at each other."

Having a plan or model to follow when faced with someone's angry outburst refocuses the attention on meaningful dialogue, productive change, and the future of a relationship. The OFTEN strategy is one template to react to another's anger. However, sometimes anger stems from not believing that the other person cares and experiencing feelings of hurt, fear, or rejection. Recognizing the value people place on apologies is important for conflict managers to consider as they work to repair damaged relationships.

CONFLICT KEY 12.1

Ultimately, happiness is a choice.

Apologies

Engaging in angry and hurtful behaviors can be the impetus for a need to apologize or to receive an apology. Taking responsibility for one's actions is an appropriate ethical behavior. Additionally, an apology perceived as sincere also carries tactical advantages. This section discusses both the personal and strategically beneficial aspects of a well-developed and effectively executed apology.

Fake, Semi, and Sincere Apologies

Should Trini, from Case 12.1, apologize to JJ for spending the majority of the lottery money on herself and not including JJ in the decision making? Maybe. If she arrives at the point where she sincerely is remorseful, an apology is appropriate.

There is a difference between a fake and a sincere apology. A **fake apology** is expedient. While going through the motions of expressing regret, inside the fake apologizer feels no remorse and still thinks the offensive behavior was fine. Fake apologies can be outright lies. They may also take the form of **semi-apologies,** which are phrased to disallow personal responsibility, such as, "I'm sorry you feel that way."

In contrast to fake apologies, **sincere apologies** arise from a genuine feeling of regret about past behaviors. If Trini doesn't feel bad about her actions, a fake apology may make things worse. If the situation continues to affect their relationship, Trini may reexamine her feelings to see if there is some part of the situation she feels responsible for that warrants expressing her regret. Perhaps she feels bad that she was not honest and upfront with JJ and went by herself to the lottery office. She could apologize for the parts of the situations that she does regret. The sincere apology covering areas where she does feel remorse could demonstrate to JJ that she recognizes how her actions affected him. Research indicates only sincere apologies are related to later forgiveness among U.S. college students (Bachman & Guerrero, 2006).

Culturally Appropriate Apologies

It is important to make a distinction between culturally appropriate indirect apologies and fake apologies. In cultures where direct conflict communication is less appropriate, a formulaic apology may be the most appropriate and culturally sensitive type (see the culture discussion in Chapter 7). A European American who says, "I'm sorry that happened" may be avoiding responsibility by using vague terms in a culture that prefers directness. Someone from a high-context culture who says, "Sometimes regrettable things happen" may be making a sincere apology because the speaker and listener share a context where indirectness is preferred over directness.

Lingley (2006) chronicles an example of how Americans and Japanese cultures approach the act of apologies on an international level. Japan was offended at what was perceived to be an insincere apology by the captain of the U.S. Navy submarine that surfaced on February 9, 2001, near Hawaii and accidently collided with the *Ehime Maru,* a Japanese ship with a group of high school students aboard. Nine Japanese died, including several students. The U.S. Navy released a statement of "sincere regret" over the incident while an investigation was launched to determine who was at fault. The American submarine Captain Waddle was silent, as was expected from U.S. norms because the investigation was still ongoing. But tensions with Japan grew as a lack of an apology stretched into weeks. The U.S. president offered an official apology and sent diplomats to Japan to deliver it personally to the families of the victims. Although respectfully received, Japan was still deeply offended by the Americans. Nineteen days after the accident, Captain Waddle offered a written letter with his "sincere regret" for the incident. The apology was rejected and considered insufficient in scope for the loss by Japan.

The families of the victims asked for Captain Waddle to demonstrate his regret and remorse in a public act of contrition, where he should accept responsibility for the accident and acknowledge the grief of the victim's families. A Japanese apology is marked by one's submission, humility, and action. If necessary, an apologizer subjugates oneself through unconditionally surrendering to the mercy of the victim. The act of apologizing is most important. Even formulaic responses are acceptable if matched by appropriate submission. Japan expected Captain Waddle to bow in submission and acknowledge the pain he caused.

In contrast, the Japanese apologies in 1972 for a group of Japanese terrorists killing several people in an Israeli airport were swift, ongoing, and shared by the Japanese people. Apologies came from Japanese youth groups, citizens from across Japan, as well as heads of state. The outpouring of regret and remorse was seemingly unending from the Japanese people. Japan's expression of accountability was never matched by the American counterparts for the 2001 accident at sea. The connection of guilt that Americans associate with the act of apologizing offers a striking contrast to the Japanese effusive and humble messages of regret. The act of apologizing holds different cultural meanings for different groups.

Barriers to Apologies

The many reasons why people won't apologize include barriers such as anger, defensiveness, feelings of virtuous superiority, not wanting to admit a wrong, seeing the offense as the end of a series of events rather than as a single event, seeing only the other's behavior and not one's own, fear of punishment, feeling morally wrong, or shame (Exline & Baumeister, 2000). Researchers determined that compounding why some may not feel an apology is warranted is the fact that "perpetrators tend to perceive their transgressions as less harmful and serious than victims do" (Exline & Baumeister, 2000, p. 140). Those who hurt others may justify their actions by saying it wasn't that big a deal or the other person shouldn't be so sensitive.

Another barrier to an apology might be that even though an individual may want to apologize, she or he fears legal action. Sometimes people are prohibited from apologizing by a third party, such as an employer or a spouse, or in Captain Waddle's case, the U.S. Navy. In Case 12.2, Warren was careless about property boundaries and cut down two of his friend's trees. He is wrong and should apologize, but Randolph has threatened to take him to court

CASE 12.2 • *The Missing Trees*

In a casual conversation, Warren and Randolph were talking about cutting firewood for the winter. Randolph mentioned there were some dead trees on the forest service land near the gate to his cabin and they would be easy to cut because they were right on the forest service road. Warren said he would check them out. The next time Randolph visited his cabin, two trees were missing from his driveway. Randolph called Warren to see if he had cut his wood yet.

When Warren thanked Randolph for the tip about the easy trees, Randolph was incensed that two of his trees had been poached. A heated conversation ensued, ending with Randolph saying if he didn't get a public apology, he would take Warren to court for the full value of the trees—$2,000 each. Warren told Randolph he didn't have any proof that would work in court, and he should put up better signs on his land boundary.

for the value of the lost property. If Warren publicly admits he cut the trees, Randolph still might sue and use the confession as evidence. Warren is sorry and wants to apologize, but he thinks it was an honest mistake and doesn't want to pay full value for the trees.

Warren's options represent a range of possible responses. He could (1) refuse to apologize and deny responsibility, (2) apologize without admitting responsibility ("I'm sorry you lost your trees"), (3) apologize without admitting responsibility and offer to help make the situation better ("I'm sorry you lost your trees. I'll buy and plant two trees if you would like me to"), (4) apologize, admit responsibility, and negotiate a reasonable compensation for the mistake ("I'm sorry I cut down your trees. It was an honest mistake and I thought you told me I could. I'm willing to buy and plant one new tree for you, and if you wish, I'd plant a second one you purchased"), (5) apologize and take full responsibility for the loss ("I'm so sorry I cut down your trees. I will take out a loan and pay you the value of the trees"), or (6) apologize, express regret, and promise not to do the behavior again ("I'm so sorry I cut down your trees. I feel horrible about it. In the future, I'm going to have you come with me and point out the trees that I can cut down near your property"). Expressing regret is useful when the harm was not intentional or was the result of an accident.

> ### *Discussion Question 12.2*
> Have you been the recipient of a fake or semi-apology? If so, how did it make you feel? Imagine that you are the recipient of Warren's semi-apology, "I'm sorry you lost your trees." How might this semi-apology affect the relationship of the two neighbors in the future?

The apology without admitting responsibility, a type of semi-apology, is less satisfying for the recipient. Warren might say, "I'm sorry about your trees" and add, "Can I help replant some trees or do something to help to make the situation better?" Part of the problem with some malpractice lawsuits is that the patient who was harmed wants an apology from the physician. An apology and sincere promise to guarantee that the issue won't happen again might settle the issue. But because an apology could be taken as an admission of guilt (in a legal sense), the apology is not forthcoming.

Restorative Justice

Apologies are a standard part of the **restorative justice** model, a view that believes justice is better served by restoring balance to an individual or a community than by mere punishment of the wrongdoer. For example, one specialized form of mediation helps people deal with the strong emotions they feel after being the victim of a crime (Umbreit, Vos, Cotes, & Brown, 2003). When victims see their offender tried in court, they may achieve retribution but are not allowed to face the offender or have a role in selecting restitution. Victims may be trapped in fear or anger and wonder why the offender picked them. In carefully screened cases, victim-offender mediation allows victims to question the offender in person and to work out a restitution plan for the offense. Victims may or may not personally forgive the offender, but they sometimes are able to let go of the fear and anger after being able to express it directly to the offender. Offenders may or may not apologize.

Swanson (2004) noted that victims of crimes want several things when they file charges against offenders: (1) They want to know why the crime happened to them. (2) They want the offender to hear their story and how the crime impacted them. (3) They need empowerment. (4) They want restitution or vindication. Apologies fit into the fourth category as a part of the restitution process.

The Strategic Side of Apology

In all contexts, there are strategic and personal advantages to a sincere apology. Refusing responsibility for one's actions can lead to negative attributions from others regarding more severe moral failings. In addition, justifying one's actions may convey a tone of superiority that elicits defensiveness from others. Over time, moral failings, negative attributions, and defensive-provoking behaviors can erode the quality of relationships and the ability to suc-ceed in personal and business contexts. Finally, not apologizing may require more effort in the long term than apologizing. Strategically, not apologizing may have more costs than benefits. Sincere apologies are an opening through which business or personal relation-ships can be repaired or sustained.

Forgiveness[1]

Defining Forgiveness

Early in the twentieth century, individuals of faith virtually were the only group to study forgiveness. Social scientists began to examine forgiveness in the 1930s, but its exploration did not flourish until the 1980s. The 1980s and 1990s saw forgiveness research explode onto the scene, with around two hundred empirical studies published (Harris, Luskin, Norman, Standard, et al., 2006). Researchers investigated questions such as these: Is the capacity to forgive related to moral development? Are there mental or physical advantages to forgiving versus not forgiving? Is the ability to forgive related to specific personality types? (McCullough, Pargament, & Thorensen, 2000).

Interpersonal forgiveness occurs when one person forgives another. Murphy (2003) explains that interpersonal forgiveness involves situations where one person *gives forgiveness* to "an unfaithful spouse, a betraying friend, a malicious colleague, a government agent by whom one has been tortured, or . . . a criminal by whom one has been victimized" (p. 5). In contrast, **group forgiveness** applies to larger frames, such as national, ethnic, or faith groups, where a *group asks forgiveness from another group*. For example, the U.S. government apologized and offered reparations to Japanese Americans subjected to the World War II internment camps.

> "The first person that forgiveness changes is the person doing the forgiving."
> —Enright, 2001, p. 9

[1]The view of forgiveness emerging in Western research is influenced by Christian theology. Other theologies may lead to other views of forgiveness (e.g., Gassin, 2001).

Part of the development of forgiveness research involves consideration of how the term should be defined. Harris et al. (2006) assert that, "Although no 'gold standard' definition of interpersonal forgiveness exists, there is general agreement among theorists and researchers about what forgiveness is not: It is not pardoning (legal term), excusing (implies good reason for offense), condoning (implies justification), denying (implies unwillingness to acknowledge), forgetting (implies failed memory, something outside conscious awareness), or reconciliation " (p. 716). For example, it is possible to forgive an abusive spouse but never consider reconciliation because the abuser has not changed.

Defining what forgiveness is seems more difficult than deciding what it is not. Luskin (2002) describes the feeling of forgiveness: "Forgiveness is the feeling of peace that emerges as you take your hurt less personally, take responsibility for how you feel, and become a hero instead of a victim in the story you tell. . . . Forgiveness does not change the past, but it changes the present. Forgiveness means that even though you are wounded you choose to hurt and suffer less" (pp. 68–69).

To some degree, forgiveness requires giving up any dreams of having had a different past. Mortensen (2006) differentiates between types of real and fake forgiveness. **Hollow forgiveness** accepts an outward apology ("He said he was sorry and brought me a present") without inner contrition ("But even though I said I accepted the apology, I still harbor deep hurt feelings and animosity toward him"). **Silent forgiveness** genuinely forgives but shows no outward sign of the forgiveness. The longer process of **genuine forgiveness** reduces personal animosity and may increases benevolence toward the transgressor.

> Life Law #9: There is Power in Forgiveness. "Open your eyes to what anger and resentment are doing to you. Take your power back from those who have hurt you. . . . Hatred, anger, and resentment eat away at the heart and soul of the person who carries them. . . . [ultimately] those who love you don't get you—they get the bitter shell of who you once were."
>
> —McGraw, 1999, pp. 200–202

Two general kinds of forgiveness emerge in the literature. **Trait forgiveness** describes a personality that tends to forgive rather than one that tends to hold a grudge. **State forgiveness** involves the act of forgiving a particular offense. Forgiveness is measured through instruments like the Acts of Forgiveness Scale, the Transgression-Related Interpersonal Motivations Inventory, and the Forgiving Personality Inventory (Lawler, Younger, Piferi, Jobe, et al., 2005).

> ### Discussion Question 12.3
>
> What is your reaction to the phrase, "Forgive and forget." What do you think is meant by the term "forget" in this phrase? Identify an example, real or fictitious, to illustrate the five types of forgiveness from Table 12.3.

Enright and Fitzgibbons (2002) discuss five forgiveness conditions (see Table 12.3). If a committed partner is unfaithful, the offended partner might only forgive after specific conditions are met, depending on the type of forgiveness being applied. **Revengeful forgiveness** might occur only after the other partner also is unfaithful. Because complete faithfulness

TABLE 12.3 *Types of Forgiveness*

Revengeful forgiveness: Forgive after you get even.
Restitutional or compensational forgiveness: Forgive after being restored or compensated.
Expectational forgiveness: Forgive because people think you should.
Lawful expectational forgiveness: Forgive because you are required to.
Social harmony forgiveness: Forgive because it is the morally right thing to do; peace is better than conflict.

cannot be restored once it is broken, within **restitutional forgiveness** or **compensational forgiveness,** the offender might be forgiven after a sincere apology and compensation (a new car) is awarded. Within **expectational forgiveness,** parents or friends pressure the victim to rise above the situation. If the partner belongs to a group or religion that advocates forgiveness, **lawful expectational forgiveness** may come into play. A victim may forgive because his faith tradition says it is the right thing to do. Finally, the victim might take a universal, **social harmony forgiveness** position that love and peace are better than anger or hate, and forgive because it is the morally right thing to do.

Examples of programs working toward forgiveness (as well as toward reconciliation) are found in areas that suffered dramatic political violence. The religious, ethnic, and racial violence in places like Bosnia, North Ireland, and South Africa gave rise to efforts to help individuals move beyond their personal tragedies (de Vries & de Paor, 2005; Gibson, 2006). Even though these programs work toward political reconciliation, personal forgiveness is the cornerstone on which the request for forgiveness is built. Pope John Paul II asked for forgiveness for historic failures of the Catholic church ninety-four times during his reign (Accattoli, 1998), including the church's indifference to the persecution of Jews during World War II, the historic oppression of women, the Inquisition, and alienation from Muslims since the Crusades. The belief that healing and awarding forgiveness are inextricably linked is a compelling motivation for these examples of public contrition.

> ### *Discussion Question 12.4*
> Wachovia Corporation, once one of largest U.S. banks, issued a public apology for its part in the exploitation of African Americans in the 1800s. What is the value of such apologies? Can reconciliation occur *without* apology and forgiveness?

Forgiving versus Unforgiving

Interpersonal rejection—being shunned, excluded, ostracized, or abandoned—may be at the heart of many grievances that result in anger, sadness, guilt, embarrassment, self-esteem loss, or isolation. A former partner or friend may simply leave or his or her last words may be "I never loved you." A parent may have given more love and attention to one sibling, abandoned her or his children, or left all the family's assets to a favorite child. Someone you wanted to be your best friend may not have wanted to be your friend. Each of these situations probably would sow feelings of rejection and resentment. Some of these actions might be difficult to forgive.

Researchers have investigated those who occupy an intermediate place between actively not forgiving and forgiving. **Unforgiveness** has been defined as mulling over an offense after the fact, "including resentment, bitterness, hostility, hatred, anger, and fear" (Harris et al., 2006, p. 716; see also Wade & Worthington, 2003). Wade and Worthington (2003) posit that actions such as taking revenge, denying the hurt, reframing the event, legal action, or justifying the offense may reduce active unforgiveness. Unforgiveness at its worst allows "vindictiveness to take over their very selves—turning them into self-righteous fanatics so involved, even joyous, in their outrage that they will be satisfied only with the utter cruel annihilation of the wrongdoer" (Murphy, 2003, p. 33). Interestingly, those who are more religious do not forgive more than nonreligious individuals (Wade & Worthington, 2003).

The benefits to relationships through the act of forgiving are well-documented. Fincham, Beach, and Davila (2004) argue that forgiveness in marriage not only stops negative conflict management strategies, but it sets the stage for reconciliation, which seems necessary for long-term survival of the relationship. They observed that positive conflict management strategies are unlikely to emerge from the smoldering embers of an unforgiven hurt. In fact, the existence of unforgiven events may be used as a justification by one partner for future retaliation or mistreatment. The ability to forgive seems to be a key conflict management skill.

The Necessity of Forgiveness

Healing takes longer than inflicting the wound. Without forgiveness, moving on with life can seem impossible. The old grudge weighs on one's thoughts and taints all relationships—it saps energy and gives the person who caused the hurt a continuing source of power. Cloke and Goldsmith (2000) comment, "Forgiveness also is a kind of boundary. It means giving up all hope of having a better past. It means releasing oneself from the conflict and letting the other person go. It means surrendering one's false expectations for how the other person ought to have behaved, releasing the other person to his or her own fate, and taking responsibility for clarifying the boundaries in one's own life" (p. 172).

> ### *Discussion Question 12.5*
> Some characterize forgiveness as the letting go of the desire to hold the other responsible for paying for the transgressions (like forgiving a debt). If you were a victim of a property crime, could you simultaneously forgive someone yet want them to compensate you for losses?

In Chapter 4 we explored how people make inferences about the behaviors of others. These inferences are put together into stories that explain reality. Cloke and Goldsmith (2000) argue that people who have suffered because of the behaviors of others can tell stories to "mend the fabric of their perceived reality" (p. 5). Unfortunately, some stories mainly keep anger and hurt alive. Conversely, healthy stories show recovery from loss or how one overcame adversity. How personal stories are framed is what makes a difference in the healing process.

Benefits of Forgiving

Those who do not forgive suffer additional harms, particularly to their mental and physical health. In a review of over five years of forgiveness research, Lawler et al. (2005; see also Maltby & Day, 2004) summarized the near universal conclusion that forgiveness is positively related to health. Those who forgive have less anxiety and depression. State forgiveness is related to fewer symptoms of poor physical health, less reliance on medication, better sleep quality, and less fatigue. The researchers concluded that not forgiving literally causes tension and stress on the body that are relieved when forgiveness occurs.

Benefits of forgiveness are relational (stops relationship deterioration and allows relationship continuance) and personal (physical and mental health improves, guilt is reduced, and self-esteem increases). Barriers to forgiveness include not wanting to cancel the debt that sustains the anger, not wanting to give something up without seeming to get anything back, fearing repetition of the act, fearing appearing weak, believing justice will not be served, losing the benefits of victim status, losing potential money in reparations, losing the justification for one's own bad behaviors or weaknesses, or missing sympathy from others (Exline & Baumeister, 2000). Table 12.4 presents several myths about forgiveness. Goens (2002) demonstrates the benefits to organizations and argues that business leaders should forgive to maintain personal integrity, ground relationships in reality, allow people's full talents and abilities to emerge, and permit transformation within organizations.

Blaming someone for your problems or hanging on to the hurt so tightly that it taints all aspects of your life *gives* the person who hurt you more power. A past grievance should not become your best friend. Holding on to a hurt can poison all other relationships and sap potential happiness. Forgiveness provides an opportunity to put the past into the past: not to forget, but to move on.

Actions Leading to Forgiveness

The steps to arrive at a place where forgiveness can occur are many and varied. Forgiveness research leads to no universal advice because everyone seems to take a personal journey toward forgiveness. Forgiveness has no timetable, and some journeys are longer than others. There is no right time to forgive—no magic amount of time before forgiveness occurs.

A few research findings are beginning to emerge that provide a path toward forgiveness. For example, merely expressively writing about the offense does not seem to reduce the negative health effects of unforgiveness (Landry, Rachal, Rachal, & Rosenthal, 2005). British researchers Matlby and Day (2004) determined that individuals who use neurotic defenses, such as fake forgiveness (saying one forgives but not meaning it) or reaction formation (demonstrating active hostility toward the other), are less likely to forgive. They conclude that some active mental transformative process is required to reap the benefits of forgiveness.

TABLE 12.4 *Myths About Forgiveness*

Forgiving is forgetting.
Forgiving tolerates what was done.
Forgiving is excusing the other person from the wrong behavior.
Forgiving means what was done was not really wrong, bad, or evil.
Forgiving shuts off seeking justice or compensation.
Forgiving invites the other person to victimize again.
Forgiveness can be conditional on the other person changing.
Forgiveness means you once again trust the person who wronged you.

One study on the efficiency of forgiveness training programs found that training did speed up forgiveness, but a majority of participants experienced no recovery during the training programs (Harris et al., 2006). Clearly, forgiveness is not easy.

Enright (2001) proposed several guideposts to forgiveness. Not everyone passes the guideposts at the same pace; some may not need every step; sometimes a step has to be revisited several times. One of Enright's guideposts for forgiving is of particular interest and closes the link in the theme of this chapter: anger, apology, forgiveness, and reconciliation. Enright's first guidepost requires the uncovering of anger. A first step is understanding that anger and shame underlie the motive for unforgiveness and that anger is not healthy. Similarly, anger is the first step in Luskin's (2002) four general stages to forgiving: identifying self-justified anger. awareness that bad feelings aren't helping. remembering how much better one felt after forgiving in the past, and becoming resistant to offense and being able to "let things go."

Although most of the forgiveness processes discussed thus far are internal and unilateral processes, other formats for forgiveness are possible. *Negotiated forgiveness* in restorative justice requires the presence of a perpetrator who is prepared to make three offers: a confession, ownership of the offending behavior, and repentance (Andrews, 2000). As was discussed earlier, victims of crimes often want to be made whole (garner restitution) and to feel some vindication. They also sometimes feel a need to forgive themselves and forgive the perpetrator. Swanson (2004) tells the story of a victim-offender mediation session between an embezzler and a business owner. The three principles of restorative justice were applied so the embezzler could see how the crime was a violation of a specific person and their relationship, that the violation created obligations, and that the embezzler had an obligation to put right to the wrong. During sessions in which the embezzler heard the owner express how deeply hurt she had been by the crime, the perpetrator sincerely apologized. Being heard and receiving a sincere apology allowed the owner to forgive; she experienced "emotional healing and closure" (p. 17). The truth and reconciliation processes discussed later in this chapter also are premised on negotiated forgiveness.

Luskin (2002), director of the Stanford Forgiveness Project, claims continued grievances are nurtured by unenforceable rules that people try to enforce. Table 12.5 lists some unenforceable rules that can make life miserable. For example, faithfulness is a choice that partners make that one person cannot enforce. If a partner chooses to be unfaithful, the "rule" can take on a life of its own and preempt any chance of forgiveness. In Luskin's view,

---

TABLE 12.5   *Unenforceable Rules*

My partner has to be faithful.
People must not lie to me.
Life should be fair.
People have to treat me with kindness.
My life has to be easy.
My past should have been better.
My parents should have loved me more.
Bad things shouldn't happen to me.

Source: Adapted from Luskin (2002).

a change in perspective must precede forgiveness when unenforceable rules are the basis for holding on to an unforgiven grudge.

Luskin (2002) suggests reframing the hurt in a grievance from a grievance story to a story that acknowledges positive intentions. A **grievance story** focuses on the bad things that happened and stars the other person as the villain. After divorce, an individual may create a story on how his life was ruined because of his wife's betrayal. As long as the betrayal story is the energy focus, he is caught in the past. A **positive intention** is an original motive. When the relationship started the positive intention was to share intimacy and have a loving family. Luskin says, "Your positive intention of having a loving family . . . has taken a hit. For the sake of this exercise picture your loss as a tire blowout on the road of intimacy. . . . This metaphorical flat tire can derail us on the road to intimacy. . . . Many will stay stuck on the side of the road complaining about how unfair this is" (pp. 144–145). Instead of deciding never to trust your car again, one needs to get back on the road. As long as the past grievance is enshrined, the positive intention of having intimacy and a loving family is less likely to happen. Remembering and focusing on the positive intention, over time, makes moving forward possible and encourages the healing process to take hold.

Rediscovering the positive intention begins by changing the story one tells from being the victim to being the hero. Dr. Luskin's work with Northern Ireland families who experienced the murder of a loved one discovered that even the darkest circumstances can uncover a positive intention. Love does not expire, it can be shared with other family members, used to help others in similar situations, build memorials, or create change.

While victims may seek the benefits of forgiving, perpetrators may have a difficult time in accepting the forgiveness of others. People stuck without self-forgiveness are full of guilt. Self-forgiveness is all about taking power over one's thoughts. An individual can make amends to those who he or she has harmed, can apologize, or can reward oneself for changing bad habits to better ones. Luskin's (2002) three basic steps can be used for self-forgiveness: Take something less personally (you are not the only person to ever make a mistake), take responsibility for your feelings (don't blame the actions of your past self for your current self's behaviors), and tell a positive intention story (don't talk about how bad you were in the past; focus on what your positive goals are for the future). Being stuck in shame doesn't help us to grow or mature. Working toward self-forgiveness allows us to move ahead toward a better life.

> "Forgiveness is not a quick fix. It is hard, sometimes painful, work. Serious emotional wounds require serious medicine."
>
> —Enright, 2001, p. 74

Reconciliation

Defining Reconciliation

As stated earlier in this chapter, reconciliation occurs when individuals rebuild a relationship. Unlike forgiveness, which can be developed without the other party, *reconciliation* requires communication among the disaffected individuals. A simple definition of reconciliation is to bring back together that which was forced apart.

Interpersonal reconciliation is the rebuilding of a relationship that was broken or tarnished. The literature on interpersonal reconciliation seems inextricably tied with social justice, international reconciliation programs, deathbed reconciliation of family members, and those who argue that forgiveness and reconciliation are obligations of the faithful.

When Reconciliation Is Right

The choice to move toward meaningful reconnection with another individual is personal. It is not, however, always a choice that is made freely. In the business context, professional reconciliation may be required before personal forgiveness or reconciliation is possible. Sometimes, we do not have the leisure of choosing not to associate with a specific person without uprooting employment, family, or other important parts of one's life. In these cases, a public partial reconciliation may be chosen to maintain employment or family harmony. For the good of the larger community, a partial reconciliation may be orchestrated.

Skilled mediators can assist individuals in negotiating the boundaries of contacts in professional or family contexts where full reconciliation has not occurred. For example, coworkers who were best friends may have an irreconcilable falling out. If their friendship dissolution affects their work, "work reconciliation" may be necessary so they can continue as coworkers, even though other aspects of their relationships have been severed.

In other circumstances, reconciliation may be chosen. Estranged family members may choose to transcend a past rift and rebuild a relationship. Sons and fathers may reconcile after years of silence. Best friends who stop talking after hurting each other's feelings may begin to communicate again. With or without forgiveness, those who reconcile find a way to reshape their relationships.

When offenses occur, forgiveness and reconciliation may or may not go together. Freedman (1998) described the four options after an offense occurs (Table 12.6). In Case 12.2, the cabin owner, Randolph, may forgive Warren and reconnect their friendship (forgive and reconcile). In the second forgiveness condition, Randolph might privately forgive but not reconnect with Warren (forgive and not reconcile). He might continue to interact without forgiveness and hold a grudge against Warren (not forgive and interact). Finally, Randolph could hold a grudge and not interact (not forgive and not interact). The choice that is made about forgiveness and further contact will alter the path of both men's futures.

Ideally, reconciliation occurs after the offending party has reformed the attitudes or behaviors that caused the original injury. Reconciliation without genuine reform and regret by the offending party is an invitation to re-victimization.

TABLE 12.6 *Forgiveness Actions*

Forgive and reconcile
Forgive and not reconcile
Not forgive and interact
Not forgive and not interact

INSERT 12.2

Political Reconciliation

Political *truth and reconciliation programs,* such as the South African Truth and Reconciliation Commission, confront an ugly past through the telling of truth from both sides in a dispute—those who committed atrocities and their victims. By telling and hearing the truth, people realize at a visceral level that all sides committed terrible acts (Gibson, 2006). In Northern Ireland, individuals who lost relatives or were otherwise harmed in the "Troubles" gathered to share stories in a safe environment. They developed empathy for the other side, desensitized people from the negative stories they were holding on to, helped people restructure how they thought about the events, and provided modeling on how to move beyond grievances into a better future (de Vries & de Paor, 2005). In the United States, the city of Greensboro attempted a reconciliation process to heal the 1979 killing of five people and wounding of ten others by Ku Klux Klan and American Nazi party members (Greensboro Truth and Reconciliation Commission, 2006). After a report documented the near genocidal treatment of Australia's indigenous population by European settlers, many cities, groups, and individuals enacted a national Sorry Day to apologize (Henderson, 2005).

Summary

Disappointment and hurt are a part of the life process. Anger is a secondary emotion that masks some primary emotion, such as fear. Anger itself can be masked through strategies such as cool posing or moderated through training programs to reduce the emotion. Trait anger is a relatively stable personality feature, whereas state anger is precipitated by a specific event. Strategies such as OFTEN can assist those who are recipients of anger.

Apologies can be fake, semi-apologies, or indicate sincere regret about a behavior. People avoid apologies for reasons such as guilt, fear of punishment, shame, viewing events differently, or seeing only the other's behavior and not one's own. Sometimes fear of legal consequences forestalls an apology. Sometimes not apologizing takes more effort and leads to worse personal consequences than apologizing.

Interpersonal forgiveness is giving up the hurt and anger toward another. Forgiveness does not condone the behavior or require reconciliation of the relationship. To reap the mental and physical health benefits of forgiveness, it must be real, not hollow or fake. Trait forgiveness describes a personality that tends to forgive, and state forgiveness is linked to specific offenses. Sometimes people put mental conditions around forgiving, such as revengeful forgiveness, compensational forgiveness, lawful expectational forgiveness, expectational forgiveness, or social harmony forgiveness. Research shows that unforgiveness, the active state of mulling over past grievances, produces negative health and psychological effects.

Forgiveness is a process rather than a single action. It may take more time for some individuals than for others. Keys to forgiveness include giving up one's anger and changing from a victim's grievance story to a positive intention. Interpersonal reconciliation is rebuilding a relationship with a person and requires direct communication.

Chapter Resources _____

Exercises

Research Topics

1. Investigate and write a report on one nation or ethnic group's reconciliation efforts.

2. Read and report on a book about reconcidiation such as Desmond Tutu's *No Future Without Forgiveness* or Nancy Friday's *My Mother, Myself.*

3. Research and identify common stages or steps to forgiveness and/or reconciliation.

4. Compare and contrast two reconcidiation models and provide your opinions on the usefulness of each model.

Essay Topics

1. "Anger is the wind that blows out the candle of the mind." How has anger affected your life or the life of someone you know?

2. Has forgiveness helped you move beyond a hurtful event?

Mastery Case

Examine Mastery Case 12, "Memory Boxes." Which concepts from the chapter can be applied to the case?

Memory Boxes

After my father's death when I was eight years old, we moved in for a short time with his mother, my paternal grandmother. Mom and Grandma's relationship always seemed a little strained, but I know that Mom was grateful for her willingness to take us in for that rough time.

Mom was a collector of memories and saw her role as the family historian. She kept newspapers of the days when her three kids were born. She had every paper that included any mention of family members—birth announcements, wedding announcements, obituaries, graduations, and anything newsworthy. She acquired this tradition from her own mother, who passed on her collection to my mom.

When Mom found a place for us to live, she was in the process of moving when she realized that the memory box of newspapers and clippings was missing. She asked Grandma about it. Grandma replied, "That box of newspapers? I threw them out. That kind of thing will just collect bugs." To make matters worse, it was clear to Mother that Grandma had gone through all of the packed boxes and got rid of "junk" that she felt was unnecessary—and helped herself to mementos of Dad's.

Mother was livid and heartsick at the same time. We left Grandma's house that day in silence. Mother refused to talk to Grandma from that day forward. Whenever anyone brings up any memory, Mother relives her anger and hurt anew about what Grandma did. Years have passed and we kids are grown, but we still have little contact with Grandma because of the newspaper incident so many years ago.

Conflict in Context

Section IV examines how conflict unfolds in several specific contexts. Each context challenges our conflict management abilities in unique ways. A conflict strategy or tactic may be effective in one context and inappropriate or ineffective in the next. Section IV offers useful information as we navigate the ubiquitous contexts of family, intimate relationships, work and society.

Managing conflict in the family setting is something that almost everyone experiences—first as a child, then as a potential partner/spouse or parent. Chapter 13 provides a base of information about family structures and family communication, and then it delves into family conflict. A focus on positive and negative patterns of conflict in romantic relationships also is addressed. Suggestions for conflict management in the family conclude the chapter.

In Chapter 14 we examine the world of employment outside the home. Given that many people spend more time interacting with coworkers than with friends and family, workplace conflict deserves special attention. How conflict is managed in the workplace makes an enormous difference in people's quality of life.

Chapter 15 places conflict in the context of the greater society. Although the book focuses on how personal conflict strategies, tactics, conceptualizations, and styles affect conflict, this chapter moves into how those same concepts bring about change in the greater society. Interestingly, the same factors that affect conflict choices and goals interpersonally find remarkable relevance in the social world.

Family Communication and Conflict

Vocabulary

Closeness	Family stories	Norm
Compadrazgo	Gay/lesbian family	Nuclear family
Consensual family	High-involvement/High-	Pluralistic family
Extended family	considerateness	Protective family
Familismo	conversational styles	Satisfaction
Family of choice	Laissez-faire family	Social learning theory
Family of origin	Machismo	Taboo topics
Family secrets	Meta-rules	Voluntary family

Objectives

After reading this chapter, you should be able to:

1. Differentiate among family types and their strengths and weaknesses
2. Discuss the factors that impact family satisfaction
3. Identify and discuss the variables that affect conflict in the family
4. Explain several tools families can use for conflict management

> "The family. We were a strange little band of characters trudging through life sharing diseases and toothpaste, coveting one another's desserts, hiding shampoo, borrowing money, locking each other out of our rooms, inflicting pain and kissing to heal it in the same instant, loving, laughing, defending, and trying to figure out the common thread that bound us all together."
>
> —Erma Bombeck, *Family— the Ties That Bind . . . and Gag!*

The Family as a Communication System

Families come in a variety of types and sizes. There are **nuclear families** (husband, wife, and their children), **extended families** (traditional or nontraditional families with multiple generations), **gay/lesbian families** (same-sex couples and their children), and **families of origin** (the family into which one was born). According to the 2005 American Community Survey (U.S. Census Bureau), 56 percent of all Americans are married. Families can live under the same roof or live in different geographic areas. Some people even create families out of friendships, called **families of choice.**

We introduced the concept of the system in Chapter 2. A family forms a unique system (Galvin, Dickson, & Marrow, 2006) where individuals develop a common view of reality that governs their family behaviors. That view of reality is (more or less) shared among family members. The degree to which family members agree about their shared identity and rules of operation, the number of conversations they have about their shared identity, and the ways in which family identity is sustained all have a deep impact on how well the family functions and the amount of dysfunctional conflict that occurs (Koerner & Fitzpatrick, 2004).

> ### Discussion Question 13.1
> In your view, what is a family?

This chapter examines the nature of family communication and how communication within the family affects and reflects its overall health. Unfortunately, much of the research on family communication and the information in this chapter has been conducted on European American, heterosexual, middle-class families (McAdoo, 2001). Until research spreads to more diverse populations, generalizing from existing research may not be appropriate in all cases. Make note of any differences that you can attribute to factors not shared by traditional research subjects.

TABLE 13.1   *The Family in Numbers*

- Fifty-nine percent of the U.S. population is married (2002).
- Ten percent of the U.S. population is divorced (2002).
- Median age at first divorce is 30.5 males and 29 females (2002).
- Median length of first marriages that ended in divorce is 7.8 years for males and 7.9 years for females (2002).
- Sixty-five percent of married people reach their tenth anniversary (2002).
- The likelihood that a new marriage will end in divorce is 43 percent (1997).
- There are over a million interracial couples (2000).

Source: U.S. Divorce Statistics (2002).

What Is a Family?

Communication scholars typically paint with a broad brush when defining the family. For example, Turner and West (1998) define a family as "a self-defined group of intimates who create and maintain themselves through their own interactions and their interactions with others; a family may include both voluntary and involuntary relationships; it creates both literal and symbolic internal and external boundaries, and it evolves through time: It has a history, a present, and a future" (pp. 7–8). The involuntary parts of a family are ties created in infancy and childhood. **Voluntary families** comprise people who chose each other for long-term commitments, through marriage, partnership, or close association. *Family boundaries* determine who is included and who is excluded. Sometimes the act of exclusion is a divorce or legal disinheritance, and sometimes the boundary is communicative—for example, when children who break custom or tradition are told they are no longer welcome in the family home or when persons who have no blood ties are informally labeled as "one of the family."

Galvin and Brommel (2000) view the family as "a system constituted, defined, and managed through its communication. Family members regulate cohesion and adaptability and develop a collective identity through the flow of patterned meaningful messages within a network of evolving interdependent relationships located within a defined cultural context" (p. 47).

Role of Communication in Families

Communication is the tool that humans use to make sense of the world, convey information, and sustain traditions. Communication is how meaning is created and shared. *Family communication* is a process through which the family system—as individuals and collectively—attributes meaning to the events in their lives, creates and sustains their interpretation of cultural rules, defines and changes relationships among each other, and carries on with everyday life. In simpler terms, communication is how a family creates its reality.

Family communication starts with what a child learns in the family of origin. When a young adult leaves home, packed among the other baggage is a template of what it means to be a family. Some aspects of the family of origin's traditions, rules, culture, or family-specific communication expectations pass down through the generations; other traditions and habits may be transformed to suit the needs of new family configurations. For example, a marriage between a Jew and a Catholic may struggle with what to do during Hanukah and Christmas or in which religion the children should be raised. Merging systems is a common area for conflict to occur.

A Typology of Family Communication

A well-developed line of research categorizes families according to their high or low degree of conformity and use of conversation (Fitzpatrick, Marshall, Leutwiler, & Krcmar, 1996; Koerner & Fitzpatrick, 2004, 2006). As Table 13.2 illustrates, **Consensual families** (high/high) encourage discussion but expect conformity. For example, we can discuss politics, and everyone is expected to participate, but we are a family of Democrats. **Pluralistic families** (low/high) encourage discussion and allow children to develop their

TABLE 13.2 *Family Types*

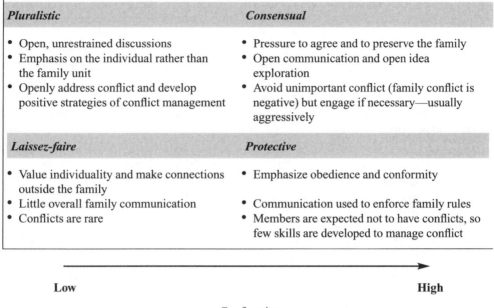

	Pluralistic	Consensual

Low ←——————————————————————————————→ High

Conformity

High ↑ Conversation ↓ Low

Pluralistic
- Open, unrestrained discussions
- Emphasis on the individual rather than the family unit
- Openly address conflict and develop positive strategies of conflict management

Consensual
- Pressure to agree and to preserve the family
- Open communication and open idea exploration
- Avoid unimportant conflict (family conflict is negative) but engage if necessary—usually aggressively

Laissez-faire
- Value individuality and make connections outside the family
- Little overall family communication
- Conflicts are rare

Protective
- Emphasize obedience and conformity
- Communication used to enforce family rules
- Members are expected not to have conflicts, so few skills are developed to manage conflict

own opinions. A pluralistic family may discuss many different kinds of religions and encourage individual exploration. **Protective families** (high/low) emphasize conformity without discussion to create an illusion of harmony. This family looks the part and acts the part of a tight knit group, although they had no idea what anyone else was thinking because they did not talk about their beliefs (Fitzpatrick et al., 1996). **Laissez-faire families** (low/low) neither encourage conversation nor pressure children to conform. Early research indicates many boys in low-conformity families may do well using self-restraint during elementary school, but they require more parental control and communication as self-restraint crumbles during middle and high school and that girls from laissez-faire families are vulnerable to social withdrawal at all ages (Fitzpatrick et al., 1996).

Additional communication differences between family types are beginning to emerge. Children reared in pluralistic families are more likely to disclose personal information to friends, behave in socially acceptable ways, and enjoy social activities. Those from protective families are more likely to be shy, try to take control, and adjust their behaviors to fit different situations (Huang, 1999). Family type does seem to affect a child's personality development and communication preferences. Laissez-faire families seem the least effective in developing a child's self-esteem and a sense of appropriate self-disclosure. Because of the association of low self-esteem and low self-disclosure with other social dysfunction, Huang surmised, "people from pluralistic families may be more likely to maintain their physical and mental health, whereas those from laissez-faire families may be more likely to have physical and mental problems and cause social problems" (p. 241). Clearly, family communication patterns make a difference in how children learn to cope with problems.

How much conformity is ideal in a family? Research indicates that families are not of one mind about conformity (Ritchie & Fitzpatrick, 1990). In the dinner scene from the film *Little Miss Sunshine,* eight-year-old Olive wants to know how her uncle Frank came to have bandages on his wrists. The father doesn't want Olive exposed to the truth of the suicide attempt brought on by Frank's unrequited love of his male graduate student. Conflict occurs when the parents, Frank, and Olive try to establish what is appropriate for an eight-year-old to know and what level of nonconformity (from Frank) would be tolerated.

Perceptions of appropriate conformity also change as children age. Krcmar (1996) compared conformity with conversation type and discovered that first- and third-grade children perceived the same messages differently depending on the *emotional affect* with which directives were delivered (i.e., was an order accompanied with a harsh or a warm tone of voice?). Younger children were more likely to obey when orders were given with a warm tone of voice. Gaining compliance by using "nice" tones disappeared for most children by third grade. The shift intuitively is sensible because younger children are more likely to accept parental authority without much thought, whereas older children challenge parental authority as a stage of their development of independent thought.

A key lesson from research on conformity and interaction is that family communication patterns change over time. Each time a child is born, the family system must readjust all of its relationships. As children progress through stages of development, relationships change again.

> **KEY 13.1**
>
> **Family patterns of communication are constantly evolving. What works in the past may be ineffective tomorrow. It is work to keep family communication functional.**

Stories Sustain the Family's Identity

Family stories sustain the vision of the family as a group and often are related to family rituals. Like the family experience in Case 13.1, the recounting of a funny episode during a family vacation or holiday gathering may start with the words "Do you remember when . . ." Family stories can be positive or negative—uplifting the family as they recount how they survived an awkward situation or demeaning an individual who is the unwilling butt of

---

CASE 13.1 • *Let's Have Flowers!*

In 1950, my mother and dad eloped on a weekend trip to Nevada during a visit to my mom's aunt. It was Memorial Day, and in those days all the shops closed down for the entire weekend in that little town. After finding out about the impending nuptials, there was a little party. Mom's aunt and her best friend became a bit tipsy, and they decided it was not going to be a proper wedding without flowers.

The next morning when Mom and Dad showed up at the chapel, it was full of fresh flowers! The room was beautifully decorated. They didn't notice until after the ceremony that the garbage cans were full of "In Memoriam" signs. Although it was over fifty years ago, someone inevitably ends up telling this story when the family gets together, usually followed by a comment of what irreverent, slightly shady, and wacky stock we come from!

TABLE 13.3 *Family Stories Function in Several Ways*

1. Family stories help keep the past alive.
2. Family stories provide family and individual identity.
3. Family stories teach moral lessons.
4. Family stories develop individual and family esteem.
5. Family stories teach members how to change.
6. Family stories provide stability.
7. Family stories pass lore from generation to generation.

family jokes. Stories can function much like a parable that teaches lessons about how one should behave (or not behave). Table 13.3 summarizes how family stories function.

Through stories, the collective meaning and social reality of a family are constructed. Family stories help children understand the changes in rules and roles as they mature. Most families tell stories that can be categorized into common types (Fiese, Tomcho, Douglas, Josephs et al., 2002). First, stories may tell *how the family came to be.* These stories relate how parents met or chronicle a birth story. A McCorkle family story relates how Fred McCorkle and Edith Neal went on their first date and he spilled a bowl of chili on Edith's lap. The moral is not to be deterred when things go wrong. In the film *Signs,* when a family is huddled in their home waiting for disaster to strike, the father (played by actor Mel Gibson) tells each of the children a story about the day of their birth to calm them and remind them of their deceased mother. The lesson was that the children were loved and had a place in the world.

Discussion Question 13.2

What stories were told in your family? Which story type best matches your family stories? Are there other types of stories that aren't part of the list in Table 13.4?

A second family story reveals that *parents are real people.* Family members or friends may tell stories of what parents were like when they were children or give examples of their human frailty. A father might relay a tale of when he made a rash purchase and ended up in debt for a car that was a lemon. The hope is that the daughter will make a better decision than he did in his youth.

TABLE 13.4 *Family Story Types*

The family creation
Parents are people too
Passages to adulthood
The family stands together
The family's core identity

The third family story theme talks about the *transition from childhood to adulthood*. These stories relate events that mark a passage to adulthood or a characteristic that earns additional privileges in the family. Parents may talk about their first jobs and how that changed their responsibilities in the family as a way of indirectly telling children to do their chores until they pass the traditional threshold of getting a job.

The extent to which *a family will stand behind its members* is the subject of the fourth theme. Stories may relate what the family did or didn't do in stressful times to help each other. Janelle's mom was the eldest girl of six kids. Her father (Janelle's grandfather) died when she was only five, requiring her mom (Janelle's grandmother) to work outside the home to keep the family afloat. A common message in Janelle's youth was "everybody pitches in" to keep the family together. Everyone should sacrifice for the benefit of the family. If that meant the ten-year-old had to cook, do laundry, and raise her siblings, it was just what you had to do.

Stories that establish a *family's core identity* are the final category. Families share stories that clarify what it means to be a member of this particular family. Family stories may emphasize "We aren't quitters" or "Everybody does a stint in the military." Another example comes from Melanie's Grandpa Reese. In the 1930s, while running cattle with his sons, he fell from a spooked horse and broke his collarbone. Although the pain was excruciating, he got back on the horse and finished the remaining three days of the long cattle drive because the cattle had to be moved. He said, "Cows don't care about collarbones." The message implicit in this story was that you *have* to take care of your responsibilities. There isn't a "quittin' time" on a farm—you work until the work is done and then rest later.

In addition to classifying family stories, research indicates that the type of story told to typify a family is associated with satisfaction within the family. Stories that illustrate care, togetherness, adaptability, and humor positively correlate with satisfaction; stories containing disregard, hostility, chaos, divergent values, and personality attributes negatively correlate with family satisfaction (Vangelisti, Crumley, & Baker, 1999).

> ### Discussion Question 13.3
> Identify a family story from your upbringing. What values or identity does the story communicate?

Rules Structure Family Behavior

Turner and West (1998) delineate the **meta-rules** that families also develop—rules about how and when to talk about rules. Often, we don't recognize a family rule or custom is until it is broken by a newcomer. For example, Tom married Stella. When Tom's sister, mother, and grandmother visited the new wife in the family, they brought along a ham and corn on the cob to share a traditional family meal. To be helpful, the new wife sliced the cold ham for sandwiches and cut the corn off the cob to make it easier to eat. The round of shocked expressions underscored that the family rituals for this type of food had been broken. A ham was a special extravagance that should be baked and lovingly basted while corn was shucked and served on the cob—all work that could be shared over conversation. Stella learned the role food preparation played in building family community and the lesson of asking questions before acting around Tom's family.

Family rules can help or hinder the communication process and be functional or dysfunctional. Sometimes rules involve **family secrets.** Implicitly or explicitly, some families know that if the illusion of family harmony is to be maintained, they can't talk about **taboo topics** such as an interfaith marriage, sex, sexual orientation, money, or psychological conditions. Other taboo subjects can be joked about or discussed only if some family members are kept out of the loop. Family members may know that their son/brother is gay, but the entire family conceals that information from the grandparents. Both functional and dysfunctional families have rules not to talk about particular topics outside of the family. In other cases, some family members may be privy to secrets that are hidden from other family members (e.g., "Don't tell Mom I bought a motorcycle.").

Imber-Black (1993) extends the concept of family taboos to delineate four types of family secrets. *Sweet secrets* have time limits and usually are related to good surprises, such as a party or a gift. For example, the entire McDonald clan banded together for months to hide preparations for Jim and Aretha's fiftieth anniversary surprise party. *Essential secrets* establish boundaries and identity among family members, such as disclosures among partners/parents that are withheld from children. As a teenager, Suzanne went with her parents to the bank while they were completing paperwork for a real estate deal. The agent asked a series of routine questions, including if either parent had been married before. Much to her surprise, her father answered that he was married and divorced once before. Later the same year, she visited her aunt's house in California and dated the boy next door. Her aunt told her she couldn't date him anymore because even though he didn't know it, the boy next door was the aunt's son. She already had too many children and fostered him to the childless neighbors for them to raise as their son. It was not unusual in the 1940s and 1950s for the parentage of a baby to be concealed. Singer Bobby Darin grew up in the 1930s with an older sister, who in reality was his mother, a secret only revealed to him as an adult. All of these secrets were known to the elder generation but concealed from the younger generation.

Toxic secrets have a destructive effect on the family or its members. Some secrets conceal substance abuse or guard the family's economic and social standing. Toxic secrets conceal information at someone's expense. If someone loses a job or flunks out of school but keeps leaving at the same time every day, it creates a lie that easily becomes a toxic situation. A murder case in Salt Lake City resulted from a husband's years of lying about his job and career prospects. He told his wife and family he had gotten into medical school. When his web of deceit started to unravel, it made more sense to him to murder his wife and claim that a stranger abducted her than to face up to his lies.

Dangerous secrets put individuals in physical harm, such as physical or sexual abuse and threats of murder or suicide. A family may know that an elder uncle molested children, but no one turned him in. Everyone instead makes sure that he is not alone with any of their kids. In terms of family rules, secret keeping is an activity that the entire family must participate in—otherwise it would not be secret (Vangelisti & Caughlin, 1997, p. 680).

Vangelisti and Caughlin's (1997) research indicates almost all families have at least one family secret—information intentionally withheld from outsiders. Most of these secrets involve taboo topics such as marital problems, substance abuse, finances, sexual preference, mental health, extramarital affairs, and physical, sexual, or psychological abuse, although some involve positive features such as family wealth.

CASE 13.2 • *New Wife, New Rules*

My folks divorced when I was eight. My birth mom's house was always the kind of place where people came in and "made themselves at home." You could put your feet on the coffee table; you sat where there was a chair open at the dinner table. If you came late to dinner, you risked having your food eaten by someone else.

Dad remarried a woman with a different view of how a house should run. Where Mom's house was informal, Dad's new house was highly structured. There were towels in the bathroom that weren't to be used because they were for show. There was a room with furniture that was rarely sat on. Feet were for the floor, and never for a couch. Dinner was a formal affair with a start time, the saying of grace, and excruciatingly proper manners. It was like we had to become completely different kids when we traveled back and forth between our parents' houses.

Norms Guide Behavior

> ### *Discussion Question 13.4*
>
> In Case 13.2, "New Wife, New Rules," what norms existed in the child's first family? How did rules in the new family conflict with past norms? How are norms learned?

Roles, rules, rituals, and norms are complex human phenomena. A **norm** is an unwritten rule that governs how people in a group behave. Stepfamilies and other family types take on additional levels of complexity as different norms, traditions, and customs collide. Communication is the means through which families avoid, negotiate, or conflict over roles, rules, rituals, and norms.

The "negotiation" of roles within a family typically occurs at certain junctures of family life (Jorgenson, 1994). When couples first decide to have a sustained relationship, norms and roles must be worked out. When a stepparent joins what formerly was a single-parent household, new relationships and roles must be forged with children. Newly married couples may have two (or more, in families of divorce) sets of in-laws with whom to work out social positioning, holiday schedules, and family practices. Elements as simple as how family newcomers are addressed are a subtext in the construction of family norms and power structures. Is a stepfather called "Dad" or "Juan"? Are in-laws addressed by their first names, called Mom or Dad, referred to as "sir," or not named at all?

CASE 13.3 • *Family Norms*

Following what she learned as a child, Pia took on the caretaker role when she married. In the first year of marriage, the new bride kept the house spotless, picked up and washed the dishes, laundered and ironed clothes, shopped, and cooked healthy meals. Five years later, she has a job, a child, and is totally worn out. She is angry that her husband, Terrence, doesn't help out around the house. Terrence says he doesn't know how to do anything around the house; besides, she does such a good job as a mother and a wife.

> **Discussion Question 13.5**
>
> Examine what occurred in Case 13.3, "Family Norms." How were norms established and why? What sustains norms in a system? How difficult is it to change a norm once it has been established?

Satisfaction in Families

One measure of how close family members feel toward each other and the overall success of their communication is a variable grounded in **social learning theory** (discussed in Chapter 2) called **satisfaction.** Generally, romantic relationship satisfaction declines if couples use negative communication such as blaming, contempt, or escalation and increases if couples use productive problem solving. If a couple calls each other derogatory names and behaves in sarcastic or snide ways toward each other, satisfaction generally decreases. If a couple works to manage and solve their difficulties without belittling one another, satisfaction tends to increase. Research shows, for wives, the social learning theory perspective holds true: Supportive communication and productive problem solving among couples correlates with long-term marital satisfaction (Gill, Christensen, & Fincham, 1999; Rogers, 2001).

The concept of marital satisfaction fits well with other research indicating couples in distressed marriages, above all else, were more negative toward one another (Gottman, Levenson, & Woodin, 2001, p. 39), especially on the nonverbal level where liking is harder to fake than on the verbal level. Compounding these results were distressed marital partners' tendency to perceive even supportive messages as negatively intended. In fact, research during marital partner's discussions could predict a marriage's stability—just from negative facial expressions (Gottman et al., 2001).

More recent research trends toward the conclusion that common interaction rules (being polite and friendly, not attempting to embarrass one's partner or make him or her feel inferior) strongly correlate to marital satisfaction (Kline & Stafford, 2004). The cumulative research in relationship satisfaction suggests that even if other variables related to satisfaction were moderated (e.g., financial stability was improved), communicative behaviors also would need to be altered if the partner's perception of emotional support and acceptance were to increase.

> **Discussion Question 13.6**
>
> What makes a family happy? Compare your list with what researchers have determined characterizes satisfactory families and relationships.

Contentment with romantic partners is one line of satisfaction research. Another line examines factors that affect the satisfaction of the rest of the family. Research indicates that fathers and sons may have more distant relationships now than during past historical periods. Furthermore, a correlation exists to suggest a connection between a son's lack of satisfaction with his relationship to his father and his degree of fear of ridicule when communicating with his father (Beatty & Dobos, 1992). Apprehension and dissatisfaction may lead to avoidance or other negative communicative behaviors.

The degree of openness about adversity may affect a family member's satisfaction levels. For example, children's satisfaction in their relationships with parents can be affected adversely by how news of an impending divorce is communicated. Even though parents may have protective intentions while hiding an upcoming divorce, children over the age of seven are keen at discerning relationship messages and deception. When the "secret" is revealed by parents who did not prepare children for a separation, long-term dissatisfaction with both parents may occur and the child's self-esteem may be lowered (Thomas, Booth-Butterfield, & Booth-Butterfield, 1995). The relationship with the noncustodial parent suffers the most permanent damage in these cases.

A concept related to satisfaction is the **closeness** that family members feel for one another. Table 13.5 summarizes a study of adult children's perceptions of ten critical moments that changed relationships with their parents—for better or for worse. Research strongly supports that families who conceal more secrets are less satisfied than families who conceal fewer secrets (Vangelisti & Caughlin, 1997).

Family Conflict Patterns

As many people from highly emotional families can attest, disagreement and loud volume does not have to result in negative outcomes. According to Peterson, Peterson, and Skevington (1986), a conflict approached calmly or managed through "heated" discussions makes no difference in overall satisfaction in the family—if the emotion is a family style, cultural, and/or moderated by positive affection. In fact, the same study suggested teenagers in healthy families gained cognitive development advantages from heated arguments.

Gottman and Silver (1999) contend that how a conflict concludes is more important to satisfaction than the intensity of the interaction. If Del yells at his wife, and she retorts with a choice name for him, this may be seen as a negative outcome. However, if, as the conflict progresses, Del smiles at his wife, and says, "This is a dumb argument—but you sure are sexy when you're all fired up." To which she says, "Well, you don't want a boring wife, now do you?" This couple is likely to report high satisfaction because the repair statement of the interaction is more influential than the expression of the conflict.

TABLE 13.5   *Closeness Change Moments*

1. An increase in physical distance
2. A time of crisis
3. A change in one's habitual communication patterns
4. The rebellious teenager years
5. Parents' acceptance of a new partner or spouse
6. Birth of a child
7. Spending more/less time on activities with parents
8. Sibling jealousy
9. Alcohol or drug abuse
10. Parental acceptance of dating or cohabitation

Source: Golish (2000).

Conflict in the Family

Believing that conflict itself is bad is a common fallacy. However, to say conflict is normal does not mean that families should experience conflict continually. Rather, the inevitable nature of conflict means that healthy families will have goal differences that create conflict situations.

Just like other interpersonal conflict, most family conflicts can be distilled to power (who has control) or self-esteem (who feels good about themselves) (Folger et al., 2005; Wilmot & Hocker, 2007). Sillars, Canary, and Tafoya's (2004) review of family conflict research found young siblings may conflict as frequent as six times an hour, much to a parent's dismay. Anyone who has been around young siblings can attest to the research finding indicating that the more contact that occurs among young siblings, the more conflict occurs.

A common cause of partner/marital conflict is *infidelity,* the breaking of a partner's trust through unfaithfulness, which can be expressed physically or emotionally. *Communication infidelity* includes behaviors such as telling a partner you love her or him without meaning it, expressing love for a cyber friend in a chat room and hiding the relationship from the at-home partner, joking about leaving a partner for someone you are attracted to, sharing flirtatious episodes with a coworker, or telling others intimate details about one's partner. One study discovered that women, more so than men, consider communication infidelity worse than physical infidelity (Podshadley & Docan, 2005-2006). Deception regarding love is a significant source of conflict among intimates. Lying and rumor telling also are significant sources of conflict for teens (Scott, 2008).

Conflict in Family Development Stages

Another way to sort the types of conflicts families experience follows stages of family development summarized by Lulofs and Cahn (2000). Each stage of family development carries with it topics that require negotiation and are potential sites of conflict. In stage one, *selecting a mate,* conflicts can arise regarding if and when to marry or formalize a bond. Stage two, *beginning marriage/partnership,* requires numerous changes for each individual, negotiation of how to live together, what parts of old systems to merge, and what to create anew, as well as what it means to be a committed couple. Stage three, *childbearing and preschool years,* require parents to rearrange their lives, social contacts, and renegotiate relationships with in-laws.

As children age, they naturally conflict with parents and siblings for control, time, attention, and self-esteem. *School-age* children's needs dominate stage four. Parents again must renegotiate their lives to reflect the often-competing transportation, economic, and interpersonal demands of children. As parents become involved in their children's activities and school, they meet and work with other adults who are coaches, teachers, or parents of the child's friends. Stage five, *adolescence,* brings more changes as children test their independence against parental needs for control. At stage six, *launching,* children leave the home. Parents must renegotiate their lives to adapt to a home without children. Families in the last two stages of *middle* and *older years* begin to deal with the issues of caring for aging parents, relationships with grandchildren, multigenerational families, children who return to the family home as adults, and/or health issues. This model, of course, is only appropriate to the roughly 50 percent of marriages that don't end in divorce. Divorced families have additional influences that bring conflict opportunities.

Patterns of Family Conflict

Conflicts happen in families. However, whether those conflicts result in strengthening the relational bonds or in eroding a loving environment will depend on how family members handle conflict.

A potential contributing factor for a positive outcome is style. Chapter 7 discussed the role of general style in the creation and escalation of interpersonal conflict. It should be no surprise that style differences also exist within families. One way to measure conversational style is differentiating between high-involvement and high-considerateness. **High-involvement conversational style** is characterized by a fast rate of speech, lots of simultaneous speech, and short pauses. **High-considerateness conversational style** exhibits slower speech rate, longer pauses within and between turns, and few overlaps while speaking. Research indicates teenagers tend to use a high-involvement style in conversing with parents, particularly with mothers, whereas parents more often exhibit a high-considerateness style (Beaumont & Wagner, 2004). The style difference offers ample opportunity for misunderstandings and conflict. For example, a teen may be quick to interrupt, argue, and pounce on potential conversational triggers with a high-involvement style mother. Parents, exhibiting high considerateness, see high involvement as a mark of disrespect, often shutting down the teen who can't seem to talk without arguing. However, being shut down only frustrates the high-involvement teen who wants nothing more strongly than to be considered as an equal. No wonder parents and teen's conversations can go so quickly awry.

The family typologies discussed earlier in this chapter are significant when understanding how families manage conflict (Table 13.6). In a study of families containing at least one teenage child, *pluralistic* families avoided conflicts less and had few examples of negative venting. *Consensual* families reported numerous conflicts and negative venting during conflicts. The social support among consensual family members, however, seemed to negate negative effects. *Laissez-faire* families tended to avoid conflict and viewed their conflicts as unimportant. *Protective* families reported conflict avoidance and negative venting.

Koerner and Fitzpatrick (2002) investigated whether the style of undergraduate students' families of origin affected how students approached conflict in romantic relationships. Not surprisingly, there was a direct influence. Students from consensual families had the most negative conflict behaviors and were very vocal and aggressive during conflicts with romantic partners. Their family of origin ill prepared them for conflict but generated a desire for open communication, which unfortunately was manifested through hostility. Those with a pluralistic family of origin grew up considering conflict normal and learned constructive management skills. Those from a pluralistic family of origin had the most productive conflicts with romantic partners. Protective family of origin individuals had unpleasant conflicts with romantic partners, with high use of avoiding and resisting behaviors. Those students were more likely to avoid conflict but be aggressive when the issue was engaged. Finally, those from laissez-faire families avoided conflict but managed it moderately effectively when necessary.

TABLE 13.6 *Conflict Style with Romantic Partners by Family of Origin*

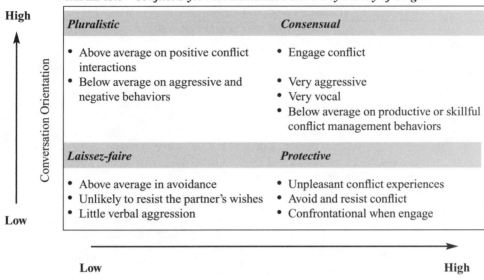

Pluralistic	Consensual
• Above average on positive conflict interactions • Below average on aggressive and negative behaviors	• Engage conflict • Very aggressive • Very vocal • Below average on productive or skillful conflict management behaviors
Laissez-faire	Protective
• Above average in avoidance • Unlikely to resist the partner's wishes • Little verbal aggression	• Unpleasant conflict experiences • Avoid and resist conflict • Confrontational when engage

(Vertical axis: Low → High, Conversation Orientation)

(Horizontal axis: Low → High, Conformity Orientation)

Discussion Question 13.7

Compare your conflict approach to the style most often exhibited in your family of origin. Does your experience match with the findings by Koerner and Fitzpatrick or in Table 13.6? If not, what do you think influenced your current style?

Conflict Styles in the Family

In general, families share the same basic choices during conflicts as individuals. When faced with conflict, one may avoid the conflict, engage the issue competitively, or use a mutual gains approach (Chapter 7). Gottman's Four Horsemen of the Apocalypse Model (1999) illustrates tactics within a negative, competitive style. Gottman identified four hurtful strategies used by intimates: criticism, contempt, denying responsibility, and stonewalling.

Criticism occurs when a partner highlights negative factors. Gottman (1999) posits that criticism is most damaging when the partner is expecting praise. For example, Lenny mows and rakes the lawn. Rather than saying how nice the lawn looks, his wife looks at the flower bed and complains that he never weeds. The criticism of the yard work is more damaging than if she had said nothing at all.

Contempt moves from criticism to insult and psychological abuse. Gottman offers examples such as name calling ("You are lazy and inconsiderate"), hostile humor, mockery ("It looks like a six-year-old did the yard rather than a grown man"), as well as disdainful body language (rolling the eyes).

The third horseman, denying responsibility, is the defensive reaction to criticism or contempt. He might become argumentative, saying, "Hey, that is not my job. You could get off your butt and come outside to help."

CASE 13.4 • *It's a Trip*

Rae and Morgan have been together for six months, but they both believe their relationship will be a lifelong commitment. Rae's family is a boisterous, come-what-may group and embraced Morgan immediately. Morgan is invited to all the family gatherings. Morgan's family, in contrast, is more reserved.

Morgan's family is getting together in Las Vegas over the winter holiday break. They will fly in from all over the country and spend four days together. By the time Rae found out about it, all of Morgan's plans were set, and Rae was not included.

Rae: "So, you're going to Las Vegas with your family?"

Morgan: "We do this every two years. It's kind of a family tradition."

Rae: "How come you didn't ask if I wanted to go? I love Vegas."

Morgan: "Well, it's a family tradition. Besides, my brother, Chuck, isn't bringing anyone."

Rae: "I know your family doesn't like me, but if they never have a chance to get to know me, how will that ever change? You should have asked me to go. You go to all my family dinners. My family loves you."

Morgan: "I've invited you to family events. You never want to go."

Rae: "You invited me to Sunday dinner once and I had a big test the next day."

Morgan: "Well, it's too late now. All the plans are set."

Stonewalling is the fourth horseman in a deteriorating relationship. Stonewalling might include avoiding the other person (work late, pretend to be asleep) or avoiding certain topics ("I can't talk right now"). According to Gottman, presence of the four horsemen in a relationship indicates trouble.

Just as adults develop patterns in conflict, so do children. Hale, Tardy, and Farley-Lucas (1995) found children's verbal explosions during school conflicts had a common underlying objective of gaining power or claiming superiority. Stein and Albro's (2001) review of how children and parents argue found that when anger was expressed by parents or children, they generally were unable to come to a resolution. Stein and Albro believe anger leads to competitive feelings of right and wrong or attempts to force the other person to change. In contrast, expressions of sadness lead to a greater probability of positive resolution.

The counterpart to competitive styles is avoidance and accommodation. A 2002 review of research on family conflict concluded that negative interaction correlated highest for divorce potential. Specifically, men tended to withdraw (avoid) more than women (similarly across all cultural groups, but highest among African American males), and most arguments were initiated over money, communication, sex, household chores, jealousy, friends, careers, in-laws, alcohol/drugs, recreation, children, or religion (Stanley et al., 2002).

Contrary to popular wisdom, women are not necessarily more self-sacrificing (compromising) in relationship conflicts than are men. Neff and Harter (2002) found 62 percent of men and 61 percent of women in heterosexual couples habitually used compromise to resolve conflicts, essentially the same rate for men and women. Those who used compromise also were more likely to perceive their partner's behavior as compromising. If the relationship was equally self-sacrificing among both partners, self-sacrificing was perceived as an authentic behavior.

However, Neff and Harter (2002) found that women who gave up their needs for their partner felt as if they acted inauthentically to their true selves, particularly if their partner turned out to be advancing a self-serving interest. For example, Dee might save money from the family budget by forgoing her spring shopping trip with her sister. However, she finds her partner Steve spent more than the money she saved to purchase a motorcycle for himself. In this situation, she feels cheated—more so than if Steve had been direct and forewarned her about his intended purchase. The research also showed that men reported positive consequences to the relationship (Steve is happy that his wife saved the money so he has some extra to buy the motorcycle)—a disconnection in how each partner perceived the situation (Steve is surprised when he learns that Dee is upset).

Culture and the Family

As noted at the beginning of this chapter, a disappointing majority of the subjects in family communication research have been white, heterosexual, upper- to middle-class families. Fortunately, the promise of more diversified research is starting to be realized. Researchers are beginning to address the significant issues of family communication in many racial, culture, ethnic, and socioeconomic groups. Initial results suggest that families of various racial and ethnic heritages may perceive "family" or "marriage" differently than has emerged thus far.

Socha and Diggs (1999) found that African American women tend to see marriage as less about the companionship and more about the spiritual and ethnic connection than her European and biracial counterparts. Biracial couples were more likely to view marriage as "work" as compared to mono-racial couples. They further theorized that African-American families most probably hold *collectivist* values about family—relying on support from the extended family and good friends, whereas European American families are more *individualistic,* expecting help only from immediate relatives.

Research on Latino families highlighted characteristics that are relevant in child custody mediation. Traditionally Latinos may value the group over the individual, particularly in **familismo,** which puts the highest value on the multigenerational family. Traditional families may embrace **machismo,** placing the father at the authoritative head of the family and the wife in a self-sacrificing caregiver role. Values of **compadrazgo,** which emphasize mutual obligation and interdependence, allow families in crisis to send children to relatives for caregiving. These values create families that are close and cooperative. Conflict in Latino families may follow patterns of brief escalations that are kept within the family. Revealing family conflict to a stranger, such as a mediator, is extremely difficult and may be perceived as humiliating, making the European American–based model of mediation problematic for this population.

A series of studies by Ting-Toomey and Oetzel relate the concept of facework to family conflict. As stated in Chapter 4, face is a person's sense of self-image. *Facework* is communication to manage self-image. Oetzel and Ting-Toomey (2003) found that families, although similar in their conflict patterns across cultures, also manifest differences. For example, Germans and European Americans share an individualistic culture, yet Germans tend to be more direct and confrontational than European Americans. Germans may see European Americans as not serious; Europeans Americans may view Germans as too blunt and pushy. Mexicans and Japanese share a collectivist culture. In a traditional Mexican family, social expectations are common that individuals will sacrifice for the family. Yet in similarly collectivist Japanese families, the needs of work may trump the needs of the family. As individuals from various root cultures marry to create blended families, a universe of misunderstandings and cultural clashes may emerge. Challenges include questions like these: "Should issues be talked out directly?" "Should everyone compromise for the greater good or does one parent have the last say in all disputes?" "How much of my time should I give to my job versus my family?"

The Dark Side of Family Conflict

In the preface of their book *The Dark Side of Close Relationships,* Spitzberg and Cupach (1998) note that it is the paradoxes of communication that give rise to the dark side (see Table 13.7). Dysfunctional families may differ from their more functional counterparts both in *what* they talk about and *how* they communicate with each other.

In a study of taped conversations of abusive and nonabusive couples, Sabourin and Stamp (1995) noted several communicative differences illustrative of how communication may create and sustain dysfunction (see Table 13.8). Abusive couples tended to use *vague, uninteresting* descriptions of their daily activities ("How was your day? Fine."). Nonabusive couples sounded more active and *precise* in describing daily events. Abusive couples *opposed* each other's statements, argued, criticized the other person, and evidenced long uncomfortable pauses while interacting. Nonabusive couples cooperatively interrupted each other, finished each other's sentences, repeated a word or phrase stated by the partner, and generally *cooperated in building a story together.* Abusive couples turned most topics into an argument about their *relationship,* complaining about each other, making controlling statements toward the other, or stating their personal feelings. Nonabusive couples collaborated and stayed on a *content* topic. Abusive couples' conversations were sprinkled with *despair,* focused on past negative events, and included statements of anger or frustration toward the partner. Nonabusive couples talked about each other in positive ways and were more *optimistic* about outcomes. Abusive couples *interfered* with each other's conversation through disagreement, complained about the other person, made disapproving

---

TABLE 13.7   *The Dark Side of Close Relationships*

- Attractiveness can be a curse.
- Openness can be costly.
- Self-esteem can be self-absorbing.
- Assertiveness can be unlikable.
- Humor can be violent and oppressive.
- Supportiveness can aggravate rather than heal.
- Cooperation and empathy are susceptible to exploitation.
- Politeness can be a reflection of oppression.
- Competence in one's communication can backfire in myriad ways.
- Friendships are often fraught with difficulties.
- Alternative models of families often are quite functional
  compared to their "normal" alternatives.

Source: Spitzberg and Cupach (1998), p. xii.

TABLE 13.8 *Abusive versus Nonabusive Couple Language*

Abusive Couples	Nonabusive Couples
Vague descriptions of activities	Precise/active descriptions of activities
Opposed each other's ideas	Build a story together
Conflict about relationship/power	Conflict about content
Despair	Optimism
Bring up negative past	Focus on future events
Interfere	Ask questions
Complaining	Complimentary

statements, and had an inability to understand the other's perspective. Nonabusive couples used *facilitative* communication strategies such as asking questions or clarifying. Abusive couples frequently *complained* about their partner; nonabusive couples were more likely to moderate complaints and to *compliment* each other.

Negative messages have significant effects on adults and children. Stafford and Dainton (1994) identified two important aspects of rejection in the family. First, a child may experience a debilitating erosion of self-esteem when parental messages consistently are disconfirming. *Disconfirming messages* either ignore the child's attempts at attention or directly label the child as worthless and bad. Telling a child "You are so stupid" runs counter to helping that child develop a positive sense of self. Second, some of the compliance-gaining strategies used by parents may be damaging, such as coercion or withdrawal of love. Some research, however, indicates that higher self-esteem moderates disconfirming messages. In romantic relationships, hurtful evaluative messages were more face threatening than similar comments about personality or appearance, with high self-esteem individuals showing less concern about disconfirmation (Zhang & Stafford, 2008).

A final dysfunctional aspect of family conflict is violence and aggression. Olson's (2002) research using European American college students who had experienced some level of aggression in their relationships found a connection between aggressive behavior and a lack of communication competence. They concluded that aggression might be used when individuals were not able to bring other communicative strategies and tactics to the situation. They also discovered that some subjects believed aggression was justifiable, thinking that aggression was biological, aggression was caused by abuse as a child, aggression was natural if it was learned in the family of origin, or aggression was fine if anger was used as a tactic to get the partner's attention. The implication of the latter finding is that it is important not only to stop excessive aggressive behaviors, but also to change people's opinions about the appropriateness of aggression.

Discussion Question 13.8

Can aggression be appropriate and/or desirable in a relationship? If so, when does aggressive behavior become dysfunctional in family communication or relationships?

Even so-called normal families have their dark side. It is a myth that at some point in history, families were happier and more successful than current families. Stafford and Dainton (1994) comment on the myth of the golden age of family relations: "During this fictitious utopian era, divorce was unheard of, children respected their elders and knew right from wrong, multiple generations dwelled blissfully in the same home, and family members spent their abundant leisure time together engaged in wholesome activities such as eating stone-ground bread that had been baked in their own ovens from plates they made themselves at their joint pottery class" (p. 261).

It is commonly held in the communication discipline that relationships require communication skills and work to keep them healthy. Sadly, many families may talk primarily about who should take out the garbage (a task) and not about issues or feelings that are critical to the relationship. Thus little time is invested in productive conflict management and relationship maintenance. Research indicates that most people believe that maintaining relationships is work; they just don't do the work (Stafford & Dainton, 1994). We may wind up practicing more careful communication with coworkers and strangers than with spouses and children.

Conflict Management Skills for Families

Families in Training

One of the most powerful ways to manage conflict in a family is to learn skills. Families can learn conflict management skills in a variety of ways. Couples can attend communication and relationship building classes. Parents can use facilitators or counselors to work out expectations and communication behaviors before stepfamilies join together. Adults can learn new skills and teach them to their families, including the adults reading this book. Children learn conflict management skills at school and can share those ideas with their parents. For change to occur, the environment must be considered safe to experiment and make mistakes. Just knowing a skill isn't enough. Diligence, desire, and practice are the means to create new habits.

As with general interpersonal conflict, listening is one of the most critical skills for family conflict management. Coakley and Wolvin (1997) emphasize that parents must learn different listening skills to use with a child as he or she ages because listening is the only way to understand what is occurring for a child during a decision-making discussion. The act of listening itself is confirming, helping the individual feel as if his or her views are valued. Parents may be deterred from effective listening for a variety of reasons, some of which are featured in Table 13.9.

KEY 13.2

Most people believe that maintaining relationships is work; they just don't do the work.

Family Meetings

Creating purposeful time for positive interactions is important for building healthy communication cultures in families. The *family meeting* or *family home night* enables families to work on issues before they become overwhelming or devolve into negative

TABLE 13.9 *Myths About Listening in the Family*

- Listening undermines parental authority.
- Listening to a child means agreeing with what the child is expressing.
- Listening obligates parents to change their views.
- Listening just leads to hearing hurtful criticism.

criticism. Simply put, a *family meeting* is a regularly scheduled time set aside for family communication and problem solving. Families may hold a particular night of the week for "family talk" or have a rule that any family member can call a meeting. Usually, families use a set agenda that includes time for "gripes" or issues, as well as mention of personal achievements and success. After the ritual sharing, the family sets an agenda of which issues to discuss and how the family can address the concern (Wilmot & Hocker, 2007).

Selecting the right time and place for a couple or a family to discuss issues is critical. Because many families have no set time when they are all together, working on family issues or conflicts rarely occurs naturally. When everyone knows that two hours are reserved to deal with a family issue, there is less impulse to drift to other activities. Typically, a family meets in a place in the home that is comfortable for everyone and away from distractions. For example, no media should intrude into the conversation and no "outsiders" should be present. Some couples who are trying to break a pattern of raising their voices with each other or cutting off a conversation early schedule a meeting to discuss issues at a restaurant, using the social setting as a reason to keep tones lower.

Mediation

When families are not able to work out their conflicts, *family mediation* is an option. Mediators facilitate family interaction in a safe setting and through a controlled agenda that encourages family members to work out their own agreements (Burrell & Fitzpatrick, 1990).

Stanley et al.'s (2002) study of conflict among Anglo-American, African American, Latino, and Asian American married couples found that negative interactions played a

CASE 13.5 • *My Family Meeting*

When my teenagers were fighting excessively—which might actually vary according to how much I could take on a particular day—I would call a family meeting. The three of us sat down at the kitchen table, and I set a few ground rules: Everybody gets an equal chance to talk without interruption and no negative comments while the other is talking. Each teenager then had a chance to vent about what was going on. Then we would brainstorm. I'd tell them that we wouldn't criticize or make faces when we were brainstorming ideas. We brainstormed how each could accommodate the other and not infringe on each other's privileges as family members. By the end of the family meeting, my teenagers would be laughing, talking together instead of fighting—coming up with the silliest ideas. In among all of the silly ideas, there always seemed to be a way through the difficulty that started their bickering.

dominant role in creating marriage dissatisfaction. They concluded, "Based on an entire body of research, we believe that successful treatment for couples will often include provision of a safe place for issues to be addressed in treatment as well as efforts to help couples develop reliable methods for talking safely and openly at home" (pp. 670–671). Specifically, couples need to learn how to refrain from hurtful comments, negative attributions of the partner's motivations, and how to stay in conversation about difficulties rather than withdrawing (a pattern of behavior in 42 percent of males and 26 percent of females).

Gottman et al. (2001) reviewed past studies showing that 50 percent of couples in distress did not perceive their partner's positive gestures as positive (compared to the observations of objective observers). They found facial expressions of anger, disgust, contempt, sadness, and fear were important predictors of negative marital outcomes. A mediator can help by observing when family members' perceptions differ and by creating a safe structure for the discussion of important issues.

Family Metaphors

How families describe themselves metaphorically can reveal their perceptions and interaction patterns. Metaphors also are a tool for active family conflict management. Does everyone in the family use the same metaphor for the family? Is the family a tree with many branches, a prison, or a nest? If family members use different descriptors, does that indicate an important difference in the perceptions of family members? When asked to describe their family using a metaphor, college students wrote primarily positive images (72 percent), such as a school of fish or a well-oiled machine. Some used negative metaphors (14 percent) such as a fragile eggshell or shattered crystal. When asked about communication in their family of origin, 34 percent wrote negative metaphors, such as a wall or radon decomposition (each year half the communication dies). Positive family communication metaphors included: the family is like different flavors of ice cream or it is deep like a pond (Pawlowski et al., 2001). Even though students generally felt positively about their families of origins, they reported low satisfaction with family communication.

Talking about how members perceive the family by comparing the family to other things metaphorically can be revealing. For example, a family that sits down to talk may discover they have no common view: "We're like cars on the freeway—we're sharing the same road but that's about it." The family could discuss how they might change that picture, for example: "Getting together in the same car instead of zipping by each other on the freeway." In this scenario, the family would discuss what they might start doing to "travel together on the freeway." Simple ideas may emerge, such as talking about their day for fifteen minutes each day, eating meals together, doing an event once a week just for the family, and so forth.

Summary

Families come in all types and sizes, from nuclear, to extended, to families of choice. Some families function well, others are at risk of losing their effectiveness when trouble occurs, and some are dysfunctional.

Family communication encompasses how the individuals attribute meaning to events in the life of the family and how rules and norms are created and sustained. Assumptions about family life and patterns of interaction were learned in the family of origin. The quality of family communication is related to family satisfaction.

Research has identified four types of families according to their high or low degree of conformity and how the family converses: Consensual families encourage discussion, but expect conformity; pluralistic families encourage discussion and allow some personal variability; protective families emphasize conformity without discussion; and laissez-faire families don't encourage anything in particular. Pluralistic families seem to provide the most beneficial social learning environment for children. Even so, the amount and type of conformity that is expected evolves over a family's lifespan as children change and age.

Family stories are a type of communication that sustains an image of the group, as well as conveying norms and life lessons. Family rituals, in contrast, are repeated behaviors that a family enacts.

In addition to stories, rituals, and traditions, families have norms and rules for interaction. Norms develop early in a couple's association and may set the standards for behaviors for a family's lifetime. Norms are customary behaviors, so they are somewhat more flexible than family rules, which strictly govern how one should behave. Some family rules include secrets, which can be sweet, toxic, or dangerous.

Research in family satisfaction finds that dissatisfied marriages are more negative and critical than more satisfied marriages. Related to satisfaction in families is their feeling of closeness and whether critical events lead to more closeness or more distance.

Two styles of family conversation, high involvement and high considerateness, may affect how family conflicts are perceived and managed. Pluralistic families provided the most effective foundation for productive conflict management. Additionally, there are significant differences in family communication and compliance behaviors across cultural groups that give rise to conflict in multicultural families.

On the dark side of family communication, researchers find differences in how abusive families and nonabusive families communicate. Abusive couples exhibited: more despair, focus on the past, negativity, anger, frustration, and long agonizing pauses. Abusive couples actively interfered with each other's goal attainment, complained more, and used many disconfirming messages.

In addition to the usual range of interpersonal conflict management skills, families may moderate conflict through changing their individual communication behaviors, establishing family meeting times, building new family metaphors, or mediation.

Chapter Resources _____

Exercises

1. In groups, select a film to view. Determine what kind of family communication is occurring and if family members have secrets that are concealed. If secrets are concealed, what are the consequences? Suggested films: *Fun with Dick and Jane, The Family Stone, Little Miss Sunshine, The Royal Tannenbaums, The Graduate, Rumor Has It, Running with Scissors, The Queen, Winter Passing,* and *The Full Monty.*
2. Compare at least two films portraying stepfamilies (recommendations from Leon & Angst, 2005: *Stepmom, The Santa Clause, Man of the House, Tumbleweeds*). What types of conflicts are portrayed in stepfamilies?

Journal/Essay Topics

1. How would you classify your family of origin? How is the style of your family of origin affecting you as an adult?

2. If you have children, or if you plan to have children someday, would you want your children to experience the same family communication style that you learned? What lessons in family conflict would/will children learn from you?

Research Topics

1. Investigate family structures and norms in a culture other than your own. What similarities and differences do you find?

Mastery Cases

Examine Mastery Case 13A, "Too Many Moms" or case 13B, "The Family Feud." What concepts from this chapter shed light on these case?

Too Many Moms

When Debbie was eight, her parents divorced. Her dad, Frank, remarried quickly and Debbie's mother, Elaine, expressed disdain for the new wife. It was clear to Debbie that her mother feared losing her children's affection and allegiance. Elaine would become jealous whenever Debbie mentioned her stepmother's birthday or if she gave her stepmother a gift on Mother's Day.

When Debbie grew up and married, her husband's mother expected Debbie to call her "Mom" like her other daughter-in-law did and like she called her husband's mother. Debbie couldn't bring herself to call her mother-in-law "Mom" and called her by her first name, Eva. Even though her own mother passed away, to call anyone else "Mom" seemed awkward or like a betrayal of her mother's memory. Eva was hurt and always winced when called by her first name instead of by "Mom," and she took the refusal to comply with her wishes very personally.

The Family Feud

Todd and Karen are brother and sister. They were very close in the past but drifted apart during their parents' prolonged illnesses. Karen provided home care for her parents for the last ten years, which dramatically affected her life. Todd refused to help. He was in his second marriage and said he had his own life and career and didn't have time, so she would just have to handle it. Karen took care of their parents until they died.

After their mother's death, probate started. In probate, all of the parents' estate must be vetted through the courts, taxes paid, and the remaining assets distributed to the children according to the will. The will named Karen and Todd as coexecutors—meaning they must work together to settle the estate. After the funeral, Karen started working on what needed to be done. Two months passed. There was a lot of tedious, time-consuming sorting to be done, and Karen wanted Todd to help. Todd agreed to meet at the family house.

It's Sunday at 2 P.M. when Todd arrives. Karen is surrounded by boxes and sorting through the items in the estate. Todd helps her carry items from the house to the garage.

Karen: "As you can see, there is a lot to do here—80 years of accumulated personal property that has to be sorted, inventoried, appraised, and distributed. I need you to help out more."

Todd: "I'm too busy with my work and my own family to get bogged down in this. I have more important responsibilities than dealing with this junk."

Karen: "You agreed to be coexecutor! That means more than picking up your check from the attorney. It's only right that you help with this stuff. I'll keep working, but you have to come by every weekend and help sort this out."

Todd: "You don't realize how hard I work. I have a life. I don't have time. You don't have Mom and Dad to take care of anymore, so you have lots of time on your hands. You can do it."

Karen: "I've worked really hard the last ten years caring for *our* parents. Where were you? I am tired and could use your help. I'm anxious to get this taken care of so I can have a life. I've been in this house for ten years taking care of our parents, and I'm ready for a change of scenery."

Todd: "I worked hard here when I was a kid. That should count for something! I shouldn't have to do much now that I have a business of my own."

Karen: "We didn't work that hard as kids, come on. Mom and Dad worked hard."

Todd: "I worked hard, whether you remember it or not."

Karen: "That was a long time ago. We need to figure out what we're going to do now."

Todd: "If I was in charge, I'd get a big dumpster and just get rid of everything! It's all crap anyway."

Karen: "You can't be serious. There's a lot of valuable stuff here—not to mention all the family pictures. How do we know what's here until we look?"

Todd: "Go ahead! Look away. I don't have time to look at all this junk when we're just going to throw most of it out. If you want me to help, I'll have to do it my way. I'll get some dumpsters in here and be done with it."

Karen: "Go for it! At least you'll be doing something. It's all in your hands. Call me when it's time for me to pick up my check on the estate settlement."

Karen leaves and slams the door. Two days later, Todd contacts Karen and says he's ready to work out a schedule to sort through the stuff. Karen says she's glad they will be working on it together.

14

Conflict at the Workplace

Vocabulary

Chain of command
Conflict management systems
Emotional labor
Flat organizational hierarchy
Groupthink
Hierarchy of authority

Leadership
Maintenance role
Mentoring
Organizational culture
Organizational misbehavior
Personal conflict coaching

Quality control circle
Role emergence
Silo mentality
Task role

Objectives

After reading this chapter, you should be able to:

1. Explain how communication in an organizational setting is similar to and different from communication in other settings
2. Understand the dynamics of new employee socialization
3. Explain how leaders can prevent some conflicts and manage conflicts that do occur
4. Recognize how roles emerge and function in organizations

The Workplace Is a Unique Context

Most people spend a significant amount of their time at work—typically more than with family or socializing with friends. Because the work environment is specialized and professional, some erroneously believe there should be little conflict at work. These same optimists believe the rare conflicts in the work setting will be about work issues. The truth is the work environment neither is immune to conflict nor limited in the types of conflicts that occur. Conflict is just as likely to emerge at work as in other contexts. Like other contexts, how conflicts are managed affects each individual in that situation.

CASE 14.1 • *You Are Not My Boss*

Jon and Marc work in the repair shop at an outdoor recreation dealership. It's spring, and everybody brought their ATVs in for tune-ups and repairs. The shop is full of equipment, and the schedule has been falling steadily behind. Marc has worked in the shop for years; Jon has been there for about a year. A third employee, Heidi, works in the sales area and comes back to talk to Marc from time to time. It is 8:30 in the morning. Jon is working on a Big Bear Honda that is due for pickup in the morning while Marc and Heidi talk over by the break room. The supervisor is out of town.

Jon: "Hey, Marc, I can't get this cover off. The bolt is rusted shut. Can you come over and give me a hand for a second?" Marc looks up and nods but keeps talking to Heidi. They both are laughing about something.

Jon: "Hey, Marc, can you come over here for a minute?"

Marc: "Just a second."

Jon waits a minute, then crawls out from under the ATV and walks over to Marc.

Jon: "What's the hold up? Can you come help me with this Big Bear?"

Marc: "Don't be so impatient. I'm talking to Heidi about some important stuff."

Jon: "That's great, but can't you two talk on break or something? We're wasting time here."

Marc: "I don't care what you think. You are not my boss. We're just working half a day today, anyway, so why get all lathered up?"

Jon: "We've got 10 people showing up at 6 A.M. tomorrow expecting to go spring hunting on their ATVs. Are you going to be there to tell them you couldn't be bothered to fix their rigs?"

Marc: "Whatever. You're such a boy scout." He and Heidi walk off, laughing.

Conflict at work is different from general interpersonal conflict in at least three significant ways. First, conflicts that occur in the workplace are inextricably tied to one's work identity. Relationship goals may be more important for some people at home or with friends than with coworkers. For others who deeply identify with their careers and "live to work," face and power goals may be paramount. The stakes are different at work than in other contexts, but they are not different in the same ways for each individual.

A second reason conflict in the workplace is different from general interpersonal conflict is the group effort required to accomplish many tasks. *Teamwork* is a buzzword of modern business that captures how employees must interconnect to accomplish tasks or provide services. Working in a group requires leadership—formal leadership from a supervisor and/or informal leadership from colleagues. When groups interact, members may see the task differently, vie for power, or offend each other's sensibilities in a number of ways, giving rise to conflict. The workplace offers numerous opportunities for coalition building, personal agendas, and power seeking. Groups can take on differentiated roles, norms, or create a unique culture all their own. Work groups use conflict in a variety of ways, including as a means to spur innovation, to inspire increased performance, to manipulate the system, or to pursue personal goals.

> **KEY 14.1**
>
> **It is not enough to be a competent leader—one must nurture competence in others and work to change the organization's culture.**

A third way that conflict differs in the work context lies in the nature of organizations. Organizations have rules, structures, hierarchies, and numerous channels of communication across and among levels. Organizational units may come into conflict or employees may vie for power within the organization. The organization may or may not provide structural outlets for productive conflict management and may or may not protect individual workers from excess conflict, bullying, or retaliation.

TOOLBOX 14.1

De-Flaming at Work

Professional conflict consultants have a saying about e-mail: "It's making us a lot of money." When an e-mail arrives at a worker's inbox, it lacks context. Despite the occasional smiley face, e-mail has little of the nonverbal or vocal nuances that help a recipient interpret a message as it was intended. Frequently e-mails are written in a hurry, and, consequently, the sender's intention can be misunderstood. When people are upset, messages may become terser or more antagonizing, a type of message awarded the searing moniker **flaming**. At worse, e-mail messages contain diatribes that one later regrets, particularly because the message was written in a format easily forwarded to others (not to mention that corporations and state agencies are required by law in many cases to keep copies of all e-mails in permanent storage). A hasty e-mail can provide a kind of fame and immortality, but it's probably not the fame anybody really wants.

E-mail may begin an escalatory conflict spiral if it (1) uses aggressive tactics, (2) is so ambiguous that it is open to negative interpretation, (3) weakens interpersonal bonds, and/or (4) is inappropriate for the problem to be solved (Friedman & Currall, 2003). The last item primarily refers to the asynchronous nature of e-mail, which makes it inappropriate for problems that require immediate attention or creative responses.

To use e-mail more professionally and with less probability of starting or sustaining a conflict, follow these guidelines:

1. Never write e-mail when you are consumed with anger or emotion. Write a draft that you can come back to later and change.
2. The more important the message, the longer it should take to write.
3. Reread all e-mails before sending, thinking about what it would be like if you received the e-mail.
4. Imagine different people reading the e-mail: your boss, your boss's boss, your coworkers, your subordinates, the media, and your mother.
5. Avoid filling colleague's inboxes with entertainment. It takes everyone's time, and it's possible that what you think is funny others may find offensive.
6. If you have had misunderstandings in the past via e-mail with the person you are writing, pick up the phone or make a face-to-face visit.
7. No flaming, ever, no matter how tempting, is permissible.
8. Put a context sentence or two at the top of every e-mail message. Include what you are referring to or responding to. Update subject lines as needed.
9. Be appropriately personal. Put the person's name at the top to remind you that you are writing to a "person." Sign your name to remind yourself that you are responsible for what you say. Avoid using your full "signature" information when e-mailing close colleagues—it's too formal.
10. Avoid piling on and gunnysacking in an e-mail. Stick to recent events as much as possible.

This chapter examines conflict in the work context. We organize this chapter by starting with the larger entity—the organization—and then moving to the building-block level of organizations—the work group. We identify what is known about common conflict patterns in the workplace. We then examine conflict among within work groups.

Workplace Communication

Although we obviously cannot give a comprehensive view of how communication is different in organizations than in interpersonal relationships, we can provide a glimpse into the worlds of group and organizational communication. To some extent, interpersonal conflict is the same wherever it occurs. But just as conflict in a family may evolve differently if the desire to remain bonded is seen as more important than the substantive issues, the nature of the workplace itself may transform how interpersonal conflict is played out.

Organizations have a **hierarchy of authority** that shapes communication from managers to workers and vice versa. In traditional management theory, the hierarchy of authority is called the **chain of command** (a military metaphor). The hierarchy of an organization is represented in an *organizational chart* that indicates who reports to whom.

In traditional organizations, the hierarchy is vertical, power is invested in top management, and messages trickle from the top of the organization down to those who create the products or do the services (workers). A **flat organizational hierarchy** has fewer layers of management between top management and workers and, theoretically, more communication flows up and down the hierarchy. To counteract the tendency of employees to communicate only with those in their unit, sometimes called a **silo mentality,** organizations may use tactics like quality control circles. In a **quality control circle,** a small group of workers from different areas of the organization meet to discuss problems and suggest solutions. When a company wanted to decrease damage during shipping of product, they started with a quality control circle comprised of a truck driver, someone in the shipping department, someone from the packing department, and a supervisor in the manufacturing unit. The group later invited a customer to sit in on the discussion. Because they all brought different ideas to the problem, the group was able to come up with a series of suggestions that helped prevent shipping damage.

> ### Discussion Question 14.1
> Who is in the chain of command at your college? Is it like the chain of command described in Insert 14.1 or different? When might it be important to understand the chain of command in your major department? For example, where would you go to make a change in the requirements for your major?

The complexity of workplace communication is measured through workplace communication assessments or audits. They may include diagnostic tests, observation of work flow and communication behaviors, interviews, network analysis, content analysis of documents, or focus groups, among other indicators. The International Communication Association Audit Process asks a series of questions about how much communication one receives versus how much information one would need to do the job (Downs & Adrian, 2004).

INSERT 14.1

Chain of Command: Who's In and Who's Out

The *formal chain of command* (named after the lines of "command" in a military organization) encompasses who reports to whom and who has authority over others. Consider the organizational chain of command in a typical university. The university president (or sometimes a provost) sits atop the formal university hierarchy, even though the president may report to a state board of education or a board of governors. Reporting to the president are several vice presidents, each having "command" in his or her area—the VP of finance supervises all the employees in that area and controls the financial operations of the university, as directed by the president. The VP of student affairs controls matters that govern student life—residential complexes, student union staff, student clubs, student grievance procedures, recruitment, and retention—as directed by the president. The VP of academic affairs governs faculty, academic units, and curriculum matters. Each of the VPs have rules and internal operating processes that constrain their actions. For example, whereas the VP of academic affairs controls the purse that funds academic programs, the faculty have control over what the content of the academic programs will be (under a concept called faculty governance). That explains why a change in a student's program of study typically goes up the chain of command on the academic side and not to the VP of student affairs.

   One factor that helps determine the chain of command is to look at who has decision-making authority or who fills in when someone is gone. If the president is away, the person who knows the most about the president's schedule is the executive assistant. The executive assistant controls the president's schedule and probably is the person most familiar with the president's thoughts on many matters. However, an executive assistant is not in the line of decision-making authority. If the president is away, decision-making authority devolves to one of the vice presidents. Typically, there are rules that govern the chain of command.

Organizations have internal sets of assumptions that are labeled an **organizational culture.** Part of every new employee's unwritten job is to learn the organization's culture and to discover how to fit in. Some firms have a formal **mentoring** process where an established employee teaches the new hire how things work. Whether there is formal mentoring or not, during the first few weeks of employment socialization occurs that either integrates new employees into the work team and their unique work culture or results in a semipermanent "outsider" status. For example, if the culture of a particular work group is that everyone goes out to lunch together on Friday and a new employee continues to go to lunch with old friends in another department, then crucial socialization time is missed and the new hire may be perceived as snobbish. Ideally, potential employees should be aware of an organization's culture before making an application to avoid accepting employment in an organization with a culture that is a bad fit. For example, two high-tech firms may both be producing new-generation microchips, but that does not mean both have modern, employee-friendly cultures.

Part of the negotiation process for employment can include the type of training and mentoring that will occur: Who specifically will train the new employee? What type of training will be offered? How many days or weeks will the trainer be available for consultation? Table 14.1 suggests a variety of methods to discover an organization's culture. Overt questions may be effective immediately after joining a company when more latitude is given to the newcomer. For example, during the first week, one might ask outright if the manager likes regular reports. Later on, a less direct strategy might be more effective, for example, asking how the manager would prefer to be kept up to date. If talking to the manager or supervisor directly seems unworkable, information can be sought from coworkers, managers in other units, or others knowledgeable about the organization. Of course, if these strategies are perceived by one's immediate supervisor as circumventing his or her authority, conflict may ensue. Testing limits, or pushing beyond the range of what one thinks the corporate culture will allow, is risky. Observing intentionally and analytically what other workers do and how they communicate with each other and with supervisors can be very revealing.

Discussion Question 14.2

Think about a place where you currently work or have worked in the past. Were you mentored when you first started your job? How were you socialized into that workplace culture? What would you tell new employees that would be helpful to their socialization?

Another way of inferring what the workplace will be like is to look at the demographic profile of workers and management. Are most workers men or women? Does the population of ethnic and racial groups in the organization parallel those of the geographic area? For example, a company in Baton Rouge whose workers all are white men would not reflect the diversity of the area. Examining the generations (see Chapter 5) represented in management may be informative. For example, if all the managers are Boomers, a Boomer culture may exist in the company.

One way that an organization's culture can be detected is how people talk about the organization. When employees at a marketing and public relations firm refer to their workplace as "the factory," going to work as "punching in at the time clock," and their supervisors as "the suits," they paint a picture of work as drudgery done only for a paycheck in an uncaring vertical hierarchy. In contrast, workers who describe going to work as "play," the workplace as "the creativity hub," and managers by their first names describe a warmer and more vibrant work culture.

Discussion Question 14.3

In one college of the university where the authors teach, the norm is that administrators are never referred to by name. Instead, they are referred to by their role: "the dean" or "the department chair" or "the provost." In the college where the other author works, people are referred to by their first names. What implications might you draw about the organizational culture of these units based on this observation?

Organizational culture is dynamic and changing. For example, the casual and/or intentional sexual and racial harassment that was common fare in the workplace of a few decades ago now is illegal. A viewing of many movies depicting a workplace from before 1980 includes scenes of sexual harassment of secretaries as a prerogative of management and ethnic/racial slurs from coworkers as an endemic reality. To escape the legal exposure from these behaviors when anti-harassment laws were passed, corporations wrote new policies, required training about illegal sexual and racial harassment, and coined terms like

TABLE 14.1   *Detecting Corporate Culture*

Read between the lines in the organization's policy manuals.
Examine the generation, age, and ethnicity in each layer of the organization.
Ask informants about the organization's culture and workplace climate.
Ask key questions during interviews.
Seek training and a mentor.
Ask direct questions.
Ask indirect questions.
Ask third parties.
Test limits.
Observe other employees.
Listen to stories about the company.

"respectful workplaces" or "diversity-friendly" employment. Behaviors, however, lag behind policy and training programs, particularly in making newcomers welcome in previously all-male or all-white workplaces.

Allen (2000) commented, "black women frequently enter workplace roles where they previously have not been welcome and where governing ideologies generally have ignored their existence or have viewed them pejoratively" (p. 183). These experiences persist among groups who historically were excluded from desirable jobs and the upper ranks of corporate America. The history of oppression also affects the socialization process and creates a paradox where one's very presence could be adverse to exclusionary cultural practices. For example, when someone breaks an employment barrier (i.e., is the first disabled, woman, openly gay, or foreign employee in a work group), routine information gathering may reinforce perceptions that someone was hired for his or her token status rather than for superior qualifications.

INSERT 14.2

Good-Natured Banter

An interesting aspect of communication in some workplace groups is called *good-natured banter*. Banter is a form of teasing. Good-natured banter is intended to be witty and a sign of inclusion in a group or friendship circle. Hurtful banter is exclusionary and intended to make someone feel bad.

If a newcomer hears coworkers jokingly calling each other names or making fun of each other's foibles, then similar remarks addressed to the newcomer may be good-natured banter. For example, if the newcomer showed up with a very pink shirt, someone might say to her. "Wow! Couldn't you find something louder to wear?" Good-natured banter of a newcomer is a test. To pass the test, one must accept the banter and respond in kind with a smile: "Hey, somebody has to class this place up." Defensive remarks confirm that the newcomer is an alien who won't fit in with the group. Saying, "You don't have any right to talk about my shirt!" fails the good-natured banter test and creates a feeling that the newcomer deserves to be excluded.

A caution about good-natured banter is prudent. Newcomers must wait for the banter and not initiate banter with the old-timers, which could be perceived as pushy or disrespectful. Participating in banter requires a firm understanding of the norms of the group and the relationships of the parties. A good rule is to observe how the norm of banter works, and with whom, before initiating it yourself.

The Nature of Groups

The group is a basic building block of an organization. A *group* is generally considered three to twelve people—large enough that dynamics kick in that are different from dyadic communication, yet small enough that all individuals can interact meaningfully with each other (Beebe & Masterson, 2006).

> "Avoiders are seldom sought out for their ideas."
> —Authors Runde and Flanagan, 2007, p. 103

Several features make a group different from the two-person interpersonal context. Although a comprehensive discussion of group dynamics is beyond the scope of this chapter, three key areas are worthy of mention: norms, roles, and leadership.

Norms

Groups develop norms that characterize their combined identity. A *norm* is an unwritten rule of behavior. For example, even though it is not written down or discussed, everyone in a group may know that it is permissible to take an extra half hour for lunch on Friday and that the boss doesn't like anyone eating at a workstation. Because norms are informal, they can be difficult to learn. It is incumbent upon the new employee to watch for the presence of normative behavior. Examples can include permissible topics, communication channels, humor, observances of time and space (including parking, equipment usage, and breaks), and even nonverbal communication. Darien worked in a convenience store where she had to wear a smock. The smock had large pockets in the front, and Darien had a habit of putting her hands in the pockets. Although she always got her work done, the boss thought that the behavior looked sloppy and told her, "Look around. Do you see anyone else standing around with hands shoved in their pockets?" Darien had violated a norm without even being aware that it existed.

Roles

Groups develop formal and informal roles. A *role* is a function performed by an individual. In the social sciences, roles commonly are classified as maintenance, task, or destructive. **Maintenance roles** are functions necessary to keep a group together—to form enough cohesion that the group can perform their jobs and see the benefit of a common identity. Table 14.2 lists maintenance roles. For example, someone needs to encourage others and moderate conflict. Another example of a maintenance role is building cohesion. Someone in an office may have appointed himself or herself as the keeper of birthdays and buys a card for everyone to sign when a birthday approaches. As units become larger and birthdays more frequent, celebrating birthdays may be turned into a task. A staff person is "tasked" to keep track of birthdays and to send an e-mail card from "the group" on each birthday.

Task roles are necessary to get the work done. Task roles may be performed by designated individuals, by management, or someone may take the role through personal initiative.

TABLE 14.2   *Maintenance Roles*

Encourager	Listening to others and praising their good work.
	Example: "That was a great job, Jamal."
Harmonizer	Moderating differences and conflict among individuals.
	Example: "We all want to get this job done, so let's try to keep focused on the best solution for the company."
Compromiser	Offering ideas to break deadlocks.
	Example: "The ideas suggested really aren't all that different. What about using some components of both to see if a combination will work?"
Tension releaser	Breaking the tension, using humor to counteract temper.
	Example: "Wow. That's quite an assignment. Let's all get our superhero suits on before we start!"
Gatekeeper	Ensuring that everyone has a chance to participate.
	Example: "Ed, you haven't commented lately. What are your thoughts about the project so far?"
Observer	Attending to individual nonverbal communication or comments to help stop misinterpretations.
	Example: "Sharon, you're looking like you have some reservations."
Follower	Supporting the leader(s) rather than contesting for leadership.
	Example: "Devon, you're the boss. I'm behind you all the way."
Feeling expresser	Making comments about the emotional tone of the group.
	Example: "I think everybody is really tired. Can we take a break?"
Standard setter	Calling for a discussion of how the group is working together.
	Example: "Can we talk about how we are treating each other? I'd like us to have some standards to help us stick together better."

Source: Most group dynamics textbooks discuss task, maintenance, and dysfunctional roles (e.g., Engleberg & Wynn, 2007; Forsyth, 2006; Rothwell, 2007).

The delegation of tasks and task roles requires leadership skills. A manager may be effective at encouraging workers to perform tasks, or a manager may dump a project on a group and then scurry back to a corner office. Understanding and practicing leadership and the various task roles that need to be performed in groups is crucial for career advancement and for the health of an organization's culture. Special projects are a good place to build competence in a variety of task and maintenance roles.

Table 14.3 lists typical task roles. For example, when you are assigned to a class group project, the instructor rarely determines who will lead the group, who will keep its records, and who will provide information. These essential roles emerge from the group. Likewise, in the work setting, every workforce has tasks that need to be accomplished for the product to be manufactured or the service accomplished. If no one in the group formally is assigned the task of making sure everyone knows how to use the software, one person usually steps up, called **role emergence,** to pick up that part of the job. If the

TABLE 14.3 *Task Roles*

Initiator	Making suggestions.
	Example: "Let's talk about our goals and criteria for success before kicking around specific project ideas."
Information seeker	Asking for facts and ideas.
	Example: "How do we know that the trend is increasing?"
Information giver	Sharing data relevant to the task.
	Example: "The report from marketing estimates a 10 percent increase in the overseas market next year."
Opinion seeker	Asking for other ideas.
	Example: "Darnell, you're the finance expert. What do you think about these projections?"
Clarifier/Summarizer	Summing up group consensus or progress.
	Example: "It sounds like everyone agrees that we should shoot for a May opening date?"
Evaluator/Devil's advocate	Bringing critical thinking to the topic.
	Example: "Are we forgetting that we can't control what will happen in the press or on the Internet?"
Procedural technician	Preparing for meetings: agenda, room arrangement, notifying participants.
	Example: "We'll need a projector and a laptop. I'll contact facilities."
Recorder	Keeping minutes/notes on what occurred and which decisions were made.
	Example: "Here is a copy of last week's minutes and our agenda of what we wanted to cover today."

Source: Most group dynamics textbooks discuss task, maintenance, and dysfunctional roles (e.g., Engleberg & Wynn, 2007; Forsyth, 2006; Rothwell, 2007).

supervisor is not present physically on the job site or chooses not to take an active role, others generally will volunteer themselves as leaders or try to take control.

Dysfunctional roles are adopted purely for personal reasons and detract from work performance (Table 14.4). For example, one person may make light of every situation (the group clown), tell inappropriately sexual jokes (the playboy/girl), or continually complain (the cynic). If these behaviors distract the group from accomplishing its goals, the behaviors are dysfunctional. Quality leadership, as well as the task and maintenance roles, is needed to curtail the damage that dysfunctional role behaviors can cause.

Leadership

Leadership is necessary to keep a group moving toward its goal and the accomplishment of the work objective. As mentioned earlier, leadership often is provided by management,

TABLE 14.4   *Dysfunctional Roles*

Aggressor	Using sarcasm and verbal aggression to push a personal agenda.
	Example: "Sure, Jenny, we can try to hit that deadline. And next week, you'll win the lottery."
Blocker	Resisting other's ideas and group progress.
	Example: "We've never needed to do that before, and we don't need to do that now."
Dominator/Stage hog	Monopolizing the discussion.
	Example: "That reminds me of when I made that sale to our competitor . . . "
Clown	Inappropriately joking and goofing off.
	Example: "Hey, look everyone—this is my favorite *South Park* clip on YouTube."
Deserter	Withdrawing active participation from the group or not showing up.
	Example: "Sorry I'm late, and I can't stay but a few minutes."
Confessor/Help seeker	Inappropriately and continuously shares personal feelings that detract from task progress.
	Example: "You won't believe what my husband said to me this morning! Does anyone have any ideas of how I can get him to be more supportive?"
Special interest pleader	Advocating for the cause of an outside group or a pet idea to the detriment of the group's interests.
	Example: "If we fly on British Airways, I can get double mileage points."
Cynic	Focusing on negatives and faultfinding.
	Example: "We tried that once; it didn't work."
Playboy/Playgirl	Uses the group as a personal dating service.
	Example: (After removing a chair from the room.) "Oh, too bad, Darla, you'll just have to sit on my lap during the meeting."

Source: Most group dynamics textbooks discuss task, maintenance, and dysfunctional roles (e.g., Engleberg & Wynn, 2007; Forsyth, 2006; Rothwell, 2007).

although a boss who has the title but provides no direction is not uncommon. Likewise, it is not unusual for a subordinate to think and act like he or she knows more than the boss or the designated leader, whether true or not. The power to lead and struggles over leadership are frequent sparks of conflict in the work setting. For example, a boss may misuse the leadership role; subordinates may try to wrestle leadership control away from the boss; subordinates may vie to establish ascendancy.

> ### *Discussion Question 14.4*
> Which do you think is the best approach in a group: to assign a leader or let a leader emerge? What are the advantages and disadvantages of each approach?

Conflict in the Work Setting

Causes of Workplace Conflict

Causes of workplace conflict run the gamut of incidents previously discussed for general interpersonal conflict, plus additional work-related causes. For example, even though workforce training manuals have long extolled the value of demonstrating to employees how to do a new task and then letting them try the task several times to gain proficiency (Graupp & Wrona, 2006), some supervisors still casually toss new jobs to employees with only vague verbal instructions—resulting in failure, inefficiency, and conflict.

Some causes of workplace conflict bubble up from personal stress and tension; some are the result of interpersonal communication with coworkers or bosses; and some conflicts center around job tasks or goals. The uncertainty that abounds in conflict, combined with goal interference and self-esteem threats, may make conflict at work the most significant of all work stress factors (Giebels & Janssen, 2005). Conflict at work threatens not only one's general well-being; it also threatens one's livelihood.

The concept of *emotional labor* was coined to describe the "work" of displaying certain emotions on the job. Service employees are expected to be happy and cheerful; collection agents may be required to be stern and demanding. When there is a mismatch between felt emotion (service employee do not feel cheerful when clients are obnoxious and grumpy), *emotional dissonance* results (Ashkanasy, Zerbe, & Hartel, 2002a). The greater the emotional labor and emotional dissonance, the more there is overall stress and the higher the necessity for an outlet. Lacking an appropriate outlet, interpersonally insensitive encounters may occur that lead to personal conflicts at work. Likewise, the reverse is true. Unlike the theme that implies bad behavior on vacation is fine because "What happens in Vegas, stays in Vegas," what happens at work does not stay at work. Conflict from work migrates from office to office and from work to home.

> "I was like a flea carrying the plague. Every person I touched was likely to be infected by the conflict I was bringing home from work."
> —Authors Runde and Flanagan, 2007, p. 7

Landau, Landau, and Landau (2001) classified the causes of workplace conflict into two groups: diversity within an organization and interdependence (see Table 14.5). Diversity in thought, style, or information arises from individual differences, professional differences, unclear vision, conflicting responsibilities, unclear responsibilities, and conflicting information. Conflicts arising from interdependence are related to scarce resources, power struggles, organizational structure, procedures, time pressures, job insecurity, and constant change. Not surprisingly, conflict management skills are positively related to success in the workplace (Sandy & Cochran, 2000). It is important to note that a homogeneous workgroup is no protection from conflict. Whether coworkers are similar or diverse, conflict can and will emerge.

> ### Discussion Question 14.5
> Identify a conflict you experienced or witnessed at work. How did the conflict affect productivity?

TABLE 14.5   *Diversity and Interdependence Conflict*

Diversity-Based Conflict	Interdependence-Based Conflict
Individual differences	Scarce resources
Professional differences	Power struggles
Unclear vision	Organizational structure
Conflicting responsibilities	Procedures
Unclear responsibilities	Time pressures
Conflicting information	Job insecurity
	Constant change

Source: Landau, Landau, & Landau (2001).

Vardi and Weitz (2004) labeled one type of workplace conflict stemming from intentional rule or norm violations as **organizational misbehavior.** Table 14.6 illustrates the three primary categories of organizational misbehavior: behaviors that benefit the self, those that benefit the employer, and those that damage the organization. Misbehavior may be intrapersonal, such as substance abuse, or interpersonal, such as incivility, insults, or bullying. For example, an employee who is about to be fired might delete all files on his workstation or intentionally misfiles important documents.

Negative communicative behaviors exacerbate conflict. Sarcasm is just as unproductive at work as it is in personal relationships. Calabrese (2000) argues that sarcasm is an expression of anger that is pervasive in the U.S. workplace. He theorizes that managers who use aggressive verbal communication or passive-aggressive tactics set in motion a series of defense responses among employees, perhaps including an "us" versus "them" mentality, antisocial behaviors, or violence. He argues that hostility (e.g., verbal aggressiveness) is the

TABLE 14.6   *Types of Organizational Misbehavior*

Misbehavior to Benefit the Self
Distorting data about work or one's performance
Theft
Selling company secrets
Harassing coworkers
Overcharging customers
Misusing facilities
Conducting private business on work time
Advancing one's career at the cost of the organization or coworkers

Misbehavior to Benefit the Organization
Falsifying records
Destroying or damaging records

Misbehavior to Damage the Organization
Sabotage equipment
Revenge-seeking behaviors
Destruction of property

Source: Vardi and Weitz (2004).

most socially acceptable way of displaying anger. Thus it prospers in the workplace: Companies tolerate sarcasm and anger to avoid physical violence and yelling. Expressions of anger and sarcasm may be disguised as humor. For example, a biting remark was made and a speaker then claimed to be "just kidding." Calabrese's research found that workers are most likely to become angry at sarcastic remarks about their work and least likely to become angry at sarcastic remarks about their appearance.

For years, one of the authors has opened conflict workshops for business groups by asking participants these questions: What are common conflicts in your workplace? What are the consequences if these conflicts are not managed well? Although not scientific, the answers to these questions are remarkably similar across types of businesses and correlate well to the causes of business conflict identified by other authors. Conflicts arise about issues like change, personality/style differences, workload, and work assignments (see Table 14.7).

A final perspective on workplace conflict can be derived from a study of troublesome people at work. Harden-Fritz (2002) itemized troublesome bosses as *the defensive tyrant* (incompetent, unethical, and fearful that others are after his or her job), *the taskmaster* (work and nonwork excessive demands), *the different boss* (exhibits a style dramatically different from those of the employees), *sand in the gears* (a backstabbing boss who brings personal problems to work), and the *extreme unprofessional* (harasses, badmouths, and overcriticizes).

> "Walk the talk. Leaders who talk a good game but do not lead by example will not be respected. Leaders must live by the traits they espouse. Anytime there is a gap between what a leader says and what that leader does, the credibility of that individual will suffer, and sometimes the cost will be too much for the leader (and the organization) to bear."
> —General Colin Powell summarized by Harari, 2002, p. 213

TABLE 14.7   *Common Workplace Conflicts*

Personality/Style Differences
One person is chatty and another needs quiet to work.

Power
One person pushes to get his or her way on new ideas and sulks when somebody else's idea is used.

Workload
One person thinks (accurately or not) that her or his workload is harder than someone else's workload. "I do all the work around here!"

Work Assignments
One person perceives (accurately or not) that his or her work assignments are a punishment or that others get more favorable assignments.

Time
Someone sees the workload (accurately or not) as more work than any one person can possibly do.

Arrogance
Some people think (accurately or not) that they know more and are better than others.

Communication
Someone cannot or will not verbally talk with coworkers.

Troublesome coworkers include the *independent other* (has a different style), the *soap opera star* (focuses on personal problems rather than work tasks), *the adolescent* (acts unprofessionally by yelling, demanding, or having tantrums), *the bully* (controlling, takes credit for other's work, intimidates), *self-protector* (shows concern only for one's own job and security), *the rebellious playboy/girl* (ignores legitimate authority, wants to be the center of attention, and sometimes sexually harasses others), the *abrasive and incompetent harasser* (peer who is bossy, sexually harasses, and fears for his or her job).

Troublesome subordinates are listed as *the intrusive unprofessional* (butts into other's business), *the backstabbing self-promoter* (advances herself or himself over the bodies of coworkers), *the harmless busybody* (is overly chatty), *the incompetent renegade* (resists orders and distracts others from work), or *the abrasive harasser* (incompetent worker who harasses).

Managing conflict with each of the different personalities requires a broad spectrum of conflict management tools. Sometimes avoidance is the best approach, especially if individual and organizational goals can be met without engaging the source of the conflict. Occasionally, accommodation is appropriate, if only temporarily, to achieve a more important goal. For example, a boss who yells or is demanding may be accommodated because fighting back means possible forfeiture of the goal of being employed. However, a decision to put up with problem behavior must be weighed in light of the long-term consequences to one's health and well-being. One should aim to fill a toolbox with a variety of conflict management skills to use in a variety of workplace situations.

Effects of Conflict in the Workplace

The consequences if conflict is not managed are similar across groups. Table 14.8 shows how effects of conflict at work can be grouped into consequences for employees, supervisors, and the company. Unmanaged conflict brings about stress. When stress goes up, productivity goes down, often resulting in people leaving or being fired.

De Dreu and Weingart (2003) conducted a meta-analysis on how conflict in groups affects team efficiency and satisfaction. (Meta-analyses use methodologies that mine the results of past studies to find important research trends.) They found that both task and relationship conflicts affect team performance negatively. Although some conflict is viewed as productive and a spur for creativity, the weight of psychological studies indicates that the mere presence of conflict takes away energy from task accomplishment. The negative effects can be mitigated when there is high trust, dissent is not viewed as a personal attack, team members feel safe, collaborative communication is more present than contentious communication, and the environment is tolerant of diverse viewpoints.

What do these studies imply for employees in today's multicultural and diverse workplace? As we discussed in Chapter 7, conflict style preferences vary across cultures. Therefore, workers cannot assume actions that would feel appropriate among a group from one's root culture are appropriate in a multicultural workplace. Likewise, attributions about intentionality during a conflict must be questioned.

TABLE 14.8 *Consequences of Unproductive Conflict in the Workplace*

To Employees
- Increased stress
- Increased physical illness
- Increased sick leave (real illness and calling in "sick" because people don't want to go near the conflict)
- People spend more time talking/worrying about the conflict

To Supervisors
- More time and energy is spent on the conflict or avoiding the conflict
- Employees lose respect for supervisors
- Upper management notices the productivity loss
- Supervisor gets a bad evaluation or is fired
- Time is taken to hire new employees
- It gets harder to hire new employees

To the Business
- Profits decrease or services suffer
- It gets harder to hire good people
- The company gets a bad reputation
- Productivity goes down
- The good people leave
- New people have to be trained

Discussion Question 14.6

What cultural variability exists in your workplace? How can you be culturally sensitive to workplace communication that has a cultural dimension?

Preventing and Managing Conflict at Work

The Role of Emotional Intelligence

Conflict experts agree that preventing all work conflicts neither is possible nor desirable. However, preventing misunderstandings and dysfunctional conflict is essential to the health of the organization and to individual workers.

In Chapter 2, the idea of emotional intelligence was introduced. Emotional intelligence and social sensitivity in the workplace are beginning to be linked by researchers to four key areas: exhibiting transformational leadership, team effectiveness, interviews, and as a moderator of job insecurity (Ashkansy, Zerbe, & Hartel, 2002b). Those who lead employees toward a clear vision and mission are better able to motivate workers if they are sensitive to social cues and feedback. Teams have less conflict if members are aware of emotional reactions within the group. Socially sensitive interviewers can detect more about applicants (and vice versa) than those who rely mostly on objective data. For example, experts who conduct job interviews are trained to look for applicants who avert their gaze when answering questions or become very agitated when asked about reliability. Individuals who score higher in emotional intelligence, and who feel their job is insecure, are more likely to "ride" that pressure to success than employees with lower emotional intelligence, who are more likely to falter under the stress. Just as self-awareness enhances personal conflict management, emotional intelligence bolsters workplace conflict management.

Conflict Management from the Supervisor/Manager's View

The very title of this section indicates what Nicotera & Dorsey (2006) identify as the primary bias of research in organizational conflict: It looks at conflict from the manager's perspective and from the top of the organization's hierarchy. We summarize some of the useful insights and research about manager conflict management.

Although the demands of each workgroup are different, mutual gains approaches generally better moderate workplace conflict in the long term than traditional power-over methods. For example, when an employee requests a shift change, the boss has the power just to say "No." Likewise, an aggressive boss who sees coworkers having a conflict probably either tells employees what to do or to "get over it" (see Table 14.9). A detached boss may say "No, it's out of my hands" without giving any explanation and then avoid the person for a week. Although these strategies manage (or successfully avoid) the immediate issue, there frequently are unintended consequences to using power, aggression, or avoidance as the route to moderate conflict. The employee may call in sick, subvert the boss, or take other anti-boss actions.

Unmanaged employee conflict is the largest reducible cost in organizations; it also is the least often realized (Dana, 1999; Slaikeu & Hasson, 1998). However, there are alternatives to aggressive or avoidant management responses. In conflict, the mutual gains boss would ask questions to determine the employee's interests in the situation, then educate the employee about policies, negotiate, or even agree that the change is better for everyone (Table 14.10).

TABLE 14.9 *Top Ten Ranked Behaviors of Aggressive Managers*

1. They are poor listeners—they "tell" but they don't listen.
2. They are adversarial—they attack and humiliate subordinates.
3. They lack people skills—they don't show compassion.
4. They use adversarial task management—they bully.
5. They get angry and are impulsive—they lose their temper or swear.
6. They are controlling and don't delegate—they show no confidence in subordinates' abilities.
7. They are autocratic—they make all the decisions and don't seek input.
8. They are arrogant—they can't accept the possibility of being wrong.
9. They are power seeking and exploitative—they steal credit for other people's work on their way to a bonus or a promotion.
10. They blame employees and are critical—they don't give positive feedback.

Source: Excerpted from Elbing and Elbing (1994).

TABLE 14.10 *Creative Problem Solving in the Workplace*

Reframe the conflict into a problem.
Develop trust.
Ensure that more than one person comes up with ideas for the solution.
Focus on interests rather than positions.
Use a structured process that allows creativity.
Brainstorm.
Evaluate solutions using objective criteria.
Use BATNA to promote new ideas.

Source: Landau, Landau, & Landau (2001).

Discussion Question 14.7

Which of the aggressive management behaviors in Table 14.9 have you observed? How did these behaviors affect productivity?

Managers spend at least 20 percent of their time working on employee "personality" conflicts (Masters & Albright, 2002). The manager's job regarding conflict is inextricably intertwined with goals for productivity. Masters and Albright (2002) itemize the goals for workplace conflict as prevent escalation, solve the real problem, depersonalize the issues, invent solutions, build relationships, and achieve workplace goals.

Runde & Flanagan (2007) argue there are four primary competencies for leaders to be "conflict competent": understanding the dynamics of conflict, knowing one's personal reactions to conflict, working toward more constructive and less destructive responses to conflict, and carrying the vision of productive conflict throughout the unit. In other words, for true leadership, it is not enough to be competent. One must nurture competence in others and change the organization's culture if necessary. Table 14.11 lists seven constructive behaviors for leaders that help manage conflict and eight destructive behaviors that may cause conflict (Runde & Flanagan, 2007). Contrary to popular thought, doing nothing can be constructive (if delaying a response) or destructive (if avoiding or yielding). Expressing emotions can be

TABLE 14.11 *Constructive and Destructive Conflict Behaviors of Leaders*

Constructive	Destructive
Perspective taking	Winning at all costs
Creating solutions	Displaying anger
Expressing emotions	Demeaning others
Reaching out	Retaliating
Reflective thinking	Avoiding
Delay responding	Yielding
Adapting	Hiding emotions
	Self-criticizing

Source: Runde and Flanagan (2007).

constructive (when telling others how their behavior affects you) or destructive (if lashing out in anger). As discussed earlier, sarcastic remarks at the expense of others may be one of the most common workplace behaviors that pierce the fabric of working relationships. The speaker may consider it "good fun," but the recipient can feel disrespected and put down.

Managers and employees can benefit from thinking creatively about all of the available power currencies (see Table 14.12). For example, a manager may not be able to change a person's hours but might be able to change the work assignment or offer perks as a reward for long-standing service. If power is perceived only as control of the budget, other options will be missed. With a broader view of the power available to a manager, better outcomes are possible.

> **Discussion Question 14.8**
>
> Discuss the subtle, and maybe not so subtle, nonverbal communication workers may use to display their displeasure or disapproval of others at work.

In addition to being creative, a manager who is thinking about evaluating someone's work must consider the most important question a supervisor or manager should ask about problematic behavior: Is the behavior affecting productivity? Just because an employee has a messy workstation doesn't mean that what a manager perceives as a "mess" isn't an efficient way of working. Numerous behaviors may annoy supervisors, but the behaviors may not affect productivity. In general, behaviors that do not affect productivity do not require supervisor intervention. In fact, some industries that altered traditional rules found either no change or an increase in productivity after relaxing the rules (e.g., rules that did not allow family pictures, outlawed plants in the office, or required rigid dress codes).

In some types of work, what one wears matters—for example, uniforms for nurses to identify them as health professionals, business attire for upscale salespeople to build credibility, or reflective safety clothing for road construction workers. For people working a phone bank where the public never visits, a uniform may be less important. Managers must

TABLE 14.12   *Power Currencies at Work*

Titles
Knowing who to contact in upper management
Technical resources
Authority to order perks (like a new chair)
Ability to alter employee assignments
Having an expensive desk
Ability to allow/take flextime
Ability to allow casual days
Authority to permit personal furnishings in the office
Influence with other employees
Where one sits at meetings
Taking/giving time off
Sending employees to training
People management skills
Speaking skills
Time in grade

sort through what is bothersome because it affects productivity and what is bothersome for personal preference reasons. Table 14.13 lists some of the decisions managers make that cause conflict.

Conflict Management from the Employee's View

How conflict management skills apply in the work setting depends on an analysis of one's role and place in the organization, as well as the role and place of the other person in the conflict. The situation can be among coworkers who are equals, among coworkers of different experience/status levels, with bosses, or with subordinates. Although it always is better to take the interests of the other party into account (see Toolbox 9.2 and Chapter 9), it is crucial when talking to a boss. For example, if employees are having difficulties that they have not been able to resolve, it is better to analyze the supervisor's "interest" in the situation and plan an approach than to demand that the boss fix the situation or to start complaining about the coworker. The boss's interests probably include having a productive workgroup that doesn't bother him or her with petty difficulties. In that case, it is best to approach the boss by explaining how the difficulty affects productivity, summarizing your attempts to resolve the issue, and then asking the boss to assist you and the other person in working out the problem. Several techniques useful to employees are discussed next.

The *echo technique* involves repeating aggressive words or startling statements back to the boss or coworker who made the comment, then pausing. Elbing and Elbing (1994) recommend the echo be made in a nonjudgmental tone. The echo helps the other person hear what she or he just said, and the pause gives that person an opportunity to rephrase the comment. For example, if the manager says, "You are an idiot!" the echo would be (said neutrally) "Idiot." The manager might change the word or might react negatively. When the latter response occurs, this is not a good technique for that person. Delicately validating the boss is a good strategy to move the conversation into safer waters. For example, "*Idiot* is a strong word and really illustrates how frustrated you must be with what's occurring. I get it."

TABLE 14.13 *Asking for Trouble*

Here are some basic ways supervisor/managers inadvertently can create conflict.

- **Set policies that can't be met.** What do you do when the policy inevitably is broken?
- **Hire the wrong people.** What do you do when an employee is incompetent or has the wrong skill set?
- **Don't give employees enough orientation/training.** What do you do when other employees train the newcomer the wrong way or the newcomer pulls the unit down because he or she can't do the job yet?
- **Allow employees to use work computers and the Internet without oversight.** What do you do when the computer is full of pornography or employees spend their work time shopping?
- **Ask for employee input when you've already made up your mind on what to do.** What do you do when employees are resentful about the decisions you make when they unanimously suggested something else?
- **Avoid the conflicts that emerge in your workgroup.** What do you do when good employees start to leave or productivity goes down?

Delayed feedback (Table 14.14) is a variation of the XYZ technique used in personal relationships (When you do X, in Situation Y, I feel Z). If an uncomfortable situation occurs in the workplace, a conversation about the potential conflict can be engaged at a later time when tempers have cooled. The formula is "When you say *A* in situation *B*, I feel my work is affected in *C* way. Because we both want goal *D*, Can we try *E*?" Any feedback given to coworkers or bosses should be delivered privately and respectfully. For example in a private area outside of others' hearing, an employee might say, "When you call me stupid in front of the other employees, my work is affected because I have to respond to that. Because we both need to get the job done, can we try to work together as a team without calling each other names?"

The *upward problem solving/suggestions technique* recognizes that modern managers are trained to kick problems back to employees. In addition, some bosses are prone to attribute suggestions from employees as a threat to their authority. These two boss perspectives make asking the boss to solve your problem or offering just one solution problematic. Instead of presenting one suggestion ("Here is what we should do to fix that problem . . ."), give the boss multiple ideas. For example, if there is a conflict with another employee about how to complete a project that the two of you can't resolve, approach the boss and say, "I don't know if you've noticed, but Lana and I can't agree on how to proceed with the Buchanan project. We're at the point where we have to have a decision. Maybe we could both give you our ideas on what to do, or maybe you have something in mind that would settle the problem, or maybe we could get somebody else to come in and help us decide how to proceed. What do you think?" Giving the boss multiple ideas informs her or him about the issue without blaming anyone, presents a menu of possible outcomes, and places the decision making with the boss.

The *style adaptation technique* recognizes that bosses and employees frequently have different work styles and those differences can cause conflict (see Chapter 7). For example, a boss who does one thing at a time may see an employee who multitasks as disorganized. Cleaning up one's work area at the end of every day would do much to allay the boss's misperception. If a coworker is thoughtful and rarely responds quickly to a new idea, the style adaptation of waiting for that person to respond rather than continuing to talk will foster better communication.

TABLE 14.14   *The Delayed Feedback Technique*

When you say *A*
In situation *B*,
My work is affected in *C* way.
Because we both want goal *D*,
Can we do *E*?

"When you are late for work in the morning, I have to open the front window and answer the general calls, which means I can't start pulling the files for today's work and the whole group gets behind. Because we all need the office to work well, can you get here on time so you can open the office?"

Consciously *questioning assumptions* also helps. Attribution errors based on cultural assumptions are a common site of conflict in the work world. For example, Shuter and Turner (1997) documented that European American and African American women see each other's behaviors in the workplace differently. African American women prefer a more direct communication style to reduce conflict. That directness was misinterpreted as pushy by European American women, who were more avoidant. Realizing that someone uses direct communication can offset a "feeling" that the other is aggressive.

Studying one's boss to determine his or her conflict management and communication style not only helps the employee interpret the boss's messages, it also helps strategize how to respond to conflict with the boss. If the boss is direct, indirect messages from employees probably will not be noticed. For instance, if a boss routinely gives directives like, "I need this report by noon," hinting there is a problem with that demand probably will not be effective (Hint: "Gee, Mrs. Washington just gave me some work to do, too"). If the boss is indirect, direct messages probably will be less well received. If the boss avoids all emotional-level discussions and runs away from conflict, asking the boss to intervene in a coworker conflict may be futile. Instead, ask the boss to find a mediator from the outside.

In general, employees need to have excellent people skills in addition to the technical skills of their chosen vocation. The New Commission on the Skills of the American Workforce commented:

> Strong skills in English, mathematics, technology, and science, as well as literature, history, and the arts will be essential . . .; beyond this, candidates will have to be comfortable with ideas and abstractions, good at both analysis and synthesis, creative and innovative, self-disciplined and well organized, able to learn very quickly and work well as a member of a team and have the flexibility to adapt quickly to frequent changes in the labor market as the shifts in the economy become ever faster and more dramatic.
>
> Tough Choices, 2007, p. 10

Groupthink

Groupthink, first postulated by Irving Janis (1972), occurs when a highly cohesive set of individuals make a series of thinking errors that lead to bad decisions, typically around taking excessive risks. As the symptoms in Table 14.15 show, part of groupthink involves protecting members from outside information, even demonizing those who disagree with the group's supposedly "superior" decisions. Outsiders are viewed suspiciously through stereotypical lenses. At the national level, groupthink is believed to have contributed to the poor decisions that led to the U.S. entry into war with Korea and Vietnam, the Bay of Pigs invasion, the Watergate burglary, and the space shuttle *Challenger* explosion (Engleberg & Wynn, 2007; Janis, 1972). Innumerable bad business decisions are made because decision makers were convinced, against all evidence to the contrary, that a product or venture could not fail. Some speculate that the insular practices of the George W. Bush White House exhibited groupthink in their advocacy for the war in Iraq and their rosy predictions of what would happen in Iraq after the invasion (Sourcewatch, 2007).

Groupthink is not inevitable, and informed leaders can prevent it. Leaders counteract groupthink by allowing dissenting opinions—coordinating differences through productive

TABLE 14.15   *Groupthink Symptoms*

- The group feels invulnerable and that it can't make a wrong decision.
- The group rationalizes away warnings.
- The group ignores ethical and moral considerations; it considers whatever it does inherently is moral.
- The group stereotypes opponents as weak or stupid.
- Group members hide their doubts because they don't want to break from the consensus.
- Any individual group member who dissents is pressured to conform.
- Each group member thinks he or she is the only one with doubts, creating an illusion of unanimity.
- Members shield each other from dissenting views and opinions.

Source: Janis (1972).

conflict management and encouraging participation. Specifically, leaders can (1) Assign the role of critical evaluator if individuals are reluctant to express their reservations, (2) refrain from expressing preferences at the outset of meetings, so group members don't feel pressured to agree with what the leader/boss wants, and (3) bring in outsiders to examine decisions.

Group Conflict

In addition to individual conflict among employees or between employees and bosses, work groups also experience conflict. Furthermore, it seems to make no difference whether a group works face to face or if they meet only online. Technology to assist groups does not positively change group conflict: Computer-mediated groups have no less conflict than face-to-face groups; their conflicts just take longer to emerge (Hobman, Bordia, Irmer, & Chang, 2002).

At least two themes of research examine conflict in groups: instrumental and developmental (Poole & Garner, 2006). The *instrumental* theme examines group conflict as an extension of interpersonal conflict that can be productive or destructive. This does not mean that groups cause conflict; rather the group is a location where interpersonal conflicts occur. As Beebe and Masterson (2006) state, "because people are unique, their different attitudes, beliefs, and values will inevitably surface and cause conflict" (pp. 169–170).

Group process scholars also identified *group development* itself as a cause of conflict. They observe that almost all new groups go through a conflict stage as they work out roles, responsibilities, power, and leadership duties. The conflict phase in groups sometimes is termed *storming* or *counterdependency* (Engleberg & Wynn, 2007; Poole & Garner, 2006). Like other places where conflict occurs, group conflict has the potential for negative or positive outcomes. In groups, the positive outcome might be greater bonding, cooperation, or clarity about roles and power structures within the group.

Even though groups are another location for conflicts, the causes of conflict in groups are similar to the interpersonal conflict realm—perceived or actual goal interference. Group communication scholars list conflict topics such as who has power in the group, who is the leader of the group, what roles are appropriate among group members, how the group should communicate among its members, what tasks the group should accomplish, how decisions are made, and who has responsibility for which tasks (Beebe & Masterson, 2006; Harris & Sherblom, 2005). Group conflicts emerge around three basic clusters: perceived scarce resources that members compete to acquire, diverse backgrounds that carry divergent expectations about communication, and varying views about task accomplishments.

Earlier in the chapter we discussed the task, maintenance, and dysfunctional roles that individuals play in groups. Managers who are focused on just the maintenance level may exacerbate conflict. A leader who is totally maintenance focused is fun and caring, but the work of the group may not get done. In contrast, a leader who overly focused on the task tries to be efficient, but the group may fall apart because relational dynamics are not seen as relevant to completing the job. Maintenance-based conflicts occur when nobody in the group diffuses tensions, builds cohesion, or pays attention to this half of group life. When conflict is not managed well in groups, trust decreases, more time is spend in disagreement that does not advance the task, efficiency decreases, emotional exhaustion increases, and individuals begin to drop out physically or mentally (Giebels & Janssen, 2005).

Getting managers to pay attention to the maintenance part of group life, and thereby decrease conflict and increase efficiency, is one aspect of the corporate world's interest in style and emotional intelligence training. When entire organizations examine individual styles and/or emotional intelligence abilities, a new vocabulary is developed to talk about style differences and group maintenance issues. All types of organizations, but particularly more traditionally "task" fields such as engineering, information technology and computer programming, are discovering that productivity is increased when the workplace culture engages the entire human being—not just the task dimension.

Conflict Management Systems

The link between conflict and turnover has motivated corporations to examine their processes. More specifically, corporations and government agencies want to reduce the costs of conflict. For example, litigation from conflicts that are mismanaged and turnover are large cost centers in some organization. The cost of turnover—including advertising, interviewing, hiring, and training—is pegged at 150 percent of the position's previous salary. For example, Texas estimates it could save $4.7 million a year if it reduced turnover by just 1 percent (Slaikeu & Hasson, 1998).

The idea of approaching conflict systematically in organizations is beginning to gain momentum. Companies accept that it is unrealistic for all supervisors to be highly skilled at managing conflict and that it is too expensive to rely solely on formal grievance procedures to settle conflicts. Instead, conflict management tools are placed throughout the organization to create a **conflict management system.** As of 1997, 17 percent of Fortune 1000 companies had conflict management systems in place (Lipsky & Seeber, 2006). A conflict management system separates regular conflict management from formal grievance or legal options. They include some combination of five elements, summarized in Table 14.16.

A conflict management system is comprehensive. It can process personnel conflicts, stretch across different departments, negotiate work condition issues, or address

TABLE 14.16 *Five Elements of an Organization's Conflict Management System*

1. *Wide scope* of application to all types of conflicts and disputes
2. *Cultural acceptance* of conflict as inevitable and often productive when well managed
3. *Multiple access points* to conflict management assistance
4. *Multiple options* for assistance
5. *Support structures* for all employees

Source: Lipsky and Seeber (2006).

any type of dispute related to work productivity. Management at all levels must support the use of the conflict management system. The system includes the formal grievance processes but creates new access points for employees to seek assistance in resolving difficulties, including problems that would never qualify in the formal grievance procedure. For example, a chatty coworker who is highly annoying to one employee probably would not qualify in the formal grievance process, but the two employees still may need help so productivity is not affected. The final component in a conflict management system is support systems. Employee assistance programs (EAPs) are offered so employees can seek private counseling for personal problems of any type—from stress, quitting smoking, family issues, or coping with divorce to alcohol/drug counseling. Training opportunities are offered in negotiation, life skills, communication, and other conflict management tools.

> **Discussion Question 14.9**
> Describe the responses to conflict present in organizations you have worked in. Were these systems adequate? If you were running a company, what formal or informal systems would you put into place?

Personal conflict coaching, sometimes called communication coaching, is an option in the list of support structures within conflict management systems. Previously, personal coaching to improve communication and conflict skills only was available to top management. Within the more modern systems view of conflict, corporations realize coaching an employee is more cost effective than letting conflict stew or firing and retraining a new hire. The coach typically has a background in mediation and other conflict management approaches (Blessing, 2006). In general, the coach listens to determine the client's goals and discovers what is preventing that individual from moving forward. Then coaching expands the perception of how communication and conflict occur and improves skills in needed areas.

Slaikeu & Hasson (1998) contend conflict management systems for organizations will be the greatest cost-control area in the future. They argue, "there is something wrong with the way most businesses, governments, schools, and religious institutions manage conflict. The failure lies in a *systemic* reliance on higher authority, power plays, and avoidance, and weak or only partial use of collaborative options" (p. 3). If systematic conflict management spreads, the quality of work life for the average employee will be vastly improved.

Summary

Communication and conflict at work occur in a context that is different from interpersonal communication in at least three ways: (1) Work goals alter the valuing of personal relationships, (2) teaming in groups is required to accomplish many work tasks, and (3) organizations contain hierarchies, multiple channels of communication, and unique rules and roles.

The hierarchy of authority in an organization is diagrammed in an organizational chart. A flat organizational hierarchy implies fewer layers of management and easier communication between workers and upper management. Organizations develop unique cultures that are conveyed to new employees during a formal or informal socialization process. Organizational culture is a dynamic feature that changes over time.

Groups are the basic building block of an organization. A group can be defined as three to twelve people. Group dynamics include norms, roles, and leadership. A norm is an unwritten rule that governs group behavior. Roles are task, maintenance, or dysfunctional behaviors adopted by group members. Task roles move the group toward accomplishing a work goal. Maintenance roles keep the individuals bonded together sufficiently to accomplish its goals. Dysfunctional roles deter the group from task accomplishment.

Leadership roles can be designated or emerge as needed from the group. Many conflicts are about who has leadership in the group.

Workplace conflict arises from an array of topics, many of which are similar to the interpersonal context. Unique sources of workplace conflict include topics such as leadership struggles, emotional labor stress, and differences on how to accomplish tasks. The effects of workplace conflict include a loss of trust in coworkers or management, stress, and productivity decreases. Effects can be categorized as consequences for employees, for managers, and for the company.

Preventing and managing conflict requires a combination of self-awareness, cultural/style sensitivity, and skill development from bosses and employees. Aggressive bosses use a variety of tactics that are conflict producing. Supervisors are estimated to spend at least 20 percent of their time managing employee conflicts. In contrast, numerous creative methods exist to help the conflict competent manager.

Workers need to analyze who a conflict is with to determine which interpersonal conflict skills are appropriate. The echo technique, the delayed feedback technique, upward problem solving, and style adaptation are positive responses to conflict producing situations.

Research into group conflict views it as instrumental (stemming from goal differences) or developmental (a unique phase that groups go through as they begin to grow and bond together). Groupthink is a danger to any highly cohesive workgroup. Strong leadership is necessary to prevent groupthink, including welcoming critical evaluation, refraining from expressing the leader's opinion first, and bringing in outsiders.

Many organizations are adopting a conflict system approach. Conflict management systems combine formal grievance procedures with employee coaching, training, mediation, and other skill development methods.

Chapter Resources _____

Exercises

1. As a group, view a pre-1980 film set in the workplace, such as *Adam's Rib* (Spencer Tracy and Katharine Hepburn, 1949). What culture is present in the workplace of that time and place? What might you infer about the workplace from its demographics? What are the sources of conflict in that workplace? How is the workplace different from one you might see today? What behaviors do you spot in the film that are illegal workplace behaviors today?

2. View a workplace film or television program, such as *The Devil Wears Prada, The Office,* or *Ugly Betty.* What norms and roles are present in the workplace? What sources of conflict are depicted in that workplace?

3. Make a list of power currencies that employees or managers have at your workplace.

4. Which of the troublesome others from Harden-Fritz's (2002) research listed in this chapter have you met in your work career (or in a group project)? How did these troublesome others affect your productivity?

5. Find an organizational chart for a local company. What does the organizational chart imply about how communication is channeled in the company?

Essay Topics

1. Describe and analyze a workplace conflict you personally experienced. Explore the types of norms, roles, and leadership that were present.

2. Write an essay about a personal experience you've had that illustrates one of the types of office incivility identified in a survey of business practices (see, "Manners," 2006). Do you agree that these behaviors are not civil: use of profanity, using a snotty tone, public reprimands by the boss, talking too loudly, cell phones ringing during meetings, speaker-phones used during meetings, talking about personal matters in meetings, micromanag-ing, and using PDAs during a meeting?

Research Topics

1. Review the published literature on work metaphors, beginning with Smith, R. C., & Eisen-berg, E. M. (1987). Conflict at Disneyland: A root-metaphor analysis. *Communication Monographs*, *54*(4): 367–380. After analyzing several studies, draw conclusions about the impact of metaphor and language on corporate culture.

2. Examine the published research literature on groupthink for the past five years. Do these studies mention electronic communication and access to information through the Inter-net? If so, how? Draw conclusions about whether the Internet, chat rooms, or other elec-tronic communication options can help alleviate groupthink.

Mastery Case

Examine Mastery Case 14, "The Faithful Fight." Which concepts from the chapter can be applied to the case?

The Faithful Fight

As prevalent as conflict is, one would imagine that it wouldn't come as a surprise when conflict occurs among people of faith. Yet, surprise—even shock—commonly is the reaction of at least one of the parties. Melanie was brought in to facilitate an organization-wide conflict at the regional level/statewide church. The participants of this denomination were as dismayed with the presence of interpersonal tension as they were with the substance of the conflict—maybe even more so. Some in the group felt that if the church leadership had been "living" their faith then they wouldn't be in conflict with other members of the organization. Others felt shame at the level of their own anger and frustration.

In addition to resolving the substantive issues, those at the meeting included leaders who wanted to rebuild the group and develop better attitudes and skills about conflict. The first step in moving the group forward was to convince them that conflict was normal and had the potential for clarification, opportunity, creativity, and growth. At the same time, they needed to see that conflict became problematic because it was avoided and handled badly when it first emerged.

Here are the principles the group adopted:

1. We recognize that we are richly diverse with a common, deep commitment to our faith.
2. Our differences make us stronger as we will see many facets of any issue we undertake.
3. We expect to disagree at times and will look at these moments as opportunities to learn, grow, and make quality decisions.
4. When we get to a point where we are unable to move beyond our disagreements, we will seek help.
5. We will strive to make collaborative decisions and value our differences as we work together.

15

Conflict and Society

Affirmative communication
  processes
Capitulation
Deficit language
Deviance

Gandhian tactics
Guerrilla tactics
Flag issue/Flag person
Negative peace
Nonviolent resistance

Polarization
Positive peace
Purgation
Risky shift phenomenon

Objectives

After reading the chapter, you should be able to:

1. Explain how the political also is personal
2. Critique the effects of polarization on decision making
3. Discuss the strategic tactics of agitation and control
4. Examine options for transforming social conflict into collaborative problem solving

> "The current generation has a relational and national task, an obligation, a require-
> ment that, whether it prefers it or not, it must undertake. The task of the current gen-
> eration can be summarized very succinctly: to create a well-functioning intercultural
> nation."
>
> —Myron W. Lustig (2005, p. 337), president,
> Western States Communication Association

Politics as Personal

"What is personal is political." This rallying cry of the early feminist movement offers
insight to the formation of many types of social conflicts. For feminists in the 1970s, politics
about equal pay, sexual harassment, reproductive choice, and access to opportunities were

not esoteric exercises. Politics deeply affected their everyday lives. Although this book has focused primarily on interpersonal conflict, the current chapter shows how the ability to analyze components of personal conflict can inform our understanding of conflict in the greater society.

In Chapter 1 we defined interpersonal conflict as a struggle occurring between a small number of interdependent people who perceive interference with goal achievement. Our definition centers on the idea that conflict stems from a perception that someone or something is thwarting important goals. Personal goals for self-determination or the desire to have a voice in decisions also may include goals for the society at large and a vision of what the future should hold. Although interpersonal conflict is limited to a small number of people, the definition of conflict expands to the social realm when we recognize that individuals make up social groups and that individual values encompass the direction one wishes that society would take. You may believe that global warming is the biggest threat facing the world and personally engage in recycling, rely on public transportation, and strive to have a minimal carbon impact on Earth. However, if you look around and see that your individual efforts will have little impact, personal goals may take on societal implications. No one may be stopping you from recycling, but the denial by others that there is cause for concern directly affects your personal goal of creating a more sustainable ecosystem. Personal goals intersect with the political realm at the point where we become interdependent with larger groups to meet our goals.

Elements of interpersonal conflict are present in societal conflicts. Barge (2001) argues that although the scope of social conflict is vast, the central thread that runs through social conflict is that they inherently are about morals. "Moral conflicts are challenging to work through," he adds, "because people's patterns of felt compulsions, permissions, and prohibitions to act in certain ways inform their identity, and when one passionately feels a particular way on a issue then changing a position on it simultaneously evokes a radical change in one's identity" (pp. 89–90). The impetus to act socially or politically is motivated by personal identities and moral views. Truly the personal is political.

This chapter (1) uncovers the personal value and moral elements involved in social conflict, (2) examines issues such as value differences, identity or face threats, and polarization as keys to understanding societal conflict, (3) explores how groups can identify and use their power resources to influence societal conflict, and (4) identifies ways to bring conflicting sides together to manage conflict productively.

Values, Beliefs, and Attitudes

Society has never lacked contentious issues. Recent social issues include freedom of speech, gay marriage, abortion rights, the war on terrorism, doctor-assisted suicides, limits on civil liberties, religious freedom, death penalty, school choice, gun control, and genetic engineering. The list is endless. A common element of social conflict is that it affects the individual as well as society as a whole. Individuals are willing to take on social issues that speak to their personal values and beliefs. In general, values are the basis for beliefs, whereas beliefs are used to explain attitudes and behaviors.

Discussion Question 15.1

Identify a social cause or conflict that you care about. Aside from how the conflict plays out in the larger society, how does the issue affect you personally?

Rokeach (1973) defined values as "an enduring belief that a specific mode of conduct or end-state of existence is personally or socially preferable to an opposite of converse mode of conduct or end-state of existence" (p. 5). Values can be understood as core constructs that we accept as right or wrong, true or false. Honesty, hard-work, self-determination, and sanctity of life may all be core values. Beliefs are the positions of right, wrong, true, or false that we take based on our values.

One may value hard work and self-sufficiency. Those values may lead to a belief that using food stamps or public assistance is undesirable or even morally wrong. Attitudes stemming from values and beliefs are the links that provide a justification for behaviors. If one is disappointed by a family member who goes on assisted housing, that disappointment may stem from a challenge to a core value. If that same person then works to overhaul the current welfare system, that core value drives that individual's political activism.

The interesting element of values important to a discussion of social conflict is that core values may be in conflict with one another, thus resulting in dissonance. A prominent media case in 2007 involved national radio talk show host Don Imus making derogatory comments about the Rutgers University women's basketball team. His long-running show consistently was edgy, regularly disdainful of others, and generally politically incorrect. The remark he made about the women's basketball team caused a national furor. Deemed both sexist and racist, it resulted in his termination, even though Imus had uttered equally racist and sexist remarks about others in the past. The Rutgers incident triggered core values that precipitated widespread outrage. Because the remarks were aimed at a group of amateur college athletes, his diatribe was particularly distasteful.

Core values that entered into the discussions about the Imus incident included both freedom of speech and the need for civility, two values held by many people. What made this situation different from his previous invectives were the values associated with the target of his comments: young women, amateur college athletes, and champions. Values regarding groups needing protection rose to the surface. Unlike previous targets who were public figures like Oprah Winfrey, Imus directed his hurtful comments toward innocents who had become champions. But ask a group whether Don Imus should have been fired and you will see how the prioritization of these competing values becomes the center of the conflict: Some value free speech more, some value civil discourse more, some value equality more, some value protecting innocents more, some value honoring champions more, and some value none of the items just listed. In a free society, should we limit speech that might be offensive? In a civil society, should we allow language that is hurtful and offensive? Reconciling competing values becomes even more difficult on a public stage as personal and political agendas enter the mix. As an aside Don Imus was hired by another major media group eight months later.

Recognizing underlying values is one part of dissecting social conflict. If values are not addressed in attempt to manage differences, the conflict will endure, making chances for reconciliation elusive.

> ### Discussion Question 15.2
> Identify a political or societal conflict. What values underlie each side of this conflict? How are those values demonstrated in beliefs and attitudes? How would each side perceive the other as thwarting their goals?

Identity (Face) Threats

In Chapter 2, we explored the way that individuals or groups conceptualize and share reality through the schema that they have constructed. Just as a "good teacher" may have a different definition depending on the construct of a teacher's role (to be more challenging or more entertaining), all value-laden terms invoke many potential schematic constructs. Constructs, such as what it means to be American or patriotic, arise from core values. When we use constructs to define ourselves, we can be threatened by competing constructs.

Patriotic American	*Patriotic American*
Doesn't criticize the president	Critiques leadership
Doesn't criticize a current war	Speaks against bad foreign policies
Supports troops verbally	Demonstrates in rallies against war
Displays the American flag	Displays the American flag

A schematic construct that seems perfectly natural and obvious to one group may be wholly unacceptable to another group; they may cherish an opposite construct that seems natural and obvious to them. For example, there are numerous ways that a "Patriotic American" may be constructed, including the following two:

In 2003, days before the U.S. start of the Iraq war, Natalie Maines, lead singer of the Dixie Chicks, publicly criticized President George W. Bush in a London concert. Maines is quoted as saying, "Just so you know, we're ashamed the president of the United States is from Texas" (Tyrangiel, 2006). The backlash in the United States reportedly cost the group half of their U.S. concert sales and resulted in numerous radio boycotts, many of which are still in effect (chronicled in the 2006 documentary, *Dixie Chicks: Shut Up and Sing*). Although some painted the Dixie Chicks as patriots, others saw them as offering support to enemies of the United States and, thereby, unpatriotic. The most extreme of the latter group delivered death threats to the group (one read, "Shut up and sing or your life will be over!").

What is an American? What is a patriot? Is there one construct that encompasses the gamut of definitions? Can one person be *more* American than another based on adherence to certain values or beliefs? Is a soldier *more* of an American or *more* patriotic than a war protester? From this example, we can see how societal conflicts have roots in how we define ourselves and what we expect from others.

CASE 15.1 • *Good Religion/Bad Religion*

I grew up as a member of the Church of Jesus Christ of Latter Day Saints (Mormon). My best friend in grade school, Bess, was Catholic. When we got into junior high we became friends with Marti, whose family attended a fundamentalist Christian church. One day Bess and I went to Marti's house and her mom asked us if we were Christians. Bess and I both said, "Yes." Then her mom asked us which religion we were, and we told her. The next day at school Marti said that her mom didn't want me to hang out with her anymore because Mormons weren't Christians. She said that Catholics aren't true Christians either, but that her mom said it was better than being Mormon. Until then I didn't realize that my religion made me bad to some people.

Discussion Question 15.3

How does the definition of Christian become the center of the conflict in Case 15.1? How might this type of conflict become a flashpoint for a societal conflict? Substitute other loaded labels such as "patriot," "illegal alien," "environmentalist," "terrorist," and consider how these terms can be a source of conflict with others.

Values and identity are two primary factors in understanding societal conflict. Another is how issues are framed to make us choose one side or another—to polarize factions into opposing camps. The next section addresses the issue of polarization.

Polarization

To have staying power, societal conflict must have adherents to the cause. Proponents must be able to identify those who are for the cause and those who are not, and then show how those who are not for the cause are wrong. The fastest means to this end is to have people choose sides.

The nature of debate and political conversation in the United States has changed significantly with the advent of television and mass media. That is not to say that social and political debate prior to television was more civil. Mudslinging, after all, is not a twenty-first-century term. However, the unique nature of television media has made the sound bite a precious commodity, and the news is influenced heavily by ratings. The need to summarize an issue quickly and present it for public consumption has resulted in complex societal discussions being watered down to two deceptively simple, opposing sides.

Tannen (1998) coined the phrase "The Argument Culture" to describe the inherently polarizing yet popular means by which we approach public dialogue about important cultural issues. She writes.

> The argument culture urges us to approach the world—and the people in it—in an adversarial frame of mind. It rests on the assumption that opposition is the best way to get anything done: The best way to discuss an idea is to set up a debate; the best way to cover news is to find spokespeople who express the most extreme, polarized views and present them as "both sides"; the best way to settle disputes is litigation that pits one party against the other; the best way to begin an essay is to attack someone; and the best way to show you're really thinking is to criticize. (pp. 3–4)

To polarize an argument is not to flesh out the nuances and underlying values—or even to provide evidence and logical support. **Polarization** is about dividing people into opposing camps and winning by establishing the other as wrong. Shades of gray are unacceptable in a polarized framework. To be a fence rider or someone who considers more than one option is seen as wishy washy, a death knell moniker for any politician. To change one's mind based on new information is characterized as flip-flopping. Tannen (1998) contrasted polarization to dialogue. She questions "using opposition to accomplish *every* goal, even those that do not require fighting but might also (or better) be accomplished by other means, such as exploring, expanding, discussing, investigating" (p. 8) and exchanging ideas. Tannen does not suggest that polarization is inherently wrong or unethical. However, she does describe it as the opposite of dialogue and as unproductive when it substitutes for reasoned decisions.

> ### *Discussion Question 15.4*
> Compare these quotes. Discuss the benefits and dangers of polarizing issues.
>
> - "If you're not with me, you're my enemy." Anakin Skywalker
> - "Only a Sith deals in absolutes." Obi-Wan Kenobi in *Star Wars Episode III: Revenge of the Sith*
> - "If you hamper the war effort of one side you automatically help that of the other. Nor is there any real way of remaining outside such a war as the present one. In practice, 'he that is not with me is against me.'" George Orwell, 1942 essay on pacifism and the war
> - "Either you are with us or you are with the terrorists." President George W. Bush's address to joint session of Congress, September 20, 2001
> - "Extremism in the defense of liberty is no vice." Barry Goldwater

Dane Scott, director of the Center of Ethics at the University of Montana, contends that the ethics of polarization are tricky. He states, "It is unhealthy and possibly dangerous for a democracy when its citizens fragment into enclaves and refuse to listen to others with opposing views. Granted, there are times when discussion should stop and the hand of friendship withdrawn, but these times should be rare, not the norm" (Radio commentary on KUFM, Montana Public Radio, 2006). The danger is that groups, when isolated, tend to become more extreme in their views. The **risky shift phenomenon,** a precursor to groupthink, occurs when individuals with relatively moderate views shift to more extreme views that they believe are supported by the group, thus making them act in more extreme ways than they would individually.

The classic study of Meyers and Bishop (1970) illustrates the power of the risky shift phenomenon. They identified levels of racial prejudice in student subjects and then placed them into groups to discuss issues of race. Groups of somewhat prejudiced students became even more prejudiced through their discussions, both in attitude and in their language choices. In contrast, unprejudiced students became even more unprejudiced the more they talked to each other. Clearly, there are costs and benefits to polarization (see Table 15.1). Benefits to the group include a clear and decisive framing of issues and allowing easy identification of supporters. However the costs to individuals and society include the oversimplification of complex issues and locking parties into opposing sides so they are unable to engage in dialogue without appearing weak.

TABLE 15.1 *Benefits and Costs of Polarizing Issues*

Benefits	Costs
Frames the debate simply	Simplifies debate to extremes
Reduces uncertainty	Waters down complex issues
Identifies supporters	Creates enemies
Appears decisive	Creates rushed and risky judgments
Proves effective for rallying groups	Cuts off reasoned discussions
Creates a group goal/mission	Locks people into positions

Scott (2006) cautions that existing factors may reinforce more polarization in society. He cites cable television, Internet blogs, and podcasting as technologies that reinforce group polarization by allowing individuals to filter any ideas that oppose their own. Sunstein (2002) notes that more and more, we are exposed to ideas that support what we already believe about the world. Someone who is a staunch conservative or a staunch liberal could find a wide array of radio and television talk show hosts and news sources that provide commentary, data, and arguments for their political predilections. With all of the choices available, one never has to go to sources outside of one's political comfort zone to get information. This selective exposure further cements already held beliefs and invites the "risky shift" mentality, thus polarizing society even more. One means of breaking the polarizing cycle is to seek diverse viewpoints and information—purposefully exposing ourselves to information that counters what we already believe and think we know.

Awareness of how societal conflict quickly turns into polarized positions provides conflict managers with indispensable insights. Many people have become conditioned to seeing only two sides to issues. Conflict specialists know that most conflicts are much more complex, much more nuanced, and require adequate time to analyze thoroughly.

> **Discussion Question 15.5**
>
> When a Russian tour guide was asked, "What do Russians think about people in the United States?" she replied, "Twenty Russians, fifty opinions." Does that comment reflect a polarized society or a nonpolarized society? Do you notice when people speak on behalf of a group (NASCAR fans, Catholics, Republicans, women, farmers, etc.) as if everyone in that group has the same opinion?

Means of Managing Social Conflict

Rummel (1976) outlined seven types of conflicts of interest and the method of resolution that would likely occur in society. Table 15.2 demonstrates how a conflict involving two groups might play out. For example, a university student organization (Group A) wants a change in policy to make Veteran's Day a recognized holiday with no classes scheduled (Goal X). The university administration (Group B) has the power to create the yearly schedules. Assuming the administration (Group B) is open to negotiating the holiday release (Goal X), the policy might be decided through a reasoned discussion (see number 4 in Table 15.2). However, administrators could say they have previously reviewed that option and will not revisit it (Goal Y), thus denying the petition of the students (see number 6 in Table 15.2). Students could then employ the manipulation approach by staging a walkout in hopes of creating change. Conversely, the administration could send the issue to the Faculty and Student Senates for review (see option number 3 in Table 15.2) with an understanding that if they allow one more holiday they will need to make it up somewhere else to meet minimum attendance standards. The nature of the competing goals and the respective power of each group affects the likelihood of one resolution method over another.

Social conflict movements stem from unresolved goal attainment. Those who did not have their goals met through resolution approaches 1 to 6 in Table 15.2 find they have only two choices left to them: give up or fight for their goal outside of the existing system (approach number 7). Rummel (1976) notes,

> Society as the social interaction between diverse individuals is a balance of order, power, and justice. Virtually all public debates, large-scale social conflict, and philosophical analyses concern how much order (security) should be sacrificed for how much justice (freedom, equality, welfare), and how much power (authoritative, coercive, force) is required to maintain the proper division between order and justice. This historical division of social interests into order, power and justice corresponds to our need for security, protectiveness, and self-assertion. And many major historical conflicts have been over the proper interpretation and balance among these concerns. (p. 28.1)

TABLE 15.2 *Conflict of Interest and Likely Resolutions*

Conflict of Interest Type	Likely Resolution Approach
1. X corresponds to a positive Y (X = $5000.00 and Y = used car)	Exchange X for Y
2. X linked to a negative Y (X = money and Y = life)	Threats and coercion
3. X is decided by norms and rules (X = president, decided by election)	Institutional/Legitimacy
4. X is decided by reason (X = best vacation, decided through reasoned discourse)	Intellectual persuasion
5. X is decided by love (X = time with kids, decided by what is best for family)	Altruism
6. X is decided by manipulation (X = curfew set at 9 P.M., decided by the person who pays for the house)	Control of resources/Outcomes
7. X is not decided on by 1 to 6	Outcome A: Abdication (give up X) Outcome B: Physical force (fight for X)

Source: Adapted from Rummel (1976).

When left to make societal change without the ability (or desire) to move through the existing system, individuals may find they have little power to affect meaningful change, so they form groups. Groups may have the advantage of making bigger waves than any one person could alone.

Identifying individuals to support a cause has become easier with the advent of the Internet. Prior to the Internet, communication to the populace relied on identifying sympathizers and getting information to them about the movement. Now individuals who have an interest in even obscure issues can find like-minded thinkers with a few keystrokes. If you wish to raise money to combat the selling of young girls into Nepalese brothels or to protest strip mining in Costa Rica, you can contact existing groups with similar goals in a matter of minutes. Warkentin (2001) argues that the Internet allows for global identity information for social movements, enticing groups from diverse areas to converge on common goals. The Internet helps develop a collective identity. Postmes and Brunsting (2002) suggest that the anonymity offered by the Internet allows for stronger group identification as people focus more on their commonalities than their differences.

The Internet does offer advantages for gaining group members, but it also contains less obvious disadvantages. Although easier to find like-minded activists, the plethora of groups to join may fragment the activists into smaller and even more polarized groups (Danitz & Strobel, 1999). Worry about outsiders infiltrating the group, being converted by control agents, or disenfranchising those without the means to get online are additional concerns (Kahn & Kellner, 2004). Maintaining group morale, energy, and cohesiveness—as well as establishing necessary boundaries—becomes challenging (Wall, 2007).

Regardless of how a social group organizes itself and communicates with its members, leaders are responsible for implementing strategies to move the group toward their common goal. The next section examines strategies of both the groups who want to make a change and those who wish to maintain the status quo.

Strategies of Group Movements

Strategies of Agitation and Control

Bowers, Ochs, and Jensen (1993) examine two elements of social conflict, those in control of the status quo and those who are agitating to change the system. By studying a variety of social conflicts, including the civil rights movement, abortion protests, and antiwar agitators, Bowers et al. highlighted strategies used to bring about change or to stop change from occurring. These strategies illustrate how individuals in conflict mobilize others through routinely employed tactics. Recognizing these strategies fosters an understanding of how groups become more polarized and less likely to work together.

Bowers et al. (1993) define *agitators* as those people outside the normal decision-making establishment who advocate for significant social change yet encounter a degree of resistance from the establishment that requires them to act with more than normal persuasion. *Control*, in contrast, involves those who have the power to decide policy and or enforce sanctions. "Agitation occurs when a group has a grievance or grievances and there is no remedy to those grievances other than challenging the social order" (Bowers et al., 1993, p. 6)

TABLE 15.3 *Types of Agitator Deviance*

Lateral Deviance	Vertical Deviance
Accepts the values of those in control	Does not accept the values of those in control
Willing to work within the existing system to affect change	Wants to overthrow the system to affect change

Agitators can engage either in vertical or lateral **deviance** against the control group (Table 15.3). *Vertical deviance* occurs when agitators accept the value system of the establishment but do not accept how the establishment distributes power. For example, Martin Luther King Jr. promoted the values of the U.S. democratic system. However, he argued that the United States was not following its own rules when applied to African Americans. *Lateral deviance*, in contrast, emerges when the agitators do not accept the values of the systems in control and wish to change it completely. The Ruby Ridge, Idaho, incident involving Randy Weaver and his family, and more recently the Ed Brown family of New Hampshire in 2007, illustrated lateral deviance when these groups refused to pay income taxes to a system they did not believe in. Both families found themselves in conflict with the system's control agents: the federal government. Fortunately, the Browns were arrested without incident, unlike the shooting of several individuals in Idaho and the death of Randy Weaver's wife Vicky.

The basic conflict between agitators and control agents can be summed up with the idea that control (people with power) want to maintain control and agitation (people who disagree with the status quo) want to influence change. Getting and holding power is the essence of the struggle. How agitation goes about influencing control affects how control will respond. Control has the advantage because they are in a position to adjust to agitation tactics and often have access to media and other institutional power resources. Going up against the powers that be (control) is a difficult endeavor, and it requires that agitation unify to gain power in numbers.

> **Discussion Question 15.6**
> Identify an example of lateral deviance and an example of vertical deviance from recent news.

Agitation Strategies

Bowers et al. (1993) determined that the path followed by agitation generally is linear and progressive and thus often predictable. Because the path is predictable and familiar, those who skip stages can be discredited as crazy or unreasonable. Knowing the stages is important both to control and to agitation. Strategies of agitation are petition, promulgation, solidification, polarization, nonviolent resistance, and escalation/confrontation (Table 15.4).

The first strategy of agitation is petition. *Petition* is the process of going through the proper channels set up by the system. If a company is seen as having unfair policies that discriminate against hiring women in management, those who seek to change the system are expected to petition the company, present reasoned arguments and evidence, and allow the control agents the opportunity to respond. Agitation carefully must choose test cases, present appropriate evidence, and navigate the appeal process strategically. The film *North Country*

TABLE 15.4 *Strategies of Agitation to Affect Change*

Strategy	Example of Tactics
Petition	Seek audience with current hierarchy File grievance Present evidence and arguments
Promulgation	Recruit members Educate public Organize meetings Seek legitimizers Stage newsworthy events
Solidification	Create unifying messages and slogans Create symbols Design in-group publications Tell stories/sing songs of unity
Polarization	Present people as either part of the problem or part of the solution Exploit "flag issue" or "flag persons" Identify friends and enemies of the cause
Nonviolent resistance	Violate unjust laws peacefully Resist policies/laws, not individuals Suffer without retaliation Be persistent and visible
Escalation/Confrontation	Use rumor to get others to over prepare Goad control to act violently Threaten disruption Be nonverbally offensive Make non-negotiable demands
Gandhi and Guerrilla	Have some agitators who will engage in violence Present majority of agitators as reasonable and work for nonviolent change

Source: Adapted from Bowers et al. (1993).

(2005) portrays a fictionalized account of the landmark sexual harassment case in 1984 against a mining company and illustrates that being right is not enough. Winning requires gathering appropriate and credible witnesses, collecting the best evidence, and strategically countering the efforts to thwart goal achievement. In another example, Rosa Parks was not the first person to refuse to give up a seat on a segregated bus, but she was the right person for agitation to champion as showing the system was wrong. Articulate, bright, and professional, Rosa Parks served well as the flash point for the modern civil rights movement. After being denied a fair resolution through petition, the agitation moved to the next step: promulgation.

Promulgation is the process of gaining social support for the cause. Staging rallies, educating people, phone calling, creating web pages, and rumor campaigns are some of the means to gain support. Promulgation may include staging events that will capture the media's attention, like Willie Nelson's efforts with the Farm Aid concerts and the worldwide Live Earth Concerts. Finding someone in the establishment to legitimize a cause is another way to gain support.

Al Gore and Leonardo DiCaprio's presence as spokespeople for the debate on global warming has taken the issue outside of scientific or policy circles and placed it firmly in the public arena. After Hurricane Katrina, people who wanted to bring attention to the conditions in New Orleans and the perceived failings of the Federal Emergency Management Agency (FEMA) in responding to the emergency sought media sources to tell their story. The media was available to put human faces to the devastation on the Gulf Coast. For example, Brad Pitt and Angelina Jolie's move to New Orleans brought media attention to the continued plight of the city.

> "The fundamental concept in social science is power, in the same sense in which energy is the fundamental concept in physics."
>
> —Philosopher Bertrand Russell

Solidification is a process that takes place primarily within the agitation group to unite the members. Slogans, songs, speakers, and symbols help rally individuals behind a cause. Slogans are also important because they frame the discussion. The terms "pro-life" or "pro-choice" are definitions of philosophies as well as identities. The labels simplify the debate for followers and the undecided. (If you are not pro-life, you are then *against* life. If you are not pro-choice, you are *against* free will.)

Symbols and slogans can lead to the next strategy of polarization: deliberate attempts to make everyone choose which side they will support. Sometimes a person inside the system is vilified and become a **flag person** to imply that all members of control are corrupt and can be painted with the same brush. For example, one may point to a member of a political party and illustrate how that person had questionable ethics or acted poorly. President Bill Clinton and Hilary Clinton became flag people for the conservatives—her involvement heading an insurance reform panel early in Bill Clinton's presidency and his high-profile infidelity became symbols suggesting Democrats were all liberal, pushy, and immoral. Likewise, a musician's claim that, "George Bush doesn't care about black people" became a way of demonizing the president after Hurricane Katrina. President Obama's previous pastor, Jeremiah Wright, provided a flashpoint for those who aimed to portray Obama as a radical during his presidential campaign.

Flag issues are topics that members of a group rally around. For example, gun control is a flag issue for some groups. Any attempt to regulate any type of firearms invigorates the group and spurs them into action.

Taking physical action against the control system is the basis of the last two strategies—nonviolent resistance and escalation/confrontation. **Nonviolent resistance** is implemented when agitators violate rules that they deem unjust. The famous sit-ins during the civil rights movement provide excellent examples of nonviolent resistance. The control system is forced to deal with the agitators, thus bringing more attention to their cause. For example, forcibly removing peaceful black protesters who were just sitting down to order lunch illustrated the meanness of segregation. Agitators depersonalize the policy and chose not to react to the control agents who were enforcing it. Those using nonviolent resistance accept sanctions without retaliating; accept violent reactions, but do not return them. Suffering demonstrates commitment to a righteous cause. The goal is to show the unreasonableness of the other side.

Escalation/confrontation strategies are grounded in the belief that control will over-react to agitation or become confused and, thus, look foolish. Agitators may purposefully overstate their numbers, threaten greater disruption than really is planned, or provoke control with words or token violence, all in hopes of eliciting an overreaction. Agitator groups may take on separate functions within an overall movement. Most of the agitators probably are committed to nonviolence, called **Gandhian tactics.** A small but powerful number, however, may be willing to engage in a full revolution or violence to achieve their ends: **guerrilla tactics.** The extremeness of the guerrilla tactics may motivate the system to meet with the more reasonable arm of the agitation movement. This tactic can backfire, of course. In the 1999 World Trade Organization (WTO) protests in Seattle, over 50,000 protesters rallied in the rain to bring attention to complaints against the WTO. A small number of protesters turned violent, grabbing the media attention and causing empathy for the police and National Guard forces who were trying to restore order. The political protest issues were lost in the media frenzy, which focused on the more photogenic fires and violence (Shah, 2001).

Strategies of Control

When an established structure is faced with the pressure of agitation, they can work with the agitation in the petition stage, or, if they are not interested in changing or relinquishing any control, they may adopt one of four rhetorical strategies: avoidance, suppression, adjustment, or capitulation (Table 15.5). Control generally follows these strategies in order.

TABLE 15.5   *Strategies of Control to Avoid Change*

Strategies	*Example of Tactics*
Avoidance	Engage in counterpersuasion
	Evade by using the bureaucracy to increase red tape, buck passing, and hoop jumping
	Be unavailable
	Postpone
	Evoke a need for secrecy
	Deny means of agitation members
Suppression	Harass agitation leadership
	Hide or destroy evidence
	Deny agitator's demands
	Banish or kill leadership
Adjustment	Adapt or modify structure
	Change the name of regulatory agency
	Sacrifice personnel
	Accept some means of agitation
	Institutionalize agitators
	Incorporate agitation's ideology
Capitulation	Replace control with agitation's personnel, ideology, and structure
	Surrender

Source: Adapted from Bowers et al. (1993).

Avoidance of the agitator's demands or concerns can be implemented through evasion tactics or by attempting to persuade the agitators that they are wrong. Evasion can include bureaucratic delays, buck passing, or entering into negotiations when control has no intention of making concessions. Control can postpone decisions by employing the "take it under advisement" strategy. Committees may be formed to study the problem, further delaying action. Control may hope that the agitators get restless, give up, or violate the rules so they can be sanctioned. Control may engage in avoidance through rationalizing that a bigger principle is involved (e.g., "It's a matter of national security") or may simply deny the agitators access to the means to organize. In a recent example, one university's administration was adverse to faculty members and graduate assistants creating a union. In an effort to thwart organizing efforts, they passed policies that forbade the use of university e-mail and mail systems to contact prospective members. They further made it explicitly against the rules to recruit during university work hours or during normal university business. Without external resources the union idea just disappeared from that campus.

Suppression is the second strategy used by control in dealing with agitation. Suppression involves the purposeful efforts to "stop the spread of [agitation's] ideology by hindering the goals and personnel of the agitative movement" (Bowers et al., 1993, p. 54). Leaders may be fired or excommunicated, documents may be destroyed, and followers may be threatened. Control may engage in harassment of leaders in hopes that it will serve as a warning to followers and that the leader will be so consumed with fighting the harassment that they cannot devote energy to their cause. A more direct means of suppression is simply saying no to the agitator's demands. This forces the agitation to move out of the system. The danger of saying no, however, is it may mobilize agitators and increase their unity. The most radical type of suppression would be **purgation:** killing the leaders of the movement.

The third option is for control to adapt or alter the status quo by way of *adjustment.* The goal for control is to appear strong even though they are making a change. The danger to control is that agitation will use the adjustment as proof that control is weak. Instead the system wants to project an image of reasonableness and strength. Sometimes adjustment is more ceremonial than real. A university had entered an agreement with a national fast-food corporation to have it sponsor its stadium in exchange for a large endowment. Protests emerged over the perception that this corporation was involved in questionable labor practices with farm workers. The protesters held public meetings and brought in national speakers on farm labor issues. The university administration attended the events. Committees were created to include some of the protesters in future decision making. A university street was renamed after Cesar Chavez. Ultimately, however, the name of the stadium remained, regardless of the concerns expressed by the protesters.

Another strategy is to sacrifice personnel. After a complaint that a national retailer had engaged in unfair business practices and failed to promote women and minorities, the board of directors simply fired the CEO.

Control may adjust by allowing the dissent or by incorporating some of the agitators into the control structure. In a public school conflict, parents were unhappy with programmatic changes to services offered for gifted children. After engaging in an extended letter writing campaign and challenging the school district in the local media, the school institutionalized the parent group. The group now has access to school meeting areas and administrative staff. The complaints still continued, but now they were "in house" and easier to control, thus proving the adage, "keep your friends close and your enemies closer."

The final strategy for control is **capitulation,** to give in to the agitators and turn over control to them. This final option is generally not done voluntarily or without pressure from superior forces. Violence or threat of violence often is the precursor to capitulation.

> ### Discussion Question 15.7
> How can the word "terrorism" be used as a control strategy?

Reframing Social Conflict

Although the strategies of agitation and control are well documented and history provides numerous examples of escalation of social conflict, we are not without options for engaging in more collaborative methods (Table 15.6). Some contend that the best approach is *transformative:* It transforms parties by affirming the worth of the people involved and working to build a bridge connecting people to create a positive future. The focus in a transformative approach is moving the parties to seeing each other in respectful, connected, and valued ways. Another approach is more directed at *problem resolution.* The goal of the latter is to achieve a level of functionality with the parties. Understanding and respect, although wonderful, are not as important as getting a resolution that allows people to manage the future more productively than they have the past. Problem resolution techniques employ the same framing that mediators use (see Chapter 9). The process usually begins with parties discussing the past grievance, identifying issues for negotiation, and—through discussion— determining options, evaluating solutions, and promising to implement solutions.

A transformative approach for community conflict can be illustrated through contrasting views of peace. Galtung (1969) laid out the difference between achieving a positive peace and a negative peace. **Negative peace** results from forced submission, not a change of heart. On the global scale, we can see many examples of how negative peace rarely is long lasting. Some may bide their time until a new government is in power; others who feel oppressed work to force more radical change faster. Hebein (1999) illustrated how people on college campuses who "lose" in a particular conflict react to exact punitive measures of their own with theft and vandalism. **Positive peace,** in contrast, is about transforming the hearts and minds of individuals to get behind a solution. Educating, sharing information, engaging in listening, and perspective taking are staples for bringing about transformation.

Barge (2001) makes a case for **affirmative communication processes** to manage societal conflict. Barge argues for framing conflicts positively instead of negatively. **Deficit**

TABLE 15.6 *Options for Reframing Social Conflict*

Transformative approach	Support the worth of parties and connections where both sides work for positive future
Problem resolution	Achieve a level of functionality between parties using mediation tools for negotiation
Affirmative communication	Framing conflicts positively, avoiding deficit language, and focusing on appreciative inquiry, capacity-focused development, and asset development

language focuses on the negative elements of conflict. For example, the "war on drugs" frames illicit drugs as the problem to be overcome. According to Barge, deficit language results in blame and disempowerment. The alternative approach would be to focus on the "best of what is" and build resolution from there. The best in a particular community might be framed as "opportunities," "strong relationships between volunteer, agencies and churches," and "commitment by many to improve the community." Instead of a "war on drugs," the focus could be on "great kids making great choices." The outcome then is framed by how we can build on our strengths to make drugs *not* the desirable option for children and promote examples of kids making positive contributions in society.

Barge (2001) delineates three elements of affirmative conflict strategies: appreciative inquiry, capacity-focused development, and asset development. The first strategy, appreciative inquiry, focuses on four steps:

1. *Appreciating and valuing the best of "what is."* Parties are interviewed to discover elements such as what is going well, moments of excellence, positive stories, and core values.
2. *Envisioning "what might be."* From the interviews, a focus on the future is maintained. Positive possibilities for the future are highlighted. Discussions about the ideal are held.
3. *Dialoguing about "what should be."* Parties are encouraged to talk about what should happen next in light of the information they have learned in the previous two stages.
4. *Innovating "what will be."* Participants plan the next steps for leading them to the future they want to create.

> "Managing conflict with communities involves cultivating our better nature."
> —Scholar Kevin Barge

The next strategy championed by Barge is *capacity-focused development.* In traditional approaches, the focus is on deficits, not capacity. After a natural disaster a community developed a list of problems and deficits in the area. This list serves to focus on negative elements, create blame and turf battles between agencies over scarce resources, and cause people to pick sides. The alternative is focusing on the capacity of the community. "Capacity-focused development aims to build communities from the inside out. . . . [It] begins by creating an asset map" (p. 94). Individuals, organizations, agencies, businesses, hospital, and so forth, list their capabilities. "A capacity-focused approach begins with the premise that there are assets within any community, and that once they are surfaced they can be mobilized for change" (p. 94). The result is a community invested in resolution. *Asset building* is going to individuals and groups and identifying capabilities, and then through actions such as empowering, education, and networking, helping others reach higher capacities. Barge contends, "The language of assets offers a common linguistic framework from which community groups can collaborate and manage conflict" (p. 95).

> ### *Discussion Question 15.8*
> Identify the benefits and disadvantages of Barge's approach for community conflict management. What factors have to exist for this approach to be considered?

At the beginning of this chapter we were reminded that the personal issues in life become the basis for political and social conflict. The reverse is also true: What is political is also personal. Social and public conflicts often are at the source of personal conflicts with others. Friendships are ruined over differences of opinions about war and religion. How social conflicts are framed, how they are argued, and how they are managed have implications for each of us.

Summary

Conflict at a social level is motivated by the same elements as personal conflict. Elements of interpersonal conflict are present in social conflicts, particularly the element of morals. Reasons for action at the social or political level are motivated by threats to personal identities, face, moral codes, and values. Values, or core constructs, lead to beliefs that we hold about what is right and wrong. Sometimes, however, core values may be in conflict with one another, causing us to feel dissonance.

Face threats on a social level can involve how we construct identities. When those identities are threatened, conflict emerges as we try to reestablish the dominance of those constructs. Social conflicts are rooted in the constructs from which we draw our identities.

A common approach to gain support for social positions is to polarize an argument. The media and their need for stories has made it easier for polarized arguments to be heard. News media has fed into Tannen's concept of the "argument culture," promoting the idea that the best way to explore an idea is to establish two polar opposites. Tannen calls for replacing the argument culture's dominance with dialogue when it is appropriate.

With the increased news sources and outlets, it is possible to listen only to partisan news or commentary. This can lead to the risky shift phenomenon where individuals take on more risky behavior and more extreme positions.

Rummel identified seven types of conflict of interest and the resolution paths to overcome them. Depending on the type of conflict, the choices include exchange, threats and coercion, institutional determination, persuasion, altruism, manipulation of resources, abdication, or physical force. In resolution the outcome can be defined as either being characterized by positive peace, where disputants choose to comply with decisions, or negative peace, where one is forced to comply with decisions. Negative peace generally does not last.

Bowers et al. examined the strategies of agitation (those who want to bring about change in the status quo) and control (those who want to maintain the power structures as they stand). Strategies of agitation include petition, promulgation, solidification, polarization, nonviolent resistance, escalation/confrontation, and Gandhi or guerrilla tactics. Control's responses to agitation can be simply to avoid the agitators to suppress, adjust, or capitulate.

Options to reframe social conflict into less confrontational approaches can be seen in transformative techniques that affirm the worth of the people involved and seek to connect sides for positive change. Another approach is to engage in problem resolution where opposing sides seek to achieve a level of functionality through techniques used in mediation: discussion of past grievances, identification of issues, and joint problem solving. A third technique involves affirmative action processes to manage social conflict, by changing deficit language that focuses on the negative elements of the conflict and shifting to language and options that build communities and commonalities. This is accomplished by highlighting what is good and focusing on what could occur in the future. The goal for parties in this approach is to have capacity-focused development of solutions.

Chapter Resources

Exercises

1. As a group, identify two examples of each of Rummel's outcomes in Table 15.2. Be prepared to argue whether you believe the outcome was fair for the specific situation.

2. Find an issue that is sparking local or national protest. Gather information about the protest group's actions and the responses to it. Identify any strategies of agitation or control used by either side.

Journal/ Essay Topics

1. For one week, listen to the news from two opposing media outlets (some suggestions are listed here). Track the top stories on each outlet (what was discussed first, second, etc.) and the slant of the stories. Write an analysis of the values implicit in the news on each outlet.

   - National Public Radio and any conservative radio station
   - FOX News and CNN
   - CBS Evening News and the BBC World News
   - Radio station news on the hour from a U.S. radio station and a BBC radio station (on the web, such as Radio Scotland)

Mastery Case

Examine Mastery Case 15, "Animal Right Protests: Terrorism or Free Speech?" Which concepts from the chapter can be applied to the case?

Animal Rights Protests: Terrorism or Free Speech?

In 2006, a New Jersey animal rights group claimed that they were engaged in free speech when it protested against companies who used animals in testing or produced animal-based products, as well as companies who have done business with those companies, such as banks. The group's tactics included "vandalism, personal warnings by e-mail and phone message, and other threats directed at family members—what's

called 'tertiary targeting'" (Knickerbocker, 2006).

Groups have engaged in intrusive and aggressive actions. Some researchers have been targeted by these groups after their home addresses became known to members. As a result, researchers and their families received "months of harassment, threats and vandalism at the homes and offices" including flooding, fire, and breaking windows (Krupnick, 2008). Researcher Edythe London (2007) of UCLA points to dangerous examples of threats of fellow researchers including "the placement of a Molotov cocktail-type of device at a colleague's home and another under a colleague's car—thankfully, they didn't ignite—as well as rocks thrown through windows, phone and e-mail threats, banging on doors in the middle of the night and, on several occasions, direct confrontations with young children."

Activists claim they need to act forcefully because the abuse of animals is unnecessary and cruel, citing examples of vivisections, dehydration, starvation, putting acid in eyes, ears, nose, and mouths of animals, and wanton cruelty. They claim that science offers alternatives to using animals and that fighting for the animal's welfare is justifiable.

Legislators and university administrators don't see the protests as appropriate, and some even call protestors "terrorists" (Krupnick, 2008). Congress enacted the 1992 Animal Enterprise Protection Act to impose sanctions on activists for harassment of companies, employees, and families. Recently sponsors of a bill to strengthen the 1992 law have proposed a bill called the "Animal Enterprise Terrorism Act."

At about the same time, the University of California sought to curtail the requirements of California's public records laws to limit publication of researchers' private information. The tide seems to be on the side of the researchers and organizations. Activists in New Jersey were convicted under the 1992 federal law, and Oregon activists with the Animal Liberation Front have been charged under the law.

But according to Knickerbocker (2006), "the crackdown by the FBI and other police agencies has not slowed activists' efforts. One anonymous group just launched a website listing the home addresses of 2,000 employees from 30 companies doing business with Huntingdon Life Sciences" (the New Jersey lab). 'From CEOs to lowly sales reps, from Alabama to Hawaii, we've sniffed them out,' activists are told. "Visit them often, and make the message clear: when you contract with HLS . . . you get us!'" The final chapter in this movement has yet to be written.

Sample Mediation Case:
The Suite Case

Note: Do not read this appendix unless told to do so by your instructor.

Mediator Case Notes

Mediator Instructions

Using the information in Chapter 11, act as the impartial and neutral third party to mediate the following case. Read only the instructions and information on this page. Do not read the confidential information for Martin/Marsha or Lyle/Lola on the next pages.

Case Information

The two parties (Martin/Marsha and Lyle/Lola) approached the student mediation center to help them with their roommate dispute.

    You received these premediation notes from your case developer:

- The two disputants live in a six-person suite in one of the residence halls.
- They both are freshmen and this is their first experience living away from home.
- Each person has a private room.
- They share the bathroom.

    Your goal as the mediator is to help the parties resolve their differences without making suggestions or intruding into "their" solution. Before beginning the mediation, think for a moment about open-ended questions or background that might be useful to ask to get the specifics of their conflict out on the table, such as these:

- How long have you been living in the residence halls?
- What are your concerns about the living situation?

- What are your views of what it means to be a good roommate?
- What are your views on appropriate [insert a concern they raise. For example, room-mates are often concerned about cleanliness or noise.]
- How long has [this issue] been a problem for you?
- What is your daily schedule like?
- When do you do your studying?

Confidential Information for Martin/Marsha

Note: Read this page only if you are assigned the role of Martin/Martha

Instructions

Your task is to play the role of Martin or Marsha. Read only the instructions and the confidential case information here. Do not read the confidential information for Lyle/Lola on the following pages. The case information may not include every detail that will come up during the role play. For example, the mediator may ask you what kind of music you like or other details that are not specifically discussed in the case information. When that happens, draw on your life experience and make up an answer. Try not to make up answers that are too exotic or bizarre. For example, if the mediator asks what your concerns are, don't make up a boa constrictor snake that gets loose in the suite.

Case Information
- You are a first-semester freshman and this is your first experience living in a suite with other students.
- You are from a small farm town in a rural part of the state. You have three brothers and two sisters.
- In your family, everybody borrowed each other's stuff, and it was never a problem. Your mom always took care of washing all the clothes, so it didn't matter who borrowed what since it all got sorted out eventually. Your mom also did all the cleaning and you really don't know how to clean or how to do laundry.
- You're never had to think about doing laundry or cleaning, so you don't.
- This is your first time away from home, and you're having a good time.
- Classes always were pretty easy for you in high school and you got good grades. However, your grades have declined considerably this semester.
- You started out liking all your roommates. You really don't see much of them since you're out with your new friends from another dorm a lot. Sometimes your friends come over to play cards in the common room on Wednesday and Thursday nights.
- Lately Lyle/Lola has been giving you dirty looks and making snide comments about the place "smelling like Martin/Marsha's family pig sty." You don't like insults about your family, so you've been rude back. Your room might be a little smelly, but you'll take your laundry home in a couple of weeks for your mom to wash.
- The other roommates in the suite are fed up with the two of you bickering and told the two of you to go to mediation or they would petition for your removal from the suite.

Your Interests
- You want to stay in the suite.
- You want Lyle/Lola to stop making rude comments.
- You want to get good enough grades to stay in college.
- You want your friends to be able to visit you.

Confidential Information for Lyle/Lola

Note: Read this page only if you have been assigned to play the role of Lyle/Lola.

Instructions

Your task is to play the role of Lyle or Lola. Read only the instructions and the confidential case information here. Do not read the confidential information for Martin/Marsha. The case information may not include every detail that will come up during the role play. For example, the mediator may ask you what kind of music you like or other details that are not specifically discussed in the case information. When that happens, draw on your life experience and make up an answer. Try not to make up answers that are too exotic or bizarre. For example, if the mediator asks what your concerns are, don't make up a boa constrictor snake that gets loose in the suite.

Case Information
- You are a first-semester freshman and this is your first experience living in a suite with other students.
- You are from the biggest city in the state and grew up with your single mom.
- Your mom worked long hours to keep the two of you housed and to save for your college tuition and expenses, so you've always had house cleaning responsibilities.
- Because you know how hard your mom worked to get you to college, you are determined to succeed. You like to have fun on weekends, but getting good grades is your first priority. You study every night.
- You liked everyone in your suite from the very start, but Martin/Marsha got out of control in a hurry. He/she parties until three in the morning at least one school night every week—so it is hard for you to study or to get to sleep for your morning classes. Maybe Martin/Marsha doesn't care about flunking out, but you do!
- You have noticed occasionally that Martin/Marsha is wearing a shirt or jacket of yours without asking. You would let him/her borrow it if asked, but are bothered at how inconsiderate this behavior is—especially when items come back dirty.
- Martin/Marsha also has turned out to be a pig. Her/his room really is smelly from the dirty laundry that has piled up and you're pretty sure that he/she never does any cleaning in the bathroom or the suite. You're sick of it.
- You have hinted around several times that she/he should help out cleaning the bathroom, and you just got these blank looks back. That fact that Martin/Marsha ignores you really ticks you off, and you have taken to making a few snide comments about

"farm kids and their pig sty houses coming to the big city." You feel a little badly about the comments, but he/she had it coming—and at least you are getting some reaction.

- The other roommates in the suite are fed up with the two of you bickering and told the two of you to go to mediation or they would petition for your removal from the suite.

Your Interests

- You have to be able to study and get good grades.
- You want to be asked before someone borrows your things, and you want them returned in the same condition they were in before being borrowed.
- You need to be able to get to sleep at a decent hour on school nights.
- You want to live in a place that doesn't stink.
- You want everybody to do their share toward the cleaning.

Glossary

The glossary gives general definitions for common terms used in conflict management studies. Particular theories or techniques may use a variation on the common meaning of a term.

A

Abstract: Ideas that are not specific or are vague.

Accommodation cultural style: A style or tactic of response to conflict to comply with the other's wishes.

Active listening: The process of purposefully attending to the speaker's expressed and unexpressed messages (see mindfulness).

Adjudication: Litigation or legal processes.

Affect/Affective event: Anything that causes an emotional response.

Affirmative communication processes: Framing messages positively rather than negatively.

Agitators: In social movements, those who oppose the current system.

Alternative dispute resolution (ADR): Conflict resolution processes that provide alternatives to legal actions, such as mediation or arbitration.

Anchor point: In negotiation over fixed items, the first offer that sets one end of the negotiation range.

Anger: A secondary emotion where one is irritated, annoyed, upset, or enraged by a stimulus that, on deeper analysis, was rooted in fear, hurt, or some other primary emotion.

Appreciative listening: Attending to the artfulness of a message.

Approach-approach conflict: The choice between two equally attractive options.

Approach-avoid conflict: The choice between two opposing options, one negative and one positive.

Arbitrator: A third party who investigates and makes a decision for the parties in a conflict (see binding arbitration).

Argument: Providing reasons to support an assertion or claim.

Argumentativeness: A tendency to defend one's position from a competitive stance.

Assertiveness: The ability to advance one's thoughts or goals without aggression.

At-risk family: A family that faces personal, health, social, or economic hardships that threaten the family's relational bonds or puts individual family members at adverse risk.

Attitude: A relatively stable predisposition to act or believe in specific ways.

Attribution error: In attribution theory, where one ascribes motivations for another's behavior to a personality or character trait when it actually results from a situational influence, or vice versa.

Attribution theory: The concept that people consistently make sense of the world by assigning meaning and motives to others' behavior.

Authority rule: A decision-making method where the most powerful person or the established leader makes the decision.

Autonomy: A state of independence from the influence of others.

Avoidance: A style or tactic in response to conflict not to engage directly in conflict.

Avoid-avoid conflict: The choice between two equally unattractive options.

Awareness wheel: An assessment tool for two people to use interactively (created by Miller, Miller, Nunally, and Wackman).

B

Balanced Model of Mediation: A mediation model that considers conciliation and problem-solving approaches equally valuable depending on the circumstances.

Bargaining: Interactions between parties for the purpose of individual and/or joint goal attainment (also called negotiation).

Bargaining range: The areas of overlap in the parties' goals where a beneficial outcome might be reached.

Barnlund's six views: A theory that each person in a conversation has three views: my view of myself, my view of you, and my view of how you view me.

Binding arbitration: A third party (arbitrator) who makes a decision where the parties have agreed that they will implement the arbitrator's decision.

Boulwarism/Boulware strategy: In negotiation, making a reasonable first offer on a take-it-or-leave-it basis without further bargaining.

Boundary management theory/Communication privacy management theory: An explanation of how individuals set limits around their personal interactions or relationships.

Brainstorming: A communication technique to spur creativity and quantity of ideas in problem solving.

Bullying: Frequent harassment over time that harms the intended recipient (also called mobbing and psychological terror).

C

Capitulation: Giving up or giving in to the demands of the other side.

Catharsis: The theory that watching something moderates the desire to do that thing (e.g., the theory that watching television violence moderates the impulse to do violence).

Chain of command: A formal or informal hierarchical ranking system where each rank has decision-making authority over those of lower rank (see also hierarchy of authority and organizational chart).

Channel/Communication channel: The medium through which a message is conveyed.

Civility: Showing respect for others.

Close-ended questions: Questions answerable with limited options, such as "yes" or "no," or other forced choice answers; opposite of open-ended questions.

Closure: The final phase in the Balanced Mediation Model where the agreement is summarized or parties told the next steps if the mediation participants fail to reach agreement.

Clusters of conflict: An assessment tool based on Mayer's Wheel of Conflict and Moore's Circle of Conflict.

Coalition: A group that unites on a particular issue to advance mutual goals.

Codependence: A pathological condition characterized by a person's overreliance on another to satisfy his or her needs, often demonstrated by the manipulation of one person by another.

Coercion/Coercive power: Forcing others to comply (also called power-over).

Collaboration: A style of conflict management where parties work until all agree that the chosen solution is the best possible solution available for all parties.

Collectivist culture: A society that values the group above the individual.

Commonality: Any issue, circumstance, or goal shared by all parties.

Communication infidelity: Being unfaithful to a partner through verbal or simulated intimacy with another person without physical sexual contact.

Compensational forgiveness: Giving forgiveness only after receiving some value to compensate for your loss (also called restitutional forgiveness).

Competitive worldview: A social construct in which the way humans interact is based on the assumption that the only choices are win, lose, or tie (also called distributive).

Comprehensive conflict checklist: An analysis tool that asks a series of wide-ranging and thorough questions to examine a conflict.

Comprehensive listening: Attending to acquire the overall meaning of a message (see also content paraphrasing).

Compromise: A style or tactic in response to conflict where each party gives up some part of goal achievement in order to reach agreement.

Concession: Something given to the other party in a negotiation.

Conciliation: The process of overcoming past difficulties or to reconcile a relationship.

Concrete/Concreteness: Very specific ideas or behaviors.

Conflict assessment: Formal analysis of a conflict using an assessment tool.

Conflict coaching: Part of a systematic response to conflict in organizations where individuals are provided with private coaching to improve their conflict and communication skills.

Conflict management style: An individual's preferred or habitual responses to conflict situations.

Conflict management system: An organization's systematic response to conflict by providing multiple formal and informal access points for the resolution of conflicts.

Conflict road map: An assessment tool for larger group situations based on Wehr's analysis instrument.

Connotative meaning: An individualized reaction to a word derived from one's personal association or experience with it.

Consensus: A decision-making method where, after all parties have weighed in on the issue, a decision emerges that all parties agree to support.

Constructive conflict: Conflict that moves toward positive outcomes.

Constructivism: An interaction theory advanced by Delia, and others, that holds individuals create meaning and interpret reality through a series of personal constructs or schemas.

Content paraphrasing: A communication technique to summarize the denotative message of the speaker.

Control/Controllers: In social movements, those who represent the status quo or the existing system.

Conventionality: Following the common path and customs.

Conversational style: Speech habits, vocal patterns, and preferred means of expression.

Cool posing: Socially appropriate behaviors adopted when one is angry and expression of anger could have severe consequences.

Cooperative worldview: The view that with work and creativity, the needs of all people can be met (also called mutual gains, interest based, or win-win).

Creating value: Using the decision-making process to create outcomes that add benefit to the individuals involved.

Cultivation theory: Posited by Gerbner and others who argued that watching media creates expectations of what real life is like.

Culture: Common assumptions, tendencies, and experiences shared by a group.

Currency/Power currency: A social exchange theory concept that controlling assets, abilities, traits, and so on, valued by others creates power.

Cyberbullies: Bullying through the Internet, text messaging, or other electronic media.

D

Defense-provoking: Types of communicative behaviors posited by Gibb to provoke protective or negative reactions.

Deficit language: Framing things negatively or as a deficiency.

Delayed feedback technique/XYZ technique: A planned pattern of response based on the model, "When you do X in situation Y, I feel Z."

Denotative meaning: The literal dictionary definition of a word.

Descriptive language/descriptive statements: Communicating direct observations about behaviors without adding evaluation or interpretation.

Destructive conflict: Conflict that moves toward destructive outcomes.

Deviance: In social science research, any variation from the norm.

Diagnostic flowchart: A tool that diagrams multiple options to isolate the probable cause of behaviors.

Dialectical tension: A pull between opposing forces.

Dialogic (relational) listening: Taking turns speaking and listening for the purpose of mutual understanding.

Directiveness: In mediation, how tightly the mediator controls the process and communication during a mediation session.

Directness: How open and clear an individual is about thoughts, goals, or interests.

Disclosiveness: The level of personal information an individual reveals to others.

Discriminative listening: Attending to particular signals; isolating particular words or sounds from the mass of background sound.

Discussant cultural style: An intercultural conflict style that is low in emotional expressiveness and high in direct communication.

Disputants: The individuals invested in the outcome of a conflict or a mediation.

Dissonance: A state where an individual holds conflicting attitudes, beliefs, or values; the presence of an attitude, value, or belief that is direct conflict with one's behavior.

Distributive conflict/Distributive negotiation: A competitive view that conflicts are win-lose where what is at stake will be divided among those in the conflict.

Dyad/Dyadic communication: Communication between two people.

Dynamic cultural style: An intercultural conflict style that is high in emotional expressiveness and low in directiveness.

Dysfunctional family: Families that create or exist in a toxic environment or that do not provide emotional or social support to its members.

Dysfunctional roles: Roles assumed for personal reasons that detract from relationship maintenance or task accomplishment.

E

Echo technique: Repeating a comment back to the speaker.

Egocentrism: Singular focus on one's personal needs and desires.

Emotional intelligence/EQ or EI: A counterpart to intellectual intelligence (IQ) that holds that individuals possess measurable levels of self-awareness, emotion management, self-motivation, awareness of others, and relationship management.

Emotional labor: The work of displaying or containing certain psychological or physical reactions to situations on the job.

Emotional paraphrase: A listening technique to show empathy and validate the feelings of others, often to the effect of decreasing the emotional affect in others.

Empathetic listening: Attending to a message in order to understand another person's perspective without evaluation or criticism.

Empathy: The ability to understand, but not necessarily share or agree with, another person's view or emotional state.

Empowerment: Identifying and making apparent power resources for the purpose of increasing an individual's independence and self-determination (also called power-to).

Enculturation: The informal process through which individuals learn social or group rules, customs, and appropriate behaviors.

Engagement cultural style: An intercultural conflict style that is high in expressiveness of emotions and high in directness of expression.

Entitlement effect: A view that one is owed privileges or special treatment.

Escalation: A communication behavior where a response is designed to expand the size, scope, or intensity of the conflict.

Essentializing: Assuming that all persons in a gender, social, racial, or ethnic group think essentially the same way or have the same experiences.

Ethnocentric errors: Thinking errors caused by cultural stereotyping or essentializing.

Evaluative (critical) listening: Attending to a message in order to judge it.

Evaluative statements: Communicating to the other an attribution of his or her motivation or to interpret behavior as having purposeful intent (generally negative).

Expectancy violation: A mismatch between what is expected and what occurs.

Expectational forgiveness: Forgiving because of social pressure or a belief that it is the right thing to do. In lawful expectational forgiveness, you are required by rule or law to demonstrate surface forgiveness.

Expert power: Power derived from having knowledge or skills valued by others.

Extended family: Individuals related but not a part of the immediate familial structure; those outside of the nuclear family—typically referring to multigenerational families.

External attribution: Assigning motive to factors external to the individual, such as the environment or outside circumstances.

Extrovert: A personality type that gains personal energy by socializing and being with other people; a personality trait where one is comfortable with personal expression.

F

Face: The public or private image one holds about oneself (also called self-face).

Face goal: Goals regarding the expression of self-worth, pride, or self-respect.

Facework: Active attempts to moderate or manage one's self-image or image presented to others; can also apply to attempts to modify the self-image of another person.

Fake apologies: Verbalizations of insincere apology.

Family: A self-defined group of intimates who create and maintain an identity among themselves and with others (see also nuclear family extended family, gay/lesbian family, nontraditional family, family of origin).

Family boundaries: Determinations of who is included in the family group and who is intentionally excluded by social or legal action.

Family communication: The quantity and quality of interactions among family members that create their unique rules, customs, style, and functionality.

Family meeting/Family home night: A ritualized time and format for a family to gather together to work on their relationship, to engage in a joint activity, or to discuss family issues.

Family of choice: A group that forms a long-term association and/or residence (also called voluntary families).

Family of origin: The family into which one was born and/or raised.

Family ritual: Customary events or repeated patterns of interaction specific to a family.

Family stories: Narratives repeatedly told about family members or family events that serve to sustain rules, customs, or teach lessons.

Fear: A primary emotion rooted in a psychological belief that harm will result if a stimulus occurs.

Feeling paraphrase: A listening technique to show empathy and validate the emotions of others, often to the effect of decreasing the emotional affect in others.

Field theory: Developed by Lewin and others; the theory suggests there are types of forces that drive conflict and forces that restrain conflict.

Flag issue/Flag person: An event or symbol that represents or champions an issue for a group.

Flaming: Attacks on others via electronic media, such as e-mail, chat rooms, blogs, or text messaging.

Flash point: The event that precipitates a conflict episode (also called triggering events).

Flat organizational hierarchy: An organization with fewer layers of management between workers and upper management.

Fogging: A technique of admitting to accusations that are true but not relevant to the issue in discussion.

Forgiveness: Accepting an apology for hurt caused by another person or group or giving up active mulling about the offense.

Fractionation: A style or tactic of conflict to respond to issues by breaking them down into smaller parts for problem solving. A fractionator is someone who uses fractionation.

Future focus: A conflict management technique that requires disputants to attend to the changes to be made in the existing circumstances instead of focusing on past events, previous problems, or root causes.

G

Game theory: A theory that models the outcomes of conflict based on choices made by players through a rational process.

Gandhian tactics: A type of nonviolent resistance where those who want change refuse to follow social mandates, actively disobey existing rules set by those in control, and refuse to defend or attack when challenged.

Gay/lesbian family: A same-sex couple and their children.

Genderlect: A hypothesis that differences in women and men's speech are caused by socialization.

Generational cohort: An age group influenced by similar events or experiences.

Genuine forgiveness: Forgiveness that is sincere and intentional.

Goal: The end or desired condition.

Gregorc styles model: A personal style classification based on whether individuals are abstract or concrete and sequential or random.

Grievance story: The portrayal of oneself in conversations to others as a victim.

Group: A small group typically includes three to twelve people who interact meaningfully with each other long enough to form norms and other group dynamic features.

Group forgiveness: The giving or asking of one group to forgive another for past injustices.

Groupthink: A phenomenon posited by Janis that explains how highly cohesive groups function to make bad decisions.

Guerrilla tactics: A wing of a social movement willing to commit violence in the name of the cause.

Gunnysacking: Holding complaints or issues (as if collecting them in a sack) until one cannot bear any more. Then the entire sack of issues is dumped on the other person.

H

Hearing: An automatic physiological process of receiving sounds.

Hierarchy of authority: A formal or informal ranking of who has designated decision-making power in a family, group, or organization (see also chain of command, organizational chart).

High-context culture: A concept developed by Hall that some cultures interpret most of the meaning in a message from the general social and physical environment where the message occurs.

Hollow forgiveness: Accepting an apology without giving up the inner hurt.

Hypothetical offer: A negotiation tactic to make an offer without actually putting the offer on the table.

I

Imagined interaction: An analysis tool to rehearse mentally different conflict tactics and strategies.

Impartiality: In negotiations, a person (usually a third party) who has no stake in the outcome of a dispute; the state of being uninvested in the outcome.

Impasse: In negotiation, a state where the parties are stuck and can make no progress toward resolution.

Impulse control: The ability to moderate emotional and spontaneous reactions.

Incompatibility: Goals or other actions that do not fit well together.

Individualistic culture: A society that values the individual over the group.

Initial goal: Goals held by individuals at the beginning of a conflict.

In-process goals: Goals that evolve and change as a conflict episode progresses.

Integrative engagement model/style: A conflict management style that is cooperative and seeks mutually beneficial outcomes for all parties.

Integrative power: The concept that the ability to influence is based on the connections between individuals.

Interaction theories: Explanations that focus on the communication that occurs between people in conflict rather than on an individual or internal processes.

Interactive conflict analysis: An assessment tool for disputants to work through past, present, and future views of an issue.

Intercultural Conflict Style Inventory: An intercultural conflict style diagnostic test that measures how directly issues and emotion are expressed.

Interdependent/Interdependence: A state where one thing or person requires another thing or person to meet goals.

Interest: A need that drives a goal.

Interest-based bargaining: Negotiating or working through conflict by discovering each person's underlying needs.

Internal attributions: Assuming a behavior was caused by factors inherent to the person, such as personality, values, or characteristics, and not some external situation.

Internal rationalizing process: The reasoning within oneself justifying one's own beliefs or actions.

Interpersonal conflict: A struggle among a small number of interdependent people (usually two) arising from perceived interference with goal achievement.

Interpersonal forgiveness: Forgiveness given or received in an interpersonal context.

Interpersonal reconciliation: Reconciliation that is experienced in an interpersonal context.

Intrapersonal communication: Communication within oneself; self-dialogue.

Intrapersonal conflict: An internal struggle with competing personal goals.

Introvert: A personality type that gains personal energy by solitude or intimate interactions; a personality trait where one may be uncomfortable expressing oneself.

Intrusiveness: In the context of mediation, a mediator who makes suggestions to the parties on what the solution could or should be.

Issue: In conflict, that which must be resolved.

"I" statement: A statement taking responsibility for one's personal feelings or thoughts.

K

Kinkeepers: Family members who sustain the family's history and traditions.

L

Latent conflict: Issues that have potential for conflict that the parties do not yet perceive to be a problem.

Lawful expectational forgiveness: Forgiving because of social pressure or a belief that it is the right thing to do. In lawful expectational forgiveness, you are required by rule or law to demonstrate surface forgiveness.

Leadership: A role assumed to channel the resources and energy of a group toward accomplishing its goal.

Legitimate power: Institutional influence derived from titles, offices held, or rightful authority within a structure.

Listening: The physical and psychological processing of aural stimuli (see active listening, appreciative listening, comprehensive listening, content paraphrase, discriminative listening, emotional paraphrase, empathic listening, evaluative listening, and feeling paraphrase).

Lose/lose: A resolution of conflict where both parties sacrifice some needs in order to reach agreement; the actual outcome of many win/lose negotiations where the loser makes sure the winner is not able to benefit from the victory.

Low-context culture: A concept developed by Hall that certain cultures gain most of the meaning in messages in the words and symbols that are used apart from the environment in which they were expressed.

M

Maintenance role: A role assumed to foster the relationship health among individuals in a dyad or a group.

Mapping: Diagramming conflict factors in order to determine primary issues and best strategies for managing negotiations; an assessment tool based on the Australian Conflict Resolution Network Needs and Fears Worksheet.

Mechanical model: The mistaken idea that communication processes work like machines where one component can be removed and understood apart from the system in which it occurs.

Mediation: The assistance of a neutral and impartial third party who facilitates the parties in creating their own mutually agreeable outcome.

Mediator monologue: A presentation of the opening statement by the mediator (also called mediator opening statement).

Meeting management: Leadership activities to coordinate group interactions and make them effective.

Mentoring: The guidance by an experienced employee given to newcomers on how to behave in an organization, how to perform a job, and/or how to achieve professional goals.

Metacommunication: Focusing discussion on the interaction process; communication about communication.

Metaphor: Describing something using the characteristics of an unrelated thing.

Metaphor analysis: A tool to examine how metaphorical comparisons are used in conflict interactions and the impact of those comparisons on perceptions and behaviors.

Meta-rules: Mandates guiding when it is and is not acceptable to talk about rules.

Mindfulness: A personal commitment and mental state to attend fully to someone without distraction (see active listening).

Mirroring: Reflecting back the same tactics or communication behaviors that another person uses.

Mixed motive: Situations where an individual's goals are somewhat cooperative and somewhat competitive.

Mulling: Reliving or obsessively replaying a past interaction.

Multitasking: Doing one thing while mentally or physically engaging in another thing.

Mutual gains: The view that through interest-based negotiations the needs of all parties can be met to some extent (also called cooperative, integrative, win-win, interest-based bargaining).

Myers-Briggs Type Indicator: A personality style test based on the Jungian theory of psychological types that assesses preferences in four dichotomous areas: extroversion/introversion, intuition/sensing, feeling/thinking, and perception/judging.

N

Nature: A theory that holds one's personality and behavior are influenced by biological development rather than social development.

Negative interdependence: A state where if one person achieves a goal, the other person will not.

Negative peace: Ending a conflict by forcing others to submit.

Negative settlement range: In bargaining, a gap between the bargaining ranges of the individuals where there is no overlap in their preferred outcomes.

Negotiation: Interactions between parties for the purpose of individual and/or joint goal attainment (also called bargaining).

Negotiation analysis: A tool used to prepare for entering a negotiation by examining factors that may impact the process; a tool used to analyze a past negotiation.

Neutral: In negotiations, a person (usually a third party) who has no relationship to the parties in a dispute or no preference for either party.

Nontraditional family: A family unit that is structurally different than the normative expectation of a mother, father, and their biological children.

Nonviolent resistance: Opposing a current system through protests and strategies that do not commit violence, even though violence may be done to them.

Norm: An unwritten rule that governs how people behave.

Nuclear family: A Western conceptualization of a family group consisting of parents (generally a mother and father) and their children; the core family unit as compared to the extended family.

Nurture: A theory that holds one's personality and behavior are influenced by social development as opposed to biological development.

O

Open-ended questions: Questions designed to elicit answers that demonstrate the speaker's opinions, perceptions, and personal experiences; opposite of close-ended questions.

Opening statement: The first phase in the mediation process where the mediator outlines the mediation process and the guidelines governing roles and expectations to be followed (also called mediator monologue).

Organizational chart: A diagram listing the formal hierarchy of authority in an organization and who reports to whom (see also hierarchy of authority and chain of command).

Organizational culture: The formal or informal norms, rules, and assumptions of how to behave and what it means to be a member of that organization; the expressed values of an organization and its members.

Organizational misbehavior: Any action that violates the organization's formal or informal rules, culture, or policies.

P

PACIER system: A six-step listening system that perceives, attends, comprehends, interprets, evaluates, and responds.

Parties: The individuals in a conflict.

Perception: The process through which stimuli is attended to, interpreted, and evaluated.

Perceptual filters: Biases, values, experiences, attitudes, and other factors that affect how stimuli are interpreted and evaluated.

Personal conflict coaching: See conflict coaching.

Personality style: A relatively stable pattern of thinking and processing information that impacts behavior.

Petition: In social movements, an agitation strategy of seeking redress by going through the official channels.

Polarization: Dividing people into opposing camps and claiming the other side is wrong; simplifying a conflict into diametrically opposed positions.

Position: A demand, proposed solution, or fixed outcome statement.

Positive intentions: The general benefit one hoped for when beginning something new or a new relationship.

Positive interdependence: A state where one person will achieve a personal goal when the other person achieves a personal goal.

Positive peace: Peace gained by transforming individuals or situations where peace is voluntarily achieved.

Positive settlement range: The overlap in bargaining positions in which a settlement may be created.

Postponement: A tactic of deferring discussion of the conflict to a specific time.

Power: The ability to influence others or to bring about desired outcomes.

Power currency: Any possession, trait, or action that is valued by someone else that can be used to gain influence with that person.

Power management: The concept that power may need to be increased or decreased when differences are too great before meaningful conflict management or negotiation can occur (formerly called power balancing).

Privilege: The taking of an advantage—whether earned or unearned; the expectation that an advantage exists.

Probing questions: Questions aimed to uncovers additional details.

Problem-solving mediation: A philosophical approach to mediation that is issue-centered and focused more on problems than on the disputant's emotions.

Process goal: In negotiation, a party's desired means of how an event should happen or a negotiation should proceed.

Promise: A tactic of stating a positive reward will occur if the other party complies with certain conditions.

Promulgation: In social movements, the stage where agitators gain support for the cause.

Provisionalness/Provisionalism: The ability to withhold judgment or offering solutions until all information is on the table; the state of being open-minded to ideas and beliefs that are not personally held.

Pseudo-conflict: Conflicts caused by misinterpretations and misinformation.

Psychodynamic theory: Freud's psychological theory that behavior is motivated by both the conscious and subconscious mind where the id, ego, and superego are all vying for control.

Purgation: In social movements, the control strategy of eliminating the leaders of the opposition.

Q

Quality control circle: A strategy adopted from Japanese management theory where individuals from different parts of the organization work together to resolve problems and make suggestions for improvement.

Quid pro quo: A negotiation strategy of offering something for something.

R

Rapport talk: Tannen's description of a cooperative conversational style engaged in for the purpose of building a relationship or affirming the connection between the parties.

Reality testing: Comparing decisions to feasibility and workability criteria.

Reconciliation: The rebuilding of a relationship broken or tarnished in conflict.

Referent power: Individual power derived from association with power sources or personality traits that others value.

Reformed sinner: A negotiation tactic of admitting to past mistakes and seeking a new beginning.

Reframing: A technique to move an issue or topic from a narrow interest or negative frame into a larger or neutral frame where defensiveness is decreased and productive negotiation is encouraged.

Relationship goal: A party's preference for the depth or type of connection to another person.

Report talk: Tannen's description of a competitive conversational style engaged in for the purpose of convincing the other, presenting definitive information, or otherwise gaining a competitive advantage in the interaction.

Responsiveness: The level of emotion displayed or information given.

Restitutional forgiveness: Forgiving after being compensated for your loss (also called compensational forgiveness).

Restorative justice: A view that fairness is better served by bringing balance to a community or a victim by requiring reparations and or acknowledgments by the offender in addition to or in lieu of punishment by the system.

Retrospective goals: What one says one's goals were after a conflict episode ends.

Revengeful forgiveness: Forgiving only after one has hurt the one who hurt you.

Reward power: Power derived from one's ability to provide benefits to others.

Rights-based: Decision-making or resolution criteria based on legal or other institutionalized rights (see adjudication).

Risky shift phenomenon: An effect where people become more extreme in their opinions through interactions with others holding similar views; a tendency of a group to engage in more risky decisions or actions than individuals would independent of the group.

Role: A function performed by an individual.

Role emergence: The process in relationships or groups where individuals choose to adopt particular task or maintenance roles.

Root culture: The cultural group a person was born into or received the most influence from as a child.

S

Scarce resources: Anything perceived to be in short supply.

Schema: A personally constructed attitudinal pattern or frame that affects how one selects and interprets stimuli.

Selective attention: Focusing only on those things that one expects to see or hear; consciously or subconsciously attending to particular stimuli and forgoing other stimuli.

Selective exposure: Focusing on or actively seeking sources of information or input while simultaneously limiting or eschewing other sources of information, usually with the result of reinforcing previously held opinions.

Selective perception: The process of filtering out input during the perception process or focusing only on what one expects to see.

Self-actualization: From Maslow's hierarchy of needs, the drive an individual has to reach or actualize one's potential.

Self-construal: A view of oneself; how people construct their personal cultural identities.

Self-concept: A relatively stable set of perceptions, values, attitudes, and beliefs an individual holds about oneself.

Self-identity: One's view of oneself.

Self-serving bias: In attribution theory, where one ascribes motivations for personal behavior to a personal character trait when it is most flattering and to situation constraints to diminish personal responsibility (the precise opposite of how motivations are attributed to others).

Semi-apologies: A statement that has the form of an apology without taking responsibility for the action that caused the offense.

Sense-making: The process by which individuals weave together facts, feelings, and inferences to explain the world.

Settlement range: The area of overlap between negotiators' offers.

Shadow negotiation: Subtle, sometimes discriminatory, tactics to reduce an individual's power and influence.

Silent forgiveness: Forgiving another individual but not telling that person.

Silo mentality: Only talking to or seeing the perspective of one's own workgroup.

Sincere apologies: Apologies that are truthful and well intended.

Social exchange theory: A relational theory suggesting individuals make choices about relationships by evaluating the personal rewards, costs, and expected profits/benefits involved in maintaining that relationship.

Social harmony forgiveness: Forgiving because one believes peace is better than conflict or forgiving to maintain good social relationships.

Socialization/Cultural socialization: Theories that explain differences in behavioral patterns, such as gendered behaviors, as learned through cultural and societal influences.

Social learning theory: A behavioral theory that holds that individuals learn what attitudes and behaviors are appropriate through observation and social interaction.

Social styles model: Interpersonal styles identified by trained observers along assertiveness and responsiveness dimensions.

Solidification: In social movements, an agitator strategy where group members bond together and generate shared symbols, slogans, and identifiers to unite the group around the cause.

State anger: Anger caused by a momentary state of mind or a situation that will abate (the opposite of trait anger).

State forgiveness: Forgiveness based on a specific situation (see also trait forgiveness).

Stereotype: A generalization that ascribes the same characteristics to all members of a group.

Stereotype confirmation: Individual evidence of observed behaviors that seem to prove a stereotype correct.

Storming: The conflict phase of group development.

Structure: The external framework, rules, setting, and processes in which a conflict occurs.

Substantive goal: Goals around tangible resources.

Systems theory: A theory that highlights the complex nature of life and holds that the interdependency of all the relationships among individuals in a system, as well as the surrounding environment, must be considered to understand the whole.

Style: A person's habitual and/or preferred way of operating in the world (see conversational style and personality style).

T

Taboo: A forbidden behavior or topic.

Tag question: A powerless form of speech that ends a statement with a question (e.g., "doesn't it?").

Taking value: Claiming resources or credit for solutions; depleting value that previously existed.

Task role: A role assumed to promote movement toward accomplishment of a task goal.

Theories: Tentative explanations for observed behaviors.

Third party: In conflict, a person who is not a party to the conflict who assists the conflicting parties to reach a settlement (see arbitration and mediation).

Threat: A tactic promising negative sanctions will occur if the other party does not comply (see coercion).

Tit for tat: A negotiation strategy of doing to the other party what they do to you.

Topic: The general conversational area in which a conflict issue may be embedded.

Toxic secrets: Family secrets that conceal information destructive to one or more family members.

Trait anger: A relatively stable personality style that responds to many situations with anger (the opposite of state anger).

Trait forgiveness: A relatively stable predisposition to forgive (see also state forgiveness).

Transformation: Moving from one state or condition to another; changing a key element that sustains a conflict.

Transactional model: The idea that communication occurs as a simultaneous, complex process.

Transactional process: A simultaneous, ever-changing, interactive flow of communication.

Trust: The belief that another person is dependable, consistent, and will do what is promised.

Truth and reconciliation process: Typically, a large group effort to admit facts about past harms to a group, accept responsibility, and begin a reconciliation process.

U

Unearned privilege: The taking of a social or other advantage on the basis of social ranking.

Unforgiveness: The active state of recalling and reliving a past hurtful event.

Universal team approach: A strategy to move competitive situations to cooperative situations by putting everyone on the same team rather than on opposing teams.

V

Validating: Recognizing the other person's thoughts or feelings without agreement or criticism (see empathic listening, emotional paraphrase, and feeling paraphrase).

Values: Deeply seated beliefs and core ideas about right and wrong.

Variable: A specific trait, behavior, factor, or pattern isolated for investigation.

Verbal aggressiveness: Ultra argumentativeness using personal attacks, name-calling, and other aggressive tactics.

W–Z

Whiteness: A concept surrounding unearned social and other privileges taken on the basis of race.

Winner's curse: Being victorious in a negotiation, but paying too much or not really wanting the outcome.

Withdraw-complain cycle: A pattern where one party avoids contact with the other person involved in the conflict, but talks about the conflict or complains about it to other people.

Zero-sum: A distributive view that resources are limited. As they are allocated, the amount of resources left ultimately will reach zero.

References

Accattoli, L. (1998). *When a pope asks forgiveness: The mea culpa's of John Paul II* (J. Aumann, Trans.). Boston: Pauline Books & Media.

Adair, W., Brett, J., Lempereur, A., Okumura, T., Shikhirev, P., Tinsley, C., et al. (2004). Culture and negotiation strategy. *Negotiation Journal*, pp. 87–111.

Adler, R. B., & Proctor, R. F. (2007). *Looking out. Looking in* (12th ed.). Belmont, CA: Wadsworth.

Afifi, W. A., & Guerrero, L. K. (2000). Motivations underlying topic avoidance in close relationships. In S. Petronio (Ed.), *Balancing the secrets of private disclosures* (pp. 165–179). Mahwah, NJ: Erlbaum.

Allen, B. J. (2000). "Learning the ropes": A black feminist standpoint analysis. In P. M. Buzzanell (Ed.), *Rethinking organizational & managerial communication from feminist perspectives* (pp. 177–208). Thousand Oaks, CA: Sage.

Allen, M. W., Coopman, S. J., Hart, J. L., & Walker, K. L. (2007). Workplace surveillance and managing privacy boundaries. *Management Communication Quarterly, 21*(1), 172–200.

Anderson, C. A., Carnagey, N. L., & Eubanks, J. (2003). Exposure to violent media: The effects of songs with violent lyrics on aggressive thoughts and feelings. *Journal of Personality and Social Psychology, 84*(5), 960–971.

Andrews, M. (2000). Forgiveness in context. *Journal of Moral Education, 29*(1), 75–86.

Ashkanasy, N. M., Zerbe, W. J., & Hartel, C. E. J. (2002a). Managing emotions in a changing workplace. In N. M. Ashkanasy, W. J. Zerbe, & C. E. J. Hartel (Eds.), *Managing emotions in the workplace* (pp. 3–22). Armonk, NY: M.E. Sharpe.

Ashkanasy, N. M., Zerbe, W. J., & Hartel, C. E. J. (2002b). What are the management tools that come out of this? In N. M. Ashkanasy, W. J. Zerbe, & C. E. J. Hartel (Eds.), *Managing emotions in the workplace* (pp. 285–297). Armonk, NY: M.E. Sharpe.

Ayoko, O. B., Callan, V. J., & Hartel, C. E. J. (2003). Workplace conflict, bullying, and counterproductive behaviors. *The International Journal of Organizational Analysis, 11*(4), 283–301.

Bacharach, S. B., & Lawler, E. J. (1986). Power dependence and power paradoxes in bargaining. *Negotiation Journal*, pp. 167–174.

Bachman, G. F., & Guerrero, L. K. (2006). Forgiveness, apology, and communicative responses to hurtful events. *Communication Reports, 19*(1), 45–56.

Bagshaw, M. (2000). Emotional intelligence: Training people to be affective so they can be effective. *Industrial and Commercial Training, 32*(2), 61–65.

Barge, J. K. (2001). Creating healthy communities through affirmative conflict communication. *Conflict Resolution Quarterly, 19*(1), 89–101.

Barnlund, D. C. (1970). A transactional model of communication. In K. K. Sereno & D. Mortenson (Eds.), *Foundations of communication theory* (pp. 83–102). New York: Harper & Row.

Barron, L. A. (2003). Ask and you shall receive? Gender differences in negotiators' beliefs about requests for a higher salary. *Human Relations, 56*(6), 635–662.

Baxter, L. A. (1988). A dialectical perspective on communication strategies in a relational development. In S. W. Duck (Ed.), *Handbook of personal relationships: Theory research and interventions* (pp. 257–273). New York: Wiley.

Baxter, L. A., & Montgomery, B. M. (1996). *Relating: Dialogues and dialectics.* New York: Guilford Press.

Bazerman, M. H., & Samuelson, W. F. (1983). I won the auction but don't want the prize. *Journal of Conflict Resolution, 27*(4), 618–634.

Beatty, M. J., & Dobos, J. A. (1992). Adult sons' satisfaction with their relationship with fathers and person–group (father) communication apprehension. *Communication Quarterly, 40*(2), 162–176.

Beaumont, S. L., & Wagner, S. L. (2004). Adolescent–parent verbal conflict: The roles of conversational styles and disgust emotions. *Journal of Language and Social Psychology, 23*(3), 338–368.

Beebe, S. A., & Masterson, J. T. (2006). *Communicating in small groups* (8th ed.). Boston: Pearson Education.

Bevan, J. L., & Samter, W. (2004). Toward a broader conceptualization of jealousy in close relationships: Two exploratory studies. *Communication Studies, 55*(1), 14–28.

Bippus, A. M. (2003). Humor motives, qualities, and reactions in recalled conflict episodes. *Western Journal of Communication, 67*(4), 413–426.

Blase, J., & Blase, J. (2003). *Breaking the silence: Overcoming the problem of principal mistreatment of teachers.* Thousand Oaks, CA: Corwin Press.

Blessing, K. (2006). Communication coaching. Mediate.com.

Bok, S. (2004). Truthfulness, deceit, and trust. In C. Menkel–Meadow & M. Wheeler (Eds.), *What's fair: Ethics for negotiators* (pp.79–90). San Francisco: John Wiley & Sons.

Bonach, K. (2005). Factors contributing to quality coparenting: Implications for family policy. *Journal of Divorce & Remarriage, 43*(3/4), 79–103.

Bonach, K., Sales, E., & Koeske, G. (2005). Gender differences in perceptions of coparenting quality among expartners. *Journal of Divorce & Remarriage, 43*(1/2), 1–28.

Boucaut, R. (2003). Workplace bullying: Overcoming organizational barriers and the way ahead. In W. J. Pammer & J. Killian (Eds.), *Handbook of conflict management* (pp. 148–168). New York: Marcel Dekker.

Bowers, J. W., Ochs, D. J., & Jensen, R. J. (1993). *The rhetoric of agitation and control* (2nd ed.). Prospect Heights, IL: Waveland.

Brett, J. M. (2000). Culture and negotiation. *International Journal of Psychology, 35*(2), 97–104.

Brew, F. P., & Cairns, D. R. (2004). Styles of managing interpersonal workplace conflict in relation to status and face concerns: A study with Anglos and Chinese. *The International Journal of Conflict Management, 15*(1), 27–56.

Brinkert, R. (2006). Conflict coaching: Advancing the conflict resolution field by developing an individual disputant process. *Conflict Resolution Quarterly, 23*(4), 517–528.

Brodnax, M., & Mazur, C. (2008). Delivering concrete results: The federal government's use of ADR. *ACResolution, 7*(3), 6–7.

Bullying at work still a major concern despite progress. (2005-2006). *Engineering Management, 15*(6), 4.

Burrell, N. A., & Fitzpatrick, M. A. (1990). The psychological reality of marital conflict. In D. D. Cahn (Ed.), *Intimates in conflict: A communication perspective* (pp. 167–186). Hillsdale, NJ: Erlbaum.

Bush, R. A., & Folger, J. P. (1994). *The promise of mediation.* San Francisco: Jossey-Bass.

Buysse, A., De Clercq, A., Verhofstadt, L., Heene, E., Roeyers, H., & Van Oost, P. (2000). Dealing with relational conflict: A picture in milliseconds. *Journal of Social and Personal Relationships, 17*(4–5), 574–597.

Cahn, D. D., & Abigail, R. A. (2007). *Managing conflict through communication.* Boston: Pearson.

Cai, D. A., & Fink, E. L. (2002). Conflict style differences between individualists and collectivists. *Communication Monographs, 69*(1), 67–87.

Calabrese, K. R. (2000). Interpersonal conflict and sarcasm in the workplace. *Genetic, Social, and General Psychology Monographs, 126*(4), 459–494.

Chapell, M., Casey, D., De la Cruz, C., Ferrell, J., Forman, J., Lipkin, R., et al. (2004). Bullying in college by students and teachers. *Adolescence, 39*(153), 53–64.

Cherniss, C., & Adler, M. (2000). *Promoting emotional intelligence in organizations.* Alexandria, VA: American Society for Training and Development Publications.

Cloke, K., & Goldsmith, J. (2000). *Resolving personal and organizational conflict: Stories of transformation and forgiveness.* San Francisco: Jossey-Bass.

Coakley, C. G., & Wolvin, A. D. (1997). Listening in the parent-teen relationship. *International Journal of Listening, 11,* 88–126.

Cohen, J. R. (2003). Adversaries? Partners? How about counterparts? On metaphors in the practice and teaching of negotiation and dispute resolution. *Conflict Resolution Quarterly, 20*(4), 433–440.

Coleman, P. T. (2000). Power and conflict. In M. Deutsch & P. T. Coleman (Eds.), *The handbook of conflict resolution: Theory and practice* (pp. 108–130). San Francisco: Jossey-Bass.

Coloroso, B. (2003). *The bully, the bullied, and the bystander.* New York: HarperCollins.

Conerly, K., & Tripathi, A. (2004, Summer). What is your conflict style? Understanding and dealing with your conflict style. *Journal for Quality & Participation,* pp. 16–20.

Cooley, J. W. (Ed.). (2005). *Creative problem solver's handbook for negotiators and mediators* (Vol. 2). Washington, DC: ABA Section of Dispute Resolution.

Cramer, D. (2002). Linking conflict management behaviours and relational satisfaction: The intervening role of conflict outcome satisfaction. *Journal of Social and Personal Relationships, 19*(3), 425–432.

Creo, R. A. (2005). Creative problem-solving techniques and tactics. In J. W. Cooley (Ed.), *Creative problem solver's handbook for negotiators and mediators* (pp. 42–54) (Vol. 2). Washington, DC: ABA Section of Dispute Resolution.

Crum, T. F. (1987). *The magic of conflict.* New York: Touchstone.

Cunningham, C. E., Cunningham, L. J., Martorelli, V., Tran, A., Young, J., & Zacharias, R. (1998). The effects of primary division, student-mediated conflict resolution programs on playground aggression. *Journal of Child Psychology and Psychiatry, 39*(5), 653–662.

Cupach, W. R., & Canary, D. J. (1997). *Competence in inter-personal conflict.* Prospect Heights, IL: Waveland.

Dana, D. (1999). *Measuring the financial cost of organizational conflict.* MTI Publications.

Dana, D. (2003). Retaliatory cycles: Introducing the elements of conflict. In J. Gordon (Ed.), *Pfeiffer's classic activities for managing conflict at work* (pp. 167–172). New York: Wiley.

Dana, D. (2005). *Managing differences: How to build better relationships at work and home.* Prairie Village, KS: MTI Publications.

Danitz, T., & Strobel, W. P. (1999). The Internet's impact on activism: The case of Burma. *Studies in Conflict & Terrorism, 22*(3), 257–269.

De Dreu, C. K. W., & Weingart, L. R. (2003). Task versus relationship conflict, team performance, and team member satisfaction: A meta-analysis. *Journal of Applied Psychology, 88*(4), 741–749.

Delia, J. G., & Crockett, W. H. (1973). Social schemas, cognitive complexity and the learning of social structures. *Journal of Personality, 41*(3), 413–429.

Deutsch, M. (2000a). Introduction. In M. Deutsch & P. T. Coleman (Eds.), *The handbook of conflict resolution: Theory and practice* (pp. 1–17). San Francisco: Jossey-Bass.

Deutsch, M. (2000b). Cooperation and competition. In M. Deutsch & P. T. Coleman (Eds.), *The handbook of conflict resolution: Theory and practice* (pp. 21–40). San Francisco: Jossey-Bass.

De Vries, J., & De Paor, J. (2005). Healing and reconciliation in the L.I.V.E. program in Ireland. *Peace and Change, 30*(3), 329–358.

Dindia, K. (2000). Sex differences in self-disclosure, reciprocity of self-disclosure, and self-disclosure and liking: Three meta-analyses reviewed. In S. Petronio (Ed.), *Balancing the secrets of private disclosures* (pp. 21–35). Mahwah, NJ: Erlbaum.

Downs, C., & Adrian, A. (2004). *Assessing organizational communication: Strategic communication audits.* New York: Guilford Press.

Duck, S., Kirkpatrick, D. C., & Foley, M. K. (2006). Difficulty in relating: Some conceptual problems with "problematic relationships" and difficulties with "difficult people." In D. C. Kirkpatrick, S. Duck, & M. K. Foley (Eds.), *Relating difficulty: The processes of constructing and managing difficult interactions* (pp. 1–14). Mahwah, NJ: Erlbaum.

Elbing, C., & Elbing, A. (1994). *Militant managers.* New York: Irwin Professional Publishing.

Emerson, R. M. (1962). Power-dependence relations. *American Sociological Review, 27,* 31–41.

Engleberg, I. N., & Wynn, D. R. (2007). *Working in groups: Communication principles and strategies* (4th ed.). Boston: Allyn & Bacon.

Enright, R. D. (2001). *Forgiveness is a choice.* Washington, DC: American Psychological Association.

Enright, R. D., & Fitzgibbons, R. P. (2000). *Helping clients forgive.* Washington, DC: American Psychological Association.

Exline, J. J., & Baumeister, R. F. (2000). Expressing forgiveness and repentance. In M. E. McCullough, K. I. Pargament, & C. E. Thorensen (Eds.), *Forgiveness theory, research, and practice* (pp. 133–155). New York: Guilford Press.

Falcone, P. (2000, February). Five questions. *HR Magazine,* pp. 129–136.

Farrell, L. U. (2002, March 15). Workplace bullying's high cost. *Business Journal.*

Field, T. (1996). *Bully in sight: How to predict, resist, challenge and combat workplace bullying.* Oxfordshire, UK: Wessex Press.

Fiese, B. H., Tomcho, T. J., Douglas, M., Josephs, K., Poltrock, S., & Baker, T. (2002). A review of 50 years of research on naturally occurring family routines and rituals: Cause for celebration? *Journal of Family Psychology, 16*(4), 381–390.

Fincham, F. D., Beach, S. R. H., & Davila, J. (2004). Forgiveness and conflict resolution in marriage. *Journal of Family Psychology, 18*(1), 72–81.

Fisher, R., Ury, W., & Patton, B. (1993). Negotiation power: Ingredients in an ability to influence the other side. In L. Hall (Ed.), *Negotiation: Strategies for mutual gain* (pp. 3–13). Newbury Park, CA: Sage.

Fitzpatrick, M. A., Marshall, L. J., Leutwiler, T. J., & Krcmar, M. (1996). The effect of family communication environments on children's social behavior during middle childhood. *Communication Research, 23*(4), 379–406.

Folger, J. P., Poole, M. S., & Stutman, R. K. (2005). *Working through conflict: Strategies for relationships, groups and organizations* (5th ed.). Boston: Pearson Education.

Foo, M. D., Elfenbein, H. A., Tan, H. H., & Aik, V. C. (2004). Emotional intelligence and negotiation: The tension between creating and claiming value. *The International Journal of Conflict Management, 15*(4), 411–429.

Forsyth, D. R. (2006). *Group dynamics* (4th ed.). Belmont, CA: Thomson Higher Education.

Fox, A. B., Bukatko, D., Hallahan, M. & Crawford, M. (2007). The medium makes a difference: Gender similarities and differences in Instant Messaging. *Journal of Language and Social Psychology, 26*(4), 389–397.

Freed, A. F. (2004). Epilogue: Reflections on language and gender research. In J. Holmes & M. Meyerhoff (Eds.), *The handbook of language and gender.* Blackwell Reference Online. Retrieved April 23, 2008, from http://www.blackwellreference.com

Freedman, S. (1998). Forgiveness and reconciliation: The importance of understanding how they differ. *Counseling and Values, 42*(3), 200–216.

Freiberg, P. (1998). Bullying in the workplace is a violence warning sign. *APA Monitor, 29*(7).

French, J. (1956). A formal theory of social power. *Psychological Review, 63*, 181–194.

Fried, S., & Fried, P. (2003). *Bullies, targets and witnesses: Helping children break the pain chain.* New York: M. Evans and Co.

Friedman, R. A., & Currall, S. C. (2003). Conflict escalation: Dispute exacerbating elements of e-mail communication. *Human Relations, 56*(11), 1325–1347.

Funk, J. B., Baldacci, H. B., Pasold, T., & Baumgardner, J. (2004). Violence exposure in real-life, video games, television, movies, and the Internet: Is there desensitization? *Journal of Adolescence, 27*(1), 23–39.

Furlong, G. T. (2005). *The conflict resolution toolbox.* Mississausa, Canada: Wiley.

Galtung, J. (1969). Violence, peace and peace research. *Journal of Peace Research*, pp. 167–191.

Galvin, K. M., & Brommel, B. J. (2000). *Family communication: Cohension and change* (5th ed.) New York: Longman.

Galvin, K. M., Dickson, F. C., & Marrow, S. R. (2006). System theory: Patterns and (w)holes in family communication. In D. O. Brathwaite & L. A. Baxter (Eds.), *Engaging theories in family communication* (pp. 309–324). Thousand Oaks, CA: Sage.

Garcia, E. (2000). Negotiating negotiation: The collaborative production of resolution in small claims mediation hearings. *Discourse and Society, 11*(3), 315–343.

Gassin, E. A. (2001). Interpersonal forgiveness from an Eastern Orthodox perspective. *Journal of Psychology and Theology, 29*(3), 187–200.

Gerritsen, M., & Verckens, J. P. (2006). Raising students' intercultural awareness and preparing them for intercultural business (communication) by e-mail. *Business Communication Quarterly, 69*(1), 50–59.

Gibb, J. (1961). Defensive communication. *Journal of Communication, 11*, 141–168.

Gibson, J. L. (2006). The contributions of truth to reconciliation: Lessons from South Africa. *Journal of Conflict Resolution, 50*(3), 409–432.

Giebels, E., & Janssen, O. (2005). Conflict stress and reduced well-being at work: The buffering effect of third-party help. *European Journal of Work and Organizational Psychology, 14*(2), 137–155.

Gill, D. S., Christensen, A., & Fincham, F. D. (1999). Predicting martial satisfaction from behavior: Do all roads really lead to Rome? *Personal Relationships, 6*, 369–387.

Glascock, J. (2003). Gender, race, and aggression in newer TV networks' primetime programming. *Communication Quarterly, 51*(1), 90–100.

Glendinning, P. M. (2001). Workplace bullying: Curing the cancer of the American workforce. *Public Personal Management, 30*(3), 269–287.

Goens, G. A. (2002). The courage to risk forgiveness. *School Administrator, 59*(2), 32–35.

Golish, T. D. (2000). Changes in closeness between adult children and their parents: A turning point analysis. *Communication Reports, 13*(2), 79–98.

Gottman, J., Levenson, R., & Woodin, E. (2001). Facial expressions during marital conflict. *Journal of Family Communication, 1*(1), 37–57.

Gottman, J. M. (1999). *The marriage clinic: A scientifically-based marital therapy.* New York: Norton.

Gottman, J. M., & Silver, N. S. (1999). *The seven principles for making marriages work.* New York: Three Rivers Press.

Graupp, P., & Wrona, R. J. (2006). *The TWI workbook: Essential skills for supervisors.* New York: Productivity Press.

Greensboro Truth and Reconciliation Commission Final Report Released. (2006, May 25).

Gregorc, A. F. (2006). *Adult's guide to style.* Maynard, CA: Gabriel Systems.

Gudykunst, W. B., & Kim, Y. Y. (2003). *Communicating with strangers: An approach to intercultural communication.* Boston: McGraw-Hill.

Hale, C. L., Tardy, R. W., & Farley-Lucas, B. (1995). Children's talk about conflict: An exploration of the voices and views of the "experts." *Discourse & Society, 6*(3), 407–427.

Hall, E. T. (1976). *Beyond culture.* Garden City, NY: Anchor.

Hammer, M. (2002). *Resolving conflict across the cultural divide: Differences in intercultural conflict styles.* Hammer Consulting.

Hammer, M. R. (2004). Crisis expertise in mediation. *ACResolution, 32*(2), 14–17.

Hammer, M. R. (2005). The intercultural conflict style inventory: A conceptual framework and measure of intercultural conflict resolution approaches. *International Journal of Intercultural relations, 29*, 675–695.

Harari, O. (2002). *The leadership secrets of Colin Powell.* New York: McGraw-Hill.

Harden-Fritz, J. M. (2002). How do I dislike thee? Let me count the ways. *Management Communication Quarterly, 15*(3), 410–438.

Hargie, O., & Dickson, D. (2004). *Skilled interpersonal communication: Research, theory and practice.* New York: Routledge.

Harris, A., Luskin, F., Norman, S. B., Standard, S., Bruning, J., Evans, S., et al. (2006). Effects of a group forgiveness intervention on forgiveness, perceived stress, and trait-anger. *Journal of Clinical Psychology, 62*(6), 715–733.

Harris, T. E., & Sherblom, J. C. (2005). *Small group and team communication* (3rd ed.). Boston: Pearson Education.

Harris, T. M. (2004). Interracial communication. *Communication Teacher, 18*(4), 132–135.

Hart, R. P., & Burks, D. M. (1972). Rhetorical sensitivity and social interaction. *Speech Monographs, 39*(2), 75–91.

Hebein, R. (1999). The prevention and cure of campus disputes. *New directions for teaching and learning, 77,* 87–95.

Henderson, M. (2005). *Forgiveness: Breaking the chain of hate* (2nd ed.). Portland, OR: Arnica.

Herrick, J. A. (2009). *The history and theory of rhetoric* (4th ed.). Boston: Allyn & Bacon.

Herrmann, N. D. S., & McWhirter, J. J. (2003). Anger & aggression management in young adolescents: An experimental validation of the SCARE program. *Education and Treatment of Children, 26*(3), 273–302.

Heydenberk, R. A., Heydenberk, W. R., & Tzenova, V. (2006). Conflict resolution and bully prevention: Skills for school success. *Conflict Resolution Quarterly, 24*(1), 55–69.

Hicks, R., & Hicks, K. (1999). *Boomers, Xers, and other strangers: Understanding the generational differences that divide us.* Wheaton, IL: Tyndale House.

Hobman, E. V., Bordia, P., Irmer, B., & Chang, A. (2002). The expression of conflict in computer-mediated and face-to-face groups. *Small Group Research, 33*(4), 439–465.

Holt, J. L., & DeVore, C. J. (2005). Culture, gender, organizational role, and styles of conflict resolution: A meta-analysis. *International Journal of Intercultural Relations, 29,* 165–196.

Honeycutt, J. M., & Ford, S. G. (2001). Mental imagery and intrapersonal communication: A review of research on imagined interactions (IIs) and current developments. In W. B. Gudykunst (Ed.), *Communication Yearbook 25* (pp. 315–345). Thousand Oaks, CA: Sage.

Hook, J. (2004, 17 October). The race for the White House. *Los Angeles Times.*

Horn, S. (2002). *Take the bully by the horns.* New York: St. Martin's Press.

House, The. (2000). C-SPAN. Retrieved June 10, 2008, from www.c-span.org/questions/weekly 39.asp

Huang, L. (1999). Family communication patterns and personality characteristics. *Communication Quarterly, 47*(2), 230–243.

Hughes, M., Patterson, L. B., & Terrell, J. B. (2005). *Emotional intelligence in action.* San Francisco: Pfeiffer.

Hullett, C. R., & Tamborini, R. (2001). When I'm within my rights: An expectancy-based model of actor evaluative and behavioral responses to compliance-resistance strategies. *Communication Studies, 52*(1), 1–16.

Imber-Black, E. (1993). *Secrets in families and family therapy.* New York: Norton.

James, J. (1986). *The slug manual: The rise and fall of criticism.* Seattle: Bronwen.

Jamieson, K. H. (1997, March 10). Civility in the House of Representatives. Annenberg Public Policy Center Report. Philadelphia: Annenberg Public Policy Center of the University of Pennsylvania.

Jamieson, K. H. (2000). *Incivility and its discontents: Lessons learned from studying civility in the U.S. House of Representatives.* Needham Heights, MA: Allyn & Bacon.

Janis, I. L. (1972). *Victims of groupthink: A psychological study of foreign-policy decisions and fiascoes.* Boston: Houghton Mifflin.

Jarecke, G. W., & Plant, N. K. (2003). *Seeking civility: Common courtesy and the common law.* Boston: Northeastern University Press.

Jorgenson, J. (1994). Situated address and the social construction of "in-law" relationships. *The Southern Communication Journal, 59*(3), 196–204.

Jost, P. J., & Weitzel, U. (2007). *Strategic conflict management: A game-theoretical introduction.* Cheltenham, UK: Edward Elger.

Jourdain, K. (2004). Communication styles and conflict. *The Journal for Quality & Participation, 27*(2), 23–25.

Kahn, R., & Kellner, D. (2004). New media and Internet activism: From the "Battle of Seattle" to "blogging." *New Media & Society, 6*(1), 87–95.

Katz, T. Y., & Block, C. J. (2000). Process and outcome goal orientation in conflict situations: The importance of framing. In M. Deutsch & P. T. Coleman (Eds.), *The handbook of conflict resolution: Theory and practice* (pp. 279–288). San Francisco: Jossey-Bass.

Kellerman, K., & Cole, T. (1994). Classifying compliance gaining messages: Taxonomic disorder and strategic confusion. *Communication Theory, 1,* 3–60.

Kelly, C. (2004). Assertion theory. In J. Gordon (Ed.), *Pfeiffer's classic activities for interpersonal communication* (pp. 91–98). New York: Wiley.

Keltner, J. W. (1987). *Mediation: Toward a civilized system of dispute resolution.* Annandale, VA: Speech Communication Association.

Kim, M.-S. (2007). The four cultures of cultural research. *Communication Monographs, 74*(2), 279–285.

Kim, M.-S., Lee, H., Kim, I. D., & Hunter, J. E. (2004). A test of a cultural model of conflict styles. *Journal of Asian Pacific Communication, 14*(2), 197–222.

Kim, M.-S., & Leung, T. (2000). A multicultural view of conflict management styles: Review and critical synthesis. In M. Roloff (Ed.), *Communication yearbook 23*, (pp. 227–269). Thousand Oaks, CA: Sage.

Kimmel, P. R. (2000). Culture and conflict. In M. Deutsch & P. T. Coleman (Eds.), *The handbook of conflict resolution: Theory and practice* (pp. 453–474). San Francisco: Jossey-Bass.

Kline, S. L., & Stafford, L. (2004). A comparison of interaction rules and interaction frequency in relationship to marital quality. *Communication Reports, 17*(1), 11–26.

Knickerbocker, B. (2006, March 7). Crackdown on animal-rights activists. *The Christian Science Monitor.*

Koerner, A. F., & Fitzpatrick, M. A. (2002). You never leave your family in a fight: The impact of family origin in conflict behavior in romantic relationships. *Communication Studies, 53*(3), 234–251.

Koerner, A. F., & Fitzpatrick, M. A. (2004). Communication in intact families. In A. L. Vangelisti (Ed.), *Handbook of family communication* (pp. 177–195). Mahwah, NJ: Erlbaum.

Koerner, A. F., & Fitzpatrick, M. A. (2006). Family communication patterns theory: A social cognitive approach. In D. O. Braithwaite & L. A. Baxter (Eds.), *Engaging theories in family communication* (pp. 50–65). Thousand Oaks, CA: Sage.

Kohn, A. (1986). *No contest: The case against competition.* Boston: Houghton Mifflin.

Kolb, D. M. (2004). Staying in the game or changing it: An analysis of *moves* and *turns* in negotiation. *Negotiation Journal, 20*(2), 253–268.

Kolb, D. M., & Williams J. (2003). *Everyday negotiation: Navigating the agendas in bargaining.* San Francisco: Jossey-Bass.

Kowalski, R. M., Limber, S. P., & Agatston, P. W. (2008). *Cyber bullying: Bullying in the digital age.* Carlton, Australia: Blackwell.

Kray, L. J., Thompson, L., & Galinsky, A. (2001). Battle of the sexes: Gender stereotype confirmation and reactance in negotiation. *Journal of Personality and Social Psychology, 80*(6), 942–958.

Kray, L. J., Thompson, L., & Lind, E. A. (2005). It's a bet! A problem-solving approach promotes the construction of contingency agreements. *Personality and Social Psychology Bulletin, 31*(8), 1039–1051.

Krcmar, M. (1996). Family communication patterns, discourse behavior, and child television viewing. *Human Communication Research, 23*(2), 251–277.

Krcmar, M., & Valkenburg, P. M. (1999). A scale to assess children's moral interpretations of justified and unjustified violence and its relationship to television viewing. *Communication Research, 26*(5), 608–634.

Krupnick, M. (2008, April 15). UC seeks law to crack down on animal rights protests. *Contra Costa Times.*

Kuhn, T., & Poole, M. S. (2000). Do conflict management styles affect group decision making? *Human Communication Research, 26*(4), 558–590.

Lancaster, L. C., & Stillman, D. (2002). *When generations collide.* New York: HarperCollins.

Landau, S., Landau, B., & Landau, D. (2001). *From conflicts to creativity: How resolving workplace disagreements can inspire innovation and productivity.* San Francisco: Jossey-Bass.

Landry, D. C., Rachal, K. C., Rachal, W. S., & Rosenthal, G. T. (2005). Expressive disclosure following an interpersonal conflict: Can merely writing about an interpersonal offense motivate forgiveness? *Counseling and Clinical Psychology Journal, 2*(1), 2–14.

Lawler, K. A., Younger, J. W., Piferi, R. L., Jobe, R. L., Edmondson, K. A., & Jones, W. H. (2005). The unique effects of forgiveness on health: An exploration of pathways. *Journal of Behavioral Medicine, 28*(2), 157–167.

Lawless, J. (2004, September 1). Britain cracks down on behavior ranging from shouting to sarcasm. *Idaho Statesman*, p. A5.

Lax., D. A., & Sebenius, J. K. (1986). *The manager as negotiator: Bargaining for cooperation and competitive gain.* New York: The Free Press.

Leary, M. R., Koch, E. J., & Hechenbleikner, N. R. (2001). Emotional responses to interpersonal rejection. In M. R. Leary (Ed.), *Interpersonal rejection* (pp. 145–166). New York: Oxford University Press.

Lee, J. H. (1991, July 6). Slaying may be linked to pair's use of sign language. *Los Angeles Times*, p. B3.

Leon, K., & Angst, E. (2005). Portrayals of stepfamilies in film: Using media images in remarriage education. *Family Relations, 54,* 3–23.

Levinson, M. H. (2006). Anger management and violence prevention: A holistic solution. *ETC, 63*(2), 187–199.

Lewicki, R. J., & Robinson, R. J. (2004). Ethical and unethical bargaining tactics: An empirical study. In C. Menkel-Meadow & M. Wheeler (Eds.), *What's fair: Ethics for negotiators* (pp. 221–220). San Francisco: Jossey-Bass.

Lewicki, R. J., & Wiethoff, C. (2000). Trust, trust development, and trust repair. In M. Deutsch & P. T. Coleman (Eds.), *The handbook of conflict resolution: Theory and practice* (pp. 86–107). San Francisco: Jossey-Bass.

Lingley, D. (2006). Apologies across cultures: An analysis of intercultural communication problems raised in the Ehime Maru incident. *Asian EFL Journal, 8*(1). Retrieved December 1, 2008, from http://www.asian-efl-journal.com/March_06_dl.php

Lipsky, D. B., & Seeber, R. L. (2006). Managing organizational conflicts. In J. G. Oetzel & S. Ting-Toomey (Eds.), *Handbook of conflict communication: Integrating theory, research, and practice* (pp. 359–289). Thousand Oaks, CA: Sage.

London, E. (2007, November 1). Why I use laboratory animals. *Los Angeles Times.*

Lulofs, R. S., & Cahn, D. D. (2000). *Conflict: From theory to action* (2nd ed.). Boston: Allyn & Bacon.

Luskin, F. (2002). *Forgive for good.* New York: HarperSanFrancisco.

Lustig, M. W. (2005). WSCA 2005 presidential address: Toward a well-functioning intercultural nation. *Western Journal of Communication, 69*(4), 377–379.

Lutgen-Sandvik, P. (2007). How employees fight back against workplace bullying. *Communication Currents.* Retrieved December 1, 2008, from www.communicationcurrents.com

Lutgen-Sandvik, P., Tracy, S. J., & Alberts, J. K. (2007). Burned by bullying in the American workplace: Prevalence, perception, degree and impact. *Journal of Management Studies, 44*(6), 837–862.

Ma, R. (1992). The role of unofficial intermediaries in interpersonal conflicts in the Chinese culture. *Communication Quarterly, 40*(3), 269–278.

MacGeorge, E. L., Feng, B., Butler, G. L., Dane, J. L., & Passalacqua, S. A. (2005). Sex differences in goals for supportive interactions. *Communication Studies, 56*(1), 23–46.

MacGeorge, E. L., Gillihan, S. J., Sampter, W., & Clark, R. A. (2003). Skill deficit or differential motivation? Testing alternative explanations for gender differences in the provision of emotional support. *Communication Research, 30*(3), 272–303.

MacIntosh, G. (2006). Tackling work place bullying. *Issues in Mental Health Nursing, 27*, 665–679.

Maltby, J., & Day, L. (2004). Forgiveness and defense style. *Journal of Genetic Psychology, 165*(1), 99–109.

Manners a top priority at work: Incivility can disrupt productivity. (2006, March 15). *Washington Times.*

Manusov, V., & Spitzberg, B. (2008). Attribution theory: Finding good cause in the search for theory. In D. O. Braithwaite & L. A. Baxter (Eds.), *Engaging theories in interpersonal communication: Multiple perspectives.* Thousand Oaks, CA: Sage.

Margolin, G., & Gordis, E. B. (2004). Children's exposure to violence in the family and community. *Current Directions in Psychological Science, 13*(4), 152–155.

Marin, M. J., Sherblom, J. C., & Shipps, T. E. (1994). Contextual influences on nurses' conflict management strategies. *Western Journal of Communication, 58*(3), 201–228.

Masters, M. F., & Albright, R. R. (2002). *The complete guide to conflict resolution in the workplace.* New York: American Management Association.

Mayer, B. (2000). *The dynamics of conflict resolution: A practitioner's guide.* San Francisco: Jossey-Bass.

Mazur, M. A., & Hubbard, A. S. (2004). "Is there something I should know?": Topic avoidant responses in parent-adolescent communication. *Communication Reports, 17*(1), 27–37.

McAdoo, H. P. (2001). Point of view: Ethnicity and family dialogue. *Journal of Family Communication, 1*(1), 87–90.

McConnell-Ginet, S. (2003). "What's in a name?" Social labeling and gender practices. In J. Holmes & M. Meyerhoff (Eds.), *The handbook of language and gender* (pp. 69–97). Boston: Blackwell.

McCorkle, S., & Gayle, B. M. (2003). Conflict management metaphors: Assessing everyday problem communication. *The Social Science Journal, 40*(1), 137–142.

McCorkle, S., & Mills, J. L. (1992). Rowboat in a hurricane: Metaphors of interpersonal conflict management. *Communication Reports, 5*(2), 57–66.

McCorkle, S., & Reese, M. J. (2005a). Computer-based collaborative negotiation: The Appleby House case. *Communication Teacher, 19*(1), 19–22.

McCorkle, S., & Reese, M. J. (2005b). *Mediation theory and practice.* Boston: Allyn & Bacon.

McCullough, M. E., Pargament, K. I., & Thorenson, C. E. (2000). The psychology of forgiveness. In M. E. McCullough, K. I. Pargament, & C. E. Thorensen (Eds.), *Forgiveness theory, research, and practice* (pp. 1–16). New York: Guilford Press.

McElhinny, B. (2004). Theorizing gender in sociolinguistics and linguistic anthropology. In J. Holmes & M. Meyerhoff (Eds.), *The handbook of language and gender.* Blackwell Reference Online. Retrieved April 23, 2008, from http://www. blackwellreference.com

McGraw, P. C. (1999). *Life strategies: Doing what works, doing what matters.* New York: Hyperion.

McIntosh, P. (1988). Unpacking the invisible knapsack. Working Paper 189. Wellesley, MA: Wellesley College Center for Research on Women.

McPherson, B., & Mensch, S. (2007). Students' personality type and choice of major. *Academy of Information and Management Sciences Journal, 20*(2), 1–18.

Meiners, E. B., & Miller, V. D. (2004). The effect of formality and relational tone on supervisor/subordinate negotiation episodes. *Western Journal of Communication, 68*(3), 302–321.

Meyers, D. G., & Bishop, G. D. (1970). Discussion effects on racial attitudes. *Science, 169*(3947), 778–779.

Millar, M. (2003, September 2). Government saves more than £6m through dispute resolution scheme. *Personnel Today*, p. 4.

Miller, S., Miller, P., Nunally, E., & Wackman, D. (1991). *Talking and listening together.* Littleton, CO: Interpersonal Communication Programs.

Missouri mom indicted in MySpace cyber-bullying, suicide case. (2008, May 15). *Information Week.*

Moore, C. W. (2003). *The mediation process* (3rd ed.). San Francisco: Jossey-Bass.

Mortensen, C. D. (2006). *Human conflict: Disagreement, misunderstanding and problematic talk.* Lanham, MD: Rowman & Littlefield.

Murphy, J. G. (2003). *Getting even: Forgiveness and its limits.* London: Oxford University Press.

Myers, D. G., & Bishop, G. D. (1970). Discussion effects on racial attitudes. *Science, 169*, 778–779.

Namie, G., & Namie, R. (2003). *The bully at work: What you can do to stop the hurt and reclaim your dignity on the job.* Naperville, IL: Sourcebooks.

Neff, K. D., & Harter, S. (2002). The authenticity of conflict resolutions among adult couples: Does women's other-orientated behavior reflect their true selves? *Sex Roles, 47*(9/10), 403–417.

Nicotera, A. M., & Dorsey, L. K. (2006). Individual and interactive processes in organizational conflict. In J. G. Oetzel & S. Ting-Toomey (Eds.), *Handbook of conflict communication: Integrating theory, research, and practice* (pp. 293–326). Thousand Oaks, CA: Sage.

O'Bannon, G., & Dennis, D. (2001). Managing our future: The generation X factor. *Public Personnel Management, 30*(1), 95–110.

Oetzel, J. G., & Ting-Toomey, S. (2003). Face concerns in interpersonal conflict: A cross-cultural empirical test of the face negotiation theory. *Communication Research, 30*(6), 599–624.

Olson, L. N. (2002). "As ugly and painful as it was, it was effective:" Individuals' unique assessment of communication competence during aggressive conflict episodes. *Communication Studies, 53*(2), 171–188.

Olson, L. N., & Braithwaite, D. O. (2004). "If you hit me again, I'll hit you back:" Conflict management strategies of individuals experiencing aggression during conflicts. *Communication Studies, 55*(2), 271–285.

O'Shea, P. G., & Bush, D. F. (2002). Negotiation for starting salary: Antecedents and outcomes among recent college graduates. *Journal of Business and Psychology, 16*(3), 365–382.

Parrott, D. J., & Zeichner, A. (2003). Effects of trait anger and negative attitudes towards women on physical assault in dating relationships. *Journal of Family Violence, 18*(5), 301–307.

Pawlowski, D. R. (1998). Dialectical tensions in marital partners' accounts of their relationships. *Communication Quarterly, 46*(4), 396–412.

Pawlowski, D. R., Thilborger, C., & Cieloha-Meekins, J. (2001). Prisons, old cars and Christmas trees: A metaphoric analysis of familial communication. *Communication Studies, 52*(3), 180–196.

Peterson, C., Peterson, J., & Skevington, S. (1986). Heated argument and adolescent development. *Journal of Social and Personal Relationships, 3,* 229–240.

Petronio, S. (2000). The boundaries of privacy: Praxis of everyday life. In S. Petronio (Ed.), *Balancing the secrets of private disclosures* (pp. 37–49). Mahwah, NJ: Erlbaum.

Petronio, S. (2002). *Boundaries of privacy: Dialectics of disclosure.* Albany, NY: State University Press.

Pipher, M. (1995). *Reviving Ophelia: Saving the selves of adolescent girls.* New York: Penguin.

Plowman, K. D. (1998). Power in conflict for public relations. *Journal of Public Relations Research, 10*(4), 237–261.

Podshadley, S., & Docan, T. (2005–2006). Issues of infidelity: Physical, emotional, and communicative acts of cheating in romantic relationships. Western States Communication Association Conference, San Francisco.

Poole, M. S., & Garner, J. T. (2006). Perspectives on work-group conflict and communication. In J. G. Oetzel & S. Ting-Toomey (Eds.), *Handbook of conflict communication: Integrating theory, research, and practice* (pp. 267–292). Thousand Oaks, CA: Sage.

Porhola, M., Karhunen, S., & Rainivaara, S. (2006). Bullying at school and in the workplace: A challenge for communication research. In C. Beck (Ed.), *Communication yearbook, 30.* Mahwah, NJ: Routledge.

Postmes, T., & Brunsting, S. (2002). Collective action in the age of the Internet: Mass communication and online mobilization. *Social Science Computer Review, 20*(3), 290–301.

Quindlen, A. (2004, July 12). A foul mouth and manhood. *Newsweek*, p. 76.

Raiffa, H., Richardson, J., & Metcalfe, D. (2002). *Negotiation analysis: The science and art of collaborative decision making.* Cambridge, MA: Belknap Press.

Raines, C., & Hunt, J. (2000). *The Xers & the boomers: From adversaries to allies—a diplomat's guide.* Menlo Park, CA: Crisp Publications.

Randall, P. (1997). *Adult bullying: Perpetrators and victims.* London: Routledge.

Raven, B. H., & Rubin, J. X. (2001). The interdependence of persons. In S. M. Schmidt, D. Geddes, S. C. Currall, & A. Hochner (Eds.), *Power and negotiation in organizations.* Dubuque, IA: Kendall/Hunt.

Reese, M. J., & McCorkle, S. (2005). Three creative problem solving techniques. In J. W. Cooley (Ed.), *Creative problem solver's handbook for negotiators and mediators* (Vol. 2) (pp. 140–144). Washington, DC: ABA Section of Dispute Resolution.

Riley, H. (2001). When does gender matter in negotiation? *Leadership* [Online]. Retrieved December 1, 2008, from http://www.ksg.harvard.edu/leadership. when_does_gender_matter_in_negotiation

Ritchie, L. D. (1997). Parent's workplace experiences and family communication patterns. *Communication Research, 24*(2), 175–188.

Ritchie, L. D., & Fitzpatrick, M. A. (1990). Family communication patterns: Measuring intrapersonal perceptions of interpersonal relationships. *Communication Research, 17*(4), 523–544.

Rogan, R. G., & La France, B. H. (2003). An examination of the relationship between verbal aggressiveness, conflict management strategies, and conflict interaction goals. *Communication Quarterly, 51*(4), 458–469.

Rogers, E. L. (2001). Relational communication in the context of family. *Journal of Family Communication, 1*(1), 25–35.

Rokeach, M. (1973). *The nature of human values.* New York: The Free Press.

Roloff, M. E., & Ifert, D. E. (2000). Conflict management through avoidance: Withholding complaints, suppressing arguments, and declaring topics taboo. In S. Petronio (Ed.), *Balancing the secrets of private disclosures* (pp. 151–163). Mahwah, NJ: Erlbaum.

Rothwell, J. D. (2007). *In mixed company: Communicating in small groups and teams* (6th ed.). Belmont, CA: Thomson Higher Education.

Rummel, R. J. (1976). *Understanding conflict and war* (Vol. 2). Beverly Hills, CA: Sage.

Runde, C. E., & Flanagan, T. A. (2007). *Becoming a conflict competent leader.* San Francisco: Wiley.

Russell, B. (1938). *Power: A new social analysis.* New York: Norton.

Sabourin, T. C., & Stamp, G. H. (1995). Communication and the experience of dialectical tensions in family life: An examination of abusive and nonabusive families. *Communication Monographs, 62,* 213–242.

Saleh, D. N. (2003). This employee benefit pays off—the ombudsman. *Accounting Today, 17*(20), 8–9.

Salgado, V. (2005). Negotiating conflict in an educational environment: Investigating conflict and peer mediation at a diverse university. Western States Communication Association Conference, San Francisco.

Sample, S. B. (2002). *The contrarian's guide to leadership.* San Francisco: Jossey-Bass.

Sandy, S. V., & Cochran, K. M. (2000). The development of conflict resolution skills in children: Preschool to adolescence. In M. Deutsch & P. T. Coleman (Eds.), *The handbook of conflict resolution: Theory and practice* (pp. 316–342). San Francisco: Jossey-Bass.

Saposnek, D. T. (1998). *Mediating child custody disputes: A strategic approach* (Rev. ed.). San Francisco: Jossey-Bass.

Schelling, T. C. (1960). *The strategy of conflict.* London: Oxford Press.

Schroth, H. A., Bain-Chekal, J., & Caldwell, D. F. (2005). Sticks and stones may break my bones and words can hurt me: Words and phrases that trigger emotions in negotiations and their effects. *International Journal of Conflict Management, 16*(2), 102–127.

Scott, D. (2006, November 15). Everyday ethics: Problems of polarization. Radio commentary, Montana Public Radio.

Scott, W. (2008). Communication strategies in early adolescent conflicts: An attribution approach. *Conflict Resolution Quarterly, 25*(3), 375–400.

Sellers, J. G., Woolsey, M. D., & Swann, W. B. (2007). Is silence more golden for women than men? Observers derogate effusive women and their quiet partners. *Sex Roles, 57,* 477–482.

Seward, K., & Faby, S. (2003). Tackling workplace bullies. *Occupational Health, 55*(5), 16–19.

Seymour, D. (1997, March-April). Charting a future for quality in higher education. *About Campus,* pp. 4–10.

Shah, A. (2001). WTO protests in Seattle. In Free Trade and Globalization [Online]. Retrieved February 18, 2001, from www.globalissues.org

Shannon, C. E., & Weaver, W. (1949). *The mathematical theory of communication.* Urbana: University of Illinois Press.

Sheehan, M., Barker, M., & Rayner, C. (1999). Applying strategies for dealing with workplace bullying. *International Journal of Manpower, 20*(1/2), 50–56.

Shuter, R., & Turner, L. H. (1997). African American and European American women in the workplace: Perceptions of conflict communication. *Management Communication Quarterly, 11*(1), 74–96.

Sillars, A. L. (1980). Attributions and communication in roommate conflicts. *Communication Monographs, 47*(3), 180–200.

Sillars, A. L., Canary, D. J., & Tafoya, M. (2004). Communication, conflict, and the quality of family relationships. In A. L. Vangelisti (Ed.), *Handbook of family communication* (pp. 413–446). Mahwah, NJ: Erlbaum.

Simpson, R., & Cohen, C. (2004). Dangerous work: The gendered nature of bullying in the context of higher education. *Gender, Work, and Organization, 11*(2), 163–186.

Slaikeu, K. A. (1996). *When push comes to shove: A practical guide to mediation.* San Francisco: Jossey-Bass.

Slaikeu, K. A., & Hasson, R. H. (1998). *Controlling the costs of conflict: How to design a system for your organization.* San Francisco: Jossey-Bass.

Slater, M. D., Henry, K. L., Swaim, R. C., & Anderson, L. L. (2003). Violent media content and aggressiveness in adolescents: A downward spiral model. *Communication Research, 30*(6), 713–726.

Snider, M., & Borel. K. (2004). Stalked by a cyberbully. *Maclean's, 76*(2), 76.

Socha, T. J., & Diggs, R. C. (1999). At the crossroads of communication, race, and family: Toward understanding black, white, and biracial family communication. In T. J. Socha & R. C. Diggs (Eds.), *Communication, race, and family: Exploring communication in black, white, and biracial families* (pp. 1–24). Mahwah, NJ: Erlbaum.

Solomon, M. (2002). *Working with difficult people.* New York: Prentice Hall.

Sourcewatch. (2007, 3 August). Groupthink. Retrieved from http://www.sourcewatch.org/wiki.phtml? title= Groupthink

Spitzberg, B. H., & Cupach, W. R. (Eds.). (1998). *The dark side of close relationships.* Mahwah, NJ: Erlbaum.

Stafford, L., & Dainton, M. (1994). The dark side of "normal" family interaction. In W. R. Cupach & B. H. Spitzberg (Eds.), *The dark side of interpersonal communication* (pp. 259–280). Hillsdale, NJ: Erlbaum.

Stanley, S. M., Markman, H. J., & Whitton, S. W. (2002). Communication, conflict, and commitment: Insights on the foundations of relationship success from a national survey. *Family Process, 41*(4), 659–675.

Stark warnings over "happy slapping." (2008, March 18). BBC News.

Stein, D. (2001). Introduction. In R. Geffner, M. Loring, & C. Young (Eds.), *Bullying behavior: Current issues, research, and interventions* (pp. 1–5). New York: The Haworth Maltreatment & Trauma Press.

Stein, N. L., & Albro, E. R. (2001). The origins and nature of arguments: Studies in conflict understanding, emotion, and negotiation. *Discourse Processes, 32*(2–3), 113–133.

Stevenson, H. C. (2002). Wrestling with destiny: The cultural socialization of anger and healing in African American males. *Journal of Psychology and Christianity, 21*(3), 357–364.

Stringer, T. (2006). Barking dog negotiations: A mediator's own story. *ACResolution, 5*(2), 34–37.

Su, S. (2006). Cultural differences in determining the ethical perception and decision-making of future accounting professionals: A comparison between accounting students from Taiwan and the United States. *The Journal of American Academy of Business, 9*(1), 147–158.

Sunstein, C. R. (2002). The law of group polarization. *The Journal of Political Philosophy, 10*(2), 175–195.

Swanson, C. (2004, summer). Friendship and forgiveness in the face of embezzlement. *ACResolution,* pp. 15–17.

Takahashi, K., Ohara, N., Antonucci, T., & Akiyama, H. (2002). Commonalities and differences in close relationships among the Americans and Japanese: A comparison by the individualism/ collectivism concept. *International Journal of Behavioral Development, 26*(5), 453–465.

Tannen, D. (1994). *Talking from 9 to 5.* New York: Morrow.

Tannen, D. (1998). *The argument culture: Stopping America's war of words.* New York: Ballantine.

Thimm, C., Koch, S. C., & Schey, S. (2003). Communicating gendered professional identity: Competence, cooperation, and conflict in the workplace. In J. Holmes & M. Meyerhoff (Eds.), *The handbook of language and gender* (pp. 528–549). Boston: Blackwell.

Thomas, C. E., Booth-Butterfield, M., & Booth-Butterfield, S. (1995). Perceptions of deception, divorce disclosures, and communication satisfaction with parents. *Western Journal of Communication, 59*(3), 228–245.

Thompson, L., & Nadler, J. (2000). Judgmental biases in conflict resolution and how to overcome them. In M. Deutsch & P. T. Coleman (Eds.), *The handbook of conflict resolution* (pp. 213–235). San Francisco: Jossey-Bass.

Ting-Toomey, S., Oetzel, J. G., & Yee-Jung, K. (2001). Self-construal types and conflict management styles. *Communication Reports, 14*(2), 87–104.

Today Show. (2004, August).

Tough Choices, Tough Times. (2007). Retrieved February 26, 2007, from http://www.skillscommission.org/pdf/ exec_sum/ToughChoices_EXECSUM.pdf

Tracy, S., Lutgen-Sandvik, P., & Alberts, J. (2005). Escalated incivility: Analyzing workplace bullying as a communicative phenomenon. International Communication Association Annual Meeting, New York, NY.

Tracy, S. J., Lutgen-Sandvik, P., & Alberts, J. K. (2006). Nightmares, demons, and slaves: Exploring the painful metaphors of workplace bullying. *Management Communication Quarterly, 20*(2), 148–185.

Twale, D. J., & De Luca, B. M. (2008). *Faculty incivility: The rise of the academic bully culture and what to do about it.* San Francisco: Jossey-Bass.

Turner, L. H., & West. R. (1998). *Perspectives on family communication.* Mountain View, CA: Mayfield.

Turner, P. K. (2003). Paradox of ordering change: I insist that we work as a team. *Management Communication Quarterly, 16*(3), 434–439.

Tyrangiel, J. (2006, 21 May). Chicks in the line of fire. *Time.*

Ulam, A. (2004). Elusive libraries of Timbuktu. *Archaeology, 57*(4), 36–40.

Umbreit, M. S., Vos, B., Cotes, R. B., and Brown, K. A. (2003). *Facing violence: The path of restorative justice and dialogue.* Monsey, NY: Criminal Justice Press.

Ursiny, T. (2003). *The coward's guide to conflict.* Naperville, IL: Sourcebooks.

U. S. Census Bureau. (2005). 2005 American Community Survey. Retrieved December 1, 2008, from http://factfinder.census.gov

U.S. Divorce Statistics. (2002). Retrieved July 27, 2006, from http://www.divorcemag.com/statistics/US.shtml

Vangelisti, A. L. (1991). The pedagogical use of family measures: "My how you've grown!" *Communication Education, 40*(2), 187–201.

Vangelisti, A. L., & Caughlin, J. P. (1997). Revealing family secrets: The influence of topic, function, and relationship. *Journal of Social and Personal Relationships, 14*(5), 679–705.

Vangelisti, A. L., Crumley, L. P., & Baker, J. L. (1999). Family portraits: Stories as standards for family relationships. *Journal of Social and Personal Relationships, 16*(3), 335–368.

Van Kleef, G., De Dreu, C., Pietroni, D., & Manstead, A. (2006). Power and emotion in negotiation: Power moderates the interpersonal effects of anger and happiness on concession making. *European Journal of Social Psychology, 36*(4), 557–581.

Van Slyke, E. J. (1999). *Listening to conflict: Finding constructive solutions to workplace disputes.* New York: American Management Association.

Vardi, Y., & Weitz, E. (2004). *Misbehavior in organizations: Theory, research, and management.* Mahwah, NJ: Erlbaum.

Vasques-Scalera, C. (2002). The diversity framework informing this volume. In J. S. Trent (Ed.), *Included in communication: Learning climates that cultivate racial and ethnic diversity.* Washington, DC: AAHE.

Vecchi, G. (2004). Active listening and communication skills for crisis negotiation mediators. *ACResolution, 3*(2), 19–23.

Verona, E., Reed, A, Curtin, J. J., & Pole, M. (2007). Gender differences in emotional and overt/covert aggressive responses to stress. *Aggressive Behavior, 33,* 261–271.

von Bertalanffy, L. (1968). *General systems theory: Foundations, development, applications.* New York: George Braziller.

Wade, N. G., & Worthington, E. L. (2003). Overcoming interpersonal offenses: Is forgiveness the only way to deal with unforgiveness? *Journal of Counseling & Development, 81,* 343–353.

Walker, P. O. (2004). Decolonizing conflict resolution. *American Indian Quarterly, 28*(3/4), 527–549.

Wall, M. (2007). Social movements and email: Expressions of online identity in the globalization protests. *New Media and Society, 9*(2), 258–277.

Warkentin, C. (2001). *Reshaping world politics: NGOs, the Internet, and global civil society.* Lanham, MD: Rowman & Littlefield.

Watzlawick, P., Beavin, J., & Jackson, D. (1967). *The pragmatics of human communication.* New York: Norton.

Wehr, P. (1998). Conflict mapping. Retrieved June 24, 2008, from www.colorado.edu/conflict/peace/treatment/cmap.htm

Weiss, A. J., & Wilson, B. J. (1996). Emotional portrayals in family television series that are popular among children. *Journal of Broadcasting & Electronic Media, 40*(1), 1–29.

Welch, M. (2001). The O.F.T.E.N. strategy for conflict management. *Journal of Educational and Psychological Consultation, 12*(3), 257–262.

Welch, W. M. (2008, May 16). Mom indicted in 'cyberbullying' case. *USA Today.*

West, R., & Turner, L. H. (2000). *Introducing communication theory: Analysis and application.* Mountain View, CA: Mayfield.

Wexler, J. A., & Zimmerman, P. (2000). In-house resolution of employment disputes. *CPA Journal, 70*(12), 62–64.

Wilmot, W. W., & Hocker, J. L. (2007). *Interpersonal conflict* (7th ed.). Boston: McGraw-Hill.

Withers, B. (2002). *The conflict management skills workshop.* New York: AMACOM.

Wood, J. (2006). *Communication in our lives* (4th ed.). Belmont, CA: Wadsworth.

Workplace Bullying and Trauma Institute. (2003). Retrieved from http://bullyinginstitute.org

Zapf, D., & Gross, C. (2001). Conflict escalation and coping with workplace bullying: A replication and extension. *European Journal of Work and Organizational Psychology, 10*(4), 497–522.

Zapf, D., & Wolfgang, J. (1999). Organisational, work group related and personal causes of mobbing/ bullying at work. *International Journal of Manpower, 20*(1/2), 70–85.

Zhang, S., & Stafford, L. (2008). Perceived face threat of honest but hurtful evaluative messages in romantic relationships. *Western Journal of Communication, 72*(1), 19–39.

Zweibel, E. B., Goldstein, R., Manwaring, J. A., & Marks, M. B. (2008). What sticks: How medical residents and academic health care faculty transfer conflict resolution training from the workshop to the workplace. *Conflict Resolution Quarterly, 25*(3), 321–350.

Name Index

Subject Index